THE CONCISE ECONOMIC HISTORY OF PORTUGAL: A COMPREHENSIVE GUIDE

COLECÇÃO ECONÓMICAS – 2ª Série
Coordenação da Fundação Económicas

António Romão (org.), *A Economia Portuguesa – 20 Anos Após a Adesão*, Outubro 2006

Manuel Duarte Laranja, *Uma Nova Política de Inovação em Portugal? A Justificação, o modelo os instrumentos*, Janeiro 2007

Daniel Müller, *Processos Estocásticos e Aplicações*, Março 2007

Rogério Fernandes Ferreira, *A Tributação dos Rendimentos*, Abril 2007

Carlos Alberto Farinha Rodrigues, *Distribuição do Rendimento, Desigualdade e Pobreza: Portugal nos anos 90*, Novembro 2007

João Ferreira do Amaral, António de Almeida Serra e João Estêvão, *Economia do Crescimento*, Julho 2008

Amélia Bastos, Graça Leão Fernandes, José Passos e Maria João Malho, *Um Olhar Sobre a Pobreza Infantil*, Maio 2008

Helena Serra, *Médicos e Poder. Transplantação Hepática e Tecnocracias*, Julho 2008

Susana Santos, *From the System of National Accounts (SNA) to a Social Accounting Matrix (SAM) – Based Model. An Application to Portugal*, Maio 2009

João Ferreira do Amaral, *Economia da Informação e do Conhecimento*, Maio 2009

Fernanda Ilhéu, *Estratégia de Marketing Internacional*, Agosto 2009

Joge Afonso Garcia e Onofre Alves Simões, *Matemática Actuarial. Vida e Pensões*, Janeiro 2010

COLECÇÃO ECONÓMICAS – 1ª Série
Coordenação da Fundação Económicas

Vítor Magriço, *Alianças Internacionais das Empresas Portuguesas na Era da Globalização. Uma Análise para o Período 1989-1998*, Agosto 2003

Maria de Lourdes Centeno, *Teoria do Risco na Actividade Seguradora*, Agosto 2003

António Romão, Manuel Brandão Alves e Nuno Valério (orgs.), *Em Directo do ISEG*, Fevereiro 2004

Joaquim Martins Barata, *Elaboração e Avaliação de Projectos*, Abril 2004

Maria Paula Fontoura e Nuno Crespo (orgs.), *O Alargamento da União Europeia. Consequências para a Economia Portuguesa*, Maio 2004

António Romão (org.), *Economia Europeia*, Dezembro 2004

Maria Teresa Medeiros Garcia, *Poupança e Reforma*, Novembro 2005

1ª Série publicada pela CELTA Editora

MARIA EUGÉNIA MATA
NUNO VALÉRIO

THE CONCISE ECONOMIC HISTORY OF PORTUGAL: A COMPREHENSIVE GUIDE

ALMEDINA

THE CONCISE ECONOMIC HISTORY OF PORTUGAL: A COMPREHENSIVE GUIDE

AUTORES
MARIA EUGÉNIA MATA
NUNO VALÉRIO

VERSÃO EM INGLÊS REVISTA
por JOHN HUFFSTOT

EDITOR
EDIÇÕES ALMEDINA, SA
Rua Fernandes Tomás, n.ºs 76, 78, 80
3000-174 Coimbra
Tel.: 239 851 904
Fax: 239 851 901
www.almedina.net
editora@almedina.net

DESIGN DE CAPA
FBA.

PRÉ-IMPRESSÃO
G.C. GRÁFICA DE COIMBRA, LDA.
Palheira – Assafarge
3001-453 Coimbra
producao@graficadecoimbra.pt

IMPRESSÃO
PAPELMUNDE, SMG, LDA.

Fevereiro, 2011

DEPÓSITO LEGAL
324011/11

Os dados e as opiniões inseridos na presente publicação
são da exclusiva responsabilidade do(s) seu(s) autor(es).

Toda a reprodução desta obra, por fotocópia ou outro qualquer
processo, sem prévia autorização escrita do Editor, é ilícita
e passível de procedimento judicial contra o infractor.

Biblioteca Nacional de Portugal – Catalogação na Publicação

MATA, Maria Eugénia, 1953-   , e outro

The concise economic history of Portugal : a
comprehensive guide / Maria Eugénia Mata,
Nuno Valério. – (Fundação económicas)
ISBN 978-972-40-4310-4

I – VALÉRIO, Nuno, 1953-

CDU   33

Contents

FOREWORD 9

INTRODUCTION 11
A – Some data about the geography of Portugal 11
B – Division of the history of Portugal into periods 28

1 – BEFORE PORTUGAL (until the 8th century A.D.) 31
A – Hunter-gatherer economies (until the 4th millennium B.C.) 31
B – Agricultural and pastoral revolution (4th millennium B.C. –
1st millennium B.C.) 37
C – Urban revolution and contacts with the Mediterranean econo-
my (8th century B.C. – 3rd century B.C.) 40
D – Integration in the Roman Empire (3rd century B.C. – 5th cen-
tury A.D.) 44
E – From the end of Roman rule to the Arab conquest (5th century
A.D. – 8th century A.D.) 50

**2 – THE BEGINNINGS OF THE PORTUGUESE NATIONAL
SOCIETY (8th-13th centuries)** 57
A – Iberian Islam 58
B – Iberian Christendom 64
C – The political evolution of Portugal (8th-13th centuries) 71
D – Early Portuguese institutions and economic life 76

**3 – THE CONSOLIDATION OF THE PORTUGUESE NATIO-
NAL SOCIETY (13th-15th centuries)** 85
A – Medieval Portugal in an epoch of prosperity (13th-14th cen-
turies) 86
B – Medieval Portugal in an epoch of crisis (14th-15th centuries) ... 94

4 – PORTUGUESE EXPANSION (15th-16th centuries) 109

A – The rationale of Portuguese expansion 110
B – The conquests in Morocco 113
C – The Atlantic islands 117
D – The exploration of the western coast of Africa 122
E – The Indian Ocean 125
F – The New World 128
G – The Far East 132
H – The consequences of the expansion for the Portuguese economy and society 135

5 – PORTUGUESE APOGEE, IBERIAN UNIFICATION AND SEPARATION FROM THE WESTERN HAPSBURG EMPIRE (15th-18th centuries) 139

A – Portuguese apogee, 1490-1580 140
B – Iberian unification at work, 1580-1640 148
C – The separation from the Western Hapsburg Empire and its consolidation, 1640-1700 155

6 – PORTUGAL IN THE EURO-ATLANTIC WORLD-ECONOMY, 1700-1793 165

A – General features 166
B – The period of Brazilian gold and Portuguese wine, 1700-1750 .. 174
C – The period of privileged companies, 1750-1777 179
D – The period of early economic liberalism, 1777-1793 184

7 – THE FAILURE OF AN EARLY TAKE OFF, 1793-1851 189

A – The wars against France and Spain 190
B – The end of the colonial status of Brazil 196
C – Political upheavals, 1820-1851 199
D – Economic performance 209
E – Institutional reforms and modernisation policies 210

8 – THE FIRST EPOCH OF GROWTH, 1851-1891 215

A – The regeneration blueprint and its implementation 216
B – Integration in the international economy 229
C – Growth and crises 234

9 – A NEW EPOCH OF STAGNATION, 1891-1914 241

A – The 1891 breakdown 242
B – New economic policies 245
C – A dismal *belle époque* 253
D – Republicans at work 262

Contents | 7

10 – THE EPOCH OF WARS AND CRISES, 1914-1947 267
A – The First World War 267
B – The post-war years 274
C – The recovery of the middle and late 1920s 278
D – The impact of the Great Depression 284
E – The Second World War 289
F – Long-term effects of the epoch of wars and crises 293

11 – THE SECOND EPOCH OF GROWTH, 1947-1974 297
A – Political evolution 297
B – European and worldwide economic links 304
C – Economic policy 311
D – The golden era of Portuguese economic growth 318

12 – THE LAST QUARTER OF THE 20th CENTURY AND THE EARLY 21st CENTURY 325
A – The transition period, 1974-1976 326
B – Towards the European Communities, 1976-1985 333
C – Towards European economic union, 1985-1992 340
D – Towards European monetary union, 1993-1999 345
E – Portugal in the economic and monetary union 348
F – Long-term trends during the last quarter of the 20th century and the early 21st century 350

FINAL REMARKS 359
A – The problem of Portuguese independence 359
B – The problem of Portugal's late take-off of modern economic growth 363
C – The future of the Portuguese society in a European and world context 369

STATISTICAL APPENDIX 373
Table 1 – Population 374
Table 2 – Towns 379
Table 3 – Active population by sectors of activity 381
Table 4 – Gross domestic product 383
Table 5 – Money supply 389
Table 6 – Bank of Portugal discount rates 395
Table 7 – Prices 396
Table 8 – Public accounts and public debt 415
Table 9 – Foreign economic relations 421
Table 10 – Exchange rates 428

CARTOGRAPHIC APPENDIX 433

Map 1 – Orography and hydrography of Continental Portugal ... 434
Map 2 – Geology of Continental Portugal 435
Map 3 – Regions and main towns of Continental Portugal 436
Map 4 – Regions and main towns of Madeira 437
Map 5 – Regions and main towns of the Azores 438
Map 6 – Provinces and main towns of the future Portuguese con-
            tinental territory during the Roman and Visigothic rules
Map 7 – Formation of Portugal 439
Map 8 – Provinces of Continental Portugal (14th-19th centuries) ... 440
Map 9 – Administrative districts of Continental Portugal (19th-
            21st centuries) 442
Map 10 – Railroads built in Portugal 443
Map 11 – Portuguese colonial empire (15th century) 444
Map 12 – Portuguese colonial empire (16th century) 445
Map 13 – Portuguese colonial empire (17th-18th centuries) 446
Map 14 – Portuguese colonial empire (19th-20th centuries) 447

BIBLIOGRAPHY 449

Foreword

This book was conceived as an introductory university text – one which students having an interest in the economic history of Portugal could turn to for fundamentals as well as direction and bibliography leading towards more advanced investigation. In the end, we prepared it for an expanded audience – one which includes the student readership originally targeted, but one which also embraces the general public. In examining the economic history of Portugal, the very evolution of the country's society is laid bare, offering insight to the economist as well as those whose interests lie in other fields – at the level of scholar and lay reader alike.

We provide more data and historical detail as the period under consideration grows more recent. This reflects the authors' philosophy that the main purpose of the study of history is to provide a better understanding of the present and that recent facts are likely to exert greater influence in shaping it than are facts which are more remote. This is not to say that we have neglected earlier epochs. Indeed, all facts are relevant to an understanding of the present, and our analysis begins some million years ago with the beginnings of human life in what will come to be the continental territory of Portugal. However, in keeping with our opinion regarding the usefulness of studying history, and the contributions which such study can make even toward policy-making, we have placed increasing emphasis on facts as they approach our own day.

We have added two appendices. The first is an updated summary of the collection of Portuguese historical statistics released by the Portuguese National Statistics Institute [Instituto Nacional de Estatística]. The second is an outline of a Portuguese historical atlas. We believe these data to be indispensable for the systematic study of economic history and decided to provide it in a more accessible form than mere reference to specialised publications.

ACKNOWLEDGEMENTS

The authors of any book of this nature are of necessity indebted to all of those researchers who have gone before them. The bibliography lists only the sources which have been drawn upon directly. Even identifying the many indirect sources is impossible, and properly acknowledging them is, unfortunately, equally impractical.

Our colleague Ana Bela Nunes read the whole manuscript and made many valuable suggestions. As we chose not to follow all those suggestions, we naturally remain responsible for any error or omission which may remain.

DEDICATION

Even though our area is history, we have always felt that, as social scientists, our greatest responsibility is to the future. This book is, thus, dedicated to our son, Duarte Pedro, to our granddaughter, Teresa, and to all those like them, who will face the challenges of the fast-changing and closely-interrelated world we are building.

MARIA EUGÉNIA MATA
Professor, Faculdade de Economia,
Universidade Nova de Lisboa

NUNO VALÉRIO
Professor, Instituto Superior de Economia e Gestão,
Universidade Técnica de Lisboa

Introduction

The origins and evolution of the Portuguese society up to and including the early years of the 21st century, with special concern for its economic life – these are the themes we shall take up in these pages. By way of setting the stage, let us first look at the thing before us in terms of its physical and temporal backdrops. This introduction is comprised of two sections, which sketch out these two dimensions: a survey of the geography of the Portuguese territories, followed by an outline of the division into historical periods which will serve as the basis, chapter by chapter, of the book's organisation.

A – Some data about the geography em Portugal

Portugal as we know it today is made up of the continental territory, located in the Iberian Peninsula, and two archipelagoes, Madeira and the Azores, both located in the Atlantic Ocean. All three taken together, usually considered as a part of the European continent, have a total area of about 92,100 square km.

These three areas have made up the geographical basis of Portugal since the country's emergence as a national entity – the continental zone between the 8th and 13th centuries, and the archipelagoes added in the 15th. Since falling into the Portuguese sphere, for that matter, none of these areas has ever lapsed in its capacity as a Portuguese territory (except for some slight adjustments in the border alignment in the continental area). Other territories of Africa, Asia, Indonesia and America have been under Portuguese control at different times between A.D. 1415 and 1999, but none of these were ever integrated totally or in the same way into the Portuguese society and all of them have ultimately passed out of Portuguese control.

Continental Portugal

Continental Portugal occupies the Southwest corner of the Iberian Peninsula, roughly between latitudes 37° and 42° N and longitudes 6° 30' and 9° 30' W, with an area of nearly 89,000 square km.

Geology

Continental Portugal belongs to the Eurasian tectonic plate and has three distinct types of geological formations:

a) The Iberian Massif – a formation of Palæozoic origin, made up predominantly of granite and schist and exhibiting infrequent volcanic and seismic activity.

b) The so-called Western and Southern Edges – formations of Mesozoic or Cenozoic origin, made up mostly of limestone, with many signs of extinct volcanic activity, and frequent current seismic activity.

c) The alluvial plains – formations of Cenozoic or Anthropozoic origin, composed mostly of clay and sandstone, devoid of volcanic activity, but showing frequent seismic activity.

The Iberian Massif is a formation that occupies the centre and the west of the Iberian Peninsula, facing the Cenozoic Cantabric mountains to the north, and the also Cenozoic Iberian and Betic mountains to the east. Within the Portuguese territory, it has an area of around 62,000 square km, and includes the zone north of the Douro, the whole of the interior, and the southern coast of Alentejo.

The Western Edge includes a section of the coast roughly located between the mouths of the Tagus and the Lis, with a small extension to the interior in a northeast direction. It has an area of approximatelly 10,000 square km.

The Southern Edge includes the southern coast, with an area of around 5,000 square km.

The main alluvial plains are those of the Tagus and Sado, having an area of about 10,000 square km, and the Vouga, with an area around 2,000 square km.

Morphology

The continental territory of Portugal has an average altitude of around 240 m, clearly lower than Eurasia (330 m) and the Iberian Peninsula (600 m). However, there is a sharp contrast between the part of the Iberian Massif north of the central range, represented in the Portuguese territory by the mountains of Estrela, Açor and Lousã, and the rest of the country. As a matter of fact, the part of the Iberian Massif north of the central range has an average altitude of around 370 m and sometimes exceeds 1,200 m, the altitude over which there is usually permanent snow during the winter. The highest altitude of the continental territory of Portugal is nearly 2,000 m in the Estrela mountains. The rest of the country has an average altitude of around 160 m, nowhere exceeding 1,200 m.

Hydrography

The main rivers of the Portuguese continental territory have their source in Spain and flow from east to west or from northeast to southwest, due to the general shape of the Iberian Massif. They are:

a) The Minho, which has its source in the Cantabric mountains and most of its course in the Spanish region of Galicia. It forms, however, 75 km of the northern border of Portugal, with

45 km traditionally navigable. The part of its basin located in the Portuguese territory is small, with an area of only around 800 square km.

b) The Douro, which has its source in the Iberian mountains, and crosses the Spanish regions of Old Castile and Leon and the continental territory of Portugal. Here, it has an extension of 322 km, of which 130 km traditionally were navigable – to these 70 km more were added during the 19th century. Its basin has an area of around 18,600 square km in the Portuguese territory.

c) The Tagus, which has its source in the Iberian mountains, and crosses the Spanish regions of New Castile and Extremadura and the continental territory of Portugal. Here, it has an extension of 275 km, of which 212 km traditionally are navigable. Its basin has an area of around 24,900 square km in the Portuguese territory.

d) The Guadiana, which has its source in the Betic mountains, and crosses the Spanish regions of New Castile and Extremadura and the continental territory of Portugal. Here, it has an extension of 260 km, of which 72 km traditionally are navigable, most of it forming part of the eastern border of the country. Its basin has an area of around 11,500 square km in Portuguese territory.

Between the Minho and the Douro, there are a few small rivers, with the whole of their courses and basins in Portuguese territory. The most important of these are:

a) The Lima, with 65 km, of which 40 km traditionally are navigable, and a basin of around 1,100 square km.

b) The Cávado, with 118 km, of which 6 km traditionally are navigable, and a basin of around 1,600 square km.

c) The Ave, with 85 km, of which 2 km traditionally are navigable, and a basin of around 1,400 square km.

Between the Douro and the Tagus, there are also a few rivers, with the whole of their courses and basins in Portuguese territory. The most important of these are:

a) The Vouga, with 136 km, of which 50 km traditionally are navigable, and a basin of around 3,700 square km.

b) The Mondego, with 220 km, of which 85 km traditionally are navigable, and a basin of around 6,800 square km.

Between the Tagus and the Guadiana, there are also a few small rivers, with the whole of their courses and basins in Portuguese territory. The most important of these are:

a) The Sado, with 175 km, of which 70 km traditionally are navigable, and a basin of around 7,600 square km.

b) The Mira, with 130 km, of which 30 km traditionally are navigable, and a basin of around 1,800 square km.

All the rivers mentioned have very irregular regimes, with floods in the winter and spring, a clear reduction of the flow during the summer and a gradual increase of flow during the autumn. These fluctuations make navigation impossible during some periods of the year and call for the building of extensive reservoirs for an efficient use for hydroelectric or irrigation purposes.

All the rivers mentioned, with the exception of the Vouga, end in estuaries that are usually good harbours, though the bars may be difficult to reach during winter storms. The Vouga presents a terminal formation usually called Ria de Aveiro, formed by a delta ending in a lagoon cut off from the sea by a sand bar.

Climate

The Portuguese continental territory has a temperate climate, varying among the Atlantic, Mediterranean and semi-continental in its character. Average temperature is usually between 15°C and 20°C, though it is around 10°C in the highlands of the interior. The yearly range of temperatures is around 10 °C near the coast and around 15 °C in the interior. Annual rainfall reaches around 1,000 mm in the north and 500 mm in the south, rising to nearly 2,000 mm in the higher altitudes.

Regions

In spite of its small area, Continental Portugal presents a rather pronounced regional physical and human variation, as the preceding considerations suggest. It is useful to study it in terms of nine regions of different geographical characteristics: Entre--Douro-e-Minho, Trás-os-Montes, Beira Litoral, Beira Alta, Beira Baixa, Estremadura, Ribatejo, Alentejo and Algarve.

Entre-Douro-e-Minho

The region of Entre-Douro-e-Minho occupies the northwest corner of Continental Portugal. To the north it faces the Spanish region of Galicia; to the east it faces the Spanish region of Galicia and the Portuguese region of Trás-os-Montes; to the south it faces the Portuguese regions of Beira Litoral and Beira Alta; to the west it faces the Atlantic Ocean. It roughly coincides with the old province of Entre-Douro-e-Minho and with the present administrative districts of Viana do Castelo, Braga and Porto. It has an area of around 7,400 square km.

From a geological point of view, Entre-Douro-e-Minho belongs to the Iberian Massif, the predominant rock being granite, in some zones replaced by schist. From a morphological point of view, it is a hilly region, open to the influence of the sea through the river valleys. The eastern border is marked by a range of mountains: from north to south they are called Peneda, Suajo, Gerês, Barroso, Alvão and Marão. From a hydrographic point of view, the region is formed by the left bank of the lower Minho, by the valleys of the Lima, the Cávado and the Ave, and by the right bank of the lower Douro.

Entre-Douro-e-Minho has a temperate Atlantic climate, with rainy, moderately cold winters, and warm, moderately rainy summers.

Agriculture and animal husbandry in Entre-Douro-e-Minho have traditionally been intensive activities, based mainly on small holdings, giving rise to high population densities. The southern part of the region became highly industrialised since the second half of the 19th century, and especially during the second half of the 20th century.

The urban life of Entre-Douro-e-Minho was traditionally centred around the towns of Braga (late Roman provincial capital; archbishopric see) in the centre of the region, and Porto (busy seaport since the medieval period) at the mouth of the Douro. A few small harbours also developed on the coast or at the end of the navigable stretches of the main rivers. Today, Porto is the second largest city of the country, with around 1.5 million inhabitants, Braga remains one of the six largest towns of the country, and many small towns have grown in the southern part of the region as the consequence of the industrialisation of that zone.

Trás-os-Montes

The region of Trás-os-Montes occupies the northeast corner of Continental Portugal. To the north it faces the Spanish region of Galicia; to the east it faces the Spanish region of Leon; to the south it faces the Portuguese region of Beira Alta; to the west it faces the Portuguese region of Entre-Douro-e-Minho. It roughly coincides with the old province of Trás-os-Montes and with the present administrative districts of Vila Real and Bragança. It has an area of around 10,900 square km.

From a geological point of view, the region of Trás-os-Montes belongs to the Iberian Massif, the dominant rocks being granite, mainly in the northwest, and schist, mainly in the east and the south. From a morphological point of view, it is a region of plateaux and valleys, screened from the influence of the sea by the mountains of the western border: Gerês, Barroso, Alvão and Marão. The northern border is also marked by a range of mountains: from west to east they are called Larouco, Coroa and Montezinho. From a hydrographic point of view, the region is formed by the right bank of the upper Douro.

Trás-os-Montes has a temperate semi-continental climate, with cold, snowy winters, and hot, dry summers.

Agriculture and animal husbandry in Trás-os-Montes have traditionally been extensive activities, based mainly on large holdings, giving rise to low population densities. Since the 17th century, however, the southwest corner of the region has specialised in the intensive cultivation of vineyards to produce port wine, giving rise to higher population densities. There has never been any significant industrialisation in any part of the region.

The urban life of Trás-os-Montes has always been centred around small towns scattered throughout the region.

Beira Litoral

The region of Beira Litoral occupies the north-central coast of Continental Portugal. To the north it faces the Portuguese region of Entre-Douro-e-Minho; to the east it faces the Portuguese regions of Beira Alta and Beira Baixa; to the south it faces the Portuguese regions of Estremadura and Ribatejo; to the west it faces the Atlantic Ocean. It roughly coincides with the coast of the old province of Beira and with the present administrative districts of Aveiro and Coimbra and the northern part of the present administrative district of Leiria. It has an area of around 8,900 square km.

From a geological point of view, Beira Litoral is divided into three distinct formations: the east belongs to the Iberian Massif, where the predominant rock is schist; the northern part of the coast belongs to the so-called Ria de Aveiro, made up predominantly of clay and sandstone; the south belongs to the so-called Western Edge, where the predominant rock is limestone. From a morphological point of view, it is a region of plains, open to the influence of the sea. The eastern border is marked by a range of mountains: from north to south they are called Montemuro, Gralheira, Caramulo, Buçaco and Lousã. From a hydrographic point of view, the region is formed by the left bank of the lower Douro, by the lower valleys of the Vouga and the Mondego, and by the valley of the Lis.

Beira Litoral has a temperate Atlantic climate, with rainy, moderately cold winters, and warm, moderately rainy summers.

Agriculture and animal husbandry in Beira Litoral have traditionally been intensive activities, based mainly on small holdings, giving rise to high population densities. The southern part of the region is one of the most important forest areas of the country. The northern part of the region became highly industrialised during the second half of the 20th century.

The urban life of Beira Litoral was traditionally centred around Coimbra (university centre since the medieval period) in the valley of the Mondego. A few small harbours also developed on the coast or at the end of the navigable stretches of the main rivers. Today, Coimbra remains one of the six largest towns of the country, and many small towns have developed in the northern part of the region as the consequence of industrialisation of that zone.

Beira Alta

The region of Beira Alta occupies the north-central interior of Continental Portugal. To the north it faces the Portuguese regions of Entre-Douro-e-Minho and Trás-os-Montes; to the east it faces the Spanish region of Leon; to the south it faces the Portuguese region of Beira Baixa; to the west it faces the Portuguese region of Beira Litoral. It roughly coincides with the interior north of the old province of Beira and with the present administrative districts of Viseu and Guarda. It has an area of around 10,500 square km.

From a geological point of view, Beira Alta belongs to the Iberian Massif, the predominant rock being granite, in some zones replaced by schist. From a morphological point of view, it is a region of plateaux and valleys, screened from the influence of the sea by the mountains of the western border: Montemuro, Gralheira, Caramulo, and Buçaco. The southern border is also marked by a range of mountains: Estrela. From a hydrographic point of view, the region is formed by the left bank of the upper Douro, and by the upper valleys of the Vouga and of the Mondego.

Beira Alta has a temperate semi-continental climate, with cold, snowy winters, and hot, dry summers.

Agriculture and animal husbandry in Beira Alta have traditionally been extensive activities, based mainly on medium-size holdings, giving rise to low population densities. There are, however, some local exceptions; the main one is the northwest corner of the region, which has shared the intensive cultivation of vineyards to produce port wine with southwestern Trás-os--Montes, since the 17th century. There has never been any significant industrialisation in any part of the region.

The urban life of Beira Alta has always been centred around small towns scattered throughout the region.

Beira Baixa

The region of Beira Baixa occupies the central interior of Continental Portugal. To the north it faces the Portuguese region of Beira Alta; to the east it faces the Spanish region of Extremadura; to the south it faces the Portuguese regions of Ribatejo and Alentejo; to the west it faces the Portuguese region of Beira Litoral. It roughly coincides with the interior south of the old province of Beira and with the present administrative district of Castelo Branco. It has an area of around 6,700 square km.

From a geological point of view, Beira Baixa belongs to the Iberian Massif, the predominant rock being schist, in some zones replaced by granite. From a morphological point of view, it is a region of plateaux and valleys, screened from the influence of the sea by the mountains of the western border: Lousã. The northern border is also marked by mountains: Estrela. From a hydro-graphic point of view, the region is formed by the right bank of the upper Tagus.

Beira Baixa has a temperate semi-continental climate, with cold, rainy winters, and hot, dry summers.

Agriculture and animal husbandry in Beira Baixa have tradi-tionally been extensive activities, based mainly on rather large holdings, giving rise to low population densities. The western part of the region is one of the most important forest zones of the country. There has never been any significant industrialisa-tion in any part of the region, except for the southern part of the Estrela mountain range.

The urban life of Beira Baixa has always been centred around small towns scattered throughout the region.

Estremadura

The region of Estremadura occupies the central coast of Continental Portugal. To the north it faces the Portuguese region of Beira Litoral; to the east it faces the Portuguese region of Ribatejo; to the south it faces the Portuguese region of Alentejo; to the west it faces the Atlantic Ocean. It roughly coincides with the coast of the old province of Estremadura and with the pre-sent southern part of the administrative district of Leiria, the present administrative district of Lisbon and the present nor-thern part of the administrative district of Setúbal. It has an area of around 5,700 square km.

From a geological point of view, Estremadura belongs to the so-called Western Edge, the predominant rock being limestone, though there are significant zones of basalt on the right bank of the Tagus mouth. From a morphological point of view, it is a region of plains and small hills, open to the influence of the sea. From a hydrographic point of view, it is formed by the valleys of a few small rivers such as the Sizandro, by the mouth of the Tagus, and by the lower Sado.

Estremadura has a temperate Atlantic-Mediterranean transition climate, with moderately cold, rainy winters, and warm, dry summers.

Agriculture and animal husbandry in Estremadura have traditionally been intensive activities, based mainly on small holdings, giving rise to high population densities. The southern part of the region has become highly industrialised since the second half of the 19th century, and especially during the second half of the 20th century. Lisbon is also one of the most important tourism regions of the country.

The urban life of Estremadura was traditionally centred around two seaports: Lisbon (having pre-Roman origins and capital of the country since the 13th century) at the mouth of the Tagus; and Setúbal (with Roman and medieval settlements of different locations) at the mouth of the Sado. It should be noted that the mouths of the Tagus and the Sado are the best natural ports of the country, as they have almost no sand formations or accessibility problems during the winter. A few small harbours also developed elsewhere on the coast. Today, Lisbon remains the largest city of the country with around 2.5 million inhabitants, Setúbal remains one of the six largest towns of the country, and many small towns have recently grown, mainly in the southern part of the region, as the consequence of the industrialisation of that zone.

Ribatejo

The region of Ribatejo occupies the centre of Continental Portugal. To the north it faces the Portuguese regions of Beira Litoral and Beira Baixa; to the east and to the south it faces the Portuguese region of Alentejo; to the west it faces the Portuguese region of Estremadura. It roughly coincides with the interior of the old province of Estremadura and with the present administrative district of Santarém. It has an area of around 6,700 square km.

From a geological point of view, Ribatejo is basically formed by the alluvial plain of the Tagus, the predominant rocks being clay and sandstone. From a morphological point of view, it is a region of plains, open to the influence of the sea. From a hydrographic point of view, it is the lower part of the Tagus valley.

Ribatejo has a temperate Atlantic-Mediterranean transition climate, with moderately cold, rainy winters, and warm, dry summers.

Agriculture and animal husbandry in Ribatejo have traditionally been extensive activities, based mainly on large holdings, giving rise to rather low population densities. The southwest corner of Ribatejo became highly industrialised during the second half of the 20th century. Fátima, in the northwest corner of the region became one of the most important tourism regions of the country during the second half of the 20th century, because of its sanctuary to the Virgin Mary.

The urban life of Ribatejo has traditionally been centred around the harbour of Santarém (having Roman or earlier origins) in the Tagus. Several small towns have also developed recently in the southwestern part of the region as a consequence of the industrialisation of that zone, and the direct influence of Lisbon is felt more and more clearly.

Alentejo

The region of Alentejo occupies the centre-south of Continental Portugal. To the north it faces the Portuguese regions of Estremadura, Ribatejo, and Beira Baixa; to the east it faces the Spanish regions of Extremadura and Andalucia; to the south it faces the Portuguese region of Algarve; to the west it faces the Portuguese region of Ribatejo, and the Atlantic Ocean. It roughly coincides with the old province of Alentejo and with the present southern part of the administrative district of Setúbal and the present administrative districts of Portalegre, Évora and Beja. It has an area of around 27,200 square km.

From a geological point of view, Alentejo is divided into two distinct formations: the Iberian Massif, where the predominant rock is schist, though in some zones granite and even limestone appear; and the alluvial plain of the Sado, where the predominant rocks are clay and sandstone. From a morphological point of view, it is a region of plains and small hills, open to the influence of the sea, except in the zones near the Spanish border. From a hydrographic point of view, the region is formed by the left bank of the upper Tagus, by the right bank and part of the left bank of the upper Guadiana, by the upper Sado, and by the valley of the Mira.

Alentejo has a temperate semi-continental climate, with cold, moderately rainy winters, and hot, dry summers.

Agriculture and animal husbandry in Alentejo have traditionally been extensive activities, based mainly on large holdings, giving rise to low population densities. There has never been any significant industrialisation in any part of the region.

The urban life of Alentejo has traditionally been centred around Évora (archbishopric see since the 16th century and university centre between the 16th and 18th centuries), located in the centre of the region. A few small towns have also developed scattered throughout the region.

Algarve

The region of Algarve occupies the south of Continental Portugal. To the north it faces the Portuguese region of Alentejo; to the east it faces the Spanish region of Andalucia; to the south and to the west it faces the Atlantic Ocean. It roughly coincides with the old province or kingdom of Algarve and with the present administrative district of Faro. It has an area of around 5,000 square km.

From a geological point of view, Algarve is divided into two distinct formations: the Iberian Massif, where the predominant rock is schist; and the so-called Southern Edge, where the predominant rock is limestone. From a morphological point of view, it is a region of plains near the coast and of small hills to the north, open to the influence of the sea. From a hydrographic point of view, the region is formed by the right bank of the lower Guadiana, and by the valleys of a few small rivers such as the Arade.

Algarve has a temperate Mediterranean climate, with warm, moderately rainy winters, and hot, dry summers.

Agriculture and animal husbandry in Algarve have traditionally been intensive activities, based on small holdings, giving rise to rather high population densities. Fishing and the fish processing industry were also traditional strong economic activities of the region, which became one of the most important tourism regions of the country during the second half of the 20th century.

The urban life of Algarve was traditionally centred around small towns scattered along the southern coast. However, today the town of Faro is gaining some prominence and a significant place among the towns of the country.

Madeira

The archipelago of Madeira is formed by one main island, also called Madeira (wood), located at latitude 32° 45' N and longitude 17° W, a small inhabited island, Porto Santo (holy harbour), located to the northeast of the main island, at latitude 33° N and longitude 16° W, and two groups of small deserted islands, located to the southeast of the main island – the Desertas (desert) at latitude 32° 30' N and longitude 16° 30' W, and the Selvagens (wild) at latitude 30° N and longitude 16° W. The archipelago has an area of around 800 square km, of which around 740 square km correspond to the main island.

The islands of the archipelago of Madeira are of volcanic origin. They are old peaks of the central Atlantic range, which moved east because of the movement in that direction of the

African tectonic plate to which they belong. Thus, the predominant rock is basalt, but there are neither active volcanic phenomena, nor frequent earthquakes.

The main island, or Madeira proper, is divided into somewhat different northern and southern parts by an east-west mountain range with a maximum altitude of around 1,850 m. The other islands of the archipelago are also hilly, but, due to their small size, do not rise to high altitudes.

The northern part of the main island has a temperate Atlantic climate, warm and moderately rainy during the whole year. The southern part of the main island and the other islands of the archipelago have a temperate Mediterranean climate with warm, moderately rainy winters, and hot, dry summers.

The small area of all the islands of the archipelago precludes the existence of any important river.

Agriculture and animal husbandry in Madeira have traditionally been intensive activities, based mainly on small holdings, giving rise to high population densities. The southern part of the main island has higher population densities, basing its agriculture on irrigation that uses water coming from the northern part of the island. Fishing has also traditionally been a very important activity in the region. There has never been any significant industrialisation in any part of the region, which became one of the most important tourism regions of the country during the 20th century.

The urban life of Madeira has traditionally been centred around the port of Funchal on the southern coast of the main island. Funchal remains today one of the six largest towns in the country.

The Azores

The archipelago of the Azores is formed by nine inhabited islands and some deserted islands, with a total area of around 2,300 square km. The islands may be divided into three groups:

the Eastern group with the inhabited islands of São Miguel and Santa Maria located between latitudes 37° and 38° N and between longitudes 25° and 26° W; the Central group with the inhabited islands of Terceira, Graciosa, São Jorge, Pico and Faial located between latitudes 38° and 39° N and between longitudes 27° and 29° W; the Western group with the inhabited islands of Flores and Corvo located between latitudes 39° and 40° N and between longitudes 31° and 32° W. The largest island is São Miguel with an area of around 740 square km.

The islands of the Azores are of volcanic origin. They are peaks of the central Atlantic range, which have just begun their westward or eastward movement (the islands of the western group belong to the North American tectonic plate and have a westward movement, while the islands of the central and eastern groups belong to the Eurasian tectonic plate and have an eastward movement). Thus, the predominant rock is basalt and there are many active secondary volcanic phenomena and frequent earthquakes.

All the islands are rather hilly. One of them – Pico – even attains the maximum altitude in Portugal – nearly 2,350 m.

The small size of all the islands in the archipelago precludes the existence of any important river.

The Azores have a temperate Atlantic climate, with moderately cold, rainy winters, and warm, moderately rainy summers.

Agriculture and animal husbandry in the Azores have traditionally been intensive activities, based mainly on small holdings, giving rise to high population densities. Fishing has been another very important economic activity. There has never been any significant industrialisation in any part of the region.

The urban life of the Azores was traditionally centred around the port of Angra on the island of Terceira, superseded during the 19th century by the port of Ponta Delgada on the island of São Miguel. Both remain among the largest towns of the country.

B – Division of the history of Portugal into periods

In the following chapters, the history of Portugal (and of the societies that existed before Portugal in the territory that later became the continental part of the country) is divided into periods based on a consideration of the larger global societies that formed the background of human life in this part of the world. In this vein, five main epochs may be identified: the epoch before the existence of Portugal (until the 8th century A.D.); the epoch of the formation of Portugal (between the 8th and 13th centuries); the epoch during which Portugal was mainly a part of medieval Western Christendom (between the 13th and 15th centuries); the epoch during which Portugal was mainly a part of the Euro-Atlantic world-economy (between the 15th and 18th centuries); and the epoch during which Portugal became a part of the contemporary world economy (since the late 18th century).

The epoch before the existence of Portugal

Chapter 1 is an overview of the history of the territory that later would become the continental part of Portugal before the formation of the Portuguese national society (that is to say, until the 8th century A.D.). Such an overview, presented in an Iberian context, contributes to an understanding of the conditions prevailing during the later formation of the Portuguese national society.

No similar overview is necessary for the archipelagoes of Madeira and the Azores, as they were not permanently inhabited until the 15th century.

The beginnings of the Portuguese national society

Chapter 2 describes the process of formation of the Portuguese national society between the 8th and 13th centuries in the context of the conflict between Islam and Western Christendom for the control of the Iberian Peninsula. The Portuguese society appeared first as the separate Counties of Portugal and Coimbra belonging to the Kingdom of Leon (between the 8th and 11th centuries), later as one united County of Portugal still belonging to the Kingdom of Leon (between the 11th and 12th centuries), and finally as the independent Kingdom of Portugal (between the 12th and 13th centuries).

Portugal as a part of Medieval Western Christendom

Chapter 3 is a summary of the main aspects of the existence of Portugal as a part of medieval Western Christendom between the 13th and 15th centuries. This was a period of consolidation of the Portuguese national society.

Portugal as a part of the Euro-Atlantic world-economy

Chapters 4, 5 and 6 deal with the period between the 15th and 18th centuries, during which Portugal was mainly a part of the Euro-Atlantic world-economy.

These chapters are separated partly on a thematic basis, partly on a chronological basis. The theme of chapter 4 is the Portuguese expansion of the 15th and 16th centuries. Chapter 5 deals with the period of apogee of Portugal, roughly between 1495 and 1580, with the period of political unification of the Iberian Peninsula, between 1580 and 1640, and with the separation of Portugal from the Western Hapsburg Empire and the consolidation of Portuguese independence, between 1640 and 1700. Chapter 6 deals with the evolution of the Portuguese society during the 18th century.

Portugal as a part of the contemporary world economy

Chapters 7 to 12 present a detailed analysis of the evolution of the Portuguese society during the 19th and 20th centuries.

These chapters are separated on a chronological basis. Chapter 7 deals with the period between 1793 and 1851, during which Portugal was unable to keep pace with the modernisation process that had started in other European countries. Chapter 8 deals with the period between 1851 and 1891, during which Portugal made its first attempt at an economic take-off. Chapter 9 deals with the period between 1891 and 1914 during which stagnation came back to the Portuguese economy. Chapter 10 deals with the inter-war period (1914 to 1947), during which the preconditions for a second modernisation effort were put into place. Chapter 11 deals with the post-World War II golden age of Portuguese economic growth (1947 to 1974). Chapter 12 deals with the problems faced by the Portuguese society during the last quarter of the 20th century and the early 21st century.

1.

Before Portugal
(until the 8th century A.D.)

This chapter presents a brief sketch of the evolution of the future continental territory of Portugal before the 8th century A.D. in an Iberian context. Section A deals with the beginnings of human life in the Iberian Peninsula and with the millennia during which man was a hunter-gatherer. The agricultural and pastoral revolution is presented in section B. The urban revolution and the early contacts with the Mediterranean world are dealt with in section C. Section D is about the integration of the Iberian Peninsula in the Roman Empire. Section E deals with the end of the Roman rule and the turmoil of invasions that followed.

A – Hunter-gatherer economies (until the 4th millennium B.C.)

Probable absence of *Australopithecus* and *Homo Habilis*

It is likely that neither *Australopithecus*, nor *Homo Habilis*, ever lived in the Iberian Peninsula. The main reason to believe in their absence is the fact that neither human remains nor undisputable lithic remains of their presence have hitherto been found. It may also be argued in support of this absence that their technology was inadequate to survive in the Iberian winter except in a few favourable places during inter-glacial periods. In fact, in spite of the existence of some uncertainties about the climatic history of the Iberian Peninsula in general and of the future continental territory of Portugal in particular, it is certain that during the Pleistocene and the Holocene the Iberian Peninsula had either cold or temperate climates. As cold and temperate climates imply freezing or near freezing temperatures during the winter, and the early *Hominidiæ* lacked the control of fire and the use of skin clothing, the Iberian Peninsula probably did not belong to their potential ecosphere.

Homo Erectus

The absence of *Australopithecus* and *Homo Habilis* means that the human occupation of the Iberian Peninsula began with the arrival of the species *Homo Erectus*.

No human remains of *Homo Erectus* have as yet been found in the Peninsula, but their lithic remains (implements of the Palæolithic type known as Acheulian) are plentiful. There are some doubts about the chronology of these implements. These doubts make it impossible to present secure dates, but it is possible to say that the arrival of *Homo Erectus* occurred between 1,000,000 and 500,000 years ago, and that their presence lasted until between 200,000 and 100,000 years ago.

It is also impossible to know whether the first groups of *Homo Erectus* came from North Africa across the Strait of Gibraltar or from Central Europe over the Pyrenees. If the first hypothesis is correct, the arrival must have occurred during the Donau or Günz glaciations, because the possibility of crossing the Strait of Gibraltar without robust flotation supposes a considerable fall in the level of the sea. If the second hypothesis is correct, the arrival might have occurred during the Donau-Günz inter-glacial period.

Homo Erectus always had a hunter-gatherer way of life, in the Iberian Peninsula as elsewhere. Collecting vegetation, fishing and hunting were the main economic activities for obtaining the basic supplies of food and clothing. Instruments were certainly made mainly of stone and wood, but only the former have survived in the archaeological register. The control of fire and the manufacture of skin clothing were also important activities, necessary for survival during the Iberian winters, as mentioned above. Details about the changes in the life of these populations, as the climate underwent the fluctuations between the cold and temperate periods of the Donau glaciation, the Donau-Günz inter-glacial period, the Günz glaciation, the Günz-Mindel inter-glacial period, the Mindel glaciation, the Mindel-Riss inter-glacial period and the Riss glaciation are only superficially known.

Homo Sapiens

Between 200,000 and 100,000 years ago, *Homo Erectus* was replaced as the dominant species in the Iberian Peninsula by *Homo Sapiens*.

The variant *Homo Sapiens Neanderthalensis* of this species provided the oldest human remains yet discovered in the Iberian Peninsula. The lithic remains of *Homo Sapiens Neanderthalensis* (implements of the Palæolithic type known as Mousterian) are also plentiful. Doubts about the chronology of these implements are quite similar to those of the *Homo Erectus* tool assemblage. These doubts again make it impossible to present more than approximate dates for the beginning of *Homo Sapiens* in the Iberian Peninsula. It is only possible to say that the arrival occurred between 200,000 and 100,000 years ago. It is likewise impossible to know whether the first groups of *Homo Sapiens* came from North Africa or from Central Europe. If the first hypothesis is correct, the arrival must have occurred during the Riss glaciation. If the second hypothesis is correct, the arrival might have occurred during the Riss-Würm inter-glacial period.

Homo Sapiens at first had a hunter-gatherer way of life in the Iberian Peninsula, as elsewhere. *Homo Sapiens Neanderthalensis* remained linked to that way of life for the whole of its existence. References made above to the main economic activities, to instruments, to the control of fire and to the manufacture of skin clothing concerning *Homo Erectus* could be repeated here concerning *Homo Sapiens Neanderthalensis*. However, some technological progress was associated with the dominance of *Homo Sapiens*. This technological progress consisted not only of a new technique for fashioning stone implements (the Mousterian technique), but also in the introduction of complex tools (combining wood and stone parts, for example).

Homo Sapiens Neanderthalensis had to face climatic changes of the same type as those faced by *Homo Erectus*, such as the Riss glaciation, the Riss-Würm inter-glacial period and the Würm glaciation in succession. Once again, the economic changes associated with these ecological changes are only understood all too poorly.

Homo Sapiens Sapiens

Some 35,000 years ago, *Homo Sapiens Neanderthalensis* was replaced as the dominant variant of *Homo Sapiens* in the Iberian Peninsula by *Homo Sapiens Sapiens*.

Human and industrial remains of the early stages of the existence of *Homo Sapiens Sapiens* in the Iberian Peninsula are plentiful. However, doubts about the chronology of these remains still continue. It is possible to date the arrival of *Homo Sapiens Sapiens* with greater precision than the arrival of his predecessors, though it is, once more, impossible to know whether the first groups of *Homo Sapiens Sapiens* came from North Africa or from Central Europe. In any case, it is certain that the arrival occurred during the Würm glaciation.

Homo Sapiens Sapiens at first had a hunter-gatherer way of life in the Iberian Peninsula, as elsewhere. References made above to the main economic activities, to instruments, to the control of fire and to the manufacture of skin clothing could be repeated here. However, further technological progress was associated with the dominance of *Homo Sapiens Sapiens*. This technological progress consisted mainly of new lithic techniques and in the systematic use of new materials such as bone and horn. The new lithic techniques gave way to Palæolithic implements of the Perigordian, Aurignacian, Gravettian, Solutrian and Magdalenian types during the Würm glaciation, that is to say until some 11,000 years ago.

Epipalæolithic and Mesolithic

The end of the Würm glaciation and the beginning of the Holocene (post-glacial) climatic period some 11,000 years ago again brought important changes in the ecological environment of human life in the Iberian Peninsula. New plants and new animals had to be used to provide the basic necessities of life. Mammals such as deer, ox, boar and rabbit appear to have been the staple meats. The vegetables used are less well known. At the same time, new lithic techniques developed, leading to the Epipalæolithic and Mesolithic implements of the Azilian, Sauveterrian, Campignyian and Tardenoisian types.

The most important sites of this period are the shell middens left on the Tagus and Sado banks by the consumers of molluscs. Some of these middens attain huge sizes, attesting to an intensive occupation of these areas. This has led some scholars to suggest that these were already sedentary societies. Besides the shells, these sites provide remains of the Mesolithic industry and of the above mentioned mammals.

Sub-Neolithic

After the middle of the 5th millennium B.C., polished stone and pottery implements begin to occur at sites located in the future continental territory of Portugal. However, as these implements are not associated with remains of cultivated plants and of domestic animals, they cannot be taken as proof that an agricultural and pastoral revolution was underway, that is to say true Neolithic communities. These materials indicate the development of Sub-Neolithic communities, that is to say, communities still with a hunter-gatherer way of life that borrowed the techniques to produce Neolithic stone implements and pottery from neighbouring Neolithic or Sub-Neolithic communities.

Peoples

The peoples that lived in the Iberian Peninsula in the 5th millennium B.C. were the result of an undetermined number of migrations coming either from Central Europe or from the Maghreb during the epoch of the Würm glaciation, and of the spread of a Maghrebian people, the so-called Capsians, in the 9th millennium B.C.

The ethnic and linguistic characteristics of these peoples are known only by conjecture based on later developments. It is certain that the inhabitants of the Iberian Peninsula before the 2nd millennium B.C. were not Indo-Europeans, because the Basque language, which has survived until the present day, is not Indo-European and was not introduced by the peoples that came to the Iberian Peninsula after that epoch. Thus, it is possible to suggest that the early inhabitants of the Iberian Peninsula belonged to a larger group, which occupied the whole of Western Europe before the arrival of the Indo-European peoples, and perhaps also the Maghreb before the arrival of the Camitic peoples.

The names that should be given to this larger group and to the tribes that lived in the Iberian Peninsula are still a matter of debate among scholars. The traditional name of West-Mediterraneans for the larger group is perhaps the best one. Concerning the tribes living in the Iberian Peninsula, it is impossible to decide between the name Iberians or Ligurians, as will be seen in more detail in section B below.

Population

The population of the Iberian Peninsula must have remained very small until the end of the glaciations and even until the agricultural and pastoral revolution. As a matter of fact, a hunter-gatherer way of life is unable to sustain a population density much above 1 inhabitant/100 square kilometre with a cold climate, or much above 1 inhabitant/10 square km with a temperate climate. As the Iberian Peninsula has an area of nearly 600,000 square km, it is likely that its population never exceeded 6 thousand inhabitants until the end of the glaciations and 60 thousand inhabitants until the 5th millennium B.C.

It is likely that the future continental territory of Portugal had a population density similar to the population density of the Peninsula as a whole. Thus, the population of the future continental territory of Portugal was certainly around one sixth of the population of the whole Peninsula: about 1,000 inhabitants until the end of the glaciations, about 10,000 inhabitants until the 5th millennium B.C.

B – Agricultural and pastoral revolution (4th millennium B.C. – 1st millennium B.C.)

Agricultural and pastoral revolution

After the middle of the 4th millennium B.C., remains of cultivated plants and domestic animals join those of polished stone implements and pottery in the sites located in the future continental territory of Portugal. This means that the agricultural and pastoral revolution was underway, and that a new way of life, based on true Neolithic and sedentary communities was gradually being adopted all over the western part of the Iberian Peninsula. Cereals such as wheat and barley and animals such as goat, sheep and ox became thereafter key elements of the economy in this part of the world.

Besides pottery, Neolithic tools and remains of these cultivated plants and domestic animals, sites of this period in the future Portuguese territory also provide remains of looms. This indicates that the use of flax and wool for weaving cloth must have begun by this same time.

Of course, traditional gathering, hunting and fishing activities remained important for a long time. At least one millennium elapsed before the agricultural and pastoral revolution was consolidated, that is to say, before the new activities began to satisfy the majority of human needs.

Consolidation of the agricultural and pastoral revolution

Consolidation of the agricultural and pastoral revolution came during the 3rd millennium B.C. This was probably associated with the introduction of the plough, but some scholars have raised doubts about this thesis, because no undisputable remains of this type of implement dating from this epoch have yet been found. In any event, the idea of an increase of the importance of animal husbandry as against agriculture is widely accepted.

Associated with the consolidation of the agricultural and pastoral revolution is the introduction of the production of gold, silver and copper implements, later improved to bronze working in the 18th century B.C.

The introduction of metallurgy certainly implied the beginning of the sectorialisation of the economy, that is to say the specialisation of at least some economic units according to specific activities, and of regional exchanges of metallic ores. Such an evolution is usually associated with a process of social differentiation that leads to social stratification. Signs of such an evolution have been pointed out, mainly with respect to burial places and rituals, and with the building of huge megalithic monuments.

Sectorialisation of the economy and social stratification did not lead immediately to an urban revolution and to the organisation of a state. The development of fortified villages, located mainly on hilltops, suggests that some aspects of such an evolution did effectively take place. However, the small size of these communities and the absence of significant differences between them make it impossible to consider the existence of a true urban revolution.

The Iberians and the Ligurians

The 2nd millennium B.C. witnessed the arrival of a new people to the Iberian Peninsula. Debates about the origins and the ethnic and linguistic characteristics of the newcomers are still going on among scholars. According to some, the newcomers were the Ligurians, belonging to the Indo-European group and coming from Central Europe. According to others, the newcomers were the Iberians, belonging to the Camitic group and coming from the Maghreb.

Those who think that the early inhabitants of the Iberian Peninsula were the West-Mediterranean Iberians and the 2nd millennium B.C. newcomers were the Indo-European Ligurians base their opinion on the existence of signs of the presence of Indo-Europeans in the Iberian Peninsula before the arrival of the Halstat Celts in the 8th century B.C. Some have even suggested that the Ligurians were an early wave of Celts (specifically, Q-Celts) that could be named Celto-Ligurians.

Those who think that the early inhabitants of the Iberian Peninsula were the West-Mediterranean Ligurians and the 2nd millennium B.C. newcomers were the Camite Iberians usually associate the Ligurians with the cradle of the so-called bell-beaker culture and the spread of that culture with migrations of the Ligurians pushed by the arrival of the Iberians.

It is impossible to retrace the details of the spread of the 2nd millennium B.C. newcomers. It is possible to say that, at the beginning of the 1st millennium B.C., the Ligurians seem to have been located mainly in the western part of the Iberian Peninsula and the Iberians in its central and eastern parts.

Population

The agricultural and pastoral revolution and its consolidation certainly lifted the 60,000 limit suggested above for the population of the Iberian Peninsula with a hunter-gatherer way of life, because of the increases of labour efficiency and labour productivity associated with its technological and organisational innovations (agriculture, animal husbandry, metallurgy, beginnings of sectorialisation of the economy). Judging by the population densities attained in other regions of the world following the agricultural and pastoral revolution, a primitive cultivation economy is able to sustain a population density of around 3 inhabitants/square kilometre. This means that the population of the Iberian Peninsula might have attained, in the early 1st millennium B.C., a figure somewhat below 2 million inhabitants.

It is likely that the future continental territory of Portugal still had a population density similar to that of the Iberian Peninsula as a whole. This means that the population of the future continental territory of Portugal might have reached, in the early 1st millennium B.C., a figure somewhat below 400,000 inhabitants.

C – Urban revolution and contacts with the Mediterranean economy (8th century B.C. – 3rd century B.C.)

Phoenician and Greek merchants in Iberia

The first seeds for the formation of a Mediterranean world-economy were laid down by Phoenician and Greek seafarers of the late 2nd millennium and early 1st millennium B.C. Their journeys reached the Iberian Peninsula as early as the 2nd millennium B.C., but intensive and systematic contacts seem to date back only to the 8th century B.C.

Iberia provided the East Mediterranean merchants mainly with raw materials: metallic ores of tin, copper, silver, gold and mercury were its staple exports. The East Mediterranean merchants brought in exchange mainly consumer goods: sophisticated textiles, pottery, and glass seem to have been the most important of Iberian imports.

The intensive and systematic contacts with these East Mediterranean merchants integrated the eastern and southern coasts of the Iberian Peninsula in the Mediterranean world-economy that gradually took shape during the 1st millennium B.C. Of course, this integration also led to the introduction and spread of new techniques. The most important was perhaps iron working, which was introduced to the Iberian Peninsula in the 7th century B.C.

Urban revolution: Tartessus

The combination of the trends resulting from the consolidation of the agricultural and pastoral revolution and of the contacts with Eastern Mediterranean traders led to the development of an undoubted urban revolution in the Guadalquivir valley during the 7th century B.C.

The first civilised society in the Iberian Peninsula was perhaps a Phoenician colony, Gadir (today Cadiz) in the mouth of the Guadalquivir. However, the population of the surrounding region soon organised itself as a state, Tartessus, which was able to control the whole Guadalquivir valley and to extend its sphere of influence to the southern half of the Iberian Peninsula.

The ethnic and linguistic characteristics of the population of the Kingdom of Tartessus are unknown. A Tartessian writing system of Phoenician affiliation developed. Unfortunately, this writing has not yet been deciphered, and it is impossible to know to which linguistic group the Tartessians belonged.

There is also little known about the institutions and evolution of the Kingdom of Tartessus. The references of classical authors are rather legendary: after three mythical kings, Gargoris, Habis and Gerion, the apogee of the kingdom would have been attained under King Arganthonius between 620 B.C. and 540 B.C.

Foreign occupation: Carthage and Massilia

The Tartessian state did not last long. Early in the 6th century B.C., the Greek city of Massilia (today Marseille) occupied the Ebro valley (or at least its coastal regions), and established privileged trade relations with Tartessus. However, the decay of Massilia after the battle of Alalia (535 B.C.), where the Greek cities of Massilia and Syracuse were defeated by an alliance of the Etruscans and the Phoenician city of Carthage, allowed a Carthaginian intervention in the Iberian Peninsula. The Carthaginians excluded the Massiliotes from the trade of Southern Iberia, and, by the end of the 6th century B.C., conquered the Kingdom of Tartessus and occupied the Guadalquivir valley and the eastern coast. They also inherited the Tartessian sphere of influence in the southern half of the Iberian Peninsula.

Things remained relatively stable until the 3rd century B.C., at which time the Carthaginian defeat in the First Punic War (264 B.C.-241 B.C.) and the alliance of Massilia with Rome led the Carthaginians to attempt an expansion of their Iberian possessions and brought Rome in as another competitor in the Iberian Peninsula.

Between 229 B.C. and 220 B.C., Carthage managed to upgrade its sphere of influence in the southern half of the Iberian Peninsula into direct administration. This Carthaginian empire was formally recognised by Massilia and Rome, but a clash over the town of Saguntum in the Ebro valley in 219 B.C. soon threw the three competitors into what came to be the Second Punic War.

Carthage managed to take the strategic initiative occupying the Massiliote possessions of the Ebro valley and sending the famous expedition of Hannibal over the Pyrenees and the Alps to Italy. Rome tried to reply with an expedition into the Iberian Peninsula in 218 B.C., but after some fighting the Roman troops were expelled in 212 B.C. However, in 210 B.C. a second Roman expedition came to the Iberian Peninsula, and by 206 B.C. the previous Massiliote and Carthaginian possessions had fallen into Roman hands.

The Celts

Meanwhile, the northern half of the Peninsula had been overrun during the 8th century B.C. by an invasion of Celts, coming from Central Europe. According to the standard view, this was the first Celtic (and perhaps even Indo-European) flow to come to the Iberian Peninsula. Other scholars, however, think this was the second Indo-European flow (and perhaps even the second Celtic flow, specifically a P-Celtic wave).

The newcomers brought the new technique of iron working, introduced roughly at the same time into the southern half of the Iberian Peninsula through contacts with the East Mediterranean traders. Their material culture belonged to the Halstat type, later replaced in the 4th century B.C. by the La Tène type.

The Celtic invasion seems to have overrun first the Ebro valley. After some time, however, the Iberians of the northeastern part of the Peninsula regained their autonomy. As the southern and eastern coasts came under the rule of the states of Tartessus, Massilia and Carthage, the Celts were restricted to the centre and northwestern parts of the Peninsula, where they tended to absorb the Iberians and the Ligurians. The tribes that resulted from such a process became known as Celtiberians.

The Iberians and the Celtiberians had a sectorialised cultivation economy, but did not experience an urban revolution until the 3rd century B.C. Their political life remained strictly tribal and they did not organise complex states similar to those that controlled the southern and eastern parts of the Iberian Peninsula.

Population

The 1st millennium B.C. certainly witnessed an increase in the population of the Iberian Peninsula, mainly in the regions where the urban revolution occurred, once again because of the increases of labour efficiency and labour productivity associated with its technological and organisational innovations (iron working, full sectorialisation of the economy). A 10 inhabitants/square km population density for the southern half of the Iberian Peninsula and the above-mentioned 3 inhabitants/square kilometre density for the northern half may be considered reasonable assumptions for the end of the period. This leads to a 3.5 million estimate for the population of the whole Iberian Peninsula at the end of the 1st millennium B.C.

It is likely that the future continental territory of Portugal by then had a population density somewhat lower than the average population density of the Iberian Peninsula, because of a less extensive impact of the urban revolution. A figure of 500,000 inhabitants may be a reasonable estimate for its population at the end of the 1st millennium B.C.

D – Integration in the Roman Empire (3rd century B.C. – 5th century A.D.)

Roman conquest

By the end of the 2nd century B.C., as a result of the Second Punic War, Roman possessions in the Iberian Peninsula included the Guadalquivir valley, the eastern coast, the Ebro valley and the western and central regions south of the Tagus.

In 197 B.C., they were divided into two provinces: Hispania Citerior (capital city, Tarraco, today Tarragona) including the Ebro valley and the eastern coast, and Hispania Ulterior (capital city, Hispalis, today Seville) including the Guadalquivir valley and the western coast.

Rome soon tried to extend its possessions. Between 179 B.C. and 149 B.C. the area between the Tagus and the Douro was brought under a precarious Roman control and added to the province of Hispania Ulterior. The Lusitanian tribes of the region revolted between 146 B.C. and 139 B.C. led by Viriatus, but his assassination in 139 B.C., and some successful campaigns between 138 B.C. and 133 B.C., which ended with the conquest of the last stronghold of the revolt, Numantium, restored the Roman rule.

The Roman civil wars of the 1st century B.C. again disturbed Roman possessions in the Iberian Peninsula. A refugee of the populist party, Sertorius, led a new Lusitanian revolt between 80 B.C. and his assassination in 72 B.C.; and the sons of Pompey, Cnæus and Sextus, kept part of the Roman possessions in the Iberian Peninsula out of central control between 48 B.C. and 44 B.C.

Two decades later, Rome decided to end with its Iberian frontier. This time the war was a short one: between 27 B.C. and 25 B.C. the north and northwest of the Iberian Peninsula were occupied. These new possessions were added to the province of Hispania Ulterior.

Roman administration

Between 16 B.C. and 13 B.C., the provincial organisation of the Iberian Peninsula underwent significant changes: the north-western and northern regions were transferred from Hispania Ulterior to Hispania Citerior, and Hispania Ulterior was divided into two provinces, Bætica (capital city, Hispalis, today Seville) including the Guadalquivir valley, and Lusitania (capital city, Emeritas, today Merida) including the region between the Guadiana and the Douro. Bætica became a senatorial province; Lusitania and Hispania Citerior became imperial provinces.

The future continental territory of Portugal south of the Douro belonged to the province of Lusitania, and was divided into thirty-four municipalities (*civitates*). Of these, twenty-eight were tributary municipalities (*oppidi stipendiarii*), where the magistrates were not Roman citizens and the old Celtiberian laws still prevailed. The other six were Latin colonies (*coloniæ Latinæ*), Roman municipalities (*municipii civium Romanorum*) or Latin municipalities (*municipii Latinii*), where the magistrates and most of the free men were Roman citizens and the Roman law was already applied. This was the case of Pax Julia (today Beja) and Scallabis (today Santarém), which were Latin colonies, of Olisipo (today Lisbon), which was a Roman municipality, and of Ebora (today Évora), Mirtilis (today Mértola) and Salacia (today Alcácer do Sal), which were Latin municipalities. The future continental territory of Portugal north of the Douro belonged to the province of Hispania Citerior and was divided into a similar number of municipalities, all of them tributary. The difference in the degrees of integration into the Roman world of the areas south of the Tagus (with four Latin colonies or municipalities), between the Tagus and the Douro (with one Roman municipality and one Latin colony both in the Tagus valley) and north of the Douro (with no Roman or Latin colony or municipality) is clear.

In any event, integration proceeded at a quick pace. Nearly one century later, in A.D. 74, all tributary municipalities received the legal status of Latin municipalities. This meant that their magistrates became Roman citizens and that Roman law applied everywhere.

In A.D. 212, Roman citizenship was awarded to all free men by the well-known Caracalla constitution. In the same year, the province of Antoniana (capital city, Bracara, today Braga) including the north and the northwest of the Iberian Peninsula was separated from Hispania Citerior, but this separation was repealed in A.D. 218.

Between A.D. 262 and A.D. 266, the Iberian Peninsula experienced a short period of disturbance during which it was, for the first time, invaded by German tribes, namely the Franks and the Alemanni. However, Roman control was soon firmly re-established.

The reforms of Diocletian in the late 3rd century A.D. included the Iberian Peninsula in the *præfectura* of Gallia and in the *diœcesis* of Hispania. The *diœcesis* of Hispania included the Iberian Peninsula and the Western Maghreb and was divided into six provinces: one was Mauretania Tingitana (capital city, Tingis, today Tangiers) in Western Maghreb; the other five were located in the Iberian Peninsula. Hispania Citerior was divided into three provinces: Callæcia (capital city, Bracara, today Braga) including the north and the northwest, Carthaginensis (capital city, Carthago Nova, today Cartagena) including the eastern coast, and Tarraconensis (capital city, Tarraco, today Tarragona) including the Ebro valley. Bætica and Lusitania remained as they had been organised in the 1st century B.C.

Trade under Roman rule

Roman rule brought the integration of the whole of the Iberian Peninsula into the Mediterranean world-economy.

The trade of the Iberian Peninsula with the rest of the Roman Empire showed the traditional pattern of the relations between the Iberian Peninsula and the Mediterranean world-economy of the 1st millennium B.C. with some improvements. The staple exports were still raw materials, such as metallic ores of tin, copper, silver, gold and mercury, to which were added some foodstuffs, such as wheat, olive oil and prepared fish. The main imports were still luxury consumer goods: sophisticated textiles and pottery. Concerning the future continental territory of Portugal, the most important export-oriented activities attested in its Roman sites were copper ore mining and prepared fish industries.

It is likely that the intensity and diversity of the exchanges increased, especially because of the improvement in the conditions of travel as a result of the building of roads and bridges by Roman authorities.

Rural life under Roman rule

Some new techniques and crops were introduced into the agriculture of the Iberian Peninsula during the centuries of Roman rule. The extension of crops such as olive and vines and the development of irrigation techniques linked to the building of dams are perhaps the most important aspects of these improvements.

Regarding the division of the land, it is clear that the south saw the development of latifundia centred in rural manors (*villæ*). The situation in the north is doubtful. The traditional view suggested a policy of replacement of the old fortified hilltop villages by manors (*villæ*) located in the lowlands. However, archaeological evidence seems not to confirm this view, suggesting that the old villages were romanised, and remained the main centres of rural life until the medieval period.

Urban life under Roman rule

During the period of Roman rule, urban life extended to the whole of the Iberian Peninsula. The main urban centres were still located in the Guadalquivir valley, on the eastern coast, and in the Ebro valley – Gades (today Cadiz), Hispalis (today Seville), Carthago Nova (today Cartagena), and Tarraco (today Tarragona): This means that none of these main urban centres were located in the future continental territory of Portugal.

Archaeological work and classical sources do not provide enough information to establish a map of the main towns of the future continental territory of Portugal. Ossonoba (today Faro), Mirtillis (today Mértola), Pax Julia (today Beja), Ebora (today Évora), Salacia (today Alcácer do Sal), Olissipo (today Lisbon), Scalabis (today Santarém), Aquæ Flaviæ (today Chaves) and Bracara (today Braga) played the main administrative and religious roles. The concentration of urban life south of the Tagus and on the right bank of that river is quite clear.

Population

Roman administration organised several censuses of the population of the Iberian Peninsula, but their results have not been fully preserved. From fragmentary data it is possible to infer a total population of around 6 million inhabitants for the whole of the Iberian Peninsula during the last centuries of Roman rule. Such a figure corresponds to a population density of 10 inhabitants/square kilometre, which is quite reasonable for a sectorialised cultivation economy integrated into a world-economy. It is likely that the bulk of the population growth occurred by the 3rd century A.D., and that demographic stagnation prevailed thereafter.

If it is supposed that the Roman rule allowed the future Portuguese territory to catch up with the average population density of the whole Iberian Peninsula, it may be concluded that its population when Roman rule came to its end might have reached nearly 1 million inhabitants.

Roman cultural heritage

Integration of the Iberian Peninsula into the Roman world was not only a political and economic matter, but also a cultural matter. Two cultural consequences of this integration must be mentioned here because their imprints have lasted until the present days: it is the case of the adoption of the Latin language and of the Christian religion.

The Latin language displaced all languages previously used in the Iberian Peninsula, with the exception of the ancestor of the Basque. Latin became the origin of all other languages used today in the Iberian Peninsula: Portuguese in the western part (with two dialects, Galician and Portuguese proper), Castilian or Spanish in the central part, and Catalan in the eastern part.

The Christian religion displaced the synthesis of Celtiberian and Roman cults that became dominant between the Roman conquest and the 4th century A.D.. Five bishoprics were organised during the 4th century A.D. in the future continental territory of Portugal: Bracara (today Braga), and Aquæ Flaviæ (today Chaves) in Callæcia; Olissipo (today Lisbon), Ebora (today Évora) and Ossonoba (today Faro) in Lusitania. In spite of the influence of a heretical group of local origin, the Priscillians, the Catholic version of Christianity was firmly established among the Hispano-Romans by the end of the 4th century A.D.

E – From the end of Roman rule to the Arab conquest (5th century A.D. – 8th century A.D.)

The end of Roman rule and the formation of the Iberian kingdom of the Visigoths

In 409, the Alans (an Iranian people, still pagan), and the Asding Vandals, Siling Vandals and Suevi (German peoples, also pagans or converted to the Arian version of Christianity), who had invaded Gaul in 406 and plundered it during the years of 407 and 408, were allowed by the Romans to cross the Pyrenees and to settle in the western part of the Iberian Peninsula as allied peoples (*fœderati*). The Siling Vandals occupied Bætica, the Alans occupied Lusitania, the Asding Vandals occupied the eastern part of Callæcia, and the Suevi occupied the western part of Callæcia.

Like other arrangements of the same type made in the same epoch by the Roman Empire, this was certainly seen as a transitory situation, only tolerated in order to take care of more pressing needs. As a matter of fact, five years later, the tribe of the Visigoths (a German people, professing the Arian version of Christianity) was sent as a mercenary army to win back these provinces to Rome. The Visigoths destroyed the Siling Vandals and the Alans on behalf of the Roman Empire (416) and settled as *fœderati* in Aquitania (417).

The Suevi and the Asding Vandals were left in Callæcia, perhaps as a Roman attempt to have an alternative power to counterbalance the Visigoths. However, attrition between them forced a new Roman intervention. The Suevi remained in Callæcia, the Asding Vandals were led to Lusitania (420), then to Bætica (421), and finally to Africa (429), where they managed to occupy the eastern Maghreb and to form a kingdom that came to be quite harmful to Rome, but did not interfere again with the Iberian Peninsula, except for a temporary occupation of the Balearic Islands. Division of the Iberian Peninsula between the Roman Empire and the Suevi lasted until the 460s with some conflicts and the advance of the Suevi into northwestern Lusitania. It should also be noted that around the middle of the 5th century the Suevi became Catholic Christians.

A few years later the Visigoths broke the alliance with the Roman Empire and came back to the Iberian Peninsula. During the 460s and 470s, after conquering Septimania in Gaul, they occupied the Roman part of the Iberian Peninsula, and established their capital city at Toletum (today Toledo). The Suevi resisted, but lost the territory they had acquired in northwestern Lusitania and were forced to revert to Arian Christianity. The Basques also resisted and were able to stay outside the Kingdom of the Visigoths.

The next stage of Visigothic expansion took place in Gaul again: it was the conquest of Provence in 481. However, in 507, the tide turned: after being defeated by the Franks at the battle of Vouillé, the Visigoths lost Aquitania and Provence, retaining only Septimania and the bulk of the Iberian Peninsula.

By the middle of the 6th century a new threat began to worry the Kingdom of the Visigoths: the Byzantine Empire. Following the conquest of Italy and the Maghreb, the Byzantines tried to profit from a Visigothic civil war to conquer the Iberian Peninsula, as well. In 554, they occupied the Guadalquivir valley and the eastern coast. Moreover, they established an alliance with the Suevi, who returned to northwestern Lusitania and became Catholic Christians again (559).

However, the last quarter of the 6th century saw a Visigothic revival: in 575 the Visigoths recovered most of the south of the Iberian Peninsula, and in 584 they conquered the Kingdom of the Suevi. Three years later, the Visigothic elite converted to Catholic Christianity.

Visigothic expansion went on during the 7th century. In 631, the Byzantines were expelled from the Iberian Peninsula (but not from the Balearic Islands) and saw a slice of the Maghreb occupied by the Visigoths. The only unfruitful war was the one waged against the Basques, who managed to preserve their autonomy. During most of the 7th century, nearly the whole Iberian Peninsula was united under the rule of the Kingdom of the Visigoths, which also included some territories in Gaul (Septimania) and in Africa (Tingitania).

Administration in the Kingdom of the Visigoths

From a legal point of view, the Hispano-Roman and Visigothic communities remained completely separated until the late 6th century. The kings of the Visigoths tried to put into writing the customary laws of the tribe – the Code of the Visigoths (*Codex Wisigothorum*) — and to separate them from the laws that ruled the Hispano-Romans – the Roman Law of the Visigoths (*Lex Romana Wisigothorum*).

The religious fusion of the late 6th century under the Catholic Church prepared the way for the end of legal separation, which occurred in the following decades. The new laws, common to all subjects of the kingdom, became known as the Book of the Judges (*Liber Iudiciorum*). The end of discrimination between the Hispano-Romans and the Visigoths was perhaps an attempt to eradicate the roots of the support that most of the Hispano-Roman population of the south of the Iberian Peninsula gave to the Byzantine reconquest.

The economic consequences of the end of Roman rule

The end of Roman rule in the Iberian Peninsula was, of course, only part of the larger process that started with the definitive division of the Roman Empire into its Western and Eastern parts in 395 and ended with the destruction of the Western Roman Empire in 476.

It may be said that such a process destroyed not only the Roman Empire as a political unit but also the world-economy of the Mediterranean created by the Phoenician and Greek seafarers of the late 2nd millennium and early 1st millennium B.C. From an Iberian point of view, this meant the loss of systematic trade contacts with the Mediterranean world and the transition to small self-sufficient economies.

Such an evolution does not, of course, mean that transformations linked with the agricultural and pastoral revolution and with the urban revolution were lost. Agriculture and animal husbandry remained the main economic activities; sectorialisation of the economy was also preserved; and even urban life remained, in spite of some decline.

The Byzantine attempts at reconquest must be seen in this context as an effort to rebuild not only the Roman Empire, but also the Mediterranean world-economy. As is well known, the effort was a failure, not only in the Iberian Peninsula, but also in the Mediterranean as a whole. During the 7th century the

Byzantine Empire shrank to a mere Balcanic-Anatolian state, most of what had been the Western Roman Empire saw the consolidation of kingdoms ruled by German dynasties, and the bulk of the Mediterranean world, at least in its southern half, became part of a new empire, the Arab Empire.

Rural life under the Visigoths

The replacement of Roman rule by Visigothic did not bring any important innovation to the rural life of the Iberian Peninsula. As a matter of fact, the new rulers claimed two thirds of the land (*sortes Gothicæ*), leaving only one third to the previous Hispano-Roman landlords (*tertia Romanorum*). The only practical result of such a change must have been an increase of pasture lands as against agricultural lands.

Urban life under the Visigoths

Urban life certainly declined as the result of the decrease of trade, though administrative and religious functions would remain the basis of the existing towns.

Some progress of Christianity led to the organisation of new bishoprics in the 5th, 6th and 7th centuries: the number of bishoprics in the future continental territory of Portugal doubled. The new sees were all north of the Tagus: Portucale (today Gaia), Lamecum (today Lamego), Veseo (today Viseu), Conimbriga (today Condeixa), later transferred to Æminium (today Coimbra), and Egitania (today Idanha-a-Velha). This means a progress towards higher homogeneity of urban life across the territory, but, of course, such an increase in homogeneity was accomplished in part by a decline of the previously more developed regions of the south.

Population

Population stagnation during the last decades of Roman rule was replaced by population decreases as soon as the turmoil of Alan and German invasions began. It is likely that war damages did not play an important role in the process, but epidemics and the increase of pasture lands as against agricultural lands were certainly crucial. Population censuses to measure population decreases are lacking. However, it is possible to point to the 3.5 million figure attained half a millennium earlier as a reasonable lower limit to the plausible drop. This means that the population of the future Portuguese territory must have declined to a figure somewhat above 500,000 inhabitants by the end of the 7th century.

The Arab conquest

The apogee of the Kingdom of the Visigoths was a short one. In 711, a civil war gave Mussa, governor of the Maghreb on behalf of the Umayyad caliph of Damascus, the opportunity to conquer Tingitania, and to send general Tarik across the strait that now bears his name to defeat the main Visigothic army at the battle of Crissus. This defeat put the whole of the Kingdom of the Visigoths at the will of the victors. Between 711 and 718, most of the Iberian Peninsula was subjugated – the exceptions being only the Asturias and the Basque country.

The Arabs then proceeded into Gaul, occupied the Visigothic possessions there, and began to enlarge them. This effort was a success until 732, when the Franks defeated the Arab army at the battle of Poitiers. It took nearly a decade to force the Arabs back to the Iberian side of Pyrenees, but by the early 740s the task was done: the Arab tide had been stopped and the Kingdom of the Franks ruled over the whole of Gaul, though the Arab Empire was firmly established in the Iberian Peninsula.

2.

The beginnings of the Portuguese national society (8th-13th centuries)

Between the 8th and 15th centuries, two civilisations – Islam and Western Christendom – fought for the control of the Iberian Peninsula. Portugal began its existence as a Christian frontier territory in the 9th century, became an independent state in the 12th century and consolidated that situation in the 12th and 13th centuries. The basis for the independence of Portugal may be found in the characteristics of political feudalism in Iberian Christendom; the basis for the consolidation of its existence was the triumph of Western Christendom over Islam in their fight for the Iberian Peninsula.

This chapter begins with an analysis of the general characteristics of the two civilisations that competed for the Iberian Peninsula during the Middle Ages: sections A and B deal with Iberian Islam and Iberian Christendom, respectively. Then it focuses on the Portuguese case in sections C and D. The political evolution of early Portugal is the topic of section C, and its economic life and institutions are the subjects of section D.

A – Iberian Islam

The Iberian Peninsula as a province of the Arab Empire, 711-756

The Arab Empire that controlled most of the Iberian Peninsula after the second decade of the 8th century was ruled from Damascus by the dynasty of the Umayyad caliphs. The Iberian Peninsula became a province of that empire with its capital city at Qurtuba (today Cordoba), and governors were appointed to administrative districts that roughly coincided with the previous bishoprics.

The Iberian Peninsula was a part of the Arab Empire only for about four decades, which were not quiet times. As a matter of fact, after the period of the conquest of the Iberian Peninsula (711-718), there followed expeditions to Gaul (718-740), and after their defeat the rivalries between the Arab, Berber and Syrian groups of the invaders and their various tribes and religious groups broke out into open conflict (740-742). Less than a decade after these upheavals settled, the overthrow of the Umayyad caliphs in 749 by the Abbasid dynasty started another war, during which Abd-al-Rahman, an Umayyad refugee, succeeded in creating a separate emirate in the Iberian Peninsula. As a consequence of this separation, the Iberian Peninsula only bowed to the Abbasid Caliphate between 749 and 756.

The Iberian Peninsula as an independent Moslem state, 756-1012

After 756, the Moslem part of the Iberian Peninsula became the Umayyad Emirate of Spain, which acknowledged the spiritual seniority of the Abbasid caliphs (settled in Baghdad after 763), but resisted all their attempts at political subjugation. Meanwhile, the struggles among the Moslems had cost them the loss of the territories north of the Douro.

2. The beginnings of the Portuguese national society | 59

The Umayyad state of Spain lasted for about two and a half centuries. This means it was able to control its internal conflicts and to resist its foreign enemies. The internal conflicts were mainly the result of the heterogeneity of the population: a majority of Christian subjects; a minority of Moslem rulers divided by their ethnic origins (several tribes of Arabs and Berbers, and Syrians) and by the existence of different religious groups (Sunnites, Shiites, and Kharidjites). In spite of a few upheavals, a mixture of tolerance and repression managed to ensure some degree of stability to the emirate under the Umayyad leaders of Arab-Syrian origin and Sunnite religious affiliation. The foreign enemies were, at the beginning, the Christian states – the Kingdom of Asturias, the Basque country and the Kingdom of the Franks (soon to become the Carolingian Empire) – and the Abbasid Caliphate of Baghdad. The Christian states of the Iberian Peninsula were easily forced to acknowledge the Moslem supremacy, though no attempt was made to bring them into direct rule. The Kingdom of the Franks launched some offensives in the late 8th and early 9th centuries, but these were stopped by the Umayyads with the loss of only Catalonia, partly compensated for by the conquest of the Balearic Islands (798).

The Abbasid Caliphate of Baghdad soon became harmless as other provincial governors followed the example of the Umayyads in Spain and began to build separate states of their own. Of these states, the closest neighbour – the Idrissid Caliphate of Morocco (founded in 789) – became especially worrying to the Umayyads, because its Shiite orientation excited the Moslem minorities in the Iberian Peninsula. However, after an unsuccessful uprising of these minorities in 823, the Umayyad emir decided to send the leaders and many followers of the rebellion across the Mediterranean to conquer Crete and organise a separate emirate there, and things became much calmer in the Iberian Peninsula. Later in the 9th century, the division of the Carolingian Empire left on the Umayyad frontier the Kingdom of

Navarre and the County of Barcelona, both unable to challenge the Emirate of Spain. At the same time, from the north of Europe there came a new threat, the Vikings: their first raid was a surprise that allowed them the sack of Isbilyia (today Seville) in 844; afterwards, however, they were rebuffed without difficulty.

The 10th century was the apogee of the Umayyads of Spain. They took the title of caliph (929), rejecting the seniority of the declining Abbasids, managed to acquire for a while a foothold in Provence (Fraxinetum), and destroyed the Idrissids and occupied their lands (967-972). For nearly half a century, the Umayyads were to hold an empire joining the Iberian Peninsula and the Western Maghreb.

The first Taifa period, 1012-1094

The apogee of the Umayyad Caliphate of Spain in the 10th century was followed by its disintegration in the early 11th century (1012). While the Maghrawanid took the Western Maghreb, the Moslem part of the Iberian Peninsula experienced what became known as the first Taifa period: it was divided into several emirates.

In the frontier regions, where the Christian threat was felt directly, the division led to the formation of only three relatively large emirates – Batalyaws (today Badajoz), including the northern part of the old Roman province of Lusitania; Tulaytula (today Toledo), including the centre of the Iberian Peninsula; and Saraqusta (today Zaragoza), including the Ebro valley. The south and most of the eastern coast of the Iberian Peninsula were divided into many small emirates – in the future continental territory of Portugal there were three of them: Martula (today Mértola), Silb (today Silves), and Harun (today Faro), all with less than 10,000 square km.

The end of the Umayyad Caliphate of Spain was certainly a good event for the Christian reconquest of the Peninsula. The regions between the Douro and the mountains of the centre of the Iberian Peninsula were lost by the Moslem states during the 11th century.

The Murabits, 1094-1144

By the end of the 11th century, a first wave of Moroccan conquerors, the Murabits, brought to an end the political division of the Moslems of the Iberian Peninsula, and halted Christian reconquest.

These Moroccan conquerors managed to rebuild during nearly half a century the union between the Moslem part of the Iberian Peninsula and the Western Maghreb, that the Umayyads had achieved for nearly the same period a century earlier. However, their intolerant approach to the previous balances of Iberian Islam prevented the consolidation of their rule. During the 1140s discontent with the Murabit rule led to rebellion and the Murabit Empire, in its own turn, fell apart.

The second Taifa period, 1144-1157

For nearly a decade, the Moslem part of the Iberian Peninsula went through what became known as the second Taifa period: it was divided again into several emirates. The political map of the future continental territory of Portugal was quite similar to the one that had existed during the first Taifa period, with a smaller Emirate of Badajoz.

The end of the Murabit Empire was again a fortuitous event for the Christian reconquest of the Iberian Peninsula. The regions between the mountains of the centre of the Peninsula and the Tagus were lost by the Moslem states by the middle of the 12th century.

The Muwahids, 1157-1269

History seemed to repeat. During the 1150s, a second wave of Moroccan conquerors, the Muwahids, brought an end to the political division of the Moslems of the Iberian Peninsula, and halted Christian reconquest.

The Muwahids managed to rebuild the union between the Moslem part of the Iberian Peninsula and the Western Maghreb that the Umayyads and the Murabits had achieved, and even to extend their empire to the Eastern Maghreb. However, they managed to retain the integrity of that empire against Christian attacks no longer than had their predecessors. In 1212, they were defeated at the battle of Las Navas de Tolosa, and thereafter their possessions in the Iberian Peninsula began to fall one after the other to the Christian kingdoms. When the Muwahid Empire disintegrated in 1269 into the three traditional blocks that it had managed to unite – the Iberian Peninsula, the Western Maghreb, and the Eastern Maghreb – the Moslem possessions in the Iberian Peninsula had been reduced to the region of Granada, Malaga and Almeria.

The Emirate of Granada, 1269-1492

The remaining Moslem territories of the Iberian Peninsula formed, after the mid-13th century, an emirate with its capital city at Garnata (today Granada). Somewhat unexpectedly, the Emirate of Granada was able to withstand the Christian offensive and to survive for nearly two and a half centuries, until the Christian attacks of the 1480s and early 1490s finally succeeded in ending the task of Christian reconquest of the whole Iberian Peninsula.

Trade in Iberian Islam

The integration of the Iberian Peninsula in the Moslem world played an economic role similar to its integration in the Byzantine Empire: it appeared as a surrogate for the integration in the Roman Empire and the Mediterranean world-economy, allowing the participation in a larger economic space.

Trade relations of the Iberian Peninsula with the rest of the Moslem world retained the traditional patterns of the trade relations between the Peninsula and the Mediterranean world-economies. The staple exports were still raw materials, such as metallic ores of tin, copper, silver, gold and mercury, and foodstuffs such as wheat, olive oil and fruits, to which were added metallic wares. The main imports were still luxury consumer goods – mainly sophisticated textiles – to which were added some exotic foodstuffs – such as sugar and rice – later introduced into the agriculture of the Iberian Peninsula.

Rural life in Iberian Islam

Agriculture benefited from new irrigation techniques based mainly on wells. Some new productions, such as rice, cotton and sugar were introduced, but they never rose to a prominent place in Iberian production. The watermill is another important innovation introduced into the Iberian Peninsula during the Moslem period.

Concerning property, all land was theoretically expropriated by the caliph, and given with a precarious status to the Moslem warriors as a basis for their livelihood. In practice, private property was maintained and operations of the *villa* type remained the standard rural unit, especially in the southern half of the Iberian Peninsula. Moreover, the Gothic and Hispano-Roman landlords that accepted the Moslem faith and the direct landworkers, regardless of their religious choices, generally kept their positions.

Urban life in Iberian Islam

Urban life certainly developed when compared to its decline in Visigothic times. However, the main towns of the Iberian Peninsula, such as Isbilyia (today Seville) and Qurtuba (today Cordoba), and even Saraqusta (today Zaragoza), Tulaytula (today Toledo) and Batalyaws (today Badajoz) lay outside the future continental territory of Portugal. Silb (today Silves), Harun (today Faro), Martula (today Mértola), Baja (today Beja), Yabura (today Évora), Usbuna (today Lisbon), Santarin (today Santarém), Antaniya (today Idanha-a-Velha) and Qulumriya (today Coimbra) seem to have been the main centres within the boundaries the future Portuguese territory during the Moslem period.

B – Iberian Christendom

The Kingdom of Asturias and the Basque country

As did the other regions of the Iberian Peninsula, Asturias received an Arab governor in 718. After some incidents with the local population, he had to flee. A punitive expedition was sent by the provincial authorities and rebuffed by the Asturians. This allowed the leader of the revolt, Pelagio, to claim the heritage of the Kingdom of the Visigoths. For the time being, however, he had to content himself with the Kingdom of Asturias and to wait for better days to organise any attempt to enlarge his realm.

Busy as they were with their expeditions in Gaul, where the sack seemed more promising, the Moslem armies did not care to crush the rebellion of Asturias, as they did not care to occupy the barren mountains of the Basque country. This allowed Asturias and the Basque country to remain out of Arab control.

The reconquest as far as the Douro valley and the Carolingian attacks

The first opportunity to enlarge the Christian territories came with the Moslem civil wars of the 840s and 850s. King Alfonso I of Asturias took advantage of it and cleared the region north of the Douro from their Moslem authorities. Thus, the Kingdom of Asturias became the Kingdom of Leon.

In the late 8th century and early 9th century, the Carolingian Empire also attempted to enlarge the Christian territories in the Iberian Peninsula. The results were somewhat mixed. The Basque country was submitted to Frank authority, Catalonia was conquered from the Umayyads, but the Balearic Islands were lost. Later in the 9th century, when the Carolingian Empire disintegrated, its possessions in the Iberian Peninsula became the Kingdom of Navarre (a Basque state) and the County of Barcelona (a Catalan state).

Christian reconquest stagnated and even receded during the 9th and 10th centuries. This was a consequence of the power of the Umayyad state, the division of Iberian Christendom and the difficulties of Western Christendom in general. The Christian states of the Iberian Peninsula had to face yet another danger, Viking raids, which disturbed the coasts of the Kingdoms of Leon and Navarre during the 9th and 10th centuries, but did not give way to any permanent settlement.

The reconquest as far as the Betic mountains

During the 11th, 12th and 13th centuries, the balance of power in the Iberian Peninsula underwent a significant change. As a matter of fact, the Taifa periods afforded advantageous opporunities for the Christian reconquest, and the Christian kingdoms of the north did not miss them. Moreover, Western Christendom as a whole managed to overcome the difficulties faced after the breakup of the Carolingian Empire and to start a period of growth, which led to attempts at external expansion, such as the Crusades. This meant the possibility of Western Christendom as a whole helping the Christian reconquest of the Iberian Peninsula.

As a consequence, the 11th, 12th and 13th centuries saw the whole region between the Douro and the Betic mountains permanently change hands. The Murabit and the Muwahid Empires may be seen, in this context, as attempts to use the Maghrebian resources to stop Christian reconquest. These attempts succeeded in the short run, as the pace of Christian reconquest slowed down when these empires were at their apogees and even suffered some setbacks. However, they failed in the long run, as the crumbling of the Muwahid possessions in the Iberian Peninsula after the decisive defeat of Las Navas de Tolosa (1212) showed.

Christian advance was at first accompanied by further political division of the Christian part of the Iberian Peninsula: the County of Castile was taken from the Kingdom of Leon by the Kingdom of Navarre in the early 11th century, and became a separate kingdom in 1035. The same year also saw the separation of the Kingdom of Aragon from the Kingdom of Navarre. Nearly one century later, it was the turn of the County of Portugal to separate as a kingdom from the Kingdom of Leon (as will be seen in greater detail in section C below). However, the first half of the 12th century was a turning point in such fragmenting trends: Aragon and Catalonia merged during the 12th century, and Castile and Leon did the same during the 13th century, starting the process of rebuilding the political union of the Iberian Peninsula.

Christian reconquest stagnated again during most of the 14th and 15th centuries. This may be explained by the demographic and economic crisis that Western Christendom, in general, and Iberian Christendom, in particular, experienced during this period.

The reconquest of the Emirate of Granada

If the Portuguese conquest of Ceuta in 1415 may be seen as a false start, it is undoubted that during the second half of the 15th century Iberian Christendom was on the move again. The Portuguese attempted to control the Atlantic coast of Morocco (as will be seen in more detail in chapter 4 below), the Kingdoms of Castile and Aragon became united under the same rulers (as will be seen in more detail in chapter 3 below), and the Emirate of Granada, the last Moslem state in the Iberian Peninsula, was conquered by the Kingdom of Castile between 1481 and 1492.

Trade in medieval Iberian Christendom

The small territories that formed the Christian kingdoms of the Iberian Peninsula during the last centuries of the 1st millennium A.D. lived, perhaps, in greater economic isolation than did any other Iberian region since the times of the Roman rule. As a matter of fact, these territories belonged to the part of the Iberian Peninsula that had always been the least involved in long-distance trade, faced a hostile Islam on their southern frontiers and were culturally linked to a Western Christendom that also tended towards local economic isolation.

This situation changed radically during the early centuries of the 2nd millennium A.D. The Christian kingdoms of the Iberian Peninsula expanded into territories that had traditionally been involved in long-distance trade, and managed to retain the economic relations of these territories with the Moslem world in spite of endemic warfare. At the same time, Western Christendom was also experiencing a process of demographic and economic growth, accompanied by the development of long-distance trade routes. This allowed the Christian kingdoms of the Iberian Peninsula to find in the other countries of Western Christendom, especially in Italy and Flanders, prosperous trade partners.

The patterns of the external trade of the Christian kingdoms of the Iberian Peninsula with the rest of Western Christendom showed some differences from the traditional patterns of external trade of the Iberian Peninsula with the Mediterranean world. Metallic ores, metallic wares and wheat were less important as exports, olive oil retained its position, and new foodstuffs and raw materials – such as salt, Mediterranean fruits and wool – joined it at the top of the export list. Consumer goods – such as sophisticated textiles – remained the most important imports. Concerning the exchanges with the Moslem world, the traditional patterns of trade with the Mediterranean world were retained.

Another important fact that fostered the relationships between the Christian kingdoms of the Iberian Peninsula and the rest of Western Christendom was the development of the pilgrimage to Santiago de Compostela in Galicia from the 10th century on. Satisfying the demand of the hundreds of thousands of pilgrims who made the route to Santiago to the supposed tomb of Saint James certainly stimulated the economy of the northern part of the Iberian Peninsula and became a strong monetising factor of its economic life.

Rural life in medieval Iberian Christendom

Rural life in Iberian Christendom showed no significant improvement until the 11th century. From then on, the diffusion of the innovations introduced in the rest of Western Christendom – such as the wheeled plough, trifoliar crop rotation, and the windmill – and of the progress made in Iberian Islam, assured an epoch of growth that lasted until the 13th century.

Concerning property, the situation was rather similar to that which prevailed in the Moslem part of the Iberian Peninsula: changes of political rule tended to imply changes of the landowners, but not of direct landworkers. In theory the king owned the land taken from the enemy and granted it to the nobles in exchange for military services. In practice land grants soon became definitive, setting the basis for more or less typical feudal institutions. However, serfdom tended to disappear among the Christian population between the 11th and 13th centuries, because of the opportunity that the advance of reconquest provided to the serfs to flee to the newly conquered lands (such movements were often stimulated by the kings themselves to increase Christian population in these newly-conquered lands). Freeholding, leaseholding and above all copyholding became the most usual status of cultivated land. Only part of the Moslem rural population of the South remained in serfdom after the Christian reconquest.

Operations of the *villa* type remained the standard rural operation in the southern half of the Iberian Peninsula even after Christian reconquest. In the northern half, however, the trend was towards the proliferation of smaller operations, a contrast that survives in Iberian agriculture today.

Urban life in medieval Iberian Christendom

It is possible to identify in the evolution of urban life in the Christian kingdoms of the Iberian Peninsula the same periods as in the evolution of external trade and of rural life. Until the 11th century, urban life was sluggish, restricted to small administrative and religious centres (the only possible exception was Barcelona). From the 11th century on, it developed mainly because the important urban centres of the southern half of the Iberian Peninsula began to fall into Christian hands. Seville (conquered in 1248) remained the largest city of the Iberian Peninsula until the 17th century.

The debates about Iberian feudalism

The question of the existence of feudalism in the Christian kingdoms of the Iberian Peninsula, especially in those of the western and central parts (Leon, Castile, and Portugal) has been much debated among historians. Some authors have underscored the similarity of economic life and institutions in Iberian Christendom and in the rest of Western Christendom and concluded that there existed in the Iberian Peninsula a more or less typical feudal regime. Other authors point to some characteristics of the institutions of Iberian Christendom, such as the early end of serfdom, the high proportion of land not subject to anyone but the king, the absence of a military monopoly of the noble class, and the high degree of centralisation of the political power in the hands of the kings, and deny that there existed a feudal regime in the western and central parts of the Iberian Peninsula.

It must be stressed that these debates focus more on terminological issues (how to define feudalism), than on descriptive issues (the characteristics of Iberian society). Thus, it is quite reasonable to sum up by saying that Iberian Christendom knew a feudal regime with some distinctions, arising from its frontier position, in more or less permanent warfare with its Moslem neighbours. As a matter of fact, it was the possibility and the need to settle the lands conquered from the Moslem states that implied the early end of serfdom among Christian subjects, it was the need to repopulate some regions that led the kings to avoid granting them to feudal lords in order to attract settlers, and it was the need to defend the same regions that led to the formation of popular levies.

The question of the high degree of centralisation of the political power is, however, a more complex one. It is possible to say that it all depends on the perspective that is adopted. In fact, the kings of Iberian Christendom retained more effective powers than did the typical king of Western Christendom. However, it should not be forgotten that most of the Christian Iberian kings (in Catalonia, Castile, Aragon and Portugal, not to mention Navarre, which inherited the tradition of Basque independence) were really just counts who had managed to separate their lands from the central power of Leon, Navarre, or the Carolingian Empire. This means that, in a certain sense, political feudalism in the Iberian Peninsula had a more radical character than in Western Christendom in general: local lords not only usurped the real political power though acknowledging the suzerainty of the king as in Western Christendom in general, but usurped the real political power and ceased to acknowledge the suzerainty of the previous king. This may be seen once more as a consequence of the frontier position of these territories, which implied a strictly local supply of public services such as defence and justice, which was provided with much more efficiency by the local lords that became kings than by a distant authority.

The ideal of the political unification of the Christian part of the Iberian Peninsula never disappeared from the minds of the ruling class. As a matter of fact, much political ingenuity was applied to attain it, as will be seen in chapters 3 and 5 below.

C – The political evolution of Portugal (8th-13th centuries)

As mentioned above, during the 740s and 750s, King Alfonso I of the Asturias expelled the Moslem authorities from the whole region north of the Douro. The southern fringe of this region, which includes the northern part of the continental territory of Portugal, lost its Moslem administration but did not immediately receive a Christian administration. For around a century it remained a frontier territory, almost completely devoid of any kind of urban life.

The first County of Portugal (9th-11th centuries)

By the middle of the 9th century, King Alfonso III of Leon tried to restore a normal administration in the region that is today the north of Portugal. This led to the organisation of a county, which gradually became known as the County of Portugal, and the appointment of Vímara Peres, a Galician noble, as the first count. Documents about the early history of this first

County of Portugal are scarce, but it seems that it included from the beginning the region of Entre-Douro-e-Minho south of the Lima and the region of Trás-os-Montes (approximately 16,500 square km). It also included some areas south of the Douro whenever the bulk of the county of Coimbra (see below) was in Moslem hands. Its main towns were Braga (archbishopric see) and Porto (bishopric see and seaport), but the counts preferred to centre their administration in the small town of Guimarães.

The first County of Portugal remained in the hands of the heirs of Vímara Peres until 1071, when Count Nuno Mendes took the losing side in a Leonese-Castilian civil war. The count died in the war, and further measures taken by the central authorities as a punishment were rather radical: the dynasty was deprived of its possessions and, as no new count was appointed, even the county ceased to exist for all practical purposes. Perhaps it was thought that a county was a solution adequate for a frontier zone, but no longer necessary, because the Christian reconquest had proceeded further south.

The County of Coimbra (9th-11th centuries)

In the late 9th century, the Kingdom of Leon also tried to set up a Christian administration in the region south of the Douro. Another county was organised, the County of Coimbra, and another Galician noble, Hermenegildo Guterres, was appointed as the first count. Documents about the early history of this County of Coimbra are scarce, as in the case of Portugal, but it seems that it included the region of Beira Litoral and the region of Beira Alta except for its eastern fringe (approximately 17,600 square km). Its main towns were Coimbra, Lamego and Viseu (bishopric sees), and the counts centred their administration in Coimbra. The county remained in the hands of the same family until the 10th century, when it disappeared as the consequence of Moslem reconquest. The remainder of its territory south of the Douro was provisionally added to the County of Portugal.

By the middle of the 11th century, the bulk of the territory of the County of Coimbra was conquered again by the Kingdom of Leon. As a consequence, the county was also organised again, and Sesnando, a Christian landowner, former Moslem subject, was appointed as the new count. The county remained in the same family only until the late 11th century, and disappeared as a separate political unit, when it was included in the County of Galicia in 1093.

An ephemeral Kingdom of Portugal (926-930)

When King Ordoño II of Leon died in 926, the kingdom was divided among his sons. One of them, Ramiro II, received the counties of Portugal and Coimbra as his lot. This was the first time that what may be called a Kingdom of Portugal existed, but it was a short-lived experiment. In 930, Ramiro II became sole king of Leon, and Portugal and Coimbra were integrated as separate counties once again into his kingdom.

The second County of Portugal (1096-1143)

In 1093, King Alfonso VI of Leon and Castile gave to his daughter and heiress, Urraca, and to her husband, Raimundo, the western part of his kingdom (Galicia proper and the counties of Portugal and Coimbra) as the County of Galicia. The new count profited from the faltering of the so-called first Taifa period to enlarge the county as far as the Tagus, conquering Lisbon in 1093. However, the Murabits soon endeavoured the task of recovering the lost ground from the Christians and by 1095 the southern frontier of the county had receded to the Mondego. Alarmed at the turn of events, and convinced that smaller counties would be more efficient, King Alfonso VI separated the territory of the former counties of Portugal and Coimbra from Galicia and organised them into a new and larger County of Portugal. Another daughter, Teresa, and her husband, Henrique, a noble of Burgundian origin, became the first rulers of this second County of Portugal.

The second county of Portugal included the regions of Entre--Douro-e-Minho, Trás-os-Montes and Beira Litoral, and the region of Beira Alta except for its eastern fringe (approximately 35,900 square km). Its main towns were the above-mentioned archbishopric and bishopric sees of Braga, Porto, Coimbra, Viseu and Lamego, but the capital town remained Guimarães during the early decades of its existence.

Henrique died in 1114, and Teresa took the government of the County together with her new husband (or lover, according to other sources) Fernando Peres de Trava, a Galician noble. In 1128, the son of Teresa and Henrique, Afonso, born in 1111, claimed the government of the County. As his mother and stepfather did not comply with his demands, he organised a revolt and drove them out of the County. Then he proceeded to impose his role as count and his autonomy from his cousin the king of Leon and Castile Alfonso VII (son of Urraca and Raimundo). After a decade and a half of an attrition war, the conflict was settled by the treaty of Zamora of 1143, negotiated by a papal emissary. Afonso was recognised as King of Portugal, but acknowledged being the vassal of the emperor of Spain, Alfonso VII.

The Kingdom of Portugal (1143-1250)

The Kingdom of Portugal that emerged from the treaty of Zamora remained legally dependent upon the emperor of Spain, but soon became fully independent.

From a formal point of view, it was the death of the emperor Alfonso VII and the division of his states in 1157 that ended the dependence. In 1176, Pope Alexander III confirmed this fact, by recognising the royal status of Portugal and accepting its direct dependence upon the Holy See. However, the real basis for the independence of Portugal was the territorial expansion that took place between 1143 and 1250.

This expansion resulted from the conquest of what is today the southern part of the continental territory of the country from Moslem states. Afonso I of Portugal had already made an expedition south of the Tagus and defeated a local garrison in 1139 at the battle of Ourique (a victory written large in Portuguese traditions, but affording no practical advantage). However, as soon as his quarrels with the emperor of Spain were settled, he recentred the administration of the kingdom in Coimbra, and tried to profit from the so-called second Taifa period to enlarge his possessions. During the rest of the 1140s, 1150s and 1160s, he managed to occupy the regions of Beira Baixa, Estremadura, Ribatejo and Alentejo, and even part of what is today Spanish Extremadura. There followed some problems with Leon, because the Leonese kings opposed the Portuguese conquest of what is today Spanish Extremadura. There was some fighting, the Portuguese were defeated and they had to abandon Badajoz, Caceres, Merida and Trujillo. Worse still was the Muwahid reaction, which deprived Portugal of most of the Alentejo previously gained. Nevertheless, the area of the kingdom had been enlarged to something around 58,000 square km. Moreover, after these conquests, Portugal encompassed three additional important towns: Santarém (conquered in 1147), Lisbon (conquered with the help of North European crusaders during the same year) and Évora (conquered in 1165).

After a pause that included the reigns of Sancho I (1185-1211) and Afonso II (1211-1223), Portugal, as did the other Christian states of the Iberian Peninsula, resumed advance after the battle of Las Navas de Tolosa (1212). During the 1220s and 1230s, King Sancho II occupied the whole Alentejo and the eastern part of Algarve. In spite of these successes, he had to face a powerful coalition of nobles and bishops that convinced Pope Innocence IV to depose him (1245). His brother, Afonso (later King Afonso III), agreed to replace him and managed to assume regency after some fighting. During the late 1240s, the new king was able to conquer the western part of Algarve. The Kingdom now had around

87,700 square km, and included four additional important towns: Beja, Mértola, Faro and Silves. Afonso III took the title of King of Portugal and of the Algarves (*Rei de Portugal e dos Algarves*), though the so-called Kingdom of the Algarves was never separated for any practical purpose from the Kingdom of Portugal.

D – Early Portuguese institutions and economic life

Economic activity

There is not much to add for Portugal to what has already been said about the economic life of Iberian Christendom. Until the 11th century, agriculture, animal husbandry, and industrial activities were performed almost exclusively for self-consumption and not for selling in the market, let alone for long-distance trade. From the 11th century on, exports of salt, olive oil and Mediterranean fruits developed, and, according to some opinions, the Portuguese economy became one of those most-linked to long-distance trade in Western Christendom (though far from the Italian or Flemish commercialisation levels).

The gradual diffusion of the innovations coming both from the Moslem world and from Western Christendom, already examined in sections A and B above, improved productivity, and slowly changed the rural life of early Portugal. The main consequence of this progress was population growth, which will be considered below.

Urban life

The growth of trade and the conquest of the more-urbanised regions of the south certainly increased the importance of urban life in Portugal. However, no Portuguese town seems to have reached the 20,000 inhabitants mark until the 13th century, and only Lisbon approached that level.

Population

The initial population of the first County of Portugal in the 9th century was certainly very low, because of the devastations that preceded its foundation. A figure of 110,000 inhabitants (which implies an average population density of nearly 7 inhabitants/square km) is perhaps a reasonable assumption.

When the first County of Portugal ceased to exist in the 11th century, the situation was certainly very different. As a matter of fact, the county had lived for more than two centuries in the relative peace and prosperity that its location near the frontier and the feudal administration allowed. An increase of 50%, raising the population density to around 10 inhabitants/square km and total population to around 165,000 seems another reasonable assumption.

The population of the first County of Portugal was concentrated mainly in the coastal region of Entre-Douro-e-Minho, which certainly had a population density clearly above that of the interior region of Trás-os-Montes. This fact was a consequence of the probable greater importance of agricultural activities in Entre-Douro-e-Minho and of animal husbandry in Trás-os-Montes, which may be explained by ecological circumstances.

*

It is likely that the evolution of the County of Coimbra during the same two centuries was somewhat different. The initial average population density was perhaps higher, because the region had not been subject to equally severe devastations until the 9th century, and the population growth was perhaps lower, because the region was subject to more-severe warfare thereafter. An initial estimate of around 125,000, and a final estimate of around 160,000 may be reasonable conjectures.

The population of the County of Coimbra was concentrated mainly in the interior region of western Beira Alta and in the valley of the Mondego, though the regional contrasts of population density were certainly lower than those in the first County of Portugal.

*

The second County of Portugal might have had an initial population of around 350,000 inhabitants, with an average population density approaching 10 inhabitants/square km. During the century and a half that elapsed until the conquest of Algarve was completed, population growth certainly continued at least at the same pace as in the most favourable circumstances of the preceding centuries, which may have increased the population density to a figure above 13 inhabitants/square km and the total population of the original territory of the county to something like 470,000 inhabitants.

The southern regions added to the kingdom during the second half of the 12th century and the first half of the 13th century presumably had a population density lower than the original northern regions, not only because of natural conditions, but also because of the devastations of more-recent warfare. An average estimate of 10 inhabitants/square km leads to a total of around 520,000 inhabitants. This population was concentrated mainly in the Tagus valley and in the Algarve, leaving the Alentejo as a region of very low population density.

Thus, the total population of the whole Kingdom of Portugal around the middle of the 13th century was approaching 1 million inhabitants. This means that by 1250 the continental territory of Portugal had recovered its maximum earlier population, which is to say, a population figure similar to that of the final centuries of Roman rule.

Population movements

The increases of the population of Portugal were partly the result of the increases in the area of the country, partly the result of an excess of births over deaths, and partly the result of net immigration coming from other Christian territories. The reconquest often led to the emigration of part of the Moslem population, as well, and the kings and landlords always tried to repopulate the newly conquered lands with Christian subjects. Immigration coming from the northern part of Iberian Christendom provided most of this new Christian population, but immigration coming from other countries of Western Christendom, mainly from France and Flanders was also important, as is attested by many surviving placenames.

Population juridical status

The juridical status of the various groups of the population was, of course, quite different. Religious minorities, common people, the aristocracy and the clergy formed different social orders.

Religious minorities

Religious minorities – Jews and Moslems – were segregated from the rest of the population and were not allowed access to public dignities and military or civil service, but enjoyed the right to the freedom of religion. Many Moslems remained serfs in the rural world, mainly in the southern part of the country. In towns, Jews and Moslems had self-governing separate areas.

Common people

Common people included Christian peasants, artisans and merchants. There were sizeable differences of wealth among these groups, but they had in common their unprivileged status: they were not allowed access to public dignities, their role in civil service was restricted to municipal magistrates, and their role in the army was subordinate, though not unimportant.

Privileged orders

The nobles and the clergy enjoyed the right to be judged only by the king or by their peers, controlled part of the country as feudal landlords, and last but not least, were, on the average, richer than the rank and file as owners of most of the land. However, no individual noble or member of the high clergy was powerful enough to become a rival of the king.

Besides individual nobles or members of the high clergy, reference must be made to the power and wealth of religious orders. There were three kinds of religious orders: traditional orders of the Benedictine type, military orders, and new orders of the preacher and mendicant type.

Traditional orders of the Benedictine type survived during the Moslem rule. After the reconquest they developed and were influenced by the reforms of Cluny origin. During the 1150s the new order centred at Citeaux also had its first Portuguese affiliate. These orders were influential in the diffusion of some agricultural innovations and in the settlement of some regions (mainly in Beira Litoral and Estremadura).

Military orders played an important role in the defence and settlement of the southern half of the country. There existed four religious military orders in Portugal. Two of them were organised in Palestine to protect the holy places there in the context of the Eastern Crusades: the Knights Templar (introduced in Portugal in 1128; centred at Tomar in Ribatejo); and the Knights Hospitaller (introduced in Portugal in 1130; centred at Crato in Alentejo). The other two were organised in the Iberian Peninsula to promote the so-called Western Crusades: the Knights of Calatrava (introduced in Portugal in 1166; centred at Avis in Alentejo) and the Knights of Saint James (introduced in Portugal in 1172; centred at Palmela in Estremadura).

The new orders of preachers (Dominicans) and mendicants (Franciscans) began to develop in the urban areas during the first half of the 13th century. They played a major role in the cultural developments of that century.

Legal and administrative background

In theory, the legal background of Portuguese life until the 13th century was still the old Visigothic Book of the Judges (*Liber Iudiciorum*) with all additional laws enacted by the kings of Asturias, Leon and Portugal. In practice, the chief legal texts were the local charters (*forais*) awarded by the kings of Asturias and Leon, by the counts of Portugal and Coimbra, by the kings of Portugal, and sometimes even by local nobles, bishops, or religious orders. These charters created feudal territories (*terras*) subject to a noble or ecclesiastical landlord, or self-governing municipalities (*concelhos*) based on assemblies of all free men.

Local charters varied widely in scope and content, affording a high degree of heterogeneity in local administration. They usually organised local courts and magistrates, headed by a judge (*juíz*), and prescribed the fiscal regime of the feudal territory or municipality. They also often included proceedings and penal codes, and rules about economic life.

*

The central administration of the Kingdom of Asturias, later Kingdom of Leon, and of the early Kingdom of Portugal was rather rudimentary. The king and a few military and civil servants formed the permanent staff. An assembly of the bishops and of the highest members of aristocracy met to assist the king in decisions about the most important questions, whenever convoked by the king.

Monetary system and prices

Until the 12th century, the kings of Asturias and the kings of Leon issued only subsidiary copper coins. The circulation of gold (and, more rarely, silver) coins depended, in practice, on the gold dinars and silver dirhams of Moslem mints.

During the 12th century, Christian military superiority and territorial growth was also translated into monetary matters. However, the coins issued by the Leonese, Castilian and Portuguese kings until the middle of the 13th century were only gold dinars with Latin inscriptions and Christian symbols, and subsidiary copper coins. This means that the Christian kingdoms of the western and central parts of the Iberian Peninsula had no monetary regime of their own, and that they simply adopted the monetary system of their Moslem rivals.

*

The absence of data makes it impossible to examine the evolution of prices in this epoch of the Portuguese society. In a certain sense, this is the consequence of the paucity of market transactions, which makes the price evolution less significant than in later epochs.

Fiscal systems

It is possible to speak of three different and interrelated fiscal systems in Portugal during the period under consideration: the feudal fiscal system, the Church fiscal system, and the State fiscal system.

The feudal fiscal system was formed by the taxes prescribed in the local charters referred to above. Most of these taxes were paid in kind, and even in personal services (either agricultural or military).

The Church fiscal system consisted of the tithe, that is to say, the right to receive the tenth of the gross product of all economic activities. The payment of the tithe was sometimes made in money, and it soon became the most important tax in quantitative terms. Of course, Church dignitaries also received revenue from feudal taxes paid by the territories that happened to have

2. The beginnings of the Portuguese national society | 83

them as landlords, and parishes had to defray the living expenses of the local clergy.

The State fiscal system included tariffs on foreign trade and various taxes on internal trade, paid mainly in money. Of course, the royal exchequer also received some revenue from the taxes prescribed in the local charters of municipalities not subject to feudal lords, and the king counted on the military service of the levies of his noble and ecclesiastical vassals and of the municipalities; but these resources should be reckoned as part of the feudal fiscal system.

3.

The consolidation of the Portuguese national society (13th-15th centuries)

With the conquest of western Algarve in the late 1240s, the continental territory of the Kingdom of Portugal took its general definitive shape and the period of the beginnings of the Portuguese national society came to an end. The rest of the medieval era was an epoch of consolidation of the Portuguese national society in the context of Western Christendom.

Growth and prosperity were the hallmarks of the long-term economic evolution of Western Christendom between the 11th and the 13th centuries. By the early 14th century, stagnation began to predominate, and by the mid-14th century, the irruption of the Black Death started a period of crisis and decline. The economic evolution of Portugal was quite similar, except for the absence of clear signs of stagnation during most of the first half of the 14th century. Section A of this chapter deals with the last century of prosperity in medieval Portugal (from the 1240s to the 1340s). Section B turns to the period of crisis (from the 1340s to the 1480s), with its long list of foreign and civil conflicts and analyses the impact of these conflicts on the consolidation of the Portuguese national society. Examination of the earliest efforts at Portuguese overseas expansion (from 1415 on) is postponed until chapter 4.

A – Medieval Portugal in an epoch of prosperity (13th-14th centuries)

Population

The Portuguese population went on growing between the mid-13th and the mid-14th centuries at the same rate at least as in previous centuries. Signs of a stagnation of population growth, general in Europe after the beginning of the 14th century, seem to appear in Portugal only in the 1340s. This yields a total of about 1.25 million inhabitants by the mid-14th century, on the eve of the Black Death.

The uneven distribution of the population among different regions of the country already noted for the previous centuries certainly continued between the 1240s and the 1340s. The part of the country conquered during the 12th century and the first half of the 13th century, included nearly 60% of the population, while the original territory included only around 40%, in spite of higher values of population density in the original territory (more than 15 inhabitants/square km), than in the more recently-conquered lands (barely exceeding 10 inhabitants/square km). Within the original territory, the region of Entre-Douro-e-Minho still had the highest population density and included perhaps 15% of the total population of the country; within the more recently conquered lands, it was the Tagus valley that had the highest population density and included perhaps 25% of the total population of the country.

Population movements

The conquest of new territories ceased to be a significant source of population growth for Portugal during this period, but the excess of births over deaths and the net immigration from other Christian territories continued as before until the mid-13th century.

Urban life

The urban life of the more-recently conquered lands was more important than the urban life of the original territory, as described for the previous centuries, but the disturbances of a more-recent reconquest contributed to a decline of southern towns that made for increased homogeneity within the country. The original territory had six bishopric sees – Braga, Porto, Lamego, Viseu, Coimbra and Guarda – and two other important towns – Guimarães and Covilhã – and the more-recently conquered lands had three bishopric sees – Lisbon, Évora and Silves – and six other important towns – Setúbal, Elvas, Beja, Lagos, Faro and Tavira.

Lisbon was the only large town of the country, reaching a population of some 25,000 inhabitants by the mid-14th century. It was only natural that it became the capital of the country during the second half of the 13th century.

Population juridical status

The juridical status of the different groups of the Portuguese population remained unchanged during the first century after the end of the reconquest. The only significant event to be mentioned in this context is the gradual dwindling of the Moslem minority by peaceful conversion to the Christian religion.

Economic activity

Population growth between the mid-13th century and the mid-14th century was accompanied by economic growth and by some structural changes in the Portuguese economy.

Extensive agricultural growth is evidenced by the awarding of new local charters to attract settlers to some regions that were still underpopulated. Such a process went on at least until the early 14th century. It is also likely that diffusion of agricultural innovations continued, at least until the epoch of the end of population growth, that is to say until the 1340s.

Concerning industrial activities, there was certainly some quantitative growth as a consequence of general economic growth, but there are no signs of important technological or organisational innovations. It is, however, important to underscore the growth of shipbuilding, as a result of the increase in long-distance trade. Such growth was certainly important in fostering the improvements that were to be decisive for the beginning of overseas explorations, and was linked to some efforts of forest plantation in the coastal region of the centre of the country. This forest plantation was also a device to prevent the incursion of sandy soils into cultivated zones.

The main structural change in the Portuguese economy was the increase in internal and foreign trade, which resulted from the higher proportion of total production brought to the market.

The increase in internal trade was mainly related to the foundation of regular market fairs. These fairs were often institutionalised with formal royal protection and played a decisive role in the growth of medium-distance trade, which could not have been expanded on a local market basis.

Foreign trade underwent a shift in its composition: relations with Western Christendom gradually replaced relations with the Moslem world. Though the patterns of trade with each one of these partners did not change significantly, this meant some changes in the most important items of Portuguese exports, and in the most important origins of traditional imports. Salt, wine and Mediterranean fruits became the most important Portuguese exports. The most-developed regions of Western Christendom became the main suppliers of sophisticated textiles and spices, even when these regions acted only as intermediaries in this trade. The role of Christian partners in Portuguese foreign trade was fostered by the intensification of the sea traffic between Italy and Flanders. This was perhaps partly a consequence of the

Christian reconquest of most of the southern coast of the Iberian Peninsula, which put that route almost completely under Christian control.

The increase of foreign trade was accompanied by the organisation of trade factories by Portuguese merchants in Italian, Flemish and English ports, and by foreign merchants in Lisbon and in other sea harbours of Portugal. This often led to formal diplomatic contacts and commercial treaties, mainly with the Kingdom of England.

In 1293, Portuguese merchants involved in long-distance sea trade organised an insurance fund, which received royal protection. This was the first case of an insurance activity created in the country.

Political and administrative evolution

The reinforcement of the central royal authority against feudal and municipal autonomy was perhaps the main aspect of Portuguese political and administrative evolution during the reigns of Afonso III (1248-1279), Dinis I (1279-1325) and Afonso IV (1325-1357), which roughly correspond to the prosperity period under consideration.

This reinforcement began during the first half of the 13th century with the so-called confirmations (*confirmações*), that is to say, the systematic verification of the legal basis of the status of feudal territories. This process led, of course, to the confirmation of the majority of the feudal possessions, but allowed the king to claim and exercise some control over the local administration provided by the feudal lords.

To enforce this control, both in feudal territories and in municipalities, the country was divided during the first half of the 14th century into six provinces: Entre-Douro-e-Minho (later called simply Minho), Trás-os-Montes, Beira (including the regions of Beira Alta and Beira Baixa, and later also the region of Beira Litoral), Estremadura (including the regions of Beira

Litoral, later transferred to the province of Beira, Estremadura and Ribatejo), Entre-Tejo-e-Guadiana (later called Alentejo), and Algarve (strictly speaking, Algarve had the rank of a kingdom separated from Portugal, but it was actually administered as a sixth province). A correction judge (*corregedor*) was appointed to each province, to control the work of local courts and of local administration. During the second quarter of the 14th century, the king went one step further, trying to replace the elected chairmen of local courts and local councils in the municipalities – the so-called ordinary judges (*juízes ordinários*) – by appointed civil servants – the so-called outside judges (*juízes de fora*). At the same time, there was a trend, both in feudal territories and in municipalities, to organise local courts and local administration on the basis of small councils that replaced traditional assemblies of all free men.

These efforts at political and administrative centralisation led, of course, to an increase in the number of civil servants working for the king. At the same time, the military staff lost part of its importance, at least in relative terms, because of the end of the wars of reconquest against the Moslem states.

As to the political system, the main change was that representatives of the most important municipalities began to be convoked to the assemblies of bishops and nobles that assisted the king in important decisions, which took the name of Courts (*Cortes*), which would remain the name of the parliament until the end of the monarchy. Such assemblies did not gather at regular intervals, but had to be convoked at least whenever the king wished to change the monetary or fiscal laws.

Reference must also be made to the efforts to separate the Portuguese branches of the Knights of Calatrava (which became known in Portugal as the Knights of Avis) and of the Knights of Saint James from their Castilian branches, and to put them under the control of the king. These efforts had some practical success in the early 14th century. At the same time, the extinction of the Knights Templar in 1312, allowed the foundation of the Knights of Christ, a strictly Portuguese religious military order, which took their place in Portugal. This means that only the Knights Hospitaller remained independent of Portuguese leadership.

No significant internal conflicts occurred between the 1240s and the 1340s, except for the friction that opposed King Dinis I and his son Afonso (later King Afonso IV) between 1320 and 1324.

Legal and administrative system

Local charters remained the basis of the Portuguese legal system, though the centralisation policy led to an increase in the number of new general laws issued by the kings.

Reference must also be made to the increasing role of the canonical law, especially after the compilations of the 13th century, because conflicts over most affairs of daily life (such as marriage) had to be settled in ecclesiastical courts.

International relations

Foreign affairs also enjoyed a rather peaceful evolution when compared to the previous reconquest period.

After 1250 the only country bordering Portugal was the Kingdom of Leon (in fact, as the definitive fusion of the kingdoms of Leon and Castile had taken place in 1230, and the Kingdom of Castile was really the more important of the two, it is better to speak of their union as the Kingdom of Castile). The tradition of feudal dependence of the Kingdom of Portugal upon the Kingdom of Leon, and Portuguese conquests over the Moslem states in regions that Castile considered as belonging to the Castilian lot of reconquest (the left bank of the Guadiana and even the Algarve) led to some friction. The treaty of Badajoz (1267) solved the problem of Algarve according to the Portuguese interests, and reduced the feudal obligations of the Kingdom of Portugal upon the Kingdom of Castile to military help in case of war. The remaining problems led to a short war between 1295 and 1297. The military operations were quite favourable to Portugal: Castilian attacks in the contested territories were rebuffed, and some territories on the left bank of the Douro were occupied by Portuguese troops. In the treaty of Alcañices of 1297, Castile was forced to recognise the Portuguese possession of the contested places, and to give up the region of Ribacoa occupied by Portugal during the war. Moreover, the feudal obligations of the Kingdom of Portugal to the Kingdom of Castile were no longer mentioned. This treaty gave the continental part of Portugal an area of around 89,500 square km, and defined an incredibly stable border that has lasted until the present day with only a small change in 1801.

A second conflict with Castile occurred between 1336 and 1339, but had no important consequences. Moreover, the threat of a Moroccan invasion of the Iberian Peninsula soon forced the two countries into an alliance. When the invasion materialised in 1340 and the combined forces of Morocco and Granada advanced into Andalusia, King Afonso IV of Portugal led the Portuguese army to Castile, and the Portuguese and Castilian forces attacked the Moslem army in the fields of Salado. The Christian allies won a clear victory that put an end to the possibility of a new Moroccan onslaught on the Iberian Peninsula.

This battle was the only significant clash between Portuguese and Moslem forces during the period under consideration. The absence of a border with Moslem states put an end to the earlier state of endemic war with these states, except for mutual piracy between Portuguese and Moslem fleets.

Monetary system and prices

The first step away from the Moslem monetary system that prevailed in Portugal until the mid-13th century was made in 1253 with the adoption of the Carolingian monetary units – the pound (*libra*), the shilling (*soldo*) and the penny (*dinheiro*). Portuguese issues of gold and silver coins remained very scarce, and the needs of monetary circulation, still not very important, were partly satisfied by foreign coins of Moslem and Christian states.

The gold and silver value of the Portuguese pound underwent a clear devaluation between 1253 and 1369, the result of manipulations by the kings to gain quick revenue for the royal exchequer. The gold value of the Portuguese pound was 2.5 g in 1253 but had dropped to 1.1 g by 1369; the silver value of the Portuguese pound was 20.0 g in 1253 and 6.6 g in 1369.

*

In spite of some increase in market transactions, the absence of data regarding prices makes it impossible, as in previous centuries, to study their evolution during this period.

Fiscal systems

There were no fundamental changes in the feudal, Church and State fiscal systems between the mid-13th and mid-14th centuries. As a matter of fact, there were increases in the revenue coming from these systems, but this was only a consequence of the economic and demographic growth.

Cultural aspects

Consolidation of the national society was also the main trend in Portuguese cultural life during the second half of the 13th and first half of the 14th centuries.

First of all, reference must be made to the adoption of Portuguese as the official language. Legal and official texts were always written in Latin until the late 12th century. During the 13th century, Portuguese began to emerge as a written language, first in poetry, later in private documents, and lastly in legal and official documents. By the end of the century, King Dinis I ordered that legal and official documents should always be written in Portuguese. Such a decision restricted the use of Latin to ecclesiastical and international affairs.

Also important was the foundation of the first Portuguese university. Its activity began in the late 1280s in Lisbon and was confirmed by Pope Nicolas IV in 1290. In 1308 it was moved to Coimbra, but came back to Lisbon in 1338, only to be moved once again to Coimbra in 1354. In 1377 it was definitively established in Lisbon for the rest of the medieval period.

B – Medieval Portugal in an epoch of crisis (14th-15th centuries)

Population

The Black Death arrived in Portugal in 1348. Its effects were quite similar to those in other countries of Western Europe. A 25 % drop in the Portuguese population, to something like 0.9 million inhabitants, is the most plausible figure for its immediate demographic impact.

Population stagnation seems to have lasted until the late 14th century. The second half of the 14th century was an epoch of recurrent epidemics, poor harvests and civil and Iberian wars. During the 15th century the situation improved, and recovery began, but it took the 15th century to undo the effects of the Black Death. Only by 1500 was the Portuguese population passing the 1.25 million mark again.

Population movements

There were no territorial changes and no significant migratory movements during the second half of the 14th century. Thus, the excess of deaths over births was the only important explanation for the drop in the Portuguese population between the mid-14th century and the early 15th century.

The 15th century was very different from the second half of the 14th century from this point of view: territorial expansion and migratory movements once again became significant. Territorial expansion and the population of the new Portuguese territories will be dealt with in chapter 4 below. Regarding the continental part of the country, emigration of settlers to the new territories was at least partly compensated for by the importation of slaves from the western coast of Africa. Thus, the excess of births over deaths was the main explanation for the increase in the Portuguese population during the 15th century.

Urban life

It is likely that the population of urban centres suffered higher mortality than did the rural population, although total urban population perhaps had a lower decline than did total rural population, because of migrations of rural population to the towns. Such a process was perhaps more important in the southern part of the country, leading to a growing contrast of population density and weight of urban life between the north and the south of Portugal: population density became clearly higher in the north, with many lands in the south reverting to pastoral uses; concentration in urban centres became clearly higher in the south.

Lisbon remained the only large town in the country. Its population increased and reached 50,000 inhabitants by the end of the 15th century, mainly because of the impact of its role in Portuguese overseas trade.

Population juridical status

Religious minorities were easy scapegoats in times of trouble. The Moslem minority had almost disappeared from Portugal in the 14th century, so the rage turned against the Jewish minority. Discriminatory rules were reinforced during the second half of the 14th and 15th century, but, as the treatment in other Iberian Christian states was harsher, there was an inflow of Jews, mainly from Castile. The growth of the Jewish community in Portugal, however, only stimulated popular and official mistrust, paving the way for the radical measures taken in the 1490s, which offered the Portuguese Jews a choice between conversion and emigration.

*

The juridical status of the Christian groups of the Portuguese population remained unchanged during the 14th century and the first half of the 15th century. However, friction between peasants and landlords in the rural world, between artisans and merchants in the urban world, and between the aristocracy and the emerging bourgeoisie became endemic in these times of distress. This friction was the social background of the political conflicts of the period, eventually exploding into riots and even revolutions to be mentioned below.

*

During the second half of the 15th century a new group was added to the Portuguese social orders: Berber and Negro slaves imported from the western coast of Africa. Their number never exceeded 1/50 of the total population, and they never played any important role in the main economic activities, as they served mainly as domestic slaves.

Economic distress and improvements

The demographic slump of the second half of the 14th century was, of course, accompanied by an economic slump.

The most visible aspect of this economic slump was the decrease of agricultural production, linked with the reduction of cultivated land, because of lack of labour. Portuguese kings reacted in the same way as many other European kings of the epoch, by enacting laws to compel agricultural labourers to work for the same wages as before, to force landlords to have their lands tilled as usual, and to forbid the emigration of rural population to towns. The practical effects of these measures were seldom felt, as has already been pointed out. Most agricultural land converted to pastoral uses, mainly in the southern part of the country.

Industrial activities were also affected by the recession, though less dramatically. The organisation of corporations among artisans was perhaps a consequence of the need to adapt to these hard times. It is also important to stress the development of the tanning activities, fostered by the increase of animal raising that accompanied the 14th-century recession.

Domestic and foreign trade do not seem to have experienced any relative decline, though the general economic recession certainly reduced their absolute amount. As a matter of fact, the activity of local markets, fairs, seaports and trade factories was seldom interrupted, even if the increase in social and military conflicts was certainly detrimental to trade relations, at least in specific zones and periods.

*

The 15th century saw a gradual recovery of economic activity linked to the simultaneous demographic recovery. Territorial expansion in Morocco, Madeira and the Azores, and the establishment of regular trade relations with the western coast of Africa were the most conspicuous signs of this economic recovery. This process will be dealt with in chapter 4, below, together with the technological and organisational innovations that allowed the extension of the geographic and economic horizon of the Portuguese society. The intermediate role played by Portugal between the newly-discovered regions and Western Christendom in general also fueled Portuguese economic activity.

However, the recovery of agricultural and industrial production was certainly the key event, even in setting the basis for overseas expansion.

Regarding agriculture, there were no significant innovations during the 15th century. The recovery was based mainly on the extension of the cultivated area, benefiting from the additional labour provided by population growth. At the same time, cash crops, such as wine and fruits, increased their share in the total agriculture production as against cereal crops, because of higher demand, mainly in foreign markets.

As for industry, some new activities were introduced in Portugal during the 15th century. The production of paper, soap and gunpowder, and printing were the leaders among these. From a quantitative point of view, however, shipbuilding related to long distance trade and overseas explorations was certainly the industrial sector experiencing the highest growth.

It must also be stressed that the development of cash crops and of the new industries clearly linked to the market decreased the share of production used for self-consumption, even if the trade related to the overseas expansion is disregarded.

Political evolution 1348-1369

During the last years of the reign of Afonso IV there were some quarrels between the king and his son Pedro (later King Pedro I) regarding the marriage of Pedro with a Castilian noble, Inês de Castro, against the will of the king. Inês was killed with the approval of the king in 1355 (an unhappy end to a love story that became one of the most popular themes of Portuguese literature, thereafter), and there followed a short civil war between the king and his son.

The reign of Pedro I (1357-1367) was calmer. However, the king started a practice that would produce later conflicts: the endowment to royal sons who were not entitled to the throne with extensive fiefs. This tended to produce powerful aristocratic houses ready to quarrel with royal authority. As a matter of fact, the sons of Inês de Castro, João and Dinis, received rich holdings, and another royal bastard, also called João, received the administration and revenue of the Knights of Avis.

Castilian dynastic troubles 1369-1383

The eldest son of Pedro I, Fernando I, spent most of his reign (1367-1383) involved in wars with Castile. These wars were linked to the endemic civil strife that plagued that country during the last third of the 14th century.

Troubles began when Pedro I of Castile, the legitimate son of Alfonso XI, and his brother Henrique, a royal bastard, quarrelled about the Castilian throne. As Henrique murdered his brother and became King Henrique II in 1369, many Castilian nobles that disliked the new king searched for another candidate for the throne.

The first candidate that tried to replace Henrique II was the king of Portugal, Fernando I, cousin of Pedro I and of Henrique II. His bid for the throne of Castile involved Portugal in the Castilian civil war between 1369 and 1371. The military operations were unfavourable to the Portuguese army, and Fernando I of Portugal had to recognise Henrique II as king of Castile in the treaty of Alcoutim.

This was short lived, however. In 1372, by the treaty of Tagilde, Fernando I gave his support to another candidate, the duke of Lancaster, John of Gaunt, son of Edward III of England and married to a daughter of Pedro I of Castile. Henrique II reacted with an invasion of Portugal in which he laid siege to Lisbon, and forced Fernando I to recognise him once again, in the treaty of Santarém.

The attempt to put an Englishman on the throne of Castile alarmed France, at that time fighting England in the so-called Hundred Years War. As a consequence, French troops were sent to Castile to help Henrique II. His death in 1380 left the Castilian throne in the hands of his son Juan I, and gave new hopes to the English contender. By 1381, he was realigning his forces with Portugal, trying to use it as a staging area for attacks on Castile. The war was unfavourable once again to the Portuguese army (and to the English expeditionary forces), and in 1383 the treaty of Salvaterra de Magos swung Portugal back to the French-Castilian side. Beatriz, the heiress to the Portuguese throne, married Juan I of Castile as a pledge of the new alliance.

Portuguese dynastic troubles 1383-1387

In 1383, it was Portugal's turn to experience dynastic trouble. King Fernando I died in October, leaving the throne to his daughter Beatriz, married to Juan I of Castile. As the young queen was absent from her kingdom, her mother Leonor became regent. Leonor was very unpopular among some aristocratic and popular groups and an affair with João Fernandes Andeiro, a Galician nobleman who threatened to become the true ruler of Portugal, made things worse. In December, João, the royal bastard of Pedro I of Portugal who was master of the Knights of Avis, led a revolt in Lisbon, murdered Andeiro, expelled Leonor, and usurped the regency. The bulk of the south of the country rallied to his side, but the majority of the north remained faithful to Beatriz, the legitimate queen.

Renewed war between Portugal and Castile was inevitable, as Juan I of Castile tried to regain the control of the whole of Portugal for his wife. As expected by now, French forces came to his aid, and a new English expeditionary force arrived to support the Portuguese revolution. In the summer of 1384, the king of Castile besieged Lisbon, where the regent managed to resist. Meanwhile a land invasion of the south of the country was stopped at the battle of Atoleiros by Nuno Álvares Pereira, who became the commanding general of the Portuguese army until the end of the war. In the summer of 1385, a full-scale Castilian invasion was defeated at the battle of Aljubarrota.

Meanwhile, the Courts had gathered in the spring of 1385 to elect a new king of Portugal. There were no supporters of Beatriz in the assembly. Thus, the two candidates to be considered were João, son of Pedro I of Portugal and of Inês de Castro, and the regent, also João and also son of Pedro I of Portugal. The supporters of the regent had a clear majority, and, after some discussion, he was formally recognised as King João I of Portugal.

By 1386 the new king of Portugal had managed to bring the whole kingdom under his authority. There followed a new Portuguese intervention in the Castilian affairs. The traditional English candidate to the Castilian throne tried once more to use Portugal as a base for his military operations, but without success. Juan I of Castile dropped his designs on the Portuguese throne, devoted himself to defending his Castilian possessions, and recognised Dinis, son of Pedro I of Portugal and Inês de Castro as king of Portugal (meanwhile, the eldest brother of Dinis, João, candidate for the throne in 1385, had died). As the attempt of Dinis to invade Portugal in 1387 failed, the war wound down and the various factions agreed to an armistice. Though this armistice was interrupted for a short period during the late 1390s and a definitive peace treaty was not signed until 1411, the result of the war left no doubt: the new dynasty of Avis was firmly established on the throne of Portugal.

The Great Schism

Meanwhile, Western Christendom had been divided by the so-called Great Schism between allegiance to the Pope of Rome or Avignon. Portugal changed its allegiance between the popes of Avignon (1378-1381), Rome (1381-1383), Avignon again (1383) and Rome again (from 1383 on), according to its current political alliances.

Long-term effects of the 1383-1387 dynastic troubles

The importance of the 1383-1387 dynastic troubles and of the triumph of the new dynasty of Avis for the future of Portugal has been a matter of much debate.

According to what may be called the standard view, this war was a decisive turning point in Portuguese history. First of all, it represented the triumph of a nationalist ideology over the legitimist ideology. In fact, the right of Queen Beatriz to the throne, as daughter of Fernando I, was unquestioned, and her substitution by a royal bastard on the basis of her marriage with the king of Castile was justified by the need to preserve the autonomy of the kingdom. Second, such a disregard for traditional succession rules met the opposition of the majority of the aristocracy, who had to flee to Castile, giving way to a bourgeois power that would promote the expansion of the 15th and 16th centuries.

There are, however, good reasons to challenge these notions. On one hand, the rise of the importance of nationalistic ideas in Portugal did not prevent new attempts at Iberian unification, including the triumph of such unification nearly two centuries later. It is also impossible to speak of a true bourgeois power. As a matter of fact, it was a new aristocracy, mainly recruited among the lower ranks of the old aristocracy, that became the dominant class in Portugal during the Avis dynasty. Moreover, it may be argued that bourgeois power is not needed to nurture expansionist policies, either by sea or by land, and that aristocratic governments are just as likely to promote them. The expansionist policies of the clearly aristocratic Castile would bear this out, even if the Portuguese case was not really similar to it.

Political evolution 1387-1474

The reign of the winner of the 1383-1387 civil war, João I (1385-1433), saw the beginnings of Portuguese overseas expansion partly by means of a military expedition to Morocco (Ceuta, 1415), and partly by the peaceful occupation of Madeira, which will be dealt with in detail in chapter 4, below. It also saw the repetition of the endowment of royal sons with rich fiefs: Pedro, the second legitimate son, became duke of Coimbra; Henrique, the third legitimate son, became duke of Viseu and master of the Knights of Christ; João, the fourth legitimate son, became master of the Knights of Avis; and Afonso, a royal bastard, received the fiefs that would allow him to become duke of Bragança. If the most powerful aristocratic houses of the second half of the 14th century had been swept away by the civil war of 1383-1387, new candidates for aristocratic troublemakers were on the way.

The short reign of the eldest son of João I, Duarte I (1433-1438), saw a disastrous military expedition to Morocco (Tânger, 1437), which will be dealt with in detail in chapter 4, below.

After the death of Duarte I there was some friction about the regency during the minority of his son Afonso V. Pedro, brother of Duarte I and uncle of Afonso V, managed to impose his authority against Leonor, wife of Duarte I and mother of Afonso V. His regency saw the beginnings of the occupation of the Azores and of trade with the western coast of Africa, which will be dealt with in detail in chapter 4, below.

In 1448, Afonso V came of age and assumed the government. The next year, he quarrelled with the former regent and Pedro was killed in a short civil war. This was the first case of aristocratic revolt against the king: the house of Coimbra disappeared and its lands were added to the royal holdings.

The main events of the reign of Afonso V (1448-1481) were the exploration of most of the western coast of Africa until the Gulf of Guinea, and new military expeditions in Morocco, which will be dealt with in detail in chapter 4, below, and an intervention in Castilian affairs (1474-1479). The successes of the expeditions in Morocco led the king to take the title of King of Portugal and the Algarves at home and overseas in Africa (*Rei de Portugal e dos Algarves de aquém e de além mar em África*) – 'Algarve at home' meaning the traditional province of Algarve, and 'Algarve overseas in Africa' meaning the Atlantic coast of Morocco.

Castilian dynastic troubles 1474-1479

The 1474-1479 intervention in Castilian affairs illustrates the survival of the idea of Iberian unification among the Portuguese rulers, and the course of the war that followed also illustrates the Castilian wishes for maritime as well as land expansion.

In 1474, King Henrique IV of Castile died leaving two potential heiresses to fight for the throne: his sister Isabel married to the king of Aragon, Ferdinand, and his daughter Juana fiancée to the king of Portugal, Afonso V. There followed a Castilian civil war that lasted until 1479. Of course, Aragon and Portugal intervened to support the wives of their kings. Most of the Castilian aristocracy supported Juana, but an equally powerful party, which included the bulk of the Castilian bourgeoisie, supported Isabel. Castilian merchants and pirates profited from the opportunity to compete with the Portuguese exploration of the western coast of Africa, using the Canary Islands as their main base, without much success. In 1476, the Portuguese and the Castilians supporting Juana were able to gain victory at the main battle of the war at Toro, but it was merely a tactical victory. During the next year the party of Isabel won the control of the country.

The Treaty of Alcáçovas of 1479 was the result of the failure of Portuguese attempts to put Juana on the throne of Castile and of the failure of Castilian attempts to interfere with Portuguese overseas expansion. Isabel was recognised as queen of Castile, and Castile recognised Portuguese monopoly of overseas explorations south of parallel 30° N. However, the Canary Islands remained in the hands of Castile.

Political evolution 1479-1495

During the reign of João II (1481-1495), the exploration of the western coast of Africa reached the Cape of Good Hope, prompting the king to add the title of Lord of Guinea (*senhor da Guiné*) – meaning the whole of the west African coast – to his already long official title, and the conflicts between the king and the main aristocratic houses came to a climax.

The houses of Bragança and Viseu led a conspiracy against the king, but failed. The Duke of Bragança was beheaded and his lands added to the royal house, the Duke of Viseu was killed by the king himself and his lands added to those of his brother, made duke of Beja as a reward for his support of the king. Ironically, some years later the death of the only son of João II allowed the Duke of Beja to become heir-apparent to the throne and later King Manuel I, adding also the lands of the former houses of Viseu and Beja to the royal holdings. However, total concentration of the most important aristocratic possessions in the hands of the king did not materialise immediately, because Manuel I restored the house of Bragança to its ducal dignity.

Further attempts at Iberian unification

The result of the Castilian civil war of 1474-1479 was not harmful to the goal of Iberian unification. As a matter of fact, if the union of Portugal with Castile failed, the union of Aragon with Castile was established once and for all. In 1489, the Iberian royal families tried to achieve the union of Aragon, Castile and Portugal, by marriage of the heir of the Portuguese throne, Afonso, to the heiress of the Castilian-Aragonese throne, Isabel. The scheme misfired, because Afonso died in 1491.

Some years later, new attempts at unification by means of royal marriages took place: in 1496, the Portuguese king, Manuel I, married Isabel, daughter of Ferdinand and Isabel, and in 1497, the death of the heir to the Castilian-Aragonese throne, Juan, made Isabel the heiress of that throne again. When she died in 1498, Miguel, the son of Manuel I of Portugal and Isabel, became heir-apparent to the thrones of the three Iberian kingdoms. However, Miguel died in 1500, and while the Portuguese throne went to a son of the second marriage of Manuel I, the Castilian-Aragonese throne went to another daughter of Fernando and Isabel, Juana, who had married the son of the German emperor Maximilian, Philip (Filipe I of Castile), and was to be the mother of the famous Charles V (Carlos I of Castile). This led to the 16th century union of Castile and Aragon with the Netherlands, Burgundy, Milan, Naples, Sicily and Sardinia (and even with the Holy Roman Empire of the German Nation under Charles V) and postponed the Iberian unification for nearly one century.

Legal and administrative background

Efforts toward legal and administrative centralisation did not cease during the second half of the 14th century and the 15th century. The main fact to be mentioned during this period is the organisation of the first compilation of Portuguese general laws – the Ordinances of King Afonso (*Ordenações Afonsinas*). This compilation, which was to replace all previous laws in civil courts (not in ecclesiastical courts, in which canonical law still prevailed) was prepared during the second quarter of the 15th century and promulgated in 1454.

A new archbishopric was also created in Lisbon in the late 14th century.

Monetary system and prices

Between 1369 and 1435, Portugal went through a period of staggering inflation, as a consequence of the attempts to finance the four wars with Castile (fought between 1369 and 1387) and the first expedition to Morocco (in 1415) partly with monetary devaluations. The gold value of the Portuguese pound, which was 1.1 g on the eve of the first war with Castile, fell to 0.5 g during the war. After the war, there was an attempt at revaluation that brought the value to 0.7 g, but, as soon as hostilities started again, gold coins ceased to be issued by the Portuguese mints, an absence which lasted until the 1430s. Rough computations based on the value of foreign coins circulating in Portugal suggest that the gold value of the Portuguese pound had dropped to 0.0007 g in the 1430s. The silver value of the Portuguese pound, which was 6.6 g on the eve of the first war with Castile, fell to 0.9 g during the war. After the war, there was likewise an attempt at revaluation that brought the value to 7.8 g, but, as soon as hostilities started again, devaluation accelerated. By the end of the century, the silver value of the Portuguese pound was 0.6 g, and by 1435 it had dropped to 0.008 g. In practice, the Portuguese mints issued only copper coins.

Such a currency devaluation implied a significant increase in prices. There are no data from effective transactions, but some information may be obtained from the official equivalence for money rent payments: they were multiplied by 5 in 1389, by 3 in 1399, by 3 1/3 in 1409, by 5 in 1417, by 2 in 1422 and by 1.4 in 1436. This implies a rent index with pre-war unitary basis of 5 in 1389, 15 in 1399, 50 in 1409, 250 in 1417, 500 in 1422 and 700 in 1436. Such an index clearly lags behind the devaluation of coins, and almost certainly behind the effective price increases, as well, but gives an idea of what was the greatest inflation in Portuguese history: an average increase of prices in excess of 10% per year during five and a half decades.

*

In 1435 a thorough monetary reform was attempted. First of all, the Portuguese pound was replaced by a new monetary unit, the Portuguese *real* (plural *reais*, later *réis*), to facilitate computations. The Portuguese real was equal to 35 Portuguese pounds, with the *conto*, equal to one million reais, as the main multiple.

Gold and silver coins were issued once again. Devaluation did not end, but went on at a moderate pace, at least when compared with the situation between the 1370s and the 1430s. The gold value of the Portuguese real was 28.7 mg in 1435, falling to 9.3 mg by 1489; the silver value of the Portuguese real was 262.9 mg in 1435, and had dropped to 92.3 mg by 1489.

In 1473 a small adjustment (multiplication by a factor of 1.2 or 1.4 according to circumstances) was made in money rent payments. Once more, the adjustment remained below the devaluation of coins, and it is likely that it also remained below the effective price increase, even if this increase did not fully correspond to the devaluation of coins.

Fiscal systems

There were no fundamental changes in the feudal and Church fiscal systems between the mid-14th and late 15th centuries. As a matter of fact, there were decreases in the revenue collected from these systems, but this was only a consequence of the economic and demographic slump.

As for the State fiscal system, the situation was quite different. The disastrous monetary consequences of the earlier three wars with Castile (1369-1371, 1372, 1381-1383) led the Courts to accept, in 1385, the introduction of the first general Portuguese tax to finance the ongoing fourth war. This tax was called excise (*sisa*). It was a tax on all transactions of capital and consumption goods, which already existed in most municipalities as a local tax.

Cultural aspects

The most important aspects of Portuguese cultural development during the 15th century were those linked with overseas expansion, which will be dealt with in chapter 4, below.

4.

Portuguese expansion (15th-16th centuries)

Between 1415 and 1580, Portuguese society went through an era of expansion, during which it made bids to control the Atlantic coast of Morocco, to occupy the archipelagoes of the North Atlantic (the Canary Islands, Madeira and the Azores), to explore the western coast of Africa, to discover a sea route to the Indian Ocean, to establish trade connections all over the Indian Ocean and the Far East, and to participate in the colonisation of the New World. These efforts began as a response to the crisis of the 14th and 15th centuries and gradually built up one upon another. At last, they brought to Western Christendom in general a great deal of new geographical knowledge, and were a contribution to the formation of the internal links and external relations of the Euro-Atlantic world-economy of the following centuries. To Portugal in particular they brought an epoch of economic prosperity and some international political power, as well as long-term consequences that are still a matter of debate.

Section A of this chapter addresses the causes and motives of Portuguese expansion as well as the national potentialities that made it feasible. Sections B to G review the various fronts of Portuguese expansion. Section H seeks to make an assessment of the consequences of expansion upon the Portuguese economy and society in the short and long run.

A – The rationale of Portuguese expansion

Causes

Portuguese expansion must be understood as, above all, a response to the challenge of the deep crisis that Western Christendom in general, and Portugal in particular, went through during the second half of the 14th and the 15th centuries. Expansion, either to prosperous Moslem territories, or to regions not yet explored as trade partners, was a means of restoring the economic prosperity lost during the decades that preceded the irruption of the Black Death. Thus, it is possible to say that Portuguese expansion must be explained, first of all, in terms of economic causes.

Of course, the goals of political expansion, that is to say, the acquisition of new possessions for the kingdom, and of religious expansion, that is to say, the conversion of new peoples to the Roman Catholic faith, were also stimuli of the expansion projects. This means that political and cultural causes also played their role.

Motives

To gain wealth by means of plunder and trade was, of course, one of the motives that drove most of the men who were responsible for the initiatives of the Portuguese expansion. It is undoubted that this motivation was a conscious and fully recognised factor for the average leader, warrior and sailor, who administrated the tasks of expansion in Lisbon, or who went to the Moroccan presidios or to the various regions integrated, one after the other, on the horizons of the Portuguese Empire. Thus, economic motives certainly played a decisive role in the minds of the agents of Portuguese expansion.

Economic motives were not alone, however. The wish for other kinds of social promotion, the wish of converting unfaithful and pagan souls to the true religion, and geographical curiosity, that is to say cultural motives, were also important for most of the leaders, warriors, sailors and missionaries who participated in the process. This means that cultural motives also played a crucial role in the minds of the agents of Portuguese expansion.

Conditions

However, objective causes and subjective motives are not enough to explain Portuguese expansion. Resources had to be marshalled, adequate technologies had to be mastered and an efficient organisation had to be set up so that the process could get underway and carry on.

Resources

The quantitative lack of resources was perhaps the greatest problem, due to the economic slump of the second half of the 14th century. Scarcity of men and money certainly retarded the possible pace of expansion until the economic expansion resulting from the first initiatives began to encourage further advances. Of course, the use of resources from other countries, for instance the participation of Italian and Flemish navigators and capitalists in the process, could help to overcome difficulties. However, the desire to retain full control of the process led Portuguese authorities to use this help rather reluctantly and sparingly.

From a qualitative point of view, Portugal was well suited to the task of expansion. Portuguese forests provided wood for the shipbuilding industry, Portuguese warriors and seamen were able to command the most sophisticated military and navigation techniques of the epoch, and Portuguese society produced during the 15th and 16th century a cadre of competent leaders who perceived the potentialities of the expansion process.

Technology

Technological challenges may be divided into three types: shipbuilding, navigation and military affairs.

Concerning shipbuilding, the Portuguese shipyards managed to combine the Mediterranean and North European traditions in new types of ships. The most important was the caravel, a ship of two or three masts equipped with lateen sails, adequate for high seas voyages because of its small crew and high manoeuvrability. The caravel was later superseded by carracks and galleons of higher tonnage for the longest voyages, and the traditional ships of the Indian Ocean were also used for local voyages.

Regarding navigation, the Portuguese navigators inherited the use of the compass for orientation, of the dead-reckoning technique to estimate sea distances, and cartography based on cardinal points from the Mediterranean tradition. Moreover, they improved on this tradition, mainly in the fields of the astronomical determination of latitude and of the systematic observation of magnetic declination, used as a very rough method of computing longitude. Further details about navigation and geographical knowledge will be given below in connection with the description of the process of mastering the Atlantic and Indian Ocean sea routes.

As to military affairs, it is enough to say that Portuguese troops managed to master the best military technology known in Western Christendom in the epoch and to produce or import its implements. Such military technology was vital in Morocco, the Indian Ocean and the Far East, where the Portuguese faced off against societies with equivalent levels of development, which were unable to resist the Portuguese at sea, but managed to block their progress into the interior of the land masses. In other regions, the Portuguese military superiority over local societies was clear and difficulties in penetrating the continents resulted mainly from natural problems, such as tropical diseases and un-navigable rivers.

Organisation

The expansion process was always a state initiative in the case of Morocco. On the maritime front, it began as a private initiative that gradually came under state control. There were, however, two different outcomes of the process. The exploration of the Atlantic Islands, the cod fisheries of the North Atlantic and the colonisation of Brazil remained mainly in private hands; state intervention in these areas was restricted to what is commonly accepted today as the provision of public goods. The exploration of the western coast of Africa and the organisation of the Cape of Good Hope route, on the contrary, became formal public monopolies, because of the concentration of resources needed to organise the voyages and above all to keep foreigners away. There was, of course, a lot of private business intermingled with the public organisation, but the principle of public monopoly remained firmly entrenched. Along the western coast of Africa, it disappeared when connection grew with Brazil, but in the Indian Ocean and the Far East it survived the 17th century failure to push out the Dutch, English and French rivals. Freedom of private trade in these regions had to wait for the end of the mercantilist era and there were even some ephemeral attempts to extend privileged schemes to the Atlantic trade.

B – The conquests in Morocco

The slow advance during the 15th century

When the Portuguese rulers decided to commit the country to a systematic expansion policy in the early 15th century, Morocco appeared as the natural target for such an expansion. As a matter of fact, the conquests in Morocco might be seen as a continuation of the reconquest of the Iberian Peninsula from Moslem rule (there was still a Moslem state left in the Iberian

Peninsula – the emirate of Granada – but it was in a geographically awkward direction for Portuguese efforts). Moreover, the coast of Morocco was the base for pirate raids against Christian shipping around the south of the Iberian Peninsula, and its control by a Christian state would improve security on sea routes linking the Mediterranean and the Atlantic. Last but not least, Morocco showed good prospects of providing revenue, not only in the form of plunder, but also from the regular taxation of busy seaports, of rich agricultural lands and of important industrial activities.

According to this policy, the first Portuguese effort at overseas expansion was a military expedition against the Moroccan city of Ceuta in 1415. The expedition was led by the king (João I) and his three eldest sons (Duarte, later king; Pedro, later regent of the kingdom after the death of his brother; and Henrique later known as 'the Navigator') and met with rather easy success. However, Ceuta proved to be an economic failure in the long term: the traffic of its port and its industrial activity dwindled after the conquest and no considerable tract of land was controlled outside the town. Thus, Ceuta became a mere presidio, that is to say, an isolated fortress in enemy territory, always demanding the expenditure of resources and providing no significant revenue in exchange.

The idea of abandoning such a burden to the royal exchequer soon arose, but it was not accepted. The Portuguese government adopted, instead, the policy of extending Portuguese rule to other towns, so that Moroccan merchants had no alternative but to use Portuguese harbours, and the rural land between the Portuguese towns also came under Portuguese control. In 1437, two decades after the conquest of Ceuta, a new expedition was sent against Tânger (today Tangiers), led by Henrique (the Navigator) and his brother Fernando. The expedition ended in disaster and Fernando had to be left as a hostage so that the Portuguese army could be extricated from the place. He died as a Moroccan prisoner, leaving the Portuguese government in humiliation.

4. Portuguese expansion | 115

Two decades elapsed before revenge was attempted: new expeditions led by the king (Afonso V) went to Morocco in 1458 to conquer Alcácer Ceguer (today Al-Qasr al-Sagir) with success, in 1460 and 1463-1464 to attack Tânger without success, and in 1471 to occupy Arzila again with success. In the same year the Moroccans abandoned Tânger, which was promptly occupied by the Portuguese army.

Portugal now had control of the northern part of the Atlantic coast of Morocco, but the economic situation of the Moroccan possessions did not improve. As a matter of fact, there remained many harbours for Moroccan trade outside the Portuguese possessions, the industrial activity of the newly gained towns declined after the conquest, as it had in Ceuta, and the rural area under Portuguese control was still very small. To put it bluntly, Portugal now had to finance four presidios instead of one.

The acceleration in the late 15th and early 16th century

In the late 15th and early 16th century, there were important changes in the pace of the Portuguese advance in Morocco. Resources flowing from other expansion achievements were used to intensify the attacks, and many conquests followed: Safim (today Safi) in 1488; Azamor (today Mulai bu Saib) in 1486; Santa Cruz do Cabo de Gué (today Agadir) in 1505; Mogador (today Essauira) in 1506; and Mazagão (today El-Jadida) in 1514. Though Mogador was abandoned in 1525, Portugal had effective control of the Atlantic coast of Morocco between the 1510s and the 1530s.

This situation allowed the fulfilment of at least one of the goals of the Moroccan campaigns: the control of Moroccan piracy. At the same time, there was some improvement in the activity of the Portuguese ports in Morocco: dressed hides, dyes and sugar became the most important exports of these ports. However, the normal course of industrial activity and, above all, the control of significant rural areas never materialised. Thus, Morocco never ceased to be a drain upon the Portuguese exchequer.

The setback of the 1540s

As long as Portugal had to face the relatively weak Marinid Emirate of Fez, the cost of maintaining the Moroccan possessions remained manageable. However, the situation changed during the 1540s. Instead of the Marinid Emirate of Fez, there emerged the new Saidian Sharifate of Marrakesh, which proved capable of increasing the burden of maintaining the presidios to a point that the Portuguese exchequer was no longer willing to bear. As Santa Cruz do Cabo de Gué was attacked in 1541 and had to surrender, the Portuguese government decided to cut its financial losses: Safim and Azamor were abandoned in 1541; Alcácer Ceguer and Arzila followed in 1550. The Portuguese possessions in Morocco were reduced to three presidios, though the dream of control of sizeable territories in Morocco did not vanish entirely.

The attempts of the 1570s

The policy of expansion in Morocco came back in the 1570s. In 1577 Arzila was occupied again, and in the next year there was an attempt to profit from a Moroccan civil war to make a full-scale invasion. However, the expedition, once more led by the king (Sebastião I), met disastrous defeat at the battle of Alcácer Quibir (today Al-Qasr al-Qebir). This episode had important consequences, as will be seen in chapter 5, below, because the king died in the battle and his death paved the way for the Iberian unification of 1580.

The end of Moroccan possessions

The outcome of the Portuguese attempts to control the Atlantic coast of Morocco between 1415 and 1580 is, of course, quite negative. As a matter of fact, the conquests in Morocco had received human and financial resources comparable to those devoted to the other expansion projects and it had been the only territory where the king eventually involved himself in person. In spite of this attention, the initial goals had not been reached. Portugal controlled only four presidios, and Morocco was the indirect cause of the Iberian unification of 1580.

No further attempts to extend Portuguese possessions in Morocco were made, and the four presidios left were lost one after the other: Arzila was abandoned in 1589; Ceuta did not recognise the government that resulted from the successful 1640 revolt against the Iberian unification and became a Castilian possession, recognised by Portugal in 1668; Tânger was awarded to England as part of the dowry of the Portuguese princess Catarina when she married Charles II and became queen of England in 1662; Mazagão was abandoned in 1769.

C – The Atlantic islands

The Canary Islands

In a certain sense, attempts to explore the Canary Islands antedated the Portuguese attacks on Morocco. During the 14th century, expeditions were sent to capture slaves from the Guancho population of the Canary Islands and to obtain furs from the seals of Canarian seas. These expeditions were, however, mainly private undertakings.

Portugal was not alone in its interest over the Canary Islands. Merchants from other Iberian and Italian countries, and even from France and England, organised similar expeditions. Portugal and Castile had, however, the best geographical position to attempt the political control of the islands, and both tried to establish that control in the early 15th century with no clear results. Pope Eugene IV decided to end this rivalry by an arbitration in favour of Castile in 1436. Portugal had to accept the decision, later confirmed by the treaty of Alcáçovas (1479), as mentioned in chapter 3, above.

Madeira

The archipelago of Madeira was not as much explored during the 14th century as were the Canary Islands, because the islands were not inhabited, a fact that prevented the taking of slaves and left furs and wood as the only interesting commodities to be obtained. However, the situation changed during the 15th century. After a Castilian expedition that did not lead to permanent control (1417), the Portuguese occupied Porto Santo in 1418 and Madeira in 1419. This occupation was never seriously contested and Prince Henrique the Navigator, who received the archipelago as a feudal possession, was able to promote the use of the islands for agriculture and animal raising.

Madeira and Porto Santo were settled with immigrants from the continental part of the country, from other European countries (mainly Italy and Flanders) and from the Canary Islands and Africa. The Canarian and African settlers were slaves, who never became the majority of the population.

The first Madeira export to become more important than furs and wood was wheat. However, the settlers soon discovered that they had a better alternative: sugar. During most of the 15th and 16th centuries, sugar became the staple export of Madeira, and nearly everything else could be listed as an import. Being a labour-intensive activity, sugar production stimulated a significant population growth: total population reached 20,000 inhabitants around 1500 and 30,000 around 1550.

During the second half of the 16th century, the sugar of Madeira lost the bulk of its market, because it was unable to compete in price with the sugar of Brazil. This led to a period of economic recession and demographic stagnation until Madeira switched its productive specialisation, converting most of its agricultural land to the vineyard, and becoming an important wine producer in the 17th century.

The island of Porto Santo is very small and its land is rather barren. This prevented it from playing a significant role in the economy of the archipelago, except as a good alternative harbour in case of bad weather. The other islands of the archipelago were never settled, as their names of Desertas (desert) and Selvagens (wild) show. They became the last refuge of seals after the hunt for furs exterminated them in the waters of Madeira proper.

Interlude: navigation in the northern half of the Atlantic Ocean

To navigate to the Canary Islands and back was relatively untaxing upon medieval technology and knowledge. The islands of Lanzarote and Fuerteventura are visible from the African coast and the islands of Gran Canaria, Tenerife, Gomera, Hierro and Palma may be seen from other islands of the archipelago. To sum up, going to the Canaries and returning is a question of quasi-coastal piloting.

Sailing to Porto Santo and Madeira and back is somewhat more difficult. The islands lie some 650 km away from the African coast and more than 800 km south-west of the Portuguese coast. However, it is possible to reach them without a compass, and without any method of computing latitude, using landmarks on the African coast as a reference.

To go further south, below the Tropic of Cancer, and come back was almost impossible with medieval technology and knowledge. Sailing in this zone encounters frequent fogs and unfavourable winds and currents on the return. Of course, it is possible to make a cautious coastal excursion, but it is very difficult to supply and control the ships in the barren and stormy coast of the Western Sahara, especially on the return, when sailing is made against the winds and currents.

The only practical alternative is to use the clockwise system of winds and currents of the North Atlantic between the equator and latitude 45° N to return, that is to say, to use westward winds and currents of low latitudes to get away from the African coast, then to profit from the northward winds and currents of the Western Atlantic to go to higher latitudes (around 35° N) where eastward winds and currents bring the ships back to Europe. Such an alternative, however, implies a trip of some 3,000 km without any land reference. An appropriate ship with a small crew, and rudimentary methods of estimating the course and distances on the high sea are needed to attempt such an alternative. The Portuguese navigators of the 1420s were able to do this using the caravel as the appropriate ship, the compass to estimate the course and the dead-reckoning process to estimate the distances. Moreover, they dared to try. As a result, in 1427 Diogo de Silves sighted the Azores for the first time, and in 1434 Gil Eanes made the voyage that started regular travel to the Western coast of Africa south of the Bojador Cape.

The Azores

The discovery of the Azores in the late 1420s was the first important result of high-seas sailing. For some years the archipelago remained an uncertain possession because it was difficult to locate the islands with the available navigation methods. However, during the 1430s the two islands of the eastern group (Santa Maria and São Miguel) and the five islands of the Central group (Terceira, Graciosa, Pico, São Jorge and Faial) were systematically identified. Formal occupation followed in 1439, and was never seriously contested. As in the case of Madeira, Prince Henrique the Navigator received the islands as a feudal possession, and promoted their settlement by immigrants from Portugal, Italy and Flanders.

Agriculture and fishing soon became important economic activities. Wheat and dyes were the staple exports of the islands, a position they retained until the 19th century. Population growth was slow during the 15th century (there were only some 10,000 inhabitants around 1500), but accelerated during the 16th century (there were some 60,000 inhabitants around 1600).

Other Atlantic islands

The two islands of the western group of the Azores (Flores and Corvo) were discovered by Diogo de Teive in 1452 as a by-product of further explorations in the North Atlantic. These islands were occupied during the 1450s and their economic life became similar to that of the rest of the archipelago.

The Cape Verde archipelago was discovered during the 1450s as a spin-off of the exploration of the western coast of Africa (see section D, below). The main islands were readily occupied (they had no previous permanent inhabitants) and their possession by Portugal was never seriously contested. However, the dry climate and the barren soil made Cape Verde a poor agricultural land. Except for some dyes, agriculture never played an important role in Cape Verde exports. The archipelago was used mainly as a base for slave trade and as a supply point for long voyages to the South Atlantic, the Indian Ocean and the Far East. The salt deposits of the island of Sal continued to be exploited, as it seems had occurred irregularly by Moslem merchants coming from the African coast before the arrival of the Portuguese. Its European-Negro cross-bred population remained scanty, hovering at around 10,000 inhabitants until the 17th century.

The islands of the Gulf of Guinea were discovered in the late 1460s and early 1470s also as a by-product of the exploration of the western coast of Africa (see section D, below). Ano Bom (today Pagalu), Fernão do Pó (today Bioko), Príncipe and São Tomé were readily occupied (only Fernão do Pó had an earlier permanent population) and its possession by Portugal was never seriously contested until the 17th century. The islands were used mainly as bases for slave trade, but São Tomé also became an important sugar producer. In spite of this, its mainly Negro population remained below 10,000 inhabitants until the 17th century.

The small islands of the high South Atlantic were discovered in the early 16th century as a by-product of the Cape route to India (see section E, below): João da Nova discovered

Ascensão and Santa Helena in 1501; Fernão de Noronha discovered Trindade and Fernão de Noronha in 1502; Gonçalo Álvares discovered Gough Island in 1505; and Tristão da Cunha discovered Tristão da Cunha in 1506. These islands were never occupied by Portugal.

D – The exploration of the western coast of Africa

The early steps

After the decisive voyage of Gil Eanes in 1434, the exploration of the western coast of Africa went on: in 1435 and 1436 Afonso Baldaia explored the Saharan coast; between 1441 and 1444 Nuno Tristão explored the Senegambia; during the 1450s Diogo Gomes explored the coast of modern Guinea (and discovered the islands of Cape Verde); in the early 1460s Pedro de Sintra explored the coasts of modern Sierra Leone and Liberia. Then, the arrival at the latitudes of the equatorial calms and of the northward winds and currents of the southern hemisphere slowed explorations down.

The coast that had been explored provided plenty of profitable trade opportunities. Gold, slaves and ivory were the staple exports of the region. These products had usually been sent across the Sahara to the Maghreb, Libya and Egypt. Now Portuguese merchants were able to undersell traditional dealers in European markets, because of the lower costs of sea transportation. The main imports of the region were textiles and metal works. The Portuguese economy provided only a small part of these imports. Most of them came from other European and Mediterranean regions on Portuguese ships.

Retaining the monopoly of this profitable trade was one of the main concerns of the Portuguese government. This did not prevent the use of foreign (mainly Genoese) capital to finance the voyages of exploration and the trade, and even the direct participation of Italian navigators and traders on the expeditions. The presence of foreign ships was, however, ruthlessly punished. During the 15th century the only significant rival was Castile. After some fighting, a settlement came with the treaty of Alcáçovas (see chapter 3, above).

Until 1465, trade with the western coast of Africa was given as a monopoly by the Crown to the Knights of Christ. Prince Henrique the Navigator until 1460, and his nephew, Fernando, between 1460 and 1465 were the leaders of that military religious order and of all related business. Between 1466 and 1471, the monopoly was leased out by the Crown to a merchant of Lisbon (Fernão Gomes). After the end of that contract, a department of the royal exchequer – the House of Guinea (*Casa da Guiné*) later House of Mina (*Casa da Mina*) – began to administrate the monopoly. Individual merchants spread all along the coast, and even penetrated into the hinterland as far as Timbuktu, but no permanent settlements were established on the African coast until the 1480s except for the fortress of Arguim in the Western Sahara. In a certain sense, they were unnecessary, because the weakness of coastal states allowed the Portuguese a free hand under the protection of their ships.

The search for a passage to the East

During the late 1460s and early 1470s João de Santarém, Pedro Escobar and Fernão do Pó explored the northern coast of the Gulf of Guinea (and discovered the islands of the Gulf). The eastward orientation of the coast made some explorers think they had arrived at the southern tip of Africa. However, in 1474-1475, Lopo Gonçalves and Rui Sequeira crossed the equator, dashing these hopes: the African coast turned southwards again.

The search for a passage to the Indian Ocean became the main concern of the Portuguese exploration of the western coast of Africa thereafter, and the pace of this exploration accelerated during the 1480s under the leadership of King João II. In 1482-

1483 Diogo Cão reached latitude 15° S; in 1485-1486 the same Diogo Cão reached 22° S; and in 1487-1488 Bartolomeu Dias finally rounded the southern tip of Africa and sailed the African coast of the Indian Ocean until 33° S.

The search for a passage to the Indian Ocean did not prevent the economic concern over the old and new possessions on the African coast. Attempts to build fortresses and to establish diplomatic relations with the local kings intensified during the 1480s. The main fortress was São Jorge da Mina on the northern coast of the Gulf of Guinea. Diplomatic efforts seemed to be very promising in the Kingdom of Congo, as it became a Portuguese protectorate and a Christian kingdom in the late 15th century. However, civil and external wars in the Kingdom of Congo, and the wish of the Portuguese merchants to establish the same trade patterns as those existing on the rest of the western coast of Africa (gold, slaves and ivory against textiles and metal works) spoiled things during the 16th century. The fortress of São Paulo de Luanda, built during the 1570s, was the symbol of the failure to make the Kingdom of Congo a Christian kingdom.

Interlude: navigation in the southern half of the Atlantic Ocean

The success of the voyage of Bartolomeu Dias did not solve the whole problem of a good route to the Indian Ocean. As a matter of fact, southward coastal navigation south of the Gulf of Guinea is as difficult as northward coastal navigation north of the Gulf of Guinea, because of the unfavourable winds and currents.

The practical solution is similar to the one already described for the northern half of the Atlantic Ocean: to use the anti-clockwise system of winds and currents of the South Atlantic between the equator and latitude 45° S to reach the southern tip of Africa, that is to say, to use westward winds and currents of low latitudes to get away from the African coast, then to profit from the southward winds and currents of the Western Atlantic to go to the higher latitudes (around 35° S) where eastward winds and currents bring the ships back to Africa. From a navigation and technological point of view the conditions to use such a route are similar to those needed to navigate the northern half of the Atlantic Ocean, and the Portuguese navigators of the 1480s had improved upon cartography and orientation methods relative to those of the 1430s; namely they had developed the astronomical process of latitude determination. Even so, nearly a decade of poorly documented expeditions was needed in order to master the new South Atlantic routes. Only in the late 1490s was the definitive attempt to reach the Indian Ocean once again made.

E – The Indian Ocean

The early expeditions

Between 1497 and 1499 Vasco da Gama led, at last, the first Portuguese voyage to India. The main geographical novelty of this voyage was the knowledge of monsoon winds, a decisive point for crossing the Indian Ocean safely.

From 1500 on, yearly expeditions were sent to India on behalf of the Portuguese king, at the beginning only for trading purposes. These expeditions filled in the map of the South Atlantic with the official discovery of Brazil (as will be seen in section F, below) and with the discovery of the small islands of the high South Atlantic (as explained in section C, above).

In spite of previous land voyages organised by the government to make contact with the Indian trade (as those of Pero da Covilhã and Afonso de Paiva during the 1480s), the Portuguese found some difficulties in adapting to its patterns. The main Indian export was pepper, but other drugs and spices, such as cinnamon, cloves, nutmeg and sandal, exotic beverages such as tea and coffee, various dyes, mordants and scents, sophisticated cotton and silk textiles, and even sophisticated pottery (porcelain) were gradually added to the list. In exchange, India did not demand textiles or metal works as did Africa, but mainly gold, silver and copper. This created some financial and mental problems, as the precious metals seemed to disappear in the Eastern vortex without real advantage to the European traders. However, the Portuguese merchants were able to undersell traditional dealers of Indian products in European markets, because of the lower costs of sea transport, and the high profits flowing from the business at last overcame the initial surprise and discomfort.

The Portuguese interference with the established patterns of the world-economy of the Indian Ocean and of the Far East in its western half met with unkind reception by the existing trade powers. Though skilful exploitation of local rivalries allowed the Portuguese to gain some allies (such as Malindi on the eastern coast of Africa, and Cochim on the coast of Malabar), the early expeditions were sometimes forced to fight their way in and out of the harbours, and this led to the organisation of powerful military fleets and to the appointment of a viceroy to take command of Portuguese ships in the Indian Ocean. Francisco de Almeida, the first viceroy, took office in 1505 and had to face a coalition of the Mamluk Empire and the Gujarati kingdom of Northern India bent upon repelling the newcomers. The Portuguese had a bad start and the viceroy's son Lourenço de Almeida met defeat and death in the battle of Chaul (1508). However, the next year the viceroy profited from the marginal superiority of Portuguese artillery over the guns of the allies to destroy their fleet off Diu, and the war ended with a Portuguese triumph.

The Indian empire

This triumph suggested that it was possible to add to the trade profits, some other revenue, coming from taxing the whole trade of the Indian Ocean. The idea was to force all ships sailing in the Indian Ocean, that is to say, using the routes that linked the eastern coast of Africa, Arabia, Persia, India and the Malay Peninsula to buy a sailing permit or navicert (*cartaz*) from the Portuguese authorities. This required a string of coastal fortresses to issue and control these permits. Afonso de Albuquerque, governor of the Indian possessions after Francisco de Almeida, tried to build the string of fortresses by taking Goa (on the Malabar coast), Ormuz (in the mouth of the Persian Gulf), Socotra (in the mouth of the Red Sea) and Malacca (to control the Malayan Straits), and by terrorising potential recalcitrants by ruthless punishment of the ships found without the sailing permit. Socotra, a mere second-best to Aden, which Albuquerque was unable to take, had to be abandoned some years later, but the backbone of the system, which also included Mozambique (on the eastern coast of Africa) and some minor fortresses, was set up by 1512. For the rest of the 16th century, the Portuguese enjoyed uncontested naval superiority, which allowed occasional valuable additions to their empire, such as Diu (in the Gujarat), and Columbus (in Ceylon), and growing unpopularity among the tyrannised sea merchants of the Indian Ocean. However, the most important states of the region, such as the Sefevid empire of Persia, the Mogul empire of Northern India, the Vijayanagar empire of Southern India, and Burma and Thailand in western Indochina managed to live without Portuguese interference and did not try to face the Portuguese State of India (*Estado da Índia*) – the official name for the Portuguese possessions east of the Cape of Good Hope – at sea.

It is also important to point out that Portuguese merchants soon began to play an important role as intermediaries in the internal relations of the world-economy of the Indian Ocean and the Far East.

F – The New World

North Atlantic islands

There is no doubt that the Portuguese navigators made exploration voyages across the Atlantic during the 15th century, and there is also no doubt that, whatever was found, it did not provoke the same enthusiasm and the same official concern as the exploration of the western coast of Africa and the search for a passage to the Indian Ocean.

The only practical results of these explorations were the discovery of the western group of the Azores in 1452 (already discussed in section B, above) and the rediscovery of the Viking routes of half a millennium earlier to Greenland and Newfoundland. Such a rediscovery implied the identification of the anticlockwise system of winds and currents between latitude 45° N and the Arctic Sea in the North Atlantic, and was a slow process. In 1474 João Corte Real and Álvaro Homem arrived at what they called Terra dos Bacalhaus (Cod Land). It is impossible to decide whether this Cod Land was Greenland or Newfoundland, as only during the last decade of the 15th century did the Portuguese navigators manage to find their way back to these lands: in 1495 Pero de Barcelos and João Lavrador established the route to Greenland; in 1500 Gaspar Corte Real established the route to Newfoundland. The cod fisheries in the Northern Atlantic (around Greenland and Newfoundland) became an important industry for Portuguese fishermen during the 16th century, but there was no attempt to control any territory in those northern latitudes.

The discovery of America and the treaty of Tordesillas

According to 15th century geographical knowledge, three alternative sea routes to the Indian Ocean and the Far East were envisioned: the western route across the Atlantic; the southeastern route around the south of Africa; and the northeastern route around the north of Eurasia. The exploration of the western coast of Africa (and the failure of the lesser known explorations in the North Atlantic) convinced the Portuguese authorities that the southeastern route was the best no later than the early 1480s. This explains why they refused to finance the plan presented in 1485 by Christopher Columbus to explore the western route.

Columbus had been employed in Portuguese expeditions in the North Atlantic, and had married the daughter of a governor of Madeira. This means that he was well versed in the techniques of navigation in the northern half of the Atlantic. When his proposal was rejected in Portugal, he looked for another source of financing. After some difficulties he found it in the Castilian government, usually interested in overseas projects that might rival those set up by the Portuguese.

Columbus' first voyage took place during the summer and autumn of 1492 and was a striking success at first sight. According to Columbus' report Asia could be reached by a three-month voyage across the Atlantic.

The Portuguese authorities found a sound basis for claiming Columbus' discoveries in the treaty of Alcáçovas (see chapter 3 section C, above). As a matter of fact, the islands discovered by Columbus were clearly south of parallel 30° N. Castile reacted and extracted from Pope Alexander VI (cardinal Ramiro Borgia of Aragonese origin, that is to say a countryman of King Ferdinand of Aragon married to Queen Isabel of Castile) a decree replacing the 30° N parallel by an ill-defined meridian (perhaps meaning 30° W). Portugal reacted in turn and negotiations between the two countries finally led in 1494 to the treaty of Tordesillas, dividing the Atlantic by meridian 45° W. East of that meridian Portugal was awarded the monopoly of explorations, with the usual exception of the Canary Islands; west of that meridian was now the region for Castilian explorations.

The rationale of the Treaty of Tordesillas is clear: meridian 45° W lies roughly half way between the Azores (the western land limit of Portuguese occupation) and the Antilles (the eastern land limit of Columbus' discoveries). Of course, the Portuguese authorities did not believe that Columbus' discoveries were located in the Far East. If they did, it is unlikely that any negotiations would lead to their cession to Castile. Indeed they thought they had given to Castile the worst share of the world. The puzzling detail is the pushing of the division from meridian 30° W to meridian 45° W, which includes a slice of South America (the eastern part of Brazil) and a slice of Greenland in the Portuguese share. It is likely that the Portuguese negotiators were trying to protect the control of Brazil (which might have been discovered during the efforts to determine the conditions of the high sea navigation in the southern half of the Atlantic after the voyage of Bartolomeu Dias in 1487-1488) and the right to use the cod fisheries of the North Atlantic; but these are mere conjectures.

It is worth retracing here the destiny of the routes to the Indian Ocean and the Far East referred to above: the southeastern route proved to be the best after the voyage of Vasco da Gama in 1497-1499; the northeastern route proved impracticable when explored by Flemish and English navigators in the 16th century (though it provided new routes to the trade with Russia); the western route led to America and to new alternative routes to the Indian Ocean and the Far East. These were the northwestern route around the north of America and the southwestern around the south of America. The northwestern route proved impracticable when explored by French and English navigators in the late 15th and 16th centuries (though it provided the stimulus for the occupation of Québec by the French and of Rupert's Land by the English). The southwestern route proved practicable but uncompetitive when it was explored by the Portuguese navigator Fernão de Magalhães (also known as Magellan) for the king of Castile.

The voyage of Fernão de Magalhães (1519-1522) is best known as the first voyage of global circumnavigation, but its real goal was the exploration of the southwestern route to the Indian Ocean and the Far East. Besides geographical knowledge, the main results of Fernão de Magalhães' voyage were the later Castilian attempts to control the Spice Islands and the Philippines. The connections of these attempts with Portuguese activities in the Far East will be dealt with in section G, below.

Brazil

The discovery of what is today known as South America was probably the result of the explorations made to determine the system of winds and currents in the southern half of the Atlantic during the 1490s (perhaps led by Duarte Pacheco Pereira). However, the official discovery of Brazil was made in 1500 by the second fleet sent to India led by Pedro Álvares Cabral.

The new land appeared at first sight less interesting from an economic point of view than Africa or the Indian Ocean and the Far East. Its early exports were mainly tropical woods and dyes – the red dye even provided the current name of the country, which came to replace the official name of Terra de Vera Cruz (land of the true cross). At first, the Portuguese government divided the country into fifteen strips, gave these strips to some nobles as feudal possessions and did not bother to organise a central administration or defence. Things began to change with France's successful attempts to get a share of Brazilian trade during the 1520s. In 1531 a governor-general was appointed and naval forces dispatched to expel the French merchants with total success. The Portuguese control of Brazil was to remain undisturbed until the 17th century.

Meanwhile, agriculture developed, as three crops – sugar, cotton and tobacco – emerged as being very profitable. At the same time, animal husbandry for locally consumed meat and exported hides also began to grow.

Sugar soon became the main product in the Brazilian economy. The high need of slave manpower for the plantations and sugar factories was decisive in shaping the Brazilian population.

The Indian population had a very low density, which prevented disastrous drops in numbers as a consequence of the contagion of European diseases, as occurred in other parts of the American continent. It also prevented the recruitment of large numbers of slaves from it (moreover, the Indian slaves always had the possibility to flee and take refuge among the tribes still free of Portuguese control). The solution was to import slaves from Africa. These were cheap and plentiful (and could not flee without a high risk of being eaten by the indigenous cannibals). They soon became the majority of the population of the Portuguese settlements in Brazil. By the end of the 16th century, there were around 25,000 inhabitants of European origin, 15,000 inhabitants of African origin, 40,000 inhabitants of mixed (mainly European-African) race and 20,000 inhabitants of local origin in these settlements.

G – The Far East

Insulindia

During the 1510s, Portuguese explorations of the Asian coast had proceeded east of the Malay Peninsula, first of all to Insulindia, where the Portuguese tried to control the Spice Islands (Moluccas) and Timor, the main producers of nutmeg and sandal, respectively. By 1520 this control had been established.

Then, there arrived the Castilian expedition led by the Portuguese Fernão de Magalhães, and Castile claimed the right to occupy the Moluccas on the basis of the treaty of Tordesillas (see section F, above). According to the Castilian thesis, the Tordesillas meridian (45° W) should be completed by its opposite (135° E) for a truly equitable division of the world. The Portuguese thesis – to divide the Pacific Ocean into equal halves just like the Atlantic had been divided in the treaty of Tordesillas – was promptly rejected by Castile, and, when negotiations to settle the question opened, discussions went on about the position of the Moluccas. As a matter of fact, they lie west of the 135° E meridian (that is to say, on the Portuguese side), as the Portuguese negotiators claimed, but, as determination of longitudes was very rough before the 18th century, the majority of geographers accepted the Castilian claim that they lay east of that meridian (that is to say, on the Castilian side). However, Castile had no practical possibility to profit from the control of the Moluccas, because the treaty of Tordesillas forbade the use of the southeastern route to the Indian Ocean and the Far East by Castilian ships, and the southwestern route was much longer (requiring an eighteen-month voyage instead of a nine-month one, on the average). After nearly a decade of negotiations, the issue was settled by the treaty of Zaragoza: Portugal paid Castile an indemnity of 250,000 ducats and the dividing meridian was pushed to 144° E (a limit that nobody cared much about thereafter). In practice, Portugal got the right to occupy the Moluccas in exchange for nearly 1 metric tonne of gold. The Moluccas remained in Portuguese hands until the 1570s. They were then lost to a local Moslem power, and Solor and Timor became the main Portuguese possessions in Insulindia.

China

By the 1510s, the Portuguese exploration of the Asian coast had gone one step further to the coast of China. There the Portuguese tried to repeat the pattern of the Indian Ocean empire: profitable trade and coastal fortresses to tax other peoples' trade. The scheme was an utter failure, as the Chinese authorities reacted by destroying the Portuguese settlements. The only exception was Macau.

The traditional story about the foundation of Macau holds that in the 1550s the Chinese authorities had some difficulty in controlling the mouth of the Pearl River, which was a traditional base of local pirates. As the Portuguese merchants used their naval power to end the activities of the pirates, the Chinese authorities decided to trade permission to carry on business for maritime security.

The success of Macau was the result of two factors. First of all, there were the links of Macau with the Castilian colony of the Philippines and indirectly with the Castilian colony of Mexico. These links were established mainly during the period of Iberian unification and allowed Mexican silver to flow from Acapulco to Manila and then to Macau to buy Chinese tea, textiles, and porcelain. Second, there was the trend towards a policy of economic autarky of China under the late Ming and the Qing (Manchu) emperors. As the pattern of the trade of Macau was favourably envisaged by Chinese authorities, they never tried to stop it, and even tended to give the Canton-Macau axis the monopoly of Chinese foreign sea trade.

Japan

Perhaps as early as the 1530s, certainly no later than 1543, Portuguese traders arrived in Japan as well. The failure of the attempt to repeat in China the pattern of the Indian Ocean empire led to a sensible emphasis on normal trade relations. As some groups of the Japanese society showed great interest in the Christian religion, there were some hopes that Japan, or at least part of it, might become a Christian state. The rise of the Tokugawa shoguns put an end to those hopes, and made Japan a country as closed as China. The Portuguese were even excluded as direct trade partners from Japan in the 17th century.

Other explorations

It is likely that Portuguese navigators made other explorations in the Far East waters, reaching regions such as New Guinea and Australia. However, no proof of such explorations survives, which means that, if they took place, they did not lead to permanent trade or settlement. That is not surprising: these regions are clearly less interesting from a commercial point of view than those where Portuguese traders settled, and Portuguese resources were certainly scarce even to control the Indian Ocean and to trade in Insulindia, China and Japan.

H – The consequences of the expansion for the Portuguese economy and society

Prosperity and power

It is tempting to summarise the short-run consequences of the Portuguese expansion for the Portuguese economy and society in the formula 'prosperity and power'.

Economic prosperity, resulting from the profitable intermediary role that Portugal played between its overseas possessions and Europe in general, is undoubted, though it was not an immediate phenomenon. As a matter of fact, the first Portuguese colonial empire – the empire of the Atlantic coast of Morocco, Madeira, the Azores and the western coast of Africa – only showed significant profits after the middle of the 15th century. It was the second Portuguese colonial empire – the empire of the Indian Ocean and the Far East – that proved really profitable, both to the state and to private merchants linked with the trade of the Cape of Good Hope route. This led to the Portuguese apogee of the 16th century, to be dealt with in chapter 5, below.

Political power is another matter. Portugal did not become an important power in a Euro-Mediterranean context. It was strong enough to prevent foreign aggressions, except in the form of piracy, but it was unable to impose itself upon its neighbours. The failure of the attempts to secure the Castilian throne for the wife of the king of Portugal in the 1470s, and the failure to fulfil the dreams of conquest in Morocco, are conspicuous signs of the political weakness of the country. In overseas endeavours, the situation was somewhat different. Portuguese naval superiority was clear nearly everywhere, but inland adventures were absolutely out of the question, not only against the powerful civilised Asian states, such as Persia, the Mogul Empire, China and Japan, but also against the barbarian African states, such as Ghana, Sonrhai, Congo and Monomotapa, even if the geographical barriers were as important as the human ones in preventing these inland adventures. Only the undeveloped societies of South America allowed for a Portuguese penetration into the hinterland, and that was a rather slow process.

Long-term effects

The conventional view about the long-term effects of Portuguese expansion for the Portuguese economy and society suggests that these effects were not especially beneficial for the development of a modern economy. According to this view, profits flowing from the trade of exotic goods attracted resources to these activities, harming the development of productive activities; and this priority in the allocation of resources to trade activities as opposed to production activities, especially of an industrial nature, was the main reason for the failure of Portuguese modernisation.

It cannot be denied that this priority in the allocation of resources to trade activities instead of production existed. A good example is the choice of the Portuguese government when faced with the problem of wood scarcity in the late 16th century: it promulgated legislative measures that gave priority to its use as shipbuilding material as against its use as industrial fuel. Thus, it should be acknowledged that the structure of the Portuguese economy was shaped by expansion in a way that was detrimental to at least some productive sectors. However, the question of long-term effects of Portuguese expansion for the development of a modern economy is not answered so simply.

Two points must be remembered. Firstly, the gross domestic product of the Portuguese economy was certainly much more important than the flow of exotic commodities coming from overseas possessions. In these circumstances, whatever the diversion of resources to overseas trade may have been, it did not hinder traditional economic activities in the mother country and only affected activities in which the advantages of Portuguese specialisation were weak. Secondly, although it seems clear today that profits flowing from colonial endeavours were not decisive for the modernisation process in any European country, it cannot be denied that, being more profitable than alternative productive activities, overseas trade afforded a larger basis for capital accumulation. Under these circumstances, overseas trade certainly was not an obstacle to such accumulation. A comparative analysis shows that, among other countries strongly dedicated to overseas expansion during the modern epoch (also diverting resources away from internal productive activities), there are cases of both early modernisation and relatively late modernisation.

For all these reasons, blaming expansion for Portugal's late economic modernisation is probably an anachronistic perspective of those days in the economy of the modern epoch. Explanations for Portugal's failure to make an early economic take off must be found elsewhere.

On the other side, it is important to underscore that overseas expansion may have been a decisive factor for Portugal's survival as an independent national state. As a matter of fact, a colonial empire seems to have been an indispensable basis for the early formation of a national state in Europe, perhaps because it formed a tributary basis much more accessible and dynamic than internal productive economic activities, larger, but less linked to the market and less dynamic. It will be seen in the next chapter that overseas resources played a possibly decisive role in the War of Restoration, the result of which (favourable to Portugal) was perhaps a necessary condition for the country to remain independent from the unified Spanish monarchy in the 18th century.

5.

Portuguese apogee, Iberian unification and separation from the Western Hapsburg Empire (15th-18th centuries)

Between the 1490s and the 1570s, Portugal was at its apogee as a significant world power. It controlled a huge colonial empire including part of the Atlantic coast of Morocco, some of the main Atlantic archipelagoes, an important number of trade factories and fortresses along the western and eastern coasts of Africa, the coasts of the Indian Ocean, Indonesia and the Asian coasts of the Pacific Ocean, and some settlements in Brazil. It experienced a demographic and economic boom at home and it managed to build the main structures of a modern state.

According to the traditional view, decline began with the defeat at the battle of Alcácer-Quibir in 1578, the Iberian unification in 1580, and the Dutch, English and French competition in the colonial empire in the 1590s. It is only fair to point out that prosperity lasted for at least another quarter of century until the 1620s. However, the country did not escape the so-called crisis of the 17th century, and when full independence was recovered in 1640, Portugal had been pushed into a very secondary position in international affairs. However, Portugal managed to win the so-called Restoration War against the Western Hapsburg Empire and to recover some economic prosperity in the late 17th and early 18th centuries.

This chapter deals with the evolution of the Portuguese economy and society between the late 15th century and the early 18th century within a chronological framework. The theme of section A is the period of apogee, the theme of section B is the period of Iberian unification, and the theme of section C is the Portuguese separation from the Western Hapsburg Empire.

A – Portuguese apogee, 1490-1580

Population

The population of the continental part of the country went on growing during the 16th century. It is likely that by the end of the century it was approaching the 2-million mark.

The regional distribution of these 2 million people presented some slight changes when compared with that which had prevailed after the end of reconquest. The most populated regions were the same, but differences in population densities were greater. The provinces of Estremadura with something less then 30% of the total, Beira with around 25% of the total and Entre-Douro-e-Minho with around 20% of the total, contained a significant majority of the Portuguese population.

Towns

Lisbon doubled its population during the 16th century, reaching 100,000 inhabitants. This means that, by the end of the 16th century, the capital of Portugal was one of the largest cities of Europe. The other Portuguese towns, however, were still very small. Only Porto and Évora approached the 10,000 inhabitants level.

Population movements

The excess of births over deaths was the only source of population growth. In fact, during the 16th century the territory remained unchanged and there was no net immigration. There was even a significant net emigration. It has been estimated that over 100,000 Portuguese settled in the Atlantic islands and in Brazil or went to the Indian Ocean and the Far East and never returned, and some 20,000 Jews may have refused the conversion to the Christian faith and had to leave Portugal. In exchange, Portugal may have received some 50,000 imported slaves, and a negligible amount of immigrants from other European countries.

Population juridical status

The conversion of the last few followers of the Moslem faith during the 15th century and the measures taken in 1496-1497 that gave the Jews the choice between conversion and emigration might have ended the problem of religious minorities among the Portuguese population. However, as the so-called New Christians (*Cristãos Novos*) resulting from the conversions among the Jewish community were denied the same rights afforded to the so-called Old Christians (*Cristãos Velhos*) that formed the bulk of the population (exclusion from the main ecclesiastical, civil and military positions, for instance), things remained much the same as before. It may be said, in fact, that things became even worse for the former Jews, because popular persecutions intensified in the early 16th century and the Inquisition courts were introduced in 1536. Formally, the Inquisition dealt with a great variety of offences, such as heresy, witchcraft and so on, but clandestine Jewish practices were always its main concern.

*

The expulsion of the Jews and the introduction of the Inquisition have been blamed by some scholars for the problems that the Portuguese economy faced during the following centuries. According to them, the loss of human resources and of accumulated capital that resulted from the expulsion was critical for the perspectives of future development of the Portuguese economy, and the persecution of rich merchants of Jewish origin disturbed the normal course of capital accumulation.

It is difficult to endorse these views in full. The loss of some valuable human resources, mainly in the entrepreneurial field, is undeniable, as the success of the Jewish communities of Portuguese origin in other European and Mediterranean countries testifies. The loss of accumulated capital associated with the expulsion must have been small, because there were strict measures forbidding capital exports. The disturbance that the Inquisition made to capital accumulation in certain groups of the Portuguese society is beyond doubt, though it is hard to believe that this had a general effect. As a matter of fact, the persecutions of the New Christian community left room for larger accumulation of other groups of the Portuguese society, and the explanation of the low propensity to save of the Portuguese economy as a whole must be sought elsewhere.

Foreign and domestic trade

Long-distance trade with overseas possessions and trade factories and the distribution of exotic products all over Europe became the most conspicuous source of economic prosperity for Portugal during this period. Gold, ivory and slaves from the west coast of Africa, pepper and other spices from the regions around the Indian Ocean and the Far East, and sugar from Madeira and Brazil, joined the traditional salt, wine and Mediterranean fruits as the main Portuguese exports to the European continent. The pattern of the main Portuguese imports began to include, besides the traditional sophisticated textiles, silver and metal works needed as re-exports in the context of colonial trade, and cereals (mainly wheat), a commodity in which Portugal was no longer self-sufficient.

Internal trade continued to graw, not only in absolute terms, as a consequence of economic growth, but also in relative terms, as a consequence of economic prosperity and of the trend to replace self-consumption with market relations. The government made some attempts to introduce uniform weights and measures throughout the country to avoid the barriers to trade resulting from the differences between standard weights and measures among municipalities. These attempts were only partially successful. The standard weights and measures of Lisbon were accepted in some parts of the south of the country, and the standard weights and measures of Porto were accepted in some parts of the north of the country, but in most of the interior of the country medieval diversity prevailed.

Agriculture and cereal supply rules

The main innovation in Portuguese agriculture during the 16th century was the introduction of maize. This new cereal spread during the 16th and 17th centuries, mainly in Entre-Douro-e-Minho and Beira Litoral.

The beginning of cereal imports as a normal source of supply led to the implementation of the cereal supply rules that prevailed until the 18th century. The city of Lisbon, the Kingdom of the Algarves (meaning Algarve proper and the Moroccan presidios) and the province of Madeira became net importers of cereals, but the rest of the continental part of the country and the province of the Azores were still self-sufficient. This was translated into laws that forbade the cereals to cross the borders of the municipalities where they were produced, except for rent payments to landlords, or for supplying the net importer regions, with the proviso that the municipalities could always retain one third of the harvest for local supply. Only Lisbon, Algarve and Madeira could import cereals, either from the rest of the country, or from abroad. A Wheat Square Warehouse (*Armazém do Terreiro do Trigo*) supervised by the municipality of Lisbon, organised imports to supply Lisbon, and eventually the other net importer regions or overseas expeditions and possessions whenever the king demanded, which occurred often.

Industry

Various industrial activities developed during the 16th century as a response to the increased demand arising from economic growth and foreign trade. However, shipbuilding remained the key industrial activity linked to long-distance trade and overseas explorations. During the 16th century, the Portuguese government enacted a host of measures to protect it from foreign competition, and also to increase the size and armament of current trade vessels to face Moroccan, French and English piracy.

Political evolution

The reign of Manuel I (1495-1521) is best known for its successes in Portuguese expansion in the Indian Ocean, in the New World and in the Far East, already described in chapter 4. This led the king to add further references to his official title, which became: King of Portugal and of the Algarves at home and overseas in Africa, Lord of Guinea, and of conquest, navigation and trade of Ethiopia, Arabia, Persia and India (*Rei de Portugal e dos Algarves de aquém e de além mar em África, senhor da Guiné e da conquista, navegação e comércio da Etiópia, Arábia, Pérsia e Índia*) — Ethiopia meaning the whole eastern coast of Africa. However, this reign also saw the last attempts to unite all of the Iberian kingdoms under the same ruler by means of royal marriages and the failure of such attempts (see chapter 3, above), the most important and successful efforts to control the Atlantic coast of Morocco (see chapter 4, above), the attempts to impose religious uniformity by means of conversion or expulsion of the Jewish community (see above) and important legal and administrative reforms (see below). In a certain sense, it was the period during which the main structures of the modern Portuguese state and the bases for the Portuguese apogee of the 16th century were set in place.

King João III (1521-1557), the regents Catarina (1557-1562) and Henrique (1562-1568) and King Sebastião I (1568-1578) reaped the harvest: Moroccan and French piracy, the introduction of the Inquisition, and scattered problems in overseas possessions did not prevent a period of nearly six decades of prosperity and peace. The defeat at the battle of Alcácer-Quibir brought political trouble and the Iberian unification (see section B, below), but economic prosperity remained basically unaffected.

Legal and administrative system

Between 1497 and 1520, there was a general reform of local charters: procedure and penal rules disappeared from them, personal services to the landlords were abolished, and local charters began to include only rules about local administration and feudal taxes. Regarding local administration, all feudal territories and municipalities became municipalities with the same kind of local councils. Feudal taxes continued to be paid, either in kind or in cash to the previous landlords of feudal territories, or to the king in previous municipalities.

The reform of local charters was followed by a second compilation of general laws – the Ordinances of King Manuel (*Ordenações Manuelinas*) – promulgated in 1521, and by the introduction of a general scheme of military service. Military service was now due only to the king: all adult male able-bodied subjects were compelled to provide military service; each municipality provided a few conscripts for the regular army each year; the other men were enrolled in a local militia (*ordenanças*).

Population growth and the reform of the administrative system required an increase in the number of correction districts.

The six provinces of the 14th century (to which should be added Madeira and the Azores) became only military districts, and they were divided for administrative purposes into a growing number of correction districts (around 30 by the end of the 16th century).

At the same time, the ecclesiastical division of the country underwent a similar evolution: new bishoprics were established in Ceuta (in Morocco), Miranda do Douro, Leiria, Portalegre, Funchal (in Madeira), and Angra (in the Azores). The see of Silves was transferred to Faro. A new archbishopric was also created in Évora.

Monetary system

Monetary stabilisation characterised the years after 1489. The gold value of the Portuguese real, which was 9.3 mg in 1489 dropped to 7.1 mg by 1555, and stabilised thereafter. The silver value of the Portuguese real, which was 92.3 mg in 1489, dropped to 79.4 mg on the eve of the Iberian unification. These were trifling devaluations when compared to the situation that the country had gone through during the late 14th century and most of the 15th century.

Prices

The Portuguese economy shared the upward trend in prices that characterised the 16th century across Europe. Quantitative analysis is still very preliminary, but it is possible to suggest that prices were multiplied by a factor of around 5 during the course of the century.

As monetary devaluation ceased, the increase in prices must be explained by the inflow of gold from Africa and of silver from Castile. However, most of this inflow must have been compensated for by economic growth and by the outflow of both precious metals for the Indian Ocean and Far East trade, which explains the moderate amount of the price increases.

Fiscal systems

The feudal, ecclesiastical and state fiscal systems saw no significant changes between the late 15th century and the late 16th century, except for the replacement of the normal payment of the excise (*sisa*) by modes in lieu of it paid by the municipalities. Of course, there were important increases in revenue resulting from economic prosperity

State accounts

Retrospective budgets (*orçamentos*) of state accounts began to be made in the late 15th century at irregular intervals. They suggest that public revenue amounted to around 50 contos in the late 15th century, 300 contos in the early 16th century and 1000 contos in the late 16th century. This was enough to cover ordinary public expenditure, but nothing extra. There were no wars, but defence of home waters against Moroccan, French and English pirates, overseas commitments (such as expeditions to Morocco, and even current trade and the efforts to control the trade of the Indian Ocean), and debt service made for public deficits that became more and more frequent.

Public debt

Deficits in state accounts led to state borrowing and the existence of a public debt. The Portuguese public debt of the 16th century took two forms: floating debt represented by bills of exchange, and funded debt represented by bonds – the so-called interest certificates (*padrões de juro*). These interest certificates were of two types: redeemable interest certificates (*padrões de juro ao quitar*) and lifelong interest certificates (*padrões de juro vitalícios*).

The first issue of Portuguese public debt was made in 1500. By the middle of the 16th century, the total amount was approaching 1,500 contos. Then came the first bankruptcy (1560). Both interest and amount were reduced, but renewed borrowing was quick to follow.

Cultural aspects

The 16th century Portuguese apogee was also significant in cultural matters. The Portuguese excelled in geographical and navigational techniques, in knowledge about African, Asian and American lands and societies, and in historical and travelling literature about their own expansion. Lyrical and dramatic poetry also flourished and the combination of the literature about overseas themes with poetry gave the masterpiece of the century, the epic poem "Os Lusíadas" by Luís de Camões.

University culture also progressed. A profound reform of the University of Lisbon, which was moved once more to Coimbra in 1537, introduced the formal teaching of the humanistic culture into the country. Two decades later, in 1559, the Jesuits established a second Portuguese university in Évora.

However, the Inquisition courts were a significant disruption to cultural progress. As a matter of fact, religious homogeneity in Portuguese society was attained at the cost of the repression of new ideas, a repression that put a significant brake on cultural development as early as the second half of the 16th century. Knowledge about the world would not materialise in the development of modern science during the 17th century.

B – Iberian unification, 1580-1640

The events

King Sebastião I died in the battle of Alcácer-Quibir (1578) leaving no descendants. The new Portuguese king was his granduncle, cardinal Henrique. The old age and ecclesiastical state of the new king made the problem of succession the main political concern of his short reign (1578-1580). According to the usual rules of succession, the first rank in the succession line was occupied by the son of the Duke of Parma, Ranuccio, and the second rank in the succession line was occupied by the wife of the Duke of Bragança, Catarina. However, the heads of the houses of Parma and Bragança thought it wiser to leave the field free for the man who occupied the third rank, Filipe, king of Castile, Aragon, the Netherlands, Burgundy, Milan, Naples, Sicily and Sardinia, usually known as Philip II, according to his Castilian title. Only António, a bastard of one of the sons of King Manuel I, master of the Knights Hospitaller, dared to oppose him. When Henrique I died, he left a council of five governors to rule the country and choose the new king. António took the lead and proclaimed himself king, but a Castilian intervention led by the Duke of Alba swept him away, and Philip II added the Portuguese throne to his collection and became Filipe I of Portugal (1580).

António managed to retain the control of the Azores with French and English help. However, in 1583 he was expelled by the forces of Filipe I, and resistance to the Iberian unification ended.

The rationale of unification from the Portuguese point of view

Iberian unification was an old dream of the rulers of the Iberian Peninsula, as the attempts of the late 15th century (see chapter 3, above) show. Its easy fulfilment during the 1580s proved that it still had the support of the leading groups of the Portuguese society. The Catholic Church was happy to see the main champion of the Catholic faith on the throne of Portugal, the Portuguese aristocracy was happy to have a king that could not give the whole of his attention to Portuguese affairs, and the Portuguese bourgeoisie was happy with the prospect of being allowed to participate in the economic exploitation of the Castilian possessions in the New World (which had proved much richer than the Portuguese rulers thought when they negotiated the treaty of Tordesillas). Only the lower ranks of the popular order rallied under the banner of the defeated António.

Political evolution

The Kingdom of Portugal remained legally and practically separated from the other Hapsburg possessions during the reigns of Filipe I (1580-1598), Filipe II (1598-1621) and Filipe III (1621-1640) – add one unit to the rank to get the more usual Castilian names of these kings. Whenever the king was absent from Portugal (Madrid was the usual seat of the royal court, but Filipe I lived in Lisbon from 1580 to 1583, and Filipe II came to Portugal in 1619), he was replaced by a viceroy (always a Portuguese aristocrat or ecclesiastic, or a member of the royal family) or by a council of governors. The rest of the legal and administrative system remained unchanged, although a third compilation of general laws – the Ordinances of King Filipe (*Ordenações Filipinas*) – was promulgated in 1603.

The frequent absence of the king from the country, and eventual friction between the central power of Madrid and local representatives of the king, allowed local oligarchies of landlords and merchants (including the lower ranks of the aristocracy) to take control of the administration of municipalities, and the higher ranks of the aristocracy to show increased independence towards the monarchy. The progression of entailments was perhaps linked to such a reinforcement of aristocratic power.

Iberian unification brought Portugal a number of foreign enemies – all the enemies of the Western Hapsburg Empire, in fact. France, England and the Netherlands were the most dangerous of these enemies, because of their attacks on overseas possessions. At first, however, warfare in Europe remained mainly a matter of worrisome but non-critical pirate raids. The main exception to this rule was an Iberian initiative, the attack of the so-called Spanish Armada (*Armada Invencível*) on England in 1588-1589 with pitiful results.

*

Things changed after 1620. First of all, the Western Hapsburg Empire began to experience some difficulties, because of wars in Europe and of the drop in silver production in its American possessions. This necessitated new sources of revenue, and Portuguese economic prosperity seemed to afford good taxable prospects. At the same time, King Filipe III and his prime minister, the Duke of Olivares, tried to increase the degree of centralisation of Hapsburg administration, through tighter control of local viceroys. These attempts to increase Portuguese taxes and decrease Portuguese autonomy in a period of colonial recession met with understandable resistance. Moreover, economic prosperity and overseas possessions began to crumble in the 1630s in the face of Dutch and English competition and military attacks (see below). The aristocratic and ecclesiastical orders grumbled and the popular classes exploded into riots (the most important were those of Évora in 1637). At the first opportunity, Portugal abandoned the Western Hapsburg Empire.

Overseas problems

Dutch, English and French attacks plagued the Portuguese overseas empire after the 1590s.

In the Indian Ocean and the Far East, these attacks were successful from the beginning. The Portuguese system of taxing the Indian Ocean trade broke up during the first decade of the 17th century, Ormuz fell to the English in 1622, and Ceylon was lost to the Dutch during the 1630s. The Portuguese government tried to cut its losses and increase the efficiency of the trade initiatives in the Indian Ocean and the Far East by leasing its monopoly of trade relations in this region to private companies organised according to the celebrated model of the Dutch East India Company. However, the Portuguese East India Company (*Companhia Portuguesa das Índias Orientais*) of the 1580s and 1590s, and the India Navigation and Trade Company (*Companhia da Navegação e Comércio com a Índia*) of the 1610s and 1620s were business failures, and once again the government had to take over the decreasingly profitable trade monopoly with those regions.

In the Atlantic Ocean, the Portuguese were able to hold out until the 1630s. Both Dutch and French forces made attempts on the main towns of Brazil and the main trade factories of the western coast of Africa, but without success (Salvador was lost in 1624, but recovered the following year). However, during the 1630s, Pernambuco and most of the northeast of Brazil fell into Dutch hands. São Jorge da Mina and Arguim, two of the main Portuguese trade factories on the western coast of Africa, were also conquered by the Dutch in 1637 and 1638, respectively.

Economic evolution

Not only did Iberian unification bring no interruption to the course of Portuguese economic prosperity, it even added a significant element to the Portuguese economic horizon: Portuguese merchants were allowed to trade and settle in the Castilian possessions of the New World. Trade with Peru, via the mouth of the River Plate and the trans-South American route, was the main result of the opening up of this freedom. As Castilian merchants did not receive a symmetric authorisation, and the Portuguese colonial empire remained legally closed to foreign merchants, even to Hapsburg subjects, it is easy to conclude that the economic result of the Portuguese integration in the Western Hapsburg Empire was clearly positive up to the 1620s.

At the same time, Brazilian sugar became one of the key elements of Portuguese economic prosperity. Brazilian producers were able to undersell every other producing region (including other Portuguese possessions such as Madeira and São Tomé) in European markets, and Portugal stood as the intermediary between what became its main overseas possession and the rest of the world. Moreover, as the Brazilian trade was not a state monopoly, it was able to sustain a larger middle class scattered all along the Portuguese coast, instead of a small group of powerful merchants concentrated in Lisbon, as the Indian Ocean and Far East trade did.

This did not prevent home products such as salt, wine and Mediterranean fruits to continue to be exported to the same European markets that absorbed Brazilian sugar, adding another element to the economic strength of the country.

*

The situation changed during the second quarter of the 17th century. First, there was the levelling off of the whole demographic and economic expansion in Europe, which spelled the end of the epoch of growing demand for the products of both Portugal proper and Portuguese overseas possessions. Second, Portugal lost part of its share of this decelerating market, because of its setbacks in the overseas world (see above). Last (and perhaps not least), the whole Western Hapsburg Empire faced growing difficulties, which led to growing Castilian hostility to the Portuguese encroachment on its American possessions and to an increasing appetite on the part of the central power for taxing what was left of Portuguese prosperity. Economic stagnation and political unrest were the offspring of these trends.

Population and towns

It is likely that population fluctuations went closely hand in hand with economic fluctuations. This means that population growth continued until the 1620s, taking the Portuguese population to around 2 million inhabitants. From then on, population growth ceased and population fluctuated around the 2 million level for the rest of the century. Increased mortality was almost certainly the key factor in this demographic evolution.

Regarding regional distribution, no fundamental changes occurred. The urban picture, however, presented some novelties. Lisbon remained the leading city, with a population above 100,000 inhabitants, but tended to level off. On the contrary, other ports flourished: the main case was that of Porto, which clearly became the second town of the country, with a population of around 25,000. The university towns of Coimbra and Évora also reached the 10,000 mark.

Monetary system

Money remained stable in Portugal during the period of Iberian unification. The gold value of the Portuguese real stayed at its 1555 level of 7.1 mg, while the silver value of the Portuguese real dropped from 79.4 mg to 75.1 mg in 1588, and remained unchanged thereafter until the 1640 revolt.

Prices

Quantitative analysis of the evolution of prices during the 17th century is no more developed than that of the 16th century. However, it is possible to say that the upward trend in prices that characterised the 16th century was replaced after the turn of the century by fluctuations around a relatively stable level. Given the general trend of economic stagnation and some plausible reduction in the outflow of precious metals for trade in the Indian Ocean and Far East, it is likely that the fluctuations of the inflow of precious metals from Africa and Castile provide the explanation.

State accounts and public debt

Economic prosperity allowed public revenue to go on growing until around 1620, regularly overcoming the 1,000 contos mark per year after the beginning of the 17th century. However, participation in the burden of the Hapsburg imperial policy meant high military expenditure, both ordinary and extraordinary. This implied that deficits in state accounts became endemic.

The increase of public debt was an inevitable consequence of this process. In 1605, there was a second suspension of payments followed by a conversion with reduction of service. Forced reductions of payments became frequent from then on.

Fiscal systems

In 1634 there was an attempt to improve the situation of public accounts through the introduction in the state fiscal system of a new tax called 'water money' (*real de água*, from the name of the monetary unit). It was a general consumption tax on wine and meat, which had previously existed in some municipalities with the explicit purpose of financing the building of water supply systems, hence its name.

The feudal and ecclesiastical fiscal systems saw no significant changes during the period of Iberian unification.

C – The separation from the Western Hapsburg Empire and its consolidation, 1640-1700

The events

The revolt of Catalonia against the Hapsburg rule in March 1640 afforded a good opportunity for a Portuguese attempt to recover full independence. On the 1st of December 1640, João Pinto Ribeiro led a palace revolt in Lisbon and proclaimed the

Duke of Bragança as King João IV. The new king was accepted without opposition throughout the Portuguese territory and overseas possessions, except in Ceuta, which remained in the hands of Filipe III.

The rationale of the separation from the Portuguese point of view

Given the international situation of the second quarter of the 17th century, it is not difficult to understand the goals of the Portuguese revolt of 1640. The idea was to avoid sharing the fate of the crumbling Western Hapsburg Empire, and to recover overseas possessions by making peace with the Dutch and the English.

The results were somewhat mixed. Portugal managed to escape from the problems of the Western Hapsburg Empire (though at the price of diminished importance on the international scene), and peace with the Dutch and the English was easily established in Europe, but the recovery of overseas possessions proved impossible without a fight.

The Restoration War

The reaction of the central government in Madrid against the Portuguese revolt of 1640 was remarkably slow, because of the problems it had to face in other parts of the empire: the revolts of the Low Countries (1566-1648), which ended with the independence of the Dutch Republic, of Catalonia (1640-1652), which was crushed, and of Andalusia (1641), which was also crushed, and the war with France linked with the so-called Thirty Years War (1638-1659). Together with some Dutch, English, French and Swedish help (spoiled only in the case of England by the support of the Portuguese government to King Charles I in the civil war of 1642-1648, which led to a war that lasted until 1654), the Portuguese government enjoyed relatively quiet times in Europe until 1659. There followed the decisive years of 1659-1665: successive invasions of the Hapsburg armies were defeated in Elvas (1659), Ameixial (1663), Castelo Rodrigo (1664) and Montes Claros (1665). Three years later, the Hapsburgs recognised Portuguese independence, with the only price being the cession of Ceuta.

The wars for the colonies

The years immediately after the separation from the Western Hapsburg Empire were disastrous for the Portuguese colonial empire. What was left of the northeast of Brazil, the remaining principal trade factories and fortresses of the western coast of Africa (São Paulo de Luanda and São Tomé) and some fortresses of the Indian Ocean and the Far East (the most important was Malacca) were lost to the Dutch.

Defeat in the Indian Ocean and the Far East was more or less definitive. There was no significant recovery of the possessions already lost either to the Dutch or to the English, and further reduction of the Portuguese possessions occurred with the cession of Bombaim (today Mumbai) to England as part of the dowry of the Portuguese princess Catarina when she married Charles II and became queen of England in 1662.

Things were rather different in the Atlantic. First of all, the Brazilian colonists were able to organise an effective resistance against Dutch rule. They won the decisive battles of Tabocas (1645) and Guararapes (1649), and recaptured the whole territory under Dutch rule by 1654. Meanwhile, a Brazilian expedition had also retaken São Paulo de Luanda and São Tomé, which were vital in the slave supply for the sugar plantations (1648). Arguim and São Jorge da Mina had been lost for good, but Portuguese trade in the regions traditionally controlled by these trade factories managed to survive. North of the Gulf of Guinea, its bases were the islands of Cape Verde, as usual, and new trade factories in Cacheu and Bissau; in the Gulf of Guinea its bases were the islands of Ano Bom, Fernão do Pó, São Tomé, and Príncipe, as usual, and a new trade factory in São João Baptista de Ajudá.

Between 1649 and 1662, there was an attempt to organise a private company with the monopoly of trade with Brazil, which would also provide the naval protection needed to prevent new foreign attacks on the Brazilian possessions and on the ships involved in the Brazilian trade. However, the Brazil Trade Company (*Companhia para o Comércio com o Brasil*) met with clear resistance from the vested interests in the Brazilian trade and had to be transformed into a state-owned department, which collected taxes from the Brazilian trade and used the money to provide the defence of Brazilian possessions and Brazilian trade. This did not prevent new attempts at organising private companies with monopolies restricted to smaller areas between the 1670s and the early 18th century: the Cape Verde and Guinea Rivers Company (*Companhia de Cabo Verde e Rios da Guiné*), the Cape Verde Islands, Bissau and Cacheu Trade Monopoly Company (*Companhia para o Monopólio do Comércio nas Ilhas de Cabo Verde, Bissau e Cacheu*), the Cape Verde and Cacheu Company (*Companhia de Cabo Verde e Cacheu*), the Pará and Maranhão Company (*Companhia do Pará e Maranhão*) – Pará and Maranhão are regions in the North of Brazil, today Brazilian states – and the Corisco Island Company (*Companhia da Ilha de Corisco*) – Corisco is another name for Fernão do Pó. None of these companies met with much success.

Just as the companies created in the late 16th and early 17th centuries having a trade monopoly in the Indian Ocean and Far East, mentioned above, these companies with a trade monopoly in certain regions of the Atlantic Ocean were created in epochs of trade recession. This helps to explain their failures. If, in the case of the Indian Ocean and the Far East, the recession was more or less definitive, in the case of the Atlantic Ocean there was a clear recovery in the 18th century. Such a recovery, however, was not favourable to the companies, because in epochs of prosperity they became subject to the hostility of the merchants, who preferred the freedom to maintain their private business. Thus, their fate was, in every case, liquidation.

*

The reasons for the problems of the Portuguese colonial empire have been the matter of some debate among historians. Two standard theses have been advanced. One finds the reason for the decadence of the Portuguese colonial empire in internal factors: the Portuguese society did not adapt efficiently to the needs of the new times, was unable to profit from the overseas endeavours and produced a greedy and corrupt colonial administration. The other explains the decadence of the Portuguese colonial empire through external factors: a small country such as Portugal was unable to resist its more powerful rivals, such as the Dutch, English and French, when they committed themselves to systematic colonial expansion policies of their own.

Both theses touch important aspects of reality, but the external one is certainly more adequate as a general explanation. Inefficiency and corruption certainly plagued the Portuguese Empire and were harmful to its long-term evolution and its contribution to Portuguese prosperity and development. Decadence of the Portuguese Empire in the Indian Ocean and the Far East (and Morocco), however, must be explained by more conspicuous reasons: both European and local Asian (and Moroccan) rivals were intrinsically stronger than the Portuguese, and the monopoly of geographical knowledge which provided the basis of Portuguese superiority during the 15th and most of the 16th centuries could not be sustained forever. Only in regions where immigration from the Portuguese mainland had created a local population deeply rooted to the spot and with strong links to the mother country did the Portuguese Empire manage to survive when the challenge of these powerful rivals came. This was the case in

Madeira, the Azores, Brazil, Goa, Macau and some possessions in Africa and in Indonesia, but not in the bulk of African and Asian possessions.

Financing the wars

The need to finance the Restoration War and the wars for the overseas possessions greatly strained the Portuguese public accounts. Monetary devaluation, new taxes and public debt were needed to pay for these wars.

Monetary evolution and prices

Monetary devaluation started in 1641 and lasted for two decades following the end of the Restoration War: the gold value of the Portuguese real dropped from 7.1 mg in 1640 to 2.054 mg in 1688, and the silver value of the Portuguese real dropped from 75.1 mg in 1640 to 31.8 mg in 1688. Only after 1688 did stabilisation come, at last.

In spite of the scant amount of research to date, it is possible to suggest that the fluctuation of prices around a relatively stable level that had characterised the early decades of the 17th century continued during this devaluation period: there was a rise between the early 1640s and the mid-1660s; a fall during the late 1660s, a new rise during the 1670s and a new fall during the 1680s. The explanation for these fluctuations is likely to be similar to that proposed for the case of the early 17th century – fluctuations in the inflow and outflow of precious metals – once the trend of economic stagnation remained. To these must be added the effects of monetary devaluation.

Fiscal evolution

In the state fiscal system, a new tax, the royal or military tithe, was introduced in 1641. This tax was an income tax from which no privileged order was exempted, though the ecclesiastical order managed to secure the right to pay a mode in lieu of it.

Once more, it is possible to say that the feudal and ecclesiastical fiscal systems saw no significant changes during this period.

Public accounts and public debt

The introduction of the military tithe allowed public revenue to rise, reaching more than 1,500 contos per year in the late 17th century, but was unable to avoid deficits in public accounts and increases in public debt, especially during the War of Restoration. Although there was no suspension of payments, forced reductions of service remained frequent until the end of the war.

Military victories: Portuguese strength and weakness

Between 1640 and the 1660s Portugal was involved in simultaneous wars with the most powerful European states of the day – the Western Hapsburg Empire, the Dutch Republic and the British Commonwealth. How was it possible to achieve the real success of maintaining its independence and clinging to a significant part of its colonial empire? Of course, the main explanation is that none of Portugal's enemies ever brought their full resources to bear against Portugal, either because of other concerns, or because it was strategically advantageous to restrict the war to some selected regions. At the same time, Portugal received some help, not only from France and Sweden, but also from its very enemies in overseas theatres to fight the Western Hapsburg Empire on European soil. However, Portugal also showed some strength during the conflict that cannot be ignored.

The most important bases for Portuguese strength were the colonial resources. As a matter of fact, the existence of a colonial empire and of a national state were almost equivalent in modern times, and Portugal managed to retain a significant colonial empire in the most prosperous zone of inter-continental trade. The Brazilian population grew at least 25% during the 17th century, reaching the level of 1.25 million, and thus Brazil was able to resist the Dutch attacks and even to regain some of the African trade factories it needed for its slave supply with little help from the mother country.

The economy of the mother country was also able to retain some measure of prosperity, in spite of the general problems of the 17th century. Exports of salt, wine and Mediterranean fruits stabilised during the third quarter of the 17th century, and the cultivation of maize, vineyards and olives progressed in the north of the country. At the same time, the Atlantic islands also regained some prosperity. The most important case was that of Madeira, which switched from sugar production to wine production, and saw its staple export gain a strong position in European markets.

The Portuguese population stagnated until the early 18th century, in spite of some regional increases, mainly in the north of the country and in the Atlantic islands. This evolution was, however, quite different from the general Iberian one. The population of the Iberian Peninsula decreased from 10.5 to 10 million inhabitants during the 17th century, the main drop being felt in Castile, which helps to explain the revolts in the peripheral regions, less touched by demographic recession, and the success of at least one of these revolts – the Portuguese one.

*

At the same time, however, Portugal also showed some weakness, which materialised in the definitive loss of any significant role in international affairs. As a matter of fact, important concessions had to be made to some of its enemies to secure peace. The cession of Ceuta to Castile, of Tânger (today Tangiers) in Morocco and of Bombaim (today Mumbai) in India to England,

and of Arguim, São Jorge da Mina, Ceylon and Malacca to the Dutch Republic were the territorial losses, but perhaps not the most important concessions. Special rights given to British and Dutch traders in Portugal were to have much more impact on the future of the Portuguese economy.

Political evolution

The accession of the dukes of Bragança to the Portuguese throne extinguished the last of the aristocratic houses that had threatened royal power since the 15th century. King João IV organised the old ducal properties as an entailment to sustain royal sons not entitled to the throne, putting an end to the temptation of extensive personal endowments.

King João IV died in 1656. His son Afonso VI was feeble-minded, and there followed a period of regency by his mother, Luísa (1656-1662), a period of direct government of the king, in fact controlled by two powerful ministers, Luís Vasconcelos e Sousa (count of Castelo Melhor) and António Sousa de Macedo (1662-1667), and a period of regency of the king's brother Pedro (1667-1683), later King Pedro II (1683-1706), during which the government was led by the Duke of Cadaval.

The economic problems of the late 17th and early 18th century

By the end of the 17th century, the Dutch Republic, England and France no longer tried to attack Portuguese overseas possessions. However, they went on challenging the economic prosperity of these overseas possessions, and even of the mother country itself, through the competition of the commodities produced in their own colonial possessions against those of Portuguese origin in the European markets. The most important example was the competition of sugar from Caribbean islands to the Brazilian sugar.

Besides the attempts to create companies with the monopoly of trade in particular regions already mentioned above, the glut of Brazilian commodities led Portugal into its first attempt at an industrialisation policy. During the 1680s, pragmatic sanctions forbade the import of foreign clothes, and state subsidies and regulations tried to foster the activity of textile industries. Other sectors, such as metallurgy, also received state help.

This policy is linked with the names of the minister Luís de Meneses (count of Ericeira), and Duarte Ribeiro de Macedo. It is usually suggested that it was inspired by French industrial mercantilism.

However, the future prosperity of the Portuguese economy did not lie in industrialisation. During the 17th century, expeditions from the Brazilian coastal settlements, mainly from São Paulo, locally called 'flags' (*bandeiras*), explored most of what today forms the interior of the country in search of slaves and precious metals. In the late 1690s, gold mines were, at last, discovered in what is today the state of Minas Gerais (general mines). Some years later, the English government offered a preferential duty on Portuguese wines in exchange for the abrogation of the pragmatic sanctions forbidding imports of English clothes, and negotiations over this led to the so-called Methuen treaty (1703). Brazilian gold and the mother country's wine would become the key elements of a new Portuguese role in the Euro-Atlantic world-economy during the 18th century.

6.

Portugal in the Euro-Atlantic world-economy, 1700-1793

In certain respects, during the 18th century the Portuguese economy and society enjoyed an era quite similar to the apogee of the 16th century, characterised by population and economic growth, and by an important role of colonial and European links in Portuguese life.

In other respects, however, things were very different: the location of the most important parts of the colonial empire had shifted from the Indian Ocean and the Far East to the Atlantic Ocean, the dreams of Iberian political unification had been replaced by rather hostile relations with Spain, and, above all, the leading role that Portugal had played in European expansion was gone forever. Political decadence became a primary concern of the Portuguese elites; and, in spite of economic prosperity, even economic backwardness gradually became a problem.

Section A of this chapter presents the general features of the evolution of the Portuguese economy and society during the 18th century. Sections B to D present the characteristics of the three periods into which that evolution may be divided: the period of prosperity linked to the exports of Brazilian gold and Portuguese wine that lasted for the first half of the century; the period of setback that led to a policy of establishing monopolistic companies during the third quarter of the century; and the period of renewed prosperity between the late 1770s and the early 1790s.

A – General features

Population

The 18th century witnessed a 50% growth in Portuguese population. As a matter of fact, from a 2-million level around 1700, it grew to 3 million around 1800.

Regional distribution did not change a great deal, though the traditional trend of increasing contrasts of population density continued to prevail. In the late 18th century, the provinces of Minho and Beira included around 1/4 of the Portuguese population each, the province of Estremadura around 1/5, the provinces of Alentejo and Trás-os-Montes around 1/10 each, the provinces of the Azores, Algarve and Madeira less than 1/20 each.

Population movements

Demographic movements repeated the pattern already seen in the 16th century: there were no territorial changes, population growth was sustained by an excess of births over deaths, there was no immigration to speak of, and many Portuguese emigrated, mainly to Brazil. According to the more widely accepted estimates, some 200,000 people left the mother country to settle in its South American colony.

Towns

Lisbon increased its population to nearly 200,000 inhabitants during the 18th century. It remained the largest city of the country, though any prominent place in the European and even in the Iberian context clearly vanished. Porto also experienced a strong growth, to nearly 50,000 inhabitants. Its second place among Portuguese urban centres was no longer challenged.

Coimbra, Évora, Braga and Setúbal in the continental part of the country, Funchal in Madeira, and Angra in the Azores exceeded the 10,000 mark by the late 18th century.

Population juridical status

The 18th century witnessed two important changes in the laws pertaining to the juridical status of the population.

The first change was the end of slavery (and of slave trade to the continental part of the country, Madeira and the Azores) in 1761. This was not a humanitarian measure. Its goal was to avoid competition of the Portuguese slave market with that of Brazil. The measure had no significant direct effect on the economic situation of Portugal, because slaves had not been an important part of its labour force since medieval times.

The other change in the population juridical status was the end of legal discrimination against the descendants of Jews. The distinction between Old Christians and New Christians was dissolved in 1768, and the Inquisition courts were taken under royal control in order to avoid their use as a device in preserving these distinctions. In spite of some unfavourable reactions from conservative groups, no popular persecutions arose, and the Jewish problem was definitively solved in the Portuguese society.

Administrative and ecclesiastical division of the country

After a pause during the 17th century, due to demographic and economic stagnation, the number of so-called correction districts began to increase again during the 18th century.

A similar evolution was seen concerning bishoprics, although Beja was the only new bishopric that proved stable. Moreover, the see of Miranda do Douro was transferred to Bragança and the archbishopric of Lisbon became a patriarchate.

Agriculture

The evolution of Portuguese agriculture during the 18th century was characterised mainly by the extension of Mediterranean crops such as the vine and olive into the north of the country and by the increase of exports of Mediterranean agricultural products such as wine, olive oil, and fruits. These trends originated in the 17th century, and were promoted in the wine sector by the preferential duty given by the Methuen Treaty in the British market, by far the most important for Portuguese exports. According to the Methuen treaty, Portuguese wines paid as import duty in England only 2/3 the normal duty charged, among others, on the French wines, their main competitors. Among all Portuguese wines, the so-called Port wine and Madeira wine were those that acquired the best international reputation. The regions of southwestern Trás-os-Montes and northwestern Beira Alta, in the case of Port wine, and the southern part of the Madeira island, in the case of Madeira wine, developed, as a consequence, a clear specialisation in their production.

From another equivalent point of view, it may be said that the basis of the prosperity of Portuguese agriculture during the 18th century was the increase in the production of cash crops.

In spite of this prosperity, the higher number of inhabitants of the country demanded an increase in cereal imports. It is almost certain that cereal production increased, but did not keep pace with population increases. As imported cereals competed in price with Portuguese cereals, and most agricultural land was diverted into more profitable uses, such as cash crops and animal husbandry, it is difficult to subscribe to the view of some contemporary authors, who blamed cereal imports for impoverishing the country and its agriculture.

Another interesting innovation in Portuguese agriculture during the 18th century was the introduction of the potato. Its immediate impact was not very important, but during the 19th century the potato would become an important product of

Portuguese agriculture and replace chestnuts as an important element in Portuguese eating habits.

At the same time, innovations of the kind that precipitated the so-called agricultural revolution of 18th-century Britain were absent from Portuguese agriculture. This was a consequence of the different ecological conditions in the two countries, which made a direct copy of such innovations difficult in a country with moderately rainy or dry summers, and of the lack of adequate adaptation of these innovations.

Industry

Portuguese industry did not flourish during the 18th century. This was mainly a consequence of the competition from cheaper commodities coming from the most-developed countries of Europe, especially Great Britain. Artisan industry producing low-quality, cheap goods managed to survive, but capitalist manufacturing producing high-quality goods met with less true success.

The Methuen Treaty has been traditionally blamed for this stagnation of Portuguese industry during the 18th century. Of course, such an explanation could only apply to the textile sector, given the fact that the treaty only stipulated the end of the prohibition on the import of British clothing. However, even concerning textiles, it is only fair to point out that the treaty did not put an end to protectionist tariffs, so that, if British clothes competed with Portuguese ones, it was because of their quality and inexpensiveness (meaning a clear advantage for the consumer). It is certainly possible to argue that the development of a strong Portuguese textile industry during the 18th century might have been a good start for a precocious modernisation of the Portuguese economy, but we must be cautious about such a counter-factual argument, because it involves the as yet unproven assumptions that the Portuguese textile industry would have been able to become fully competitive in the long run and that other sectors would have developed under the influence of the textile sector. As a matter of fact, none of these assumptions is clearly supported by similar experiences abroad.

The technological innovations related to the so-called first industrial revolution of 18th-century Britain were almost absent from the Portuguese industry of the time. Experimental steam engines were built, but none were applied to economic uses. Mechanical devices tapping water power were known, but were not much of an advantage in a country that lacked steady flows in its rivers throughout the whole year.

Domestic trade

Further steps in the ongoing process of increasing the role of market schemes and decreasing the role of self-consumption in Portuguese economic life are undoubted during the 18th century.

The improvements in the network of internal transportation that were so important in other European countries in the 18th century were, however, almost absent in Portugal. Regarding canals, for example, the geographical and climatic conditions of the country made it impossible to build them in large numbers. There were some projects, but the irregular flow of Portuguese rivers (and some shortage of capital) prevented them from being realised. Paved roads only appeared at the end of the 18th century on the routes between the main towns of the country. The sea and the 800 km of navigable stretches of rivers (though often hindered by flood in winter and by drought in summer) remained the main avenues for domestic trade – after all, they served around 54,000 square km, that is to say around 60% of the continental territory of the country, and, of course, the Atlantic archipelagoes.

It should be stressed that the absence of significant progress in internal transportation was an obstacle to a greater integration of large areas of the interior of the country in the Euro-Atlantic world-economy. It is true that this contributed to the survival of traditional activities, especially industrial activities, that otherwise could have been destroyed by foreign competition. In the long run, however, it is difficult to believe that such a situation could have been beneficial to Portuguese development, as no true proto-industrialisation, let alone a modernising industrialisation, could rest on such a basis.

Residual trade in the Indian Ocean and Far East

During the 18th century, Portugal retained some trade factories and fortresses in the Indian Ocean and the Far East: Mozambique, Goa, Damão, Diu, Solor, Timor and Macau were the most important of these possessions.

However, the Portuguese role in the trade of the Indian Ocean and Far East was clearly residual. Only small quantities of Asian commodities flowed through Portugal to Europe.

Triangular trade in the Atlantic

In stark contrast to the reduced Portuguese role in the Indian Ocean and Far East, Portugal played a major role in the triangular trade of the Atlantic. The so-called colonial pact, which forbade the colonies of each country to trade directly with foreign countries and ruled out competition between economic activities of the colonies and the mother country, restricted the Portuguese role in the triangular trade in the Atlantic to the Portuguese possessions on the west coast of Africa and Brazil, but ensured the intermediate role of Portugal in most of the economic life of these possessions.

The first element of the triangular trade in the Atlantic Ocean was the flow of exports of European commodities to Africa and Brazil. Textiles and metal wares remained the main demands from Africa. Mediterranean agricultural products such as wine, olive oil and fruits joined textiles and metal works as important demands from Brazil. The Portuguese economy was able to provide the bulk of agricultural exports and some industrial exports for this trade, but most industrial exports were mere re-exports of commodities coming into Portugal from other European countries.

The second element of the triangular trade in the Atlantic Ocean was the flow of exports of African and Brazilian commodities to Europe. African exports to Europe declined in relative and even in absolute importance: gold deposits became exhausted, and the slave trade dwindled (and was even forbidden in 1761, as explained above). Thus, ivory remained the only important African export to Europe. The Brazilian trend was just the opposite: the exports of gold, sugar, cotton, tobacco and dressed hides to Europe clearly increased during the 18th century.

The third element of the triangular trade in the Atlantic Ocean was the flow of slaves from Africa to America (in the Portuguese case mainly from Angola and Guinea to Brazil). This flow clearly increased during the 18th century, as a consequence of higher Brazilian demand and of higher availability in Africa, in spite of the definitive loss of the market of Castilian colonies to Great Britain after the end of the War of Spanish Succession. Such trends were certainly detrimental to the conditions of slave life on the Atlantic routes and in Brazil.

European links

The pattern of Portuguese foreign trade with its main European partners saw no fundamental changes during the 18th century. Portugal remained mainly an exporter of primary products, such as salt, wine and Mediterranean fruits, and an importer of industrial commodities, such as textiles and metal works, and of wheat.

The quantitative increase of these trade relations was, however, very important. Portugal was willing and able to import more, because of the population and economic growth, and of the inflow of Brazilian gold. The European trade partners were willing and able to buy more Portuguese goods, also because of their population and economic growth. The role of the improvement in sea transportation, mainly the consequence of the building of larger and better ships, and of trade treaties should not be forgotten, however. Besides the Methuen Treaty, Portugal tried to establish trade treaties with other European countries, especially with those that traditionally played lesser roles as consumers of Mediterranean and colonial products, such as Prussia and Russia, with some success.

The balance of trade and the balance of payments

For most of the 18th century, Portuguese foreign trade showed large deficits. The inflow of cheap Brazilian gold and the rise of prices that was the consequence of such an inflow were the main causes of this situation, which caused much concern among Portuguese writers on economic themes. In spite of some official efforts to alter the situation, it only began to change when the inflow of Brazilian gold tended to dwindle in the second half and especially the last quarter of the 18th century.

The deficit of the official trade balance was, indeed, compensated by gold exports (usually illegal), mainly to Great Britain. This is an economically natural situation, given that Portugal (or, more precisely, its Brazilian colony) was at this time the largest gold producer of the world, making it normal that it became an exporter of that commodity. However, the concerns of Portuguese authors on economic subjects referred to above, as they were dominated by a mercantilist perspective, were only exacerbated by this fact.

Another common subject for complaint about the situation of the Portuguese foreign trade was the role that British merchants played in its business. Profiting from the special rights awarded by the Portuguese government in the wake of the 17th century wars, many British merchants established themselves in Portugal, mainly in Lisbon, Porto and Funchal, and were able to take control of most of the Portuguese foreign trade, especially of Port and Madeira wines. Lack of entrepreneurial capacity prevented Portuguese merchants from playing a similar role in Portuguese foreign trade relations.

B – The period of Brazilian gold and Portuguese wine, 1700-1750

During the first half of the 18th century, Brazilian gold and Portuguese wine were the main conspicuous sources of short-term prosperity for the Portuguese economy.

Brazilian gold, money and prices

During the first half of the 18th century, more than 500 metric tonnes of gold were imported from Brazil to Portugal. The official policy towards this gold was typically mercantilist: exports of gold were legally restricted, so that the abundance of precious metals might assure the prosperity of the country and the power of the state. In practice, things were, of course, very different: huge amounts of gold went abroad to finance the deficit of the balance of payments, and the excess that remained in the country was more harmful than useful to the Portuguese economy.

Concerning exports, this was a natural fact, as pointed out above. Restrictions and prohibitions only stimulated the growth of bureaucracy, and of smuggling, mainly to Great Britain.

As to the effects of gold in Portuguese economic life, it certainly contributed to monetary stability and to a high price level. As a matter of fact, between 1688 and 1750, the gold value of the Portuguese real remained unchanged, and the silver value of the Portuguese real was changed only twice, with a drop from 31.8 mg to 28.0 mg, a sharp contrast with the evolution between 1640 and 1688. However, it is also likely that the abundance of gold contributed to a higher price level than would have otherwise existed. Research into prices is not yet fully developed, but it seems to point to the following conclusions: after a sharp rise until around 1715, perhaps linked not only with the inflow of gold, but also with the effects of the War of Spanish Succession, prices showed some decline for nearly a decade, and stabilised from the late 1720s on.

Monetary stability was, of course, a good thing, which might have been achieved with less gold and fewer restrictions on its movements, as later experience proved. The high price level was detrimental to the economic situation of the country, because it prevented an easy competition of Portuguese commodities, both in the foreign markets and in the home and colonial markets. It is likely that less gold and fewer restrictions to its movements would have been much better for the economic development of the country.

Portuguese wine and agriculture in general

By giving a preferential duty to the Portuguese wines as against the French, the Methuen Treaty stimulated the switch of the demand of the British consumer from French to Portuguese suppliers of wine. Portuguese exports both of high quality wines such as Port and Madeira and of ordinary wines boomed, and the planting of vineyards spread in all Portuguese regions.

Complaints about the switch of landowners and peasants from the cultivation of cereals to the planting of vineyards, and about the disastrous consequences such a choice would have on Portuguese agriculture soon arose. As has been pointed out above, such complaints certainly miss the key point about the true situation of Portuguese agriculture. In any event, by the mid-18th century, wine production levelled off, as its markets began to show some saturation.

Portuguese industry

There is not much to add to what has been observed above about the relative decay of the Portuguese industrial sector during the first half of the 18th century. However, it is important to point out that, besides artisanal and domestic industry, some factories of size were able to survive in the silk and iron sectors, though only with state support.

The War of Spanish Succession

In 1700, King Carlos II of Castile (and of the other remaining Western Hapsburg Empire possessions – the southern half of the Low Countries, Milan, Naples, Sicily, Sardinia and Aragon) died, leaving his domains to be disputed between a candidate from the French royal house (Filipe), and a candidate from the Austrian imperial house (Carlos) supported by an Anglo-Dutch alliance.

The strategic position of Portugal as a neighbour of the Iberian Hapsburg possessions led both sides to ask for the Portuguese alliance. The Portuguese government hesitated and tried to find compensations for its support in territorial gains in the Iberian Peninsula and in the awarding to Portuguese merchants of the contract (*asiento*) of slave supply to the Castilian possessions in America. In the end, Portugal chose the Austrian (Anglo-Dutch) side – a strategic decision to avoid English and Dutch attacks on the remaining Portuguese overseas possessions, though it implied a conflict at home with Castile, which supported the French candidate. Most of the so-called War of Spanish Succession was spent in border skirmishes, but the 1706 campaign saw the Portuguese troops take Madrid and proclaim there King Carlos III, while the 1707 campaign saw the Castilian troops drive the Portuguese back. At the end of the war, the Western Hapsburg Empire was divided between the two candidates, the Iberian Hapsburg possessions (from now on correctly called

Spain) and its colonies being the lot of the candidate from the French royal house, Filipe V of Spain. Portugal received none of the compensations its government had sought.

*

This does not mean that the War of Spanish Succession was irrelevant for Portugal in the long run. The combined results of the so-called War of Restoration and of the War of Spanish Succession were decisive for Portugal's future, because it is reasonable to speculate that if Portugal had still been a Hapsburg possession in the early 18th century, it is likely that it would have been included in the Iberian lot of Filipe V and merged forever into the Kingdom of Spain (with no other European connections) that existed thereafter. In other words, the War of Restoration and the War of Spanish Succession drew the political map of the Iberian Peninsula of the following centuries (even in details such as the British presence in Gibraltar, also a consequence of the War of Spanish Succession).

Political evolution, 1713-1750

The rest of the first half of the 18th century was a quiet period for Portuguese international relations, except for the participation in the naval episodes of the 1716-1719 war of some Christian powers (mainly Austria and Venice) against Turkey. In particular, Portugal managed to remain neutral during the so-called Wars of Polish Succession (1731-1735) and Austrian Succession (1740-1748).

Colonial events were less quiet: Maratha pressure put Goa, the vice-regal capital of the possessions of the Indian Ocean and Far East in danger, and quarrels about the borders between Brazil and Spanish America were endemic, mainly on the left bank of the mouth of the River Plate, because the Portuguese colony of Sacramento and the Spanish colony of Montevideo tried to control the area (today Uruguay) with inconclusive results. Both problems were to be solved only during the second half of the 18th century.

Building on economic prosperity and on neutrality in European conflicts, King João V (1706-1750) and his ministers, Diogo Corte Real and cardinal Mota, managed to ensure calm, from the point of view of internal policy, during the first half of the 18th century.

Administration

In 1736, the central administration was divided into what was then called the secretaries of state (later to be called ministries), each one headed by a politician chosen by the king. During the 18th century, secretaries of state for financial, domestic, military, colonial and foreign affairs were created.

State accounts and fiscal systems

The War of Spanish Succession put some pressure on the treasury of the Portuguese state, because of the increased expenditure needed to sustain military operations. The inflow of Brazilian gold and economic prosperity in general, however, allowed an increase of public revenue from around 1,650 contos in the late 17th century to around 3,800 contos in the second decade of the 18th century. The war was fought with some increase in public debt, but without monetary devaluation.

After the war was over, it was even possible to reduce the military tithe, even if increases in indirect taxes compensated the loss of revenue to the exchequer. Expenditure was reduced and the state accounts remained roughly balanced during the following decades.

Church and feudal fiscal systems underwent no change during this period, though their revenue certainly increased as a consequence of economic prosperity.

C – The period of privileged companies, 1750-1777

During the third quarter of the 18th century, the Portuguese economy faced some short-term problems, mainly as a consequence of the relative exhaustion of Brazilian gold mines and the stagnation of the exports of metropolitan commodities. The Portuguese government tried to respond to these problems by organising a system of privileged companies, vested with production and trade monopolies, not only in colonial trade, but also in metropolitan economic activities.

Privileged companies in colonial trade

Colonial trade was, of course, the fundamental field of privileged companies. The East Trade Company (*Companhia para o Comércio com o Oriente*) received the monopoly of the trade with India and the Far East; the Great Pará and Maranhão Company (*Companhia do Grão-Pará e Maranhão*) – Pará and Maranhão are regions of the north of Brazil, today Brazilian states – and the Pernambuco and Paraíba Company (*Companhia de Pernambuco e Paraíba*) – Pernambuco and Paraíba are regions of the centre of Brazil, today Brazilian states – received the monopoly of the trade with most of the west coast of Africa and most of northern and central Brazil; and the Mujaos and Macuas Trade Company (*Companhia para o Comércio dos Mujaos e dos Macuas*) – the Mujaos and the Macuas are tribes of the east coast of Africa – received the monopoly of the trade with the east coast of Africa. They were formed during the 1750s and 1760s, and met with unequal success: the Atlantic companies managed to earn money, but the Indian Ocean and Far East companies were unable to do the same. When the tide turned in favour of free trade during the late 1770s and 1780s, the Indian Ocean and Far East companies disappeared and the Atlantic companies were deprived of their privileged status.

Privileged companies in industry

Supporting industrial development was another policy of the government. The textile sector was the main concern. As it was impossible to prohibit the import of British textiles, because of the Methuen Treaty (see section A, above), subsidies, fiscal exemptions, and regulations (and some tariff protection) were the main instruments in advancing the development of Portuguese production of sophisticated textiles. The new factories managed to survive until the early 19th century, but were ruined during the turmoil of the Peninsular War (see chapter 7, below).

Among other sectors, the main efforts were directed towards the sugar refining, ceramics, glass, metallurgy and paper industries. Some of these factories managed to survive and become the basis of important industrial sectors – as was the case of the ceramics, glass and paper industries. Others, such as metallurgy, shared the fate of the textile factories: they survived until the early 19th century, but disappeared altogether during the turmoil of the Peninsular War.

From a geographical point of view, the regions where this industrial spurt was more important were those of the Atlantic seaboard between the south of Entre-Douro-e-Minho and Estremadura, the Beira Baixa, and the north of Alentejo.

Privileged companies in agriculture and fishing

Even some primary activities were subject to the privileged companies system. This was the case of the Port wine production with the Upper Douro Vineyards Agriculture Company (*Companhia para a Agricultura das Vinhas do Alto Douro*) organised to counter the predominance of English merchants in the port wine trade, the tunny fisheries in Algarve with the Kingdom of Algarve General Royal Fisheries Company (*Companhia Geral das Reais Pescas do Reino do Algarve*), and whaling in Brazil with the

Brazilian Coast Whaling Company (*Companhia para a Pesca da Baleia na Costa do Brasil*).

Of all these companies, the only that survived the drive towards economic liberalism in the last quarter of the 19th century was the Upper Douro Vineyards Agriculture Company, which went out of business only in the mid-19th century.

Cereal trade rules

At the same time, however, attempts were made to decrease the restrictions imposed by the cereal trade rules prevailing since the 16th century (see chapter 5, above). Free domestic trade of cereals and direct control of cereal imports by the central authorities using the old Wheat Square Warehouse were the main legal measures taken during the 1760s. Municipalities reacted against these measures and, though they were never repealed, it is difficult to say that they were fully respected until the 19th century regarding the domestic free cereal trade.

The earthquake of 1755

Mention must also be made of an event that caused a terrific capital loss to the country. On the 1st of November, 1755, a massive earthquake, followed by a tsunami, destroyed most of the city of Lisbon and of the coast of Algarve.

The rebuilding of the capital required the mobilisation of many resources during the third quarter of the 18th century. The centre of the city was rebuilt with a typical 18th century plan, which was a marked improvement for urban life, and eventually became one of the most interesting architectural features of the city. The bulk of the work was finished around 1780, when the first public lighting system went into operation in Lisbon.

Political evolution 1750-1777

In politics, the third quarter of the 18th century was more turbulent than the first half of the century.

First of all, Portugal became involved in the final campaigns (1761-1763) of the so-called Seven Years War (1756-1763) on the British and Prussian side against France and Spain. Military operations were not favourable to the Portuguese army, but, as the Portuguese allies won the war, no unpleasant consequences followed.

Colonial problems saw some steps toward stable solutions. In India, the wars against the Marathas ended with the exchange of a few isolated coastal settlements for some territories around Goa and Damão. Moroccan pressure led to the withdrawal from the last Moroccan presidio (Mazagão 1769). The treaties of Madrid (1750) and of Santo Ildefonso (1777) with Spain defined a western border of Brazil which was much more favourable to Portugal than that which had been allowed by the treaty of Tordesillas, in exchange for the cession of the islands of Fernão do Pó (today Bioko) and Ano Bom (today Pagalu) in the Gulf of Guinea (to allow Spain to look after its own slave supply), and for the Portuguese withdrawal from Sacramento and the recognition of the Spanish control of both banks of the River Plate. At the same time, both countries agreed to put an end to the autonomous territories (*reduções*) that the Jesuits controlled in Paraguay.

At home, King José I (1750-1777) and his minister, Sebastião de Carvalho e Melo (later count of Oeiras and marquis of Pombal), carried on a policy of reinforcement of royal power and, as some groups among the clergy, the aristocracy and even the bourgeoisie tried to resist, there was some friction. The expulsion of the Jesuits and the ruthless repression of the main aristocratic leaders, however, ensured some success to the centralisation policies. The changes in the juridical status of the population already described above must be highlighted as being among the most important measures of the period.

Cultural measures

Reference must also be made to some measures taken by the government in the cultural field.

First of all, a nation-wide network of primary schools, paid for by the state, was organised. The real network lagged far behind official plans, which called for one school in each municipality, but the project lasted, and its goals were gradually achieved.

As for universities, the expulsion of the Jesuits led to the end of the University of Évora, which had been organised and sustained by the Society of Jesus. There was an attempt to thoroughly reform the University of Coimbra, with the introduction of modern scientific knowledge in the curricula.

Last but not least, a few specialised technical schools were created in Lisbon in the fields of business, technology, and architecture, among others.

The decline of the Inquisition also had cultural repercussions that should not be undervalued, given the restrictive effects that such an institution had had in Portuguese life during the previous centuries.

Fiscal systems

During the third quarter of the 18th century, there were two changes in the state fiscal system. One was the creation of a new tax on wine production, officially called literary subsidy (*subsídio literário*), to finance the expenditures of the reforms of primary and university education. The other was the restoration of the royal or military tithe with its original rules during the Portuguese intervention in the Seven Years War.

Church and feudal fiscal systems saw no significant change.

State accounts

State revenue continued to grow until a level of around 6,000 contos in the 1760s. This level meant that it was possible to balance current expenditure, and to ask for public loans only on occasions of war. As Portugal remained neutral during most of the European conflicts of the 18th century, public debt grew very moderately and no danger of bankruptcy haunted the Portuguese state until the 1790s.

Meanwhile, an institutional reform in 1762 created the Royal Treasury (*Erário Régio*) to centralise the accounts and prepare a yearly budget.

Money and prices

Stability was the main characteristic of the Portuguese monetary system during the third quarter of the 18th century. No changes occurred in the gold and silver value of the Portuguese real.

In spite of the usual problems about the state of the research, it is possible to suggest that prices remained stable during the third quarter of the 18th century. In the absence of monetary devaluations and in the presence of the gold inflow from Brazil, however reduced, economic growth must be the main explanation of this stability.

D – The period of early economic liberalism, 1777-1793

For a short period during the last quarter of the 18th century, short-term prosperity came back to the Portuguese economy. This was mainly a consequence of new increases in the exports of colonial and metropolitan commodities, which began during the War of Independence of the United States of America.

Prosperity allowed the first experiment with some economic liberalism. Its results are almost impossible to ascertain, because soon the Portuguese economy and society were to be disrupted by the effects of the struggle between Great Britain and revolutionary and imperial France.

The limits of early economic liberalism

First of all, it is important to define the limits of this first experiment at economic liberalism. The regime of privileged companies set up during the third quarter of the 18th century was brought to an end, colonial trade became free for all Portuguese subjects even on routes traditionally monopolised by the state, and regulations of industrial activity were gradually abandoned. However, the rules of the so-called colonial pact were maintained, and many industrial activities still survived only through public subsidies.

Agriculture

There is not much to add concerning Portuguese agriculture during this period. Production and exports rose, links to the market increased, the switch from traditional crops to cash crops and animal husbandry certainly intensified.

Industry

There is also not much to add regarding industry. Most of the large factories set up during the previous period went on working with official subsidies, but no new significant industries were founded.

Eastern trade

Some recovery of Portuguese trade in the Indian Ocean and Far East occurred in the late 18th century, but this was more a consequence of the general growth of the trade of the Indian Ocean and of the Far East (a prelude to the full integration of these regions in the contemporary world economy), than a consequence of an increase of the relative Portuguese role in the area.

Brazil

Brazilian trade also increased, especially in the cotton sector, because the country became an important supplier of the British cotton industry during the War of Independence of the United States of America.

By the second half of the 18th century, Brazil had grown to a demographic and economic size on the same order as Portugal. Its population doubled during the 18th century, from 1.25 million inhabitants to 2.5 million, and rough calculations suggest a gross domestic product of around two thirds that of Portugal's.

In such a context, it was only natural that the independence of the United States of America excited conspiracies for Brazilian independence. These conspiracies were, however, put down by the Portuguese authorities without much difficulty.

African colonies

The situation in the African colonies was quite different: slave and ivory trade remained the most important economic activities, and only in Angola were the first steps being taken to extend Portuguese rule to more than just the coastal settlements. This included the first attempt to cross the southern part of the African continent from Angola to Mozambique on a voyage of exploration. This attempt was made by Lacerda Almeida in 1787, and again in 1797, without success.

6. Portugal in the Euro-Atlantic world-economy | 187

Political evolution, 1777-1793

The royal couple, Maria I + Pedro III (1777-1786), and Queen Maria I (1786-1792) and her minister, the Duke of Lafões, showed a clear formal rejection of the principles of the policy followed by King José I and his minister, Sebastião de Carvalho e Melo, until 1777. However, as none of the most important laws enacted during the previous period were repealed, it is fair to say that the policy of the new government changed more in style than in substance.

In 1790, all remaining administrative and judicial powers of feudal landlords were abolished. At the same time, the map of the correction districts was completely revised, the number of districts reaching nearly fifty.

Concerning foreign relations, Portugal managed to remain neutral during the War of Independence of the United States of America (1776-1783).

In 1792, Queen Maria I went mad, and her son, João (later King João VI), assumed the regency. The next year, Portugal became involved in the wars against revolutionary France, and a new epoch of Portuguese life began.

Cultural measures

Aside from the efforts to complete the primary school system network, reference must be made to the foundation in Lisbon of the Academy of Sciences. This institution sought to contribute to the spread of knowledge regarding the innovations that underpinned the early British modern economic growth and to promote a systematic effort of investigation into the natural resources of the country. These efforts were certainly important in the late 18th and early 19th centuries, but the political and social upheavals that followed made them almost fruitless, as will be seen presently in the next chapter.

Money and prices

Stability remained the main characteristic of the Portuguese monetary system between the late 1770s and early 1790s. No changes occurred in the gold and silver value of the Portuguese real.

However, the behaviour of prices, still not yet fully studied, underwent some changes: between the 1770s and 1790s the price level rose by roughly one third. The gold inflows from Brazil, even if clearly reduced, were the cause of the price increase, in the absence of monetary devaluations and in the presence of economic growth.

State accounts and fiscal systems

No fundamental changes occurred in the state accounts during this period: they remained roughly balanced at a level of around 6,000 contos until the outbreak of the wars against France in 1793. At that moment, the total public debt was around 12,000 contos.

Regarding the Church and feudal systems, there were also no significant changes. Even the end of administrative and judicial powers of the landlords was not accompanied by the loss of the associated revenue, because the state went on paying the revenue of feudal taxes to the previous landlords.

7.

The failure of an early take-off, 1793-1851

During the late 18th century and the first half of the 19th century, Great Britain imposed its hegemony over world affairs, in both the economic and political fields, profiting from the advantage gained by its precocious advance into modern economic growth. At the same time, however, modern economic growth began to spread from its cradle in Great Britain and in some other regions of northwestern Europe, to some great powers of continental Europe, such as France and Germany, and even to the other side of the Atlantic, to the United States of America.

Portugal, as did the rest of southern Europe and the Mediterranean world, failed to share in the early economic take-off of the second generation of economies advancing into modern economic growth. Traditional views have blamed this Portuguese economic backwardness on British influence in Portuguese affairs. Other perspectives put the stress on the political and economic upheavals of the period. Modern specialists try to look for explanations related to general characteristics of Portuguese economic and social life, common to those of the other countries of southern Europe and the Mediterranean world that also fell behind.

The global performance of the Portuguese economy during the period under consideration will be discussed in section D, after the main political upheavals – such as the wars against France and Spain (section A), the loss of Brazil (section B) and political instability (section C) – have been examined. The attempts at economic reforms made after the triumph of the liberal regime in the 1830s will be discussed in section E.

A – The wars against France and Spain

The Campaign of Roussillon, 1793-1795

In 1793, the Portuguese government was persuaded to participate in the coalition against revolutionary France that was being organised over most of Europe. Ideological reasons – the wish to destroy liberal and democratic ideas before they spread from France to Portugal – and strategic reasons – the pressure of Britain and Spain, the main neighbours of the country, one by sea, the other by land – explain this break of the 18th century tradition of neutrality.

The role assigned to Portugal by the strategic leaders of the coalition was to send an expeditionary force to Catalonia to invade the French province of Roussillon. This was carried on in the campaigns of 1793 and 1794 without any particular military advantage going to either side, and was interrupted during the 1795 campaign by the withdrawal of Spain from the alliance against France. Lacking the indispensable strategic support in Catalonia, the Portuguese troops had to be repatriated, an event which was executed without problem. The so-called war of the first coalition against France went on until 1797 without Portuguese participation, and the peace treaties did not affect the country.

However, the whole affair was not without detrimental consequences for Portugal. The Portuguese government was left in very difficult financial straits, further aggravated during the following years by the need to prepare the defence against a possible attack of the coalition of Spain and France. These financial difficulties had unpleasant monetary consequences, as will be seen in section D, below.

The War of the Oranges, 1801

Portuguese naval forces cooperated with the British navy during the war of the second coalition against France, but there were no land operations until the winter of 1801. Then, Spain mounted a swift campaign against the Portuguese province of Alentejo. This campaign, usually known as the War of the Oranges, was a military triumph, and, in the Treaty of Badajoz, Spain forced Portugal to give up Olivença, one of the two bits of Portuguese territory on the left bank of the Guadiana. This was the only significant change of the Portuguese border that occurred since 1297, and reduced the continental part of the country to its present form, with an area of around 89,000 square km.

During the following years, the Portuguese government tried to maintain a neutrality policy. In a certain sense this was just the consequence of the prevailing financial difficulties and of the adverse results of the Campaign of Roussillon and the War of the Oranges.

The Peninsular War, 1807-1814

Portugal managed to remain neutral during the wars of the third and fourth coalitions against France, but could not do so in the so-called Continental Blockade, that is to say, the trade boycott against Great Britain imposed by the French government in 1807. As participation would almost certainly have meant the loss of the Portuguese colonial empire to British control, the Portuguese government preferred not to participate. France and Spain reacted by occupying the continental part of the country in the autumn of 1807.

As the continental part of the country came under the regency of the commander of the French invading force, General Junot, the Portuguese government withdrew to Brazil and established its capital in Rio de Janeiro. The archipelagoes of the Azores and Madeira and the whole of the Portuguese colonial empire remained under formal Portuguese control, though Madeira and some key points of the Portuguese colonies were garrisoned by British forces. As a matter of fact, the British showed much annoyance about the lack of any spirited resistance by the Portuguese army to the invading French and Spanish forces, and wanted to prevent further French attacks and possible Portuguese diplomatic moves towards France. In South America, Brazilian resources were used to occupy French Guiana and Spanish Uruguay as retaliation for the invasion of the continental part of Portugal. Furthermore, the so-called colonial pact was abrogated concerning Brazil, a far-reaching measure, as will be seen in section B below.

If the Portuguese army surrendered to the invading French and Spanish forces without appreciable resistance, the same did not happen with the populace of the country. Resistance against the invaders became endemic during the spring of 1808, and in the provinces of Trás-os-Montes, Minho and Beira, threw off the control of the French troops (mainly located in the south of the country), when the Spanish troops (mainly located in the north of the country) withdrew after the Spanish revolt of May 1808 against Joseph Bonaparte, the new king of Spain imposed by the French government. A Portuguese regency was set up in Porto, and a British force under the leadership of Arthur Wellesley (later Lord Wellington) landed in the north of the country to support the army organised by that regency. After two unsuccessful attempts to prevent the Anglo-Portuguese forces to march on Lisbon, Junot signed an armistice and the French troops were withdrawn to France on British ships.

The first French invasion of Portugal was over, but the French threat remained, because Spain was under the control of a French occupational army. The Portuguese government stayed in Brazil, and British troops were left in Portugal to support the defence against impending renewed French attacks.

The first of these attacks (the second French invasion) came in the summer of 1809. Marshall Soult, who was in command in Galicia, led an expeditionary force into Trás-os-Montes and Entre-Douro-e-Minho and managed to occupy Porto. However, he could not resist the Anglo-Portuguese counter-attack and soon had to withdraw.

*

The third French invasion was a more serious matter. In the summer of 1810, Marshall Massena managed to lead a French army to the gates of Lisbon, in spite of the resistance of the frontier fortress of Almeida and an attempt of the Anglo-Portuguese forces to stand in Buçaco. After some fighting around Lisbon that lasted for nearly one year, the French army was forced to withdraw in the summer of 1811.

Now came the turn of the Anglo-Portuguese forces to intervene in Spain. During the years of 1812 and 1813 the Iberian Peninsula was cleared of the French occupational army, and in 1814 the British, Spanish and Portuguese forces proceeded into southern France. Though their role in the so-called Campaign of France was a minor one, they managed to occupy the southwestern corner of the country. This was the end of the war for Portuguese troops, which did not intervene in the events of the so-called Hundred Days in 1815.

The Congress of Vienna

The Congress of Vienna came to two decisions relating to Portugal. The most important allowed the Portuguese government to rid itself of the external war debt towards Great Britain (800,000 pounds sterling) by means of compensations with war indemnities to be paid by France. The other involved the exchange of some territories occupied during the previous wars, and had as the only consequence that French Guiana was restored to its former ruler. As a matter of fact, neither Olivença (the Portuguese territory that had become Spanish in 1801), nor Uruguay (the Spanish territory occupied by Portugal in 1807) were affected in any practical way. Olivença has remained Spanish until today, and Uruguay became an independent country, in spite of Portuguese (later Brazilian) and Spanish efforts at control.

At the same time, the British government obtained from the Portuguese government the prohibition of slave traffic in Portuguese African possessions north of the equator and the promise to abolish it altogether within reasonable due time.

The consequences of the wars against France and Spain

The wars against France and Spain were certainly very detrimental to the Portuguese economy: the prosperity of most of the last quarter of the 18th century gave way to a slump, from which recovery proved very slow. The destruction and plundering of the country by the Spanish and French armies, the monetary and financial problems triggered by the wars, the increase of British influence in Portuguese affairs, and the economic independence of Brazil have been blamed as the main consequences of the wars that left the Portuguese economy in such an unhappy state.

Destruction and plundering by the Spanish and French armies that occupied the continental part of Portugal in 1801, 1807-1808, 1809 and 1810-1811 (six months of total occupation, nearly seventeen additional months of partial occupation, mainly in the regions of Beira, Estremadura and Ribatejo) were the most striking immediate consequences of the wars against France and Spain. However detrimental in the short run, occupation was also, perhaps, the least important of the consequences of these wars in the long run. As a matter of fact, if the other consequences had been absent, it is likely that the direct demographic and economic effects of destruction and plundering would have been overcome without much difficulty.

The monetary and financial problems brought on by the wars proved harder to cope with. As will be seen in section D, below, monetary normality returned only during the 1830s and, in a certain sense, financial stability came back only during the 1850s. However, it must be stressed once more that later events had at least as much impact on the slow recovery as the direct effects of the wars themselves.

The increase of British influence in Portuguese affairs was partly a result of the role of the British aid in the liberation of Portugal from French occupations, partly an affair of normal diplomatic pressure of the leading world power, and partly the effect of the commercial treaty of 1810 between Portugal and Great Britain. The role of the British aid in the liberation of Portugal from French occupations would later have had trifling consequences without the subsequent role of British officers in the Portuguese army. As a matter of fact, because of the lack of Portuguese officers, many British officers had been appointed to take command of Portuguese units during the war, and some of them remained after 1815. Most important of all, Marshall Beresford remained in the supreme command of the Portuguese army. This gave the British the unpopular image of being a kind of second occupation army replacing the French. British diplomatic pressure was decisive in the evolution of the relations with Brazil and even in strictly internal affairs, as will be seen in more detail below. However, the main economic effects came from the commercial treaty of 1810, which gave British commodities almost free access both to the Portuguese and the Brazilian markets. This treaty was much blamed for the decay of Portuguese industry thereafter. It is undeniable that it discriminated heavily against the foreign competitors of British goods, but it is also equally true that Portuguese industry was not discriminated against, but simply lost protection. In any event, as some degree of protection was perhaps needed to recover from the destruction and plundering of the war period, it is possible to argue that, if the free competition of the British products in the Portuguese and Brazilian markets did not ruin Portuguese industry, it at least prevented its recovery from the low point of the war period.

The most important consequence of the wars fought by Portugal against France and Spain between 1793 and 1814 was, however, the beginning of the process that led to the independence of Brazil. As the process shall be considered as a whole, it will be examined in a separate section.

B – The end of the colonial status of Brazil

The end of the colonial pact (1808)

As soon as it arrived in Brazil in the beginning of 1808, the Portuguese government decided to abrogate all laws related to the so-called colonial pact, and, in particular, to open Brazilian ports to the ships of all friendly nations. For the time being that meant British and American ships, almost exclusively.

Fearful of attempts to return to the pre-war situation, Great Britain tried to obtain a formal promise to keep the Brazilian ports open. This was the main purpose of the commercial treaty of 1810 mentioned above, which also gave British products the same treatment as Portuguese products in Brazilian markets.

The United Kingdom of Portugal, Brazil and Algarves (1815)

After the war, the Portuguese government remained in Brazil against all expectations. Moreover, it went one step further towards the consolidation of Brazilian autonomy, by putting an end to its formal status as a colony. In 1815, Brazil was declared to be a separate kingdom, and the former Kingdom of Portugal and Algarves took the name of United Kingdom of Portugal, Brazil and Algarves.

The proclamation of independence (1822)

The last attempt to bring Brazil back under Portuguese control was made by the government of the first liberal period between 1820 and 1822 (see section C, below). The attempt was an utter failure, and its main consequence was the Brazilian declaration of independence (September 7, 1822).

The recognition of Brazilian independence by Portugal (1825)

The Portuguese troops that remained in Brazil tried to oppose the declaration of independence, and there followed some inconclusive fighting. However, the strategic situation was entirely favourable to the new authorities, because of the British support. Britain controlled the sea, and could prevent the Portuguese government from sending fresh troops to crush the rebellion. Moreover, the economic and political situation of Portugal did not leave many resources free for any attempt to restore the previous situation in Brazil by force. Thus, negotiations for the recognition of Brazilian independence by Portugal soon opened. They led to the treaty of Rio de Janeiro, signed in 1825.

The main clauses of the treaty were the recognition of Brazilian independence by Portugal and the assumption by Brazil of the Portuguese foreign public debt (1,500,000 pounds sterling) as compensation. Moreover, Portuguese troops were withdrawn from Brazil, and the king of Portugal was allowed to use the honorific title of Emperor of Brazil without wielding any substantial power.

The consequences of the independence of Brazil

The economic independence of Brazil, which was the result of the end of the colonial pact in 1808, had two far-reaching consequences for Portugal: the loss of the intermediary position in Brazilian foreign trade, and the loss of a protected market for the export of Portuguese goods.

The loss of the intermediary position in Brazilian foreign trade meant a sharp reduction in the activity of the Portuguese merchant navy, the Portuguese ports, especially the port of Lisbon, and the Portuguese dealers of Brazilian goods. Thus, it was a mighty blow to what had been the prosperous tertiary sector of the Portuguese economy in the late 18th century.

The loss of protection for the export of Portuguese goods to the Brazilian market meant an increase in the competition of foreign goods, especially British goods, in that market, and certainly a reduction of the Brazilian demand for Portuguese goods. The precocity of British industrialisation had given its products a competitivity that assured them the control of the Brazilian market. The amount of the reduction of the Brazilian demand for Portuguese goods and its sectorial composition have been the matter of much debate, but it is reasonable to accept that it had a strong impact on some important sectors of Portuguese industry, mainly textiles.

To sum up: the economic independence of Brazil was undoubtedly detrimental to the prosperity of the Portuguese economy. However, it would be quite wrong to overstate its importance concerning its long-term development: prosperity based on the economic distortions arising from the prohibition of the best trade routes and from the protection of inefficient producers is certainly not a sound basis for long-term development. This means that the control of the Brazilian economy could not have provided a solid basis for long-lasting development in the Portuguese case.

*

The formal end of the colonial status of Brazil in 1815 and its political independence in 1822 merely confirmed what had happened in 1808. They had no great repercussions on Portuguese economic life, though they played an important role in the political evolution of the country, as will be examined in section C, below.

However, the prohibition of the slave traffic in the Portuguese African possessions north of the equator in 1815, and the separation of Brazil from the United Kingdom of Portugal, Brazil and Algarves in 1822 threatened to raise some problems: Brazil feared a shortage in the supply of slaves, which came mainly from the Portuguese African possessions; Portugal feared possible Brazilian attempts to occupy the Portuguese African possessions to ensure a regular slave supply. After the 1825 recognition of Brazilian independence, there was a tacit arrangement: Brazil gave up any attempt to get African possessions; Portugal gave all possible facilities for slave traffic to Brazil in the Portuguese African possessions south of the equator.

C – Political upheavals, 1820-1851

The first liberal period (1820-1823) and the first absolutist restoration (1823-1826)

The political situation in Portugal in the years that followed the end of the wars against Spain and France was one of creeping tension. The Portuguese government stayed on in Brazil even after all reasons that had forced its transfer ended (meanwhile, Queen Maria I died in 1816, and her son, João, who had been regent for more than two decades, became King João VI). British officers remained in leading positions in the Portuguese army even after the end of the war – namely Marshall Beresford, who was appointed commander-in-chief of the Portuguese army. Last but not least, the relations with Brazil failed to return to what they had been before 1808. This situation provided fertile ground for the liberal propaganda. A first conspiracy for a revolution failed in Lisbon in 1817, but the second attempt in Porto, in 1820, was a success.

The goals of the liberal revolution of 1820 are easily understandable: the revolutionaries wanted to end the British interference in Portuguese affairs and to bring Brazil back to colonial status; the replacement of the absolutist regime by a constitutional regime was, in some sense, secondary. It is also easy to see that, in this context, the revolution was a failure in its true goals: British interference in Portuguese affairs did not end, though it became more discrete for a while (and British officers disappeared from the Portuguese army, allowing comfortable promotions for Portuguese officers); and the attempts to restore Brazil to colonial status only led to its declaration of independence. As a consequence, the Constitution prepared between 1820 and 1822, with much concern for delicate balances among the various forces of Portuguese society (and, above all, between the Portuguese and Brazilian halves of the kingdom) came under general criticism, and was dropped in April 1823 after an absolutist revolt (usually known as Abrilada). The constitution had been the fundamental law of the country for only seven months. A moderate absolutist government was able to rule the country without much trouble between 1823 and 1826, retaining a few reforms of the first liberal period, such as the definitive abolition of the Inquisition.

The second liberal period (1826-1828) and the second absolutist restoration (1828-1834)

The quiet situation that prevailed between 1823 and 1826 was upset in 1826 by a succession problem: King João VI died, leaving the throne to his eldest son, Pedro, who was Emperor Pedro I of Brazil and became King Pedro IV of Portugal (as the king was in Brazil, his sister, Isabel, became regent). The possibility of a personal union of the two states was promptly rejected under British pressure. The decision of Pedro IV was to grant a rather conservative Constitutional Charter in an attempt to reconcile the absolutist and constitutionalist parties, and to abdicate the crown of Portugal to his daughter, Maria, who should marry her uncle, Miguel (the younger brother of Pedro IV), as soon as possible. According to the Constitutional Charter, there was a parliament (*Cortes*) formed of one aristocratic hereditary chamber (*Câmara dos Pares*) and one elected chamber (*Câmara dos Deputados*) – the suffrage was indirect and restricted to rather wealthy citizens; the king nominated the government without any interference of the parliament and had the right of veto on legislation passed by parliament.

The whole scheme failed. To begin with, the regent refused to promulgate the Constitutional Charter until a military coup forced her to do so. There followed absolutist revolts in some parts of the country, and a British flotilla had to be sent to the mouth of the Tagus to protect the constitutional government. However, as soon as Miguel, a radical absolutist, became regent in 1828, he decided to ignore the Constitutional Charter and to become King Miguel I, without marrying his niece.

The civil war (1828-1834)

The liberal party rallied under the banner of the young Queen Maria II, deprived of the throne by her uncle, but was almost completely defeated. The liberals retained control only of the island of Terceira in the Azores, from which they managed to secure the rest of the archipelago in 1831. Meanwhile, ex-King Pedro IV of Portugal had also become ex-emperor of Brazil. He assumed the formal regency of Portugal on behalf of his daughter and put his talents to the task of recovering the kingdom for her. In 1832 a military expedition was sent to the continental part of the country and occupied Porto. The absolutist army sieged the city, but was unable to prevent the arrival of supplies and reinforcements to the liberal army by sea. In July 1833, the decisive naval battle of São Vicente led to the destruction of the absolutist navy and to the occupation of Lisbon by the liberals. The winner of the civil war had been found, though the piecemeal occupation of the rest of the country by liberal troops would take another year.

The liberal triumph allowed the liberal government to introduce many fundamental reforms in the legal and administrative structure of Portuguese life. These reforms, which were intended to have stimulating effects on economic growth, will be dealt with in section E, below.

Conservatives and progressists (1834-1851)

The liberal triumph did not bring political stability back to the country. The conservative government that came to power in 1834 was overthrown by a progressist coup (usually known as the September Revolution) in Porto in 1836. The progressist party resisted an attempt of a conservative coup (usually known as Belènzada) in 1836 and a conservative revolt (usually known as the Marshals Revolt) in 1837, prepared a new constitution, enacted in 1838 – the main differences when compared with the Constitutional Charter were the reduction of the powers of the king and the replacement of the aristocratic chamber by an elected senate – and remained in power until 1842. Then, a conservative coup in Porto restored the Constitutional Charter, and started a second conservative period that lasted until 1846.

In the spring of 1846, popular riots in the province of Minho (usually known as the Maria da Fonte) overthrew the conservatives and put the progressists in power again for five months. In October 1846, the conservatives tried to regain power by means of another coup in Lisbon, but did not manage to control the whole country. Between October 1846 and June 1847 the conservative government of Lisbon and the progressist government of Porto fought a civil war (usually known as the Patuleia), which ended in a conservative victory, aided by an intervention of British, French and Spanish troops.

However, the third conservative period was even shorter than the second. In April 1851, a progressist coup in Porto known as the Regeneration (*Regeneração*) brought to power a moderate government that was, at last, able to introduce some political stability.

International and colonial evolution

There is not much to say about the international and colonial position of Portugal after the end of the wars against France and the independence of Brazil. Portugal played no significant role in international affairs until the 1850s and the Portuguese colonial empire remained quite unimportant in international and even domestic life, except as a supplier of slaves to Brazil. In 1836, the progressist government enacted a law forbidding slave trade in all Portuguese possessions, but it is fair to say that the law was not respected until the 1850s.

D – Economic performance

Monetary evolution and prices

In 1796 and 1797, the Portuguese government tried to raise a public loan of 4,800 contos to consolidate the floating public debt accumulated from the Campaign of Roussillon and other exceptional expenditure arising mainly from military needs. The loan was a failure, and the government used an expedient to force part of it upon the market: to issue 1,200 contos of unconvertible paper money, legally equivalent to the metallic specie.

Once the expedient was introduced, legal and common sense limits were soon forgotten. Between 1797 and 1799, 16,514 contos of paper money (that is to say, almost fourteen times the amount legally authorised) were issued. As a consequence, paper money began to circulate at a discount. It was rejected altogether outside of Lisbon and Porto, and even in these towns it was not used in most transactions. Depreciation of the Portuguese currency in the exchange markets soon followed, and prices began to soar. There was also some hoarding of metallic currency. The government tried to fight these problems by stopping the further issue of paper money, but it was impossible to remedy the effects of the foolish amount that had been issued.

British subsidies and loans allowed the Portuguese government to avoid issuing large amounts of new paper money during the decisive years of the war against France: additional issues were made only in the amount of 663 contos. At the same time, British coins (and French and Spanish coins during French and Spanish occupations) were accepted as legal tender in Portuguese monetary circulation. Meanwhile, the rise in prices did not stop: between 1793 and 1812, the price level roughly doubled.

After the war, prices began to fall at a rate similar to the previous rate of increase, until they stabilised in the 1830s at a level similar to that attained in the early 1790s. Monetary normality, however, was harder to regain.

*

It was during the first liberal period that the first serious attempt to redeem paper money was made. The plan that was presented to the parliament in 1821 was to create a discount bank, which should lend to the government the amounts needed for the redemption of paper money in exchange for the right to issue convertible bank notes. The plan was accepted and a law was passed creating the Bank of Lisbon (*Banco de Lisboa*), the first Portuguese bank, which began its activities in 1822, with its headquarters in Lisbon and a branch in Porto created in 1825. However, only half of the intended capital of 5,000 contos was underwritten, and the whole scheme failed. In a certain sense, the only significant result of this attempt to redeem paper money was to add a new item to the Portuguese money supply: besides gold, silver and copper coins, and the paper money, there were now in circulation the convertible notes of the Bank of Lisbon.

Also during 1822, there was a reform of gold currency, which changed the gold value of the Portuguese real to 1.753 mg (a 15% depreciation).

*

It was only in 1835, after the definitive triumph of the liberal regime, that a second attempt to redeem paper money was made. This time, a foreign loan provided the resources for redemption, and, in spite of some problems, it may be said that paper money disappeared from Portuguese monetary circulation by the late 1830s.

In 1835, there was a reform of silver money, which changed the silver value of the Portuguese real to 27.141 mg (a depreciation of 3%). At the same time, new gold and silver coins, following a decimal reform were introduced by law. However, as the redemption of paper money had to be made with imported foreign coins, because it was impossible to recoin them as quickly as desired, the circulation of foreign coins – mainly British gold coins and Spanish and Mexican silver coins – had to be accepted as a permanent feature of Portuguese monetary life.

Also in 1835, the second Portuguese discount and issuing bank, the Commercial Bank of Porto (*Banco Comercial do Porto*), was authorised by law and started its activities in Porto. During the early 1840s several savings banks were also established, but their activities did not progress very much.

*

The political events of 1846 and 1847 brought new trouble to the Portuguese monetary system. In May 1846, the notes of the Bank of Lisbon became inconvertible and were given the status of legal tender. Effects similar to those of the first issue of paper money soon followed: circulation of the notes of the Bank of Lisbon at a discount, rejection of these notes outside of Lisbon and Porto and even in these towns, depreciation of the Portuguese currency in the exchange markets, price increases and hoarding of metallic currency. The government tried to fight these problems by giving legal tender status to some gold and silver foreign coins (British, Spanish, Latin American and French). The civil war fought between October 1846 and June 1847, however, prevented any recovery of the monetary situation, and some foolish measures were taken during the conflict: the Bank of Lisbon was merged with another bankrupt financial company that had been formed in 1844, the National Confidence Company (*Companhia Confiança Nacional*), to form the Bank of Portugal (*Banco de Portugal*), which was allowed to issue inconvertible notes under the old name of the Bank of Lisbon and convertible notes under the new name of Bank of Portugal; many foreign coins (British, Spanish, Latin American, North American and French) were given legal tender status with values not very rigorously tied to their precious metal content; and judicial repression of refusals to accept the notes of the Bank of Lisbon at par value was attempted. The results were monetary chaos and an intensification of the problems already visible before. At the same time there was a devaluation of the gold value of the Portuguese real to 1.643 mg (a reduction of 6%). The only positive measures were a limit on the value of notes of the Bank of Lisbon in circulation – 5,000 contos – and the announcement of an amortisation scheme – 18 contos, later to be increased to 50 contos per month. Their effects were, however, felt only in the long run.

During the following years, the situation improved. The laws regarding the use of the notes of the Bank of Lisbon at par value were repealed; the discount on the notes of the Bank of Lisbon diminished, because of their gradual amortisation; and the situation of the Bank of Portugal stabilised. In 1850, it was awarded the monopoly of bank note issuing in the administrative district of Lisbon until the 1870s. Total normalisation, however, had to wait until the mid-1850s.

State accounts

The Portuguese state lived in a situation of chronic financial problems between the 1790s and the middle of the 19th century.

Between 1793 and 1814, the situation may be easily explained by the wars fought against France and Spain. Besides the paper money issue of more than 17,000 contos and the foreign public debt towards Great Britain of 800,000 pounds sterling (nearly 2,845 contos) already mentioned, these wars left a financial burden of more than 11,000 contos of internal public debt (meaning that total public debt more than doubled). They also left new taxes in the state fiscal system: the stamp tax (*imposto de selo*) enacted in 1800, and taxes on house rents (*contribuição das rendas de casa*) and on servants and horses (*imposto de criados e cavalgaduras*) enacted in 1801. Though the foreign public debt disappeared by means of compensations with war indemnities as explained in section A, above, the service of the new internal debt and the reduction in tariff revenue resulting from the end of the monopoly of the Brazilian trade were enough to put the state finances into a permanent deficit situation.

Between 1815 and 1828, more than 9,000 contos of internal public debt and 1,500,000 pounds sterling (around 6,200 contos) of foreign public debt were borrowed by the Portuguese government. Though the foreign public debt became Brazilian debt as the price of recognition of independence as explained in section B, above, when the civil war between the absolutist and constitutionalist parties broke out, total public debt reached around 32,000 contos.

Being deprived of a significant tributary basis and the internal capital market (internal war loans borrowed in the Azores and Porto amounted only to around 1,500 contos), the constitutional government had to borrow abroad to finance the war. A nominal amount of 4,600,000 pounds sterling (nearly 19,000 contos) was added to the foreign public debt of the country, given the fact that the constitutional government won the war. Meanwhile, the absolutist government was also forced to borrow 40 million francs (around 6,500 contos) abroad. However, this amount was repudiated by the constitutional government after the war.

A new loan of 1,000,000 pounds sterling (around 4,100 contos) to pay the redemption of the paper money was the last borrowing opportunity open to the new Portuguese government abroad. In 1836 an attempt at conversion to reduce the interest of the debt was still possible, but it did not prevent a suspension of payments in 1837. As public accounts continued to show systematic deficits, attempts to resume payments and to convert the debt to a consolidated form in 1841 and to convert the debt to a redeemable form with a reduction of interest in 1844 were unable to restore the situation to a sound basis. The political upheavals of 1846 and 1847 led to a new suspension of payments.

Demographic evolution during the first half of the 19th century

Population growth went on during the first half of the 19th century at a rate similar to that of the 18th century, well below 0.5% per year. Thus, the population of the country was still clearly below 4 million inhabitants by the mid-19th century.

Regional distribution of the population did not change in any appreciable way. Population densities higher than the average remained concentrated along the coast north of Lisbon and in the archipelagoes of Madeira and the Azores.

Towns

The population of Lisbon levelled off during the first half of the 19th century below 200,000 inhabitants, while the population of Porto grew significantly and passed the 50,000 mark. The higher demographic growth of the main town of the north of the country corresponded also to greater political activity: Porto was the cradle of the liberal revolutions during the 1820s and 1830s and of all successful revolutions between the 1830s and 1860s. It is likely that this also corresponded to a higher economic growth, though it is impossible to confirm this hypothesis with the available data.

Braga, also in the north of the country, Funchal in Madeira and Ponta Delgada in the Azores were the other towns of the country that clearly exceeded the 10,000 inhabitants level.

Economic evolution during the first half of the 19th century

Economic growth accompanied general population growth, showing a clear slump during the period of the French invasions. This means that per capita income showed no significant upward trend and remained rather stable in the long run, in spite of short-term fluctuations.

Innovations linked with the early steps of modern economic growth began, however, to appear in Portugal during the first half of the 19th century. These included the steam engine, introduced during the 1820s. It was only during the 1840s, however, that a greater number of steam engines began to be used in several industrial firms in the country.

E – Institutional reforms and modernisation policies

The liberal blueprint

The final establishment of the liberal regime in the mid-1830s meant, not only a significant change in the political life of the country, but also a new policy of promoting the modernisation of the Portuguese economy. Institutional reforms (in the legal, administrative, fiscal, educational and property fields) and public works were the main items of the liberal blueprint. The main institutional reforms were implemented by the mid-1830s. Public works had to wait for nearly a decade to see the first practical efforts.

The legal reform

Besides the definitive implementation of a written constitutional text, two legal reforms of the 1830s must be mentioned. Firstly, the end of all juridical differences among social orders, all nobility titles becoming merely honorary, and, secondly, the promulgation of a Commercial Code in 1834. This corresponded to the compilation, according to the codification spirit typical of the epoch, of all rules regarding commercial activity and even most economic activity.

The administrative reform

The chief elements of the administrative reform were the clear separation of judicial functions from strictly administrative ones, and the replacement of the old correction districts by new judicial and administrative districts. At the same time, most of the small municipalities disappeared in terms of their legal designation, in a process aimed at giving all municipalities a minimum size, and civil administration was also implemented at the level of the old ecclesiastical parishes. This completed the administrative and judicial system that has survived until the present day.

The fiscal reform

The most important aspect of the fiscal reform was certainly the abolition of Church and feudal taxes. Church activities depended thereafter upon state funding (far less, of course, than the previous revenue from Church taxes), and feudal lords lost their fiscal revenue altogether.

As for the state fiscal system, there were also important changes: the excise tax was abolished, export duties were reduced to very low levels, and a registration tax (*contribuição de registo*) on sales, gifts and inheritances (except those that benefited descendants, ascendants and spouses) of land and construction was created.

Tariff reform

Some years later, in 1837, a tariff reform was implemented. Import duties were raised and special protectionist measures for cereal production, which had been instigated in the early 1820s, were reinforced.

The education reform

In the education field, the main concern was to restore the municipal network of primary schools damaged by the foreign and civil wars. Moreover, there was an effort to build a network of secondary and technical schools in all administrative districts. Once more, the reality was slow to meet the official plans.

The property reform

The most important measure in the property field was the abolition of all religious orders, the confiscation of their property by the state and the selling of this property. This led to a massive transfer of land and buildings to new owners, though it is unlikely that such a reform improved the technology or the management methods in agriculture, because the majority of the land continued to be cultivated by small leaseholders.

The attempts to build public works in the 1840s and their failure

While the first part of the liberal blueprint – institutional reforms – was rather easy to promulgate and even to implement, the second part – public works – was not as easy to realise, because it demanded public expenditure, and, as was pointed out above, the state funds were lacking.

A serious attempt to begin an ambitious programme of public works, including a road network covering the whole country, an artificial harbour in Porto, and a railroad between Lisbon and the Spanish border, was undertaken during the second conservative period, between 1844 and 1846. A limited liability company, the Portugal's Public Works Company (*Companhia das Obras Públicas de Portugal*) was formed to build and manage these public works, but the upheavals of 1846 forced it to suspend its activity. It was liquidated a few years later with some losses, having built only a few roads in the regions of Entre-Douro-e-Minho and Estremadura.

The effects of the modernisation policies

The poor overall performance of the Portuguese economy during the first half of the 19th century outlined above shows that the implementation of the modernisation policies called for in the liberal blueprint remained far behinds the goals.

This does not mean that the modernisation policies had no positive effects on the Portuguese economic situation. However, the incomplete fulfilment of the original programme, either because public works were not built at the same time as institutional reforms were implemented, or because the benefits of some institutional reforms were felt only in the long term, prevented the Portuguese economy from meeting all of its challenges.

8.

The first epoch of growth, 1851-1891

By the middle of the 19th century, Portugal managed to obtain political stability and to start a period of economic growth. This period of growth lasted for nearly four decades – the 1850s, 1860s, 1870s and 1880s – and allowed the Portuguese economy to make up part of the distance by which it had lagged behind the world leaders since the first half of the 19th century. At the same time, the Portuguese economy took part in the process of intensification of international economic relations and the transformation of the old Euro-Atlantic world-economy into a true world economy.

The analysis of this first epoch of Portuguese economic growth must begin with the discussion of the implementation of the liberal blueprint (as defined in section E of chapter 7) that occurred between 1851 and 1891. This is the theme of section A. Section B deals with the integration of the Portuguese economy within the international economy during the same period. Section C analyses the performance of the Portuguese economy during these decades of economic growth.

A – The regeneration implementation of the liberal blueprint

Political stabilisation

The military coup of April 1851, usually known as the Regeneration, replaced the conservative government, which had been in power since the 1846-1847 civil war, with a progressist government. There followed a reshuffling of political parties: most of the previous progressist and conservative groups formed a new Regeneration Party (*Partido Regenerador*) to support the government; the remaining Progressist Party became known as the Historical Progressist Party (*Partido Progressista Histórico*); and the remaining conservatives became known as the Conservative Party (*Partido Conservador*). In 1852, the parliament enacted a constitutional reform, which established direct suffrage, and tighter formal control of the government by the elected chamber.

Somewhat surprisingly, this reorganisation of the Portuguese political scene was a success. There followed some decades of political stability, institutional reforms, and high public investment in transportation facilities. The liberal blueprint was at last fully implemented, and the Portuguese economy knew its first period of strong economic growth.

It is not necessary to add much else about political life between 1851 and 1891. The Regeneration Party and the Historical Progressist Party alternated in power (and for some time made a coalition) during the rest of the reign of Maria II (until 1853), the regency of her husband, Fernando II (1853-1855), the reign of her eldest son, Pedro V (1855-1863), and the beginning of the reign of her second son, Luís I (1863-1889). Between 1868 and 1870, the project of a fiscal reform and the short-term problems linked with the Paraguay War (see section C below) led to a short period of political instability, triggered by the appearance of two new small parties, the Reformist Party [*Partido Reformista*], a dissidence from the Historical Progressist Party, and the Constituient Party [*Partido Constituinte*]. During this period, there were some projects of an Iberian Union, profiting from the fall of the Bourbon dynasty in Spain. However, Fernando II and Luís I of Portugal rejected the idea of becoming kings of Spain, and the projects were dropped.

By 1871, stability had been restored. The Regeneration Party and a new Progressist Party (*Partido Progressista*) (resulting from the fusion of the Reformist Party and the Historical Progressist Party) alternated in power again during the 1870s and 1880s. Some steps towards universal suffrage were taken in the 1870s, and a new constitutional reform was enacted in 1885, replacing the aristocratic chamber with an elected senate.

A reference should be made to the man, António Maria de Fontes Pereira de Melo, who became the symbol of this epoch of economic growth, known ever since by his name, fontism (*fontismo*). As a young army officer, he fought in the civil war of 1846-1847 on the conservative side; he became a progressist deputy in the late 1840s, Minister of Finance in the first Regeneration government in 1851, first Minister of Public Works in the following year, prominent figure of the Regeneration Party during the 1850s and 1860s, and head of government for periods that add up to more than a decade during the 1870s and 1880s until his death in 1886.

Fiscal reforms

Between 1852 and 1882, a general reform of direct taxation was gradually enacted. The old military tithe was replaced by a set of new taxes: the land tax (*contribuição predial*) on land and buildings created in 1852; the industrial tax (*contribuição industrial*) on profits and the earnings of liberal professions created in 1860; and the interest tax (*contribuição de juros*) on interests, which corresponded to the remaining levy. One decade later, there was an attempt to complete the system with a general income tax (*imposto de rendimento*) modelled after the British example, but in 1882 most of the income tax was repealed, leaving only the levy on bond interests and salaries of civil servants.

Changes in indirect taxation during the same period included a repeal of the literary subsidy in 1857, and an ephemeral merger of the taxes on house rents and on servants and horses into a personal tax (*contribuição pessoal*), in 1860. In 1872, the personal tax was divided into the old tax on house rents (*contribuição das rendas de casa*) and a new tax on conspicuous luxury consumption (*contribuição sumptuária*).

The registration tax was extended to inheritances to ascendants and spouses in 1870.

Tariff reform

During the 1850s there was a tariff reform that reduced the import duties, especially those on foreign cereals. Though far from full-fledged free trade, the country was to continue until 1889 without overwhelming import duties, especially those on agricultural goods.

Monetary reform

The awkward measures of 1846 and 1847 had left the Portuguese monetary system in complete disarray. In 1851, a first step towards normalisation was made: foreign gold coins, with the exception of British coins, were recoined into Portuguese issues. Meanwhile, the discount on the notes of the Bank of Lisbon was reduced by their gradual amortisation.

However, the complete normalisation came only in 1854, with the adoption of the gold standard. The Portuguese real was defined as 1.625 mg of gold. Portuguese and British gold coins remained legal tender, foreign silver coins were recoined into Portuguese issues, and Portuguese silver coins became subsidiary money, as copper coins had been earlier.

8. The first epoch of growth | 219

Such measures were unusual at the time (only Great Britain, among the main economic powers, had adopted such a regime) and caused much controversy in the country. However, they worked well for nearly four decades and were, of course, reinforced when the international monetary system moved towards it.

The banking system

Between the mid-1850s and the mid-1870s several new issuing banks were formed in the north of the country: the Mercantile Bank of Porto (*Banco Mercantil Portuense*) in 1856, the Union Bank (*Banco União*) in 1861, the New Public Utility Company (*Nova Companhia de Utilidade Pública*) also in 1861 and the Alliance Bank (*Banco Aliança*) in 1863, with their headquarters in Porto; the Bank of Minho (*Banco do Minho*) in 1864 and the Commercial Bank of Braga (*Banco Comercial de Braga*) in 1873, with their headquarters in Braga; and the Bank of Guimarães (*Banco de Guimarães*) also in 1873, with its headquarters in Guimarães. For a while, Portugal remained in the situation of a monopoly issue of the Bank of Portugal in the region of Lisbon, and a competitive issue of the Bank of Portugal and the other issuing banks in the region of Porto, with an absence of much circulation of bank notes in the rest of the country.

At the same time, several commercial banks were also formed between the mid-1860s and the mid-1870s, taking advantage of the new law regarding corporation firms (see the reference to economic legislation below). The most important of them was the National Overseas Bank (*Banco Nacional Ultramarino*), with its headquarters in Lisbon, which became the issuing bank for the Portuguese colonies. Most of the new banks, however, were located in the north of the country, as a consequence of the fact that it was from this region that came most Portuguese emigrants, and one of the main activities of the banks came to be the channelling of remittances from these Portuguese emigrants in Brazil to their families back home. Branches of the London &

Brazilian Bank were also created in Lisbon and Porto, as a result of the same phenomenon. Merchant bankers still managed to retain a sizeable share of the banking market.

Savings banks and mortgage banks also flourished during this period. The Savings Bank of Lisbon (*Caixa Económica de Lisboa*), created during the 1840s, remained the main Portuguese savings bank, though a state savings bank, the Portuguese Savings Bank (*Caixa Económica Portuguesa*), was established during the 1880s. The most important mortgage bank was the Portuguese General Company of Property Credit (*Companhia Geral do Crédito Predial Português*). Investment banks, however, were completely absent from the Portuguese banking system of the time.

The expansion of the banking system was halted by a banking crisis in 1876. There was a bank run, and a suspension of gold convertibility of bank notes in August. By the end of the year, normality had returned, but many commercial banks had gone bankrupt, and the movement towards an increased role of bank deposits in the Portuguese money supply, which had started during the early 1870s, was cut short for several decades.

*

During the 1876 banking crisis, the issuing banks in the north of the country tried for the first time to enlist the aid of the Bank of Portugal as a kind of lender of last resort. The scheme was not a complete success, but as the performance of the Bank of Portugal during the crisis was much better than the performance of the other issuing banks, the idea of concentrating the note issue for the whole country in the Bank of Portugal soon arose. However, it met with strong opposition from the other issuing banks, and they managed to postpone its enactment as law until 1887. Even after the law was passed, the other issuing banks tried to oppose the measure through some passive resistance. It was only during a new bank run in 1891 that practical unification of note issue under the auspices of the Bank of Portugal was obtained (see chapter 9 section A).

Metric system

Another important institutional reform was the adoption of the metric system in 1853. Portuguese governments had tried in vain to implement the unification of the standards for weights and measures between the 16th and 19th centuries. At last, after the unavoidable transition due to the slow abandoning of old habits, the metric system became the basis for this unification all over the country.

Economic legislation

During the 1860s, some important measures concerning property rights were enacted.

In 1863, the old institution of entailments was abolished. In the same year, a new law regarding corporate firms was enacted. This law replaced the rule of government authorisation for the legal existence of a corporation, by completely freeing up the founding of such firms: their legal existence coming to depend on a mere registration procedure.

Four years later, the first Portuguese Civil Code (*Código Civil*) replaced the old Ordinances of King Filipe (*Ordenações Filipinas*), introducing many restrictions to all schemes of division of property rights on the same good, and compelling equal division among heirs of at least half of the inherited property.

It is also worth noting that the death penalty (which had not been applied since the 1840s) was abolished in the same year of 1867.

The 1870s and 1880s did not witness legislative changes of similar importance, though a new Commercial Code was enacted in 1888, replacing the 1834 text. It should be noted that the 1888 Commercial Code is still in force, although with many changes.

Public works

However important these new institutional reforms were, the main novelty of the period was the beginning of the creation of an ambitious programme of public works throughout the country. In 1852, a new Public Works Ministry was formed to manage the public works programme, and field works soon began.

Railroads

The building of railroads was certainly the most important element of the programme of public works.

In 1853, the Portugal Central Peninsular Railway Company (*Companhia Central Peninsular dos Caminhos de Ferro de Portugal*) was formed to build and run the Portuguese section of a Lisbon-Madrid line. By 1857, 68 km between Lisbon and Santarém had been built and opened to traffic. Then the company failed, and the government had to buy the line.

In the same year, a new contract with Sir Morton Peto was signed to build a rail line between Lisbon and Porto extending the Lisbon-Santarém section. This time the results were even worse, because no track was laid at all.

In 1860, the Spanish entrepreneur José de Salamanca formed the Royal Portuguese Railway Company (*Real Companhia dos Caminhos-de-Ferro Portugueses*), bought the Lisbon-Santarém line, and began to build the East and North lines (from Lisbon to the Spanish border, and from Lisbon to Gaia, on the left bank of the Douro, opposite Porto, respectively, with a common section from Lisbon to Entroncamento, a new town formed in the middle of the Ribatejo as a railway centre). By 1864, 438 km had been built and opened to traffic. The central part of the country at last had its main railway lines, later linked to Madrid in 1866.

Meanwhile, the first line in the southern part of the country had also been built. In 1854, the South of the Tagus National Railway Company [*Companhia Nacional dos Caminhos-de-Ferro do*

Sul do Tejo] was formed to build a railroad from Barreiro (on the left bank of the Tagus, opposite Lisbon) to the Alentejo and the Algarve. By 1861, 70 km between Barreiro and Setúbal and between Barreiro and Vendas Novas, with a small common section between Barreiro and Pinhal Novo, had been completed and opened to traffic. The company then failed and the government had to buy out the line.

In 1864 a new South Eastern Portugal Railway Company (*Companhia dos Caminhos-de-Ferro do Sueste de Portugal*) was formed. It bought the Barreiro-Setúbal and Barreiro-Vendas Novas lines, and built 150 km between Vendas Novas and Beja. In 1866, the company failed and the government again had to buy the line. The rest of the line to the Algarve (225 km) was built directly by the government.

Further progress occurred during the 1870s and 1880s. A new company, the Beira Alta Railway Company (*Companhia dos Caminhos-de-Ferro da Beira Alta*) was formed to build a line between Figueira da Foz and Vilar Formoso (which had an extension of 252 km). The line crossed the North line at Pampilhosa, and was linked to the Spanish network (and indirectly to the French and European network) in 1882. The Royal Portuguese Railway Company built two new lines: the Beira Baixa line between Abrantes (on the East line) and Guarda (on the Beira Alta line), which had an extension of 212 km, and the West line between Lisbon and Figueira da Foz, which had an extension of 242 km. Moreover, a bridge over the Douro (designed by the famous French engineer Gustave Eiffel) linked the North line with the city of Porto in 1877, and a shortcut in the Lisbon-Madrid line was ready in 1880. The government also built two new lines: the Minho line between Porto and Valença (which had an extension of 149 km), linked with the Spanish network in 1886; and the Douro line between Porto and Barca de Alva (which had an extension of 204 km), linked with the Spanish network in 1887. Several regional lines were also added to these main trunk lines.

There has never been any railway line in the islands of Madeira or the Azores.

*

The impact of railroads on the Portuguese economy has been the subject of some debate among historians. Around 1890 the railway network had a total extension of more than 2,000 km. Considering that about 400 km merely duplicated navigable stretches of rivers, it added about 1,600 km to the extension of good transportation facilities, and reduced the area of the country to which these facilities were not available to about 12,000 square km (13% of the continental part of the country). The increase in accessibility is undeniable, and even for the regions already served by waterways, considering the increase in the speed and regularity of transportation (free, for instance, of the problems caused by floods in winter and by droughts in the summer), the advantages were not imignificant. All of this certainly contributed to greater economic integration among the various regions of the country, which was one of the main goals of the public works policy. Yet the impact was not as important as in other countries, regarding transported passengers and cargo. This fact is probably best explained by the lower level of Portuguese economic development itself.

Roads

The road network was another concern of the Portuguese governments during the period under consideration, mainly as a connection of the bulk of the country with the railway network. There were only around 200 km of paved roads at the beginning of the 1850s, but this figure had grown to nearly 10,000 km by the beginning of the 1890s. All of the roads were built by the government and no turnpike system was implemented.

Ports

Leixões, Figueira da Foz, and Lisbon, in the continental part of the country, and Ponta Delgada in the Azores, were the most important Portuguese ports where modern passenger and cargo facilities were built, mainly during the 1880s. This was a natural complement to railway building, because, together with the international links of the railroad network, sea ports were the main physical link of the Portuguese economy with the international economy.

Leixões was an artificial harbour built to replace the traditional natural harbour of Porto on the Douro. It was located in a neighbouring municipality, linked to Porto by railroad. The change was needed because the harbour of Porto usually had to be closed for a few weeks every winter, due to bad weather.

Most of the other sea and river ports of the country declined as trade ports and remained important only as fishing ports, because railroads increased the concentration of trade in the main ports. However, several small ports in Algarve managed to survive as trade ports.

The development of sea ports was, however, impossible without the complement of lighthouses. During the 1880s and 1890s a network of modern lighthouses was installed along the Portuguese coast, putting an end to its notoriety as a dark and dangerous place.

Posts, telegraph and telephone

During the 1850s, the postal administration underwent a profound reform with the introduction of the postage stamp. The development of the transportation network during the following decades ensured that its service became more and more efficient. It also became linked with the post offices of other countries in the context of the International Postal Union.

The telegraph made its appearance in Portugal during the 1850s. The main network of the continental part of the country was ready during the 1860s. International and overseas links by submarine cable came during the following decades: in 1870 with Great Britain, in 1873 with Madeira, Brazil and America, in 1893 with the Azores, during the 1890s with the main Portuguese colonies. The administration of the telegraph network was given to the postal administration.

Telephones began to operate in Lisbon in 1882 and soon spread, first to Porto, then to the whole country. A British firm, the Anglo-Portuguese Telephones, obtained the administration of the Lisbon and Porto networks. In the rest of the country, it was the post and telegraph administration that was charged with the development of the telephone network.

Financing of public works, public accounts and public debt

The public works programme described above was, of course, an expensive one; and an important part of its financing came from government direct investment and government subsidies, even in the case of private railway companies.

Such an effort put a heavy strain on public finances. In the early 1850s, this was acknowledged as an unavoidable step towards the development of the country. There was a successful attempt to convert the public debt in favourable terms in 1852, so that public current accounts might have surpluses, but further borrowing was necessary to pursue public works. The increase in taxes resulting from economic development was pointed out as the basis for servicing the increasing debt in the more or less near future.

These financial schemes did not work as well as their devisers imagined. As a matter of fact, heavy borrowing occurred between 1851 and 1891, public works were carried on extensively as was pointed out above, and economic growth followed, as will be seen below. However, there were three drawbacks. First of all, current public accounts became impossible to balance. Administration, defence and, above all, the ever-growing service of public debt, made for regular deficits, which reached a maximum in the difficult period of the late 1860s (see section C, below), but remained on the average at around 20% of public expenditure. Secondly, uneasy expectations about the evolution of the Portuguese capacity to service its public debt implied that attempts to issue standard 3% consolidated bonds met with very low prices (or very high effective interest rates, usually around 7%). Last but not least, politics at home made tax increases difficult, and economic growth did not promote higher proportions of taxes in national income. As a consequence, by the late 1880s public debt was approaching 80% of gross domestic product and the service of public debt was approaching 50% of public revenue.

Public enterprises

The liberal blueprint was duly liberal in the sense that it accepted government intervention in order to foster economic growth, but rejected the existence of public enterprises as a rule. However, exceptions to this rule of rejection of public enterprises had to be accepted, partly as a way to provide certain services to some regions of the country (as in the case of the Portuguese Savings Bank already mentioned), partly as an unintended consequence of purchases of nearly-bankrupt firms that had to be kept in operation (as in the case of the majority of the railway lines north of the Douro and south of the Tagus), partly as a device to increase public revenue (as in the case of the tobacco sector, where there was an attempt to establish a government monopoly between 1888 and 1891).

Cultural measures

Education was not a priority in the regeneration programme of the liberal blueprint. The contrast between the concern with public works and the lower priority given to education may be illustrated by two facts. First, while public expenditure on public works grew and attained rather high levels, public expenditure on education remained stable and low. Second, while nobody thought of dismantling the Ministry of Public Works, which existed following 1852, two attempts to organise a Ministry of Public Instruction in 1870 and 1890 were short lived.

In any event, the general trend of economic growth and the increase of public expenditure benefited the education sector, too. Around 1890, the great majority of the parishes of the country already had at least one primary school. This afforded some sense to the attempt to make primary school attendance legally compulsory, but, for the time being, such an attempt was a total failure. The proportion of adult illiterate people was still around 85% in the mid-19th century, decreasing only to around 75% in 1890.

At the same time, the goal of having one secondary school in each administrative district had already been met.

At the university level, Coimbra was able to retain a formal monopoly. However, many schools of university level, mainly in the technical fields, began to be established in Lisbon, Porto, and even in Goa (Portuguese India).

To sum up, there was some progress in the cultural field, but it clearly lagged behind the progress being made in the economic field. Demand for education by families for their children spread only slowly. The use of child labour and the lack of interest in instruction (at least beyond reading, writing and elementary arithmetic) contributed, regardless of the weakness of the spatial distribution of the school network, to the slow spread of education. It is likely that such a situation acted as a brake on economic growth in the long run.

B – Integration in the international economy

Foreign trade

International transportation and communication certainly promoted a higher degree of integration of the Portuguese economy in the international economy during the decades under consideration. However, foreign trade in general did not show significant upward trends. Exports remained somewhat below 5% of gross domestic product, imports somewhat above that level. This means that Portugal continued to run a systematic trade deficit. Estimates based on partial official data suggest that the accumulated trade deficit between 1851 and 1891 may have reached nearly 80 million pounds.

The low level of the ratios of foreign trade to gross domestic product does not mean that the Portuguese economy grew less dependent upon foreign supplies of some vital goods. Cereals, because of the end of the protectionist legislation during the 1850s, and fuel – mainly coal – because of the development of modern industrial units based on the use of the steam engine, are perhaps the most important examples. Machinery was, of course, also a major constituent of Portuguese imports, because its domestic production was almost non-existent.

The reduction of cereal production led to the improvement of animal husbandry, and animal products and livestock became, for a while, important Portuguese exports. However, wine retained its leading position among Portuguese exports, in spite of some stagnation in demand and of some blights in the vineyards (see section C, below). Cork was another staple Portuguese export. In the industrial field, only canned fish played a large role among Portuguese exports.

The Portuguese merchant navy was unable to recover from the setbacks of the first half of the 19th century, and the country remained dependent upon the British merchant marine for the bulk of its foreign trade.

Emigration and emigrants' remittances

If Portuguese foreign trade failed to show a significant upward trend in general, emigration clearly increased. It had already reached an average of around 10,000 people per year by the middle of the 19th century, and by the late 1880s it had trebled.

Brazil was the main destination of the Portuguese emigrants, especially those leaving the continental part of the country. Following the end of the slave trade in the 1850s, demand for unspecialised free labour increased, in spite of the existence of a residual slave population, and workers from southern Europe poured into the country. For Portugal, this meant the replacement of an emigration of relatively high-level workers, to be employed mainly as salary earners in the services sector, with frequent cases of personal success, by an emigration of relatively low-level workers, to be employed chiefly as wage earners in the primary sector, with few cases of personal success. As a consequence, reflux rates, which had been sizeable, shrank.

Emigrants from the archipelago of Madeira also went mainly to the South American continent. Emigrants from the archipelago of the Azores went primarily to the North American continent, especially to the American states of Massachusetts, New York and California, and to the Sandwich Islands (the future American state of Hawaii) in the Pacific.

All of these flows played an important role in the Portuguese balance of payments, because of emigrants' remittances. Technically speaking, these remittances included not only true remittances, but also capital imports brought by immigrants returning home, and capital revenue flowing from assets held abroad by returned immigrants. In all, they were vital in compensating for the regular deficit in the foreign trade relations of the Portuguese economy. Rough estimates based on partial official data suggest that between 1851 and 1891 total accumulated emigrants' remittances may have amounted to around 60 million pounds.

An overall assessment of the consequences of emigration upon the Portuguese economy must take into account, besides financial flows resulting from remittances in the broad sense, the loss of population it represented. If remittances contributed positively to the balance of payments, the loss of population cannot be treated in the same way, especially from a qualitative point of view. Emigration drained away mainly the relatively young, active, male population, probably with training and abilities above the average. It is impossible not to admit that there was a significant loss in terms of human resources.

Capital movements

Besides emigrants' remittances in a broad sense, capital movements were also important in compensating for the trade deficit. Public loans abroad reached 89 million pounds, and brought a cash flow of 42 million pounds to the country (the difference results from the low quotations that Portuguese bonds obtained in international financial markets). It is impossible to present even rough estimates for private capital movements.

Of course, these capital imports implied the payment of interest and profits. The service of foreign public debt amounted to around 38 million pounds between 1851 and 1891. This means that the net sum brought to the country by public debt operations came to only around 4 million pounds (it is possible that such an estimate is still exaggerated, because a large part of the Portuguese foreign public debt was held by Portuguese bondholders, who preferred to hold foreign debt because they thought it was better protected against default by possible pressures from foreign governments). Once again, it is impossible to present even rough estimates for private capital movements.

Balance of payments

Adding the 80 million pounds of trade deficits and the 17 million pounds of increase of foreign gold coins in circulation not compensated by silver exports (there were significant silver exports during the 1850s because of the decision to abandon silver as a monetary standard) on one side, and the 60 million pounds of emigrants' remittances in a broad sense and the 4 million pounds of net public capital and interest movements on the other side, there is still a 33 million pound inflow gap to be explained. These 33 million pounds of errors and omissions may be explained by private capital movements net of profit and interest payments, but it is hard to believe in a net balance of such a magnitude. This has led some authors to suggest that trade statistics are grossly inaccurate and present a higher trade deficit than what actually was, either because of unregistered movements, or because of undervaluation of registered exports. This issue is still under scrutiny.

Colonial evolution

The colonial empire did not play an important role in Portuguese life during the decades under consideration. In a certain sense its economic value even decreased with the implementation of the legal abolition of the slave trade during the 1850s.

In any event, the Portuguese government tried to retain control of the possessions that already existed, and even to enlarge some of them, with varying degrees of success.

The main expansion took place in Angola and Mozambique. After a dispute with Great Britain about the control of the region of Lourenço Marques (today Maputo) in Mozambique, which was settled in favour of the Portuguese claims by American arbitration, the Portuguese authorities tried to fulfil the old dream of an overland crossing from Angola to Mozambique. Explorations led by Serpa Pinto, Hermenegildo Capelo and Roberto Ivens crossed the southern part of the African continent during the 1870s and set the basis for the claim presented by Portugal after the Conference of Berlin of 1885 to occupy the whole territory that corresponds today to Angola, Malawi, Mozambique, Zambia and Zimbabwe. This claim was accepted by the main colonial powers of the region – Belgium, France and Germany – with the exception of Great Britain, on the basis of a "pink map" that led to a diplomatic conflict between Portugal and Great Britain in 1890: Portuguese attempts to implement effective control over the region of Nyasaland met with a British ultimatum to withdraw the troops sent for the purpose. Portugal had to accept the ultimatum, and later negotiations ended with the British acquisition of Rhodesia (today Zambia and Zimbabwe) and northern Nyasaland (today Malawi) – Portugal had to content itself with southern Nyasaland, from then on included in Mozambique. In any event, Portugal acquired two huge colonies in southern Africa, the western one – Angola – with an area of around 1,245,000 square km, and the eastern one – Mozambique – with an area of around 785,000 square km.

An aborted attempt at expansion took place on the northern coast of the Gulf of Guinea, with the proclamation of a protectorate over Dahomey in 1885. French opposition forced Portugal to drop the claim, and Portuguese possessions in the area were restricted to the islands of São Tomé and Príncipe and to the fortress of São João Baptista de Ajudá, with an area of slightly under 1,000 square km.

Further north, a small bit of the coast (Portuguese Guinea) with an area of around 36,000 square km and the archipelago of Cape Verde with an area of around 4,000 square km were also retained.

In India there were no changes to the Portuguese possessions, which had an area of around 4,000 square km. They became a marginal neighbour of the British Indian Empire.

The weakening of China after the so-called Opium War (1840-1842), and especially during the period of the Taiping and

Niam revolts (1850-1875), allowed the Portuguese authorities to establish full control over the territory of Macau (16 square km) and to obtain some extra-territorial rights in China proper.

Events in Insulindia took an opposite direction. Solor and most of the western part of Timor had to be abandoned to the Dutch East Indies, and the Portuguese possessions were restricted to the eastern part of Timor, a small bit of the western part of the same island and two small neighbouring islands (Ataúro and Jaco) with an area of around 19,000 square km.

C – Growth and crises

Population

Population growth accelerated during the period under consideration, attaining an annual accumulated rate around 0.7%. As a consequence, there were 4 million people living in Portugal around 1860, and more than 5 million in 1890. This higher growth was the consequence of a drop in mortality rate, which may be explained by the increase in the standards of living and the end of traditional famines and epidemics, and of a stability of the birth rate. Of course, the higher emigration figures mentioned above acted as a brake on this growth.

Regional distribution of population

Trends in the regional distribution of the population clearly favoured the south of the country, to the detriment of the north and the islands during the decades under consideration. Of course, the north retained the majority of the population and the higher population densities, but the south was gradually closing the gap in relative terms.

From a demographic point of view, this evolution was mainly a consequence of the absence of a significant emigration flow from the south, while the north and the islands provided the bulk of Portuguese emigration.

From an economic point of view, this evolution was a consequence of the higher economic growth of the south, which was, in turn, a consequence of the higher foreign demand for its typically mediterranean agricultural products and of its higher industrial growth.

Towns

The ratio of the urban population to total population clearly increased during the decades under consideration: it was below 10% around 1850 and had outstripped that level by around 1890.

The greatest increase of urban population occurred in Lisbon. The capital of the country resumed its growth during the second half of the 19th century, reaching the 300,000 mark around 1890. The growth of Porto proceeded at a similar rate, and its population was approaching 150,000 around 1890. However, the role Porto had played in Portuguese life during the first half of the 19th century, because of the stagnation of Lisbon as explained in chapter 7, was completely lost. For instance, no further successful revolutions broke out in Porto from 1868 on.

The number of towns having more than 10,000 inhabitants also grew. By 1890, this group included Braga, Coimbra, Covilhã, Évora, Setúbal and Varzim in the continental part of the country, Funchal in Madeira, and Angra and Ponta Delgada in the Azores. However, only Braga had passed the 20,000 mark.

Macroeconomic aggregates

Real gross domestic product growth clearly exceeded population growth. It attained a yearly accumulated rate of more than 1.7%, which means that per capita real gross domestic product grew on average more than 1% per year.

After a sharp increase in the early 1850s (see more about the problems of the 1850s below), the price level did not show any marked upward or downward trend during the period under consideration. This means that monetary variables adapted rather smoothly to the real growth of the economy.

Structural changes

Portuguese economic growth between 1851 and 1891 involved, as would be expected, some important structural changes in the economy.

Available estimates of output by sectors suggest that the yearly accumulated growth of the output of agriculture was clearly below the average (less than 1%), and that the yearly accumulated growth of the output of industry was clearly above the average (perhaps around 3%). No similar estimate is available for the services sector, but it is likely that its growth was at least as important as the growth of the industrial sector. As a consequence, the share of agriculture in gross domestic product must have decreased (perhaps from more than two thirds to less than one half), and the shares of industry and services in gross domestic product must have increased (perhaps from less than one fifth each to more than one fourth each).

Census data about the labour force show that, in 1890, the share of labour force in agriculture was around 60%, and that the shares of labour force in industry and services were around 20% each. This means that productivity in the agriculture sector was clearly below the average and that productivity in the industry and services sectors was clearly above the average, as would be expected.

Disaggregation of the output from agriculture leads to the conclusion that the cereals output grew below the average, that the wine output grew more or less the same as the average and that the fruits, vegetables and animal products output grew above the average. Such structural changes were the consequence of an allocation of resources resulting from the opening of the Portuguese market to less expensive foreign cereals, as pointed out in section B, above.

The evolution of wine production deserves some additional attention. Its growth was twice disturbed during the decades under consideration by blights in the vineyards: the oidium during the 1850s and the phylloxera during the 1870s. These blights curbed the growth trend for some time and increased production costs because of the chemical treatments and vine replantings needed to fight them. However, they cannot be blamed for the loss of market share that occurred among the main European consumers, because these same blights also affected the main competitors of Portuguese production. Taste changes and some drop in the average quality of the Portuguese production are better explanations for these problems.

From a regional point of view, the growth of potato production mainly in Trás-os-Montes and Beira Alta, rice production in the alluvial plains of Estremadura and Beira Litoral and mediterranean fruits in the Azores were the most important novelties.

Disaggregation of the product of industry shows that the most dynamic sectors were the canned fish and cork industries geared towards the export markets. The textile industry, mainly in the cotton sub-sector, and other sectors producing consumer goods (food, other than canned fish, ceramics, glass, etc.) also developed, but these sectors were mainly turned toward the internal market. Modern heavy industry and capital goods production were still only just beginning. Lisbon in most industrial sectors, Porto in the cotton textiles (and some neighbouring centres in special sectors such as canned fish and goldsmithery), Covilhã in wool textiles, and several small centres in Algarve in the canned fish and cork activities were the main industrial regions of the country.

No data are available as to the disaggregation of the services sector. It is, however, possible to suggest that modern sectors, such as transportation, communications, trade, education, health and public administration were more dynamic than traditional personal services. This was, most likely, the consequence of the public and private investments and of the urbanisation process already mentioned.

All of these structural changes went, of course, hand in hand with a growing role of market schemes and a decreasing role of self-consumption schemes in Portuguese economic life.

Technological changes

There is not much to add to the references made above to transportation and communication novelties, such as the railroads and the telegraph. Of course, the use of the steam engine spread among the main industrial units of the country, but the majority of production units, both in agriculture and in industry, remained technologically traditional. In particular, mechanisation in the agricultural sector was almost restricted to transformation operations on a few large latifundia of the Alentejo.

Social movements

Industrial growth led to the development of a trade union movement similar to that which occurred in other European countries. However, as agriculture remained more important than industry, and rural population more important than urban, the impact of the trade unions in Portugal during the period under consideration was restricted to firm conflicts.

During the 1870s a Socialist Party (*Partido Socialista*) duly linked to the Socialist International was created. Its role in the Portuguese political life was, however, irrelevant. It was soon superseded by the Republican Party (*Partido Republicano*) as a full-fledged opposition party to the prevailing political order.

Short-term fluctuations

In a certain sense, the 1850s still belong to the stagnation period that the Portuguese economy went through during the first half of the 19th century. As a matter of fact, poor harvests, the oidium blight in the vineyards, and epidemics of cholera and yellow fever, together with the impact of the British and international crisis of the mid-1850s (linked with the consequences of the Crimean War), made the mid-1850s very difficult years, indeed, for the Portuguese society. However, political stability and the beginning of the large public works programmes certainly heralded the take-off of the early 1860s.

The early 1860s were an important turning point in Portuguese economic history. As was pointed out above, the main trunk railway lines were built (and soon linked with the Spanish network), some institutional reforms were achieved, and a banking boom started. At the same time, the period of strong economic growth began.

During the second half of the decade this bright picture was somewhat tarnished by the reduction of emigrants' remittances from Brazil due to the Paraguay War. The Paraguay War was fought by a coalition made up of Brazil, Argentina and Uruguay against Paraguay, between 1864 and 1870, and its early impact coincided with the impact of the British and international crisis of the mid-1860s (linked with the aftermath of the American Civil War). Between 1865 and 1869 growth ceased, only to be resumed during the early 1870s.

The new decade opened with a spectacular boom that increased real per capita gross domestic product by nearly 30% by 1875. However, in 1876 growth was temporarily halted by a crisis, certainly linked to the British and international crisis of the mid-1870s and also to the problems arising from the phylloxera blight in the vineyards. As pointed out above, there was a banking crisis, and growth halted again between 1876 and 1879.

The 1880s seemed to repeat the story of the preceding two decades. It began with a boom between 1880 and 1888, and ended with a stagnation period in 1889. This time, however, there was no upward swing at the beginning of the following decade.

9.

A new epoch of stagnation, 1891-1914

The 1891 crisis analysed in section A was an important turning point in the evolution of the Portuguese economy: it put an end to the first period of noteworthy economic growth and heralded in a period of economic stagnation that lasted until the inter-war years. The contrast with the international background of the epoch, known as the 'belle époque' and characterised by growth in the world economy and increasing international economic relations, is striking. Instead of keeping pace with the growing trend of the international economy, the Portuguese economy enhanced whatever traits of backwardness that it may still have retained in 1891.

The liberal blueprint (presented in chapter 7, above), implemented between the 1830s and the 1880s (as explained in chapters 7 and 8, above), faded out. This led to its replacement by different ideas on how to develop the Portuguese economy. These ideas are described in section B. The general evolution of the Portuguese economy between the 1891 crisis and the First World War is the theme of section C. The political takeover of the republicans and its early consequences are dealt with in section D.

A – The 1891 breakdown

The end of growth in the late 1880s

The first sign of the coming problems was perhaps the levelling off of economic growth in the late 1880s. 1888 was a peak year regarding real gross domestic product and real per capita gross domestic product. As a matter of fact, only after the mid-1920s were the levels of economic activity and the standard of living attained in Portugal in 1888 to be systematically exceeded.

The Brazilian upheavals, 1888-1891

More or less at the same time, the Brazilian society began to face a very difficult political and economic situation. The political problems were the result of the abolition of slavery (March, 1888), followed by the republican revolution that overthrew the monarchy (November, 1889) and a period of political instability that lasted until 1891. The economic problems were the result of the international economic crisis usually known as the Baring crisis.

These Brazilian upheavals led to a temporary reduction of the emigrants' remittances to Portugal. Considering what was said in chapter 8 about the role of Brazil as the main destination of Portuguese emigrants, and about the role of emigrants' remittances in the balancing of Portuguese foreign payments, it is easy to understand that the Portuguese economy was facing a hard shortage of international liquidity.

The Baring crisis

Similar problems had occurred in the preceding decades, for instance during the Paraguay War, a quarter of century earlier (as explained in chapter 8, above) without profound long-term consequences – usually because some foreign loans had been obtained to ease the situation of the balance of payments. This time, however, things became more difficult because the Baring Brothers banking house, which was the banker of the Portuguese government in London, one of the most important creditors of the Portuguese government, and a traditional short-term credit supplier for the Portuguese government at difficult moments, was fully prostrated by the crisis, and could provide no help.

Domestic political problems

Some domestic political problems worsened this picture. In the wake of the British ultimatum of January 1890 reagarding the occupation of Nyasaland (see section B of chapter 8, above), the traditional rotative scheme broke down and coalition and extra-parliamentary governments supported mainly by the new King Carlos I (1889-1908) held power for a period of nearly three years.

This situation, and the loss of prestige for the monarchy resulting from the need to give up the Portuguese claims to 1,260,000 square km in southern Africa under British pressure, led to an outbreak on the part of the Republican Party to over-throw the monarchy. On the 31st of January 1891, a republican revolt broke out in Porto. It was promptly suppressed, but it did nothing to help improve confidence in the political and financial stability of the country.

The tobacco affair

In 1891 the Portuguese government abandoned the attempt to develop the tobacco sector as a state monopoly (see section A of chapter 8, above), and leased the tobacco monopoly to a private company, the Tobacco Company of Portugal (*Companhia dos Tabacos de Portugal*). At the same time, there was an attempt to issue a 10 million pound foreign loan, with a guarantee in the tobacco monopoly lease fee, in the London and Paris markets. The aim was to consolidate floating debt and to overcome the shortage of international liquidity. The loan was a failure (it was sold at 45% of the par value), because of the international crisis and of the loss of confidence in the stability of the Portuguese situation (to all this may be added a campaign led in France by Reillac, an aristocrat who sought to force the Portuguese government to again endorse the war loans of the absolutist government of 1828-1834).

Inconvertibility

During the spring of 1891, it became clear that, deprived of sufficient revenue from the tobacco loan and of the traditional help of the Baring Brothers, the Portuguese government could have to turn to the Portuguese banks (especially to the Bank of Portugal) to ensure the normal flow of payments.

The main consequence of this situation was a bank run, leading to a moratorium (May 9), and a provisional suspension of banknote convertibility (July 9). The issuing banks in the north of the country went bankrupt, and had to surrender their issuing rights to the Bank of Portugal, according to the 1887 legislation mentioned above in section A of chapter 8. Thus, the Bank of Portugal became the only issuing bank for the whole country, and the Portuguese money supply underwent a complete transformation: the overwhelming majority of gold coins was replaced by an overwhelming majority of banknotes. As the Portuguese currency began to depreciate in the exchange markets, a return to convertibility soon became more of a dream than a real possibility. Needless to say, this replacement of the gold standard by a conventional monetary system in a period when gold standard was the hallmark of monetary normality ruined what was left of international financial credibility of the country.

Partial bankruptcy

Internal government payments were maintained with the help of the Bank of Portugal (the monetary consequences of the process will be considered below) and by imposing an income tax of 30% on the interest of internal public debt. However, it was impossible to maintain external payments in the same way without driving the gold and exchange reserves of the Bank of Portugal to exhaustion. After one year of resistance, the Portuguese government gave up: in July 1892 it suspended the amortisation of foreign public debt and reduced the interest payments to one third of the contractual level (the tobacco loan of 1891 was exempted from these measures). As easily imagined, bondholders protested and the Portuguese government could no longer reach international capital markets.

Main consequences of the 1891 breakdown

Aside from the short period of political instability, the end of the gold standard, and the end of foreign loans mentioned above, the 1891 breakdown brought on an important change in the long-term economic policy of the Portuguese government, and precipitated a period of economic stagnation, as pointed out in the introduction. The new long-term economic policy and the economic stagnation were the main features of the course of the Portuguese economy between the early 1890s and the First World War.

B – New economic policies

The end of the liberal blueprint: failure or achievement?

It is possible to argue that, from an economic point of view, the Regeneration implementation of the liberal blueprint had been a success: the growth of the Portuguese economy between the 1860s and 1880s is undeniable, even if it was a consequence of more than the prevailing long-term economic policy.

From a financial point of view, however, things were completely different. The end of the gold standard and the partial bankruptcy of the government were an unwelcome by-product of the whole scheme: economic growth proved insufficient to increase public revenue enough to balance the public accounts and to service the public debt incurred in building public works. As stagnation became the dominant feature of the Portuguese economic situation, the financial scheme of the liberal blueprint was no longer meaningful, and there was a call for new ideas.

The answer of the monarchic parties and governments was, at first, mainly the reinforcement of protectionism. However, many social groups, and especially the intellectual elite, began to put their hopes in the Republican Party, whose programme was to give priority to education and the colonies, as the bases of a Portuguese revival.

Protectionism

The first protectionist measures were taken in 1889 and were geared only to cereal production. The idea was to ensure that all domestic production was sold regardless of the price, by requiring government authorisations for cereal imports and by granting these authorisations only in exchange for commitments to buy domestic production.

In 1892 a new tariff involving an increase of specific duties on most products was adopted. As a matter of fact, the upward trend of international prices during the following decades reduced the protectionist impact of the tariff reform, but both the increase of international prices and the increase of tariffs afforded some room for higher domestic production of most industrial goods.

In 1899 protectionist measures on cereal production were reinforced.

As will presently be seen in section C, below, these measures stimulated cereal and industrial production, as they were intended to do. Their contribution to the economic development of the country is, however, doubtful. They favoured the allocation of resources to inefficient economic activities, a dangerous course of action, especially in a small economy such as Portugal's.

Education

The claim of a higher commitment on the part of the government to develop public education had, above all, political goals for the Republican Party. High illiteracy and low average school instruction were deemed to be factors in the reactionary politics of the country. Thus, primary instruction was considered to be the first priority in the development of the education programme to encourage increased participation of the Portuguese in public affairs and to stimulate deeper feelings of citizenship.

Education as an instrument to improve human capital was not ignored, however. Thus, technical education was taken as the second priority in the development of the education programme.

As the republican ideas began to gain support in public opinion, the monarchic governments also tried to demonstrate greater concern for education than they had before. The increase of public expenditure in education was, however, small, and its outcome was rather poor in the short term. On the eve of the First World War, the proportion of adult illiterate people in Portugal still hovered around 70%.

Colonies

Profiting from their colonies, as the most-developed countries were doing, was the other feature of what may be called the republican blueprint. To channel the traditional flow of emigrants to the Portuguese colonies, especially to Angola and Mozambique, instead of to Brazil, was the key dream of these colonial projects.

Although, as in the case of education, the triumph of these ideas in public opinion forced the monarchic governments to give higher priority to the colonial endeavours, practical matters were, of course, very different from these intentions.

First of all, it was necessary to control the territories and to subdue restless indigenous tribes. Colonial military campaigns with this goal were often necessary in the years between the 1890s and the First World War. These campaigns did not demand large public expenditures, nor did they entail significant human losses, because they usually ended in easy victory for the Portuguese expeditionary troops. The only exception was the 1895-1896 campaign against the Vátuas (a branch of the Zulu tribe living in Mozambique), which met with stiff resistance, but, of course, ended with victory for the Europeans.

Organising an administrative network proved more difficult and expensive. The solution adopted in Mozambique was to grant the administration and exploitation of a large part of the territory to private companies. Three companies, the Nyasa Company (*Companhia do Niassa*), the Mozambique Company (*Companhia de Moçambique*) and the Zambezia Company (*Companhia da Zambézia*), mainly financed by British capital, received control of most of the north and centre of the colony. The Nyasa Company controlled around 200,000 square km (more than one fourth of the area of the colony) in the north. The Mozambique Company controlled around 140,000 square km (nearly one fifth of the area of the colony) in the centre. The Zambezia Company controlled around 100,000 square km (more than one eighth of the area of the colony), also in the centre. The government administration was restricted to the south and to small areas of the north and centre of the colony. This arrangement remained peculiar to that colony, however, and was not adopted anywhere else.

After the end of the Portuguese protectorate in Dahomey (see chapter 8, above), all Portuguese colonies had a full colonial regime. Governors and higher administrative authorities were nominated by the central government, fundamental legal regimes were enacted by the parliament or by the central government, the lower ranks of the administrative personnel were nominated by the governors of each colony and particular legal regimes were enacted by the governors of each colony. As a general rule, the inhabitants of the colonial territories were divided into two groups: those of European origin and the assimilated natives (*assimilados*) were awarded full citizenship and had the same rights and duties towards the state as the metropolitan population; the rest of the population, the indigenous (*indígenas*), had separate legal regimes, meaning limited civil rights. Of course, the assimilated natives (in practice, literate people with permanent jobs in the modern economic sector) were a tiny minority of the native population.

The last (but not least) condition for profiting from the colonies was to invest in basic economic equipment. It is easy to imagine that the resources for such a massive investment were totally absent. Because of that, there was some call for foreign private investment, but its flow was, as would be expected, small, even in comparison with other regions of Africa.

As for the economic regime, each colony was a separate national economy. There was, of course, some coordination of economic policies by the central government, and the tariff regime usually gave a preferential treatment to the other Portuguese territories. However, there were different economic laws, different fiscal systems, different monetary rules and tariffs – all in an effort to profit from specific local situations.

Administration by private companies certainly improved the economic situation in the case of Mozambique, which became an important producer of cotton, sugar and tea. Mozambique was also favoured by the fact that the British colonies of Nyasaland and Rhodesia and part of the independent states of Orange and Transvaal (later, British colonies) were located in the hinterland of its main ports – Lourenço Marques (today Maputo) in the territory administered by the government, and Beira in the territory administered by the Mozambique Company. This ensured busy and profitable railway and port traffic. Temporary emigration of workers from Mozambique to Transvaal, mainly for mining, soon also became an important basis for economic prosperity. The population of Mozambique stood at around 2.5 million inhabitants in the early 20th century, growing to around 7 million by the 1970s, when decolonisation took place. No more than 5% of this population was of European origin.

The situation in Angola was quite different: there were no private companies to administer and develop the territory, and the colony long remained far behind its east-coast rival as far as economic prosperity is concerned. However, three important railways were built: one in the north to link the port of Luanda with its hinterland, which became a coffee producing region; another in the centre to link the port of Benguela with the regions of Lunda in Angola, and Katanga (today Shaba) in the Congo (later the Belgian colony of Congo, later Democratic Republic of Congo or Zaire), which became important diamond and copper producers; and a third one in the south to link the port of Moçâmedes with its hinterland, which became an iron ore producer. Lobito, which gradually replaced Benguela, and Luanda were able to develop as important ports, and the plateau region of the centre of the colony became a corn exporter to its eastern mining neighbours of Katanga, leading to the development of three important interior urban centres: Nova Lisboa (today Huambo), Sá da Bandeira (today Lubango) and Silva Porto (today Cuito). At the same time, there was a sizeable immigration of European origin. The population of Angola was under 3 million in the early 20th century and grew to around 5 million by the 1970s, when decolonisation took place. At the beginning, the percentage of the population of European origin was about the same as that in Mozambique, but its weight later increased to around 15%.

The other Portuguese colonies were much smaller and had little economic significance.

Cape Verde developed mainly as a merchant navy supplier, though it was unable to match its main neighbouring competitor, Dakar. Its agriculture was severely hurt by frequent droughts. Its population stood at around 100,000 inhabitants in the early 20th century, growing to around 250,000 by the 1970s, when decolonisation took place. The bulk of this population was of mixed European-African origin.

Portuguese Guinea became a tropical fats producer, mainly controlled by a branch of the most important Portuguese chemical firm, the Industrial Union Company (*Companhia União Fabril*, see section C, below). Its population stood at around 300,000 inhabitants in the early 20th century, growing to around 600,000 by the 1970s, when decolonisation took place. The bulk of this population was of African origin, but there was a significant social elite of immigrants from Cape Verde.

São Tomé e Príncipe became a cocoa producer mainly controlled by Portuguese landowners. Its population fluctuated between 50,000 and 70,000 inhabitants during the 20th century, according to the fluctuations of cocoa prices in international markets. The bulk of this population was of African origin, many of them immigrants from Angola. The fortress of São João Baptista de Ajudá on the Dahomey coast remained a part of this colony.

Goa developed as one of the ports of the province of Maharashtra in British India, though it was unable to match its main neighbouring competitor, Bombay. The rest of Portuguese India, that is to say, the territories of Damão, Diu, Dadrá and Nagar-Aveli, were of little significance. Total population stood at around 500,000 inhabitants in the early 20th century, growing to around 650,000 by the 1960s, when the colony was occupied by

India. The bulk of this population was of Indian origin, and there was a significant local social elite.

Macau developed as one of the ports of the province of Guangdong in China, though it was unable to match its main neighbouring competitor, Hong Kong. Its population fluctuated between 150,000 and 500,000 inhabitants during the 20th century, according to the situation in the neighbouring Chinese regions. The bulk of this population was of Chinese origin, many of whom were often transient refugees, and there was a strong local social elite.

Timor became mainly a coffee producer. Its population stood at around 400,000 inhabitants in the early 20th century, growing to around 700,000 by the 1970s, when it was occupied by Indonesia. The bulk of this population was of Malay origin.

*

It is worth noting that the traditional informal alliance between Portugal and Great Britain became a formal treaty during this epoch on account of a colonial affair. Great Britain needed Portuguese help during the Boer War (1899-1902) because the Afrikaner states of Orange and Transvaal were located in the hinterland of the port of Lourenço Marques in Mozambique, and it was much less costly to use this port than the ports of the British colonies of the Cape and Natal for delivering troops and supplies to the war. Portugal agreed to a defensive alliance in European affairs and a general alliance in colonial affairs, which was signed in 1899, paving the way for an indirect Portuguese intervention against the Boer states.

Another colonial affair also led Portugal into the only formal war in which it was engaged during this period. Portugal was one of the eleven countries to which China addressed a declaration of war during the so-called Boxer rebellion in 1900. In fact, no Portuguese troops participated in the expedition to Beijing that followed, and the only consequences of the war for

Portugal were a trifling indemnity and the reinforcement of the extra-territorial rights in China.

C – A dismal *belle époque*

Population

Population growth continued during the period under consideration at a yearly accumulated rate of around 0.7%, only slightly lower than the rate attained after the middle of the 19th century. As a consequence, there were around 6 million people living in Portugal on the eve of the First World War. This small drop in the rate of population growth was the consequence of increased emigration, which trebled between 1891 and 1913, and of stable birth and death rates.

Regional distribution of population

The trends in regional distribution of the population in the continental part of the country were similar to those between 1851 and 1891: a relative increase of the less-populated south of the country; a relative decrease of the more-populated north of the country. In the Atlantic islands, however, there was some change: instead of a declining share both in Madeira and the Azores, there was an increase in the weight of Madeira and a decrease in that of the Azores.

As for the continental part of the country, the demographic and economic explanations of these regional trends are also similar to those for the period between 1851 and 1891: absence of significant emigration from the south; lower economic growth of the north. In the case of the Atlantic islands, the Azores were facing some problems with the exports of mediterranean fruits, which would lead to their replacement by the production of pineapples in hothouses, especially on São Miguel, the largest island, while Madeira was enjoying a period of prosperity based on wine and banana exports and its first tourism boom.

Towns

Urban growth between 1891 and 1914 was restricted to Lisbon, which reached nearly 450,000 inhabitants on the eve of the First World War, and Porto, with nearly 200,000 inhabitants at the same time.

The number of towns having more than 10,000 stagnated between 1891 and 1914, losing Angra in the Azores, as a consequence of the economic problems in the central part of the archipelago, and adding Olhão, the most important centre of the canned fish industry in the Algarve.

Macroeconomic aggregates

Real gross domestic product growth and population growth proceeded at almost the same yearly accumulated rate between the 1891 crisis and the First World War, which means that per capita real gross domestic product levelled off on average during the period under consideration. Some authors have raised doubts about the stagnation of real per capita gross domestic product during the 1890s, in light of some signs of a significant increase in agricultural output, mainly in the cereal and wine sub-sectors. The matter should be considered to be unresolved. However, stagnation following the turning of the century seems to be a certainty.

The price level showed a 15% increase between the 1891 crisis and the First World War. This increase, for which the paper money regime adopted in 1891 was blamed, caused much concern at the time. The explanation was perhaps wrong and the concern perhaps exaggerated. The protectionist measures of domestic cereal production certainly contributed to the rise in the cost of living more than purely monetary factors, especially in the main urban centres. At the same time, the international economy was experiencing the well-known period of gold inflation that preceded the First World War, resulting from the South African gold discoveries. Such international factors certainly contributed to Portuguese inflation as well, and ensured that it was not because of price increases that the Portuguese economy went through a listless period.

Structural changes

Structural changes were not in great evidence between 1891 and 1914. The distribution of labour force by sectors showed only a slight decrease in agriculture and a slight increase in industry, and the distribution of value added by sectors showed a significant increase only in industry (from around one fourth to around one third), compensated by slight decreases in the weights of agriculture and services.

As a matter of fact, the yearly accumulated growth of industrial output was certainly higher than the average (perhaps around 1.5%), while the growth of agricultural output was certainly lower than the average (perhaps around 0.5%). No similar estimate is available for the services sector, but it is likely that its growth was at least as slow as that of the agricultural sector, reflecting the absence of urban dynamism in most of the country.

Disaggregation of the agricultural output leads to the conclusion that the cereal output grew at an above-average rate, that the wine output grew at more or less the same as the average and that the output of fruits, vegetables and animal products grew below the average. Such structural changes were the consequence of an allocation of resources resulting from the closing of the Portuguese market to cheaper foreign cereals, as pointed out in section B, above.

Disaggregation of industry shows that the most dynamic sectors were still the canned fish and cork industries geared towards the export markets, and that the textile sector also developed, mainly in the cotton sub-sector. Modern heavy industry, however, showed new signs of life, especially in the chemical sector (production of fertilisers and chemicals to fight agricultural blights). The Industrial Union Company (*Companhia União Fabril*), which was to become the centre of one of the most powerful Portuguese economic groups, was created in this sector by the entrepreneur Alfredo da Silva during the period under consideration. It started its activities in Lisbon in the last decade of the 19th century, and extended to new factories in Barreiro on the left bank of the Tagus during the first decade of the 20th century.

No data are available depicting the disaggregation of the services sector. It is possible to suggest, however, that modern sectors, such as transportation, communications, trade, education, health and public administration were more dynamic than traditional personal services.

All these structural changes, of course, went hand in hand, with a growing role of market schemes and a decreasing role of self-consumption schemes in the Portuguese economy. It is possible to suggest that on the eve of the First World War self-consumption was no longer a significant part of the Portuguese economic activity.

Technological changes

The most important technological change of the period was certainly the systematic use of electricity. Lighting and urban public transportation were its most important early uses, though some replacement of steam engines by electric motors in industrial plants was already underway on the eve of the First World War.

The replacement of horse drawn tramways by electric tramways was certainly the most important change related to electricity during the period under consideration. It occurred in Lisbon around the turn of the century and involved the leasing of the public transportation system of Lisbon by the Portuguese Lisbon Iron Rails Company (*Companhia dos Carris de Ferro de Lisboa*) to the British Lisbon Electric Tramways Company. During the following years electric tramways began to operate in Porto and Coimbra, as well. These networks were operated by Portuguese companies.

Electric generators in Portugal during this period were all of the thermal type. This situation contributed to a continuation of the dependence upon foreign coal for energy production.

In agriculture there was some increase in the use of machinery and the beginning of the use of fertilisers, especially in the latifundia of the Alentejo. However, technological and productivity backwardness remained a characteristic of Portuguese agriculture, a situation to which protectionism contributed a good deal.

It was also during this period that automobiles began to circulate on Portuguese roads. However, their numbers were still small and they had no significant economic impact before the First World War.

Social movements

The late 19th and early 20th centuries saw some growth of the trade union movement, coupled with a radicalisation that brought it gradually under the control of left-wing republican and anarchist groups, at the expense of the traditional socialist groups.

Public accounts and public debt

The partial bankruptcy of 1892 led to huge efforts to balance public finances and to stop the growth of public debt. Though public accounts closed more often with deficits than with surpluses between 1893 and 1914, and the government went on borrowing, it is fair to say that the situation had changed completely: deficits became much smaller, a few surpluses appeared, and the ratio of public debt to gross domestic product decreased.

The evolution of the situation of foreign public debt was especially important. Negotiations with foreign creditors to settle the conflict resulting from the 1892 partial suspension of payments dragged on for a decade. In 1902 an agreement was at last reached. The Portuguese government agreed to pay off half the interest it paid before 1892, to resume amortisation (to be concluded by 2001) and to pledge the country's customs revenues to ensure the payments. No further foreign debt was incurred until the First World War.

Fiscal reforms

The increase of government revenue needed in order to bring the budget into near balance was obtained by means of increased fiscal revenue. This increase came through higher tax rates and a number of formally temporary sur-taxes (renewed every year). Deeper fiscal reforms were almost absent. The only significant exception was a revision of the rules of the land tax pertaining to buildings in 1899.

Public enterprises

The origins of public enterprises have already been described in section A of chapter 8, above. In 1908, there was a general reform of their management with the aim of increasing their revenue to the Treasury. The savings bank, now called General Deposits Savings Bank (*Caixa Geral de Depósitos*), the State Railways (*Caminhos-de-Ferro do Estado*), and the Posts and Telegraphs (*Correios e Telégrafos*) were the most important of these public enterprises. The reform succeeded in its revenue aims until the First World War.

Monetary evolution

The huge public deficits of 1891 and 1892 were financed by public loans at the Bank of Portugal, which in turn issued bank notes in large numbers. This process allowed the replacement of more than 100,000 contos worth of gold coins in circulation with around 50,000 contos in bank notes, an amount further increased to around 70,000 contos by a similar process during the 1890s. Somewhat surprisingly, bank notes spread relatively easily throughout the country. Silver and copper coins retained their role as subsidiary means of payment, and the use of cheques, transfers and other means of payment with bank deposits remained restricted to a small fringe of the population. There was an apparent increase in the velocity of circulation, as the average economic unit was less interested in holding inconvertible notes, than in holding the older gold coins with intrinsic value.

In the wake of the new monetary regime, gold coins were exported or hoarded. Gold coin exports reached some 15 million pounds by the First World War, according to official figures. Gold coin hoarding was already a tradition, especially in the rural areas of the country's north, and certainly increased with the new monetary situation.

After the turn of the century, the monetary evolution was rather stable. Government borrowing at the Bank of Portugal almost stopped and the increase of bank notes in circulation slowed to near zero, as well. This evolution adapted without any problem to the stagnant situation in the real sector of the economy.

Balance of payments

Trade deficits, huge emigrants' remittances and sizeable private capital movements remained the main aspects of Portuguese foreign economic relations between the 1891 crisis and the First World War. The main difference with the period between the 1830s and 1890s was the absence of public loans abroad.

Trade deficits increased, both in absolute figures and in relation to gross domestic product, mainly because imports increased faster than exports. The ratio of exports to gross domestic product remained below 5%, and the ratio of exports to gross domestic product approached 10%. As a consequence, total trade deficits between 1891 and 1914 amounted to around 140 million pounds.

At the same time, the increase in emigration led to higher emigrants' remittances: 100 million pounds is a reasonable estimate for the whole period under consideration.

The service of foreign public debt decreased as a consequence of the partial bankruptcy of 1892 and increased as a consequence of the 1902 conversion, as pointed out above. Total payments during the period under consideration came to around 34 million pounds.

Adding the 140 million pounds of trade deficits and the 34 million pounds of the service of public debt on one side, and the 100 million pounds of emigrants' remittances in a broad sense and the 15 million pounds of gold outflows on the other side, there is still an inflow gap of 59 million pounds to be explained. The situation is quite similar to that seen in the period between 1851 and 1891: as 59 million pounds seems to be too high an estimate for private capital movements net of profit and interest payments, some authors have suggested that trade statistics are inaccurate and show a higher trade deficit than what was actually the case, either because of unregistered movements, or because of undervaluation of registered exports. This issue is still under investigation.

Exchange rate

As soon as the suspension of convertibility was announced, the exchange rate broke away from the par value of 1 British pound = 4,500 Portuguese réis. Between 1891 and 1897, the Portuguese currency depreciated until it reached a low point of 1

British pound = 7,800 Portuguese réis. Then it began to appreciate, and in 1907 it came back to par value. There followed several small fluctuations, with the lowest quotation at 1 British pound = 5,600 Portuguese réis in 1909. As far as it is possible to ascertain, the fluctuations of the exchange rate seem to be related to the fluctuations of the emigrants' remittances: to increases in the remittances there corresponds a higher demand for Portuguese currency in the exchange markets and thus a drive towards its appreciation; and conversely to decreases in the remittances.

In spite of the rather low depreciation, no serious attempt to resume convertibility or to introduce any kind of surrogate gold standard was made. The fear of a run into the gold reserves of the Bank of Portugal, which usually remained below 20% of the banknote circulation, was perhaps the most important reason for such passiveness of the monetary authorities.

Political evolution, 1891-1910

As soon as the crisis of the early 1890s was over, political stability came back, with the Regeneration and Progressist Parties alternating in power between 1893 and 1906. In 1896 a constitutional reform replaced the elected senate with a senate of life-term members chosen by the king. At the same time, an administrative reform greatly reduced the autonomy of the administrative districts in the continental part of the country (but not in Madeira and the Azores).

By the mid-1900s the Regeneration and Progressist Parties disaggregated. Alarmed at the situation, the king supported a dictatorship of one of the dissident groups of the Regeneration Party (the so-called Liberal-Regenerators). The results were tragic: on the 1st of February 1908, the king and the heir apparent to the throne were murdered by republican radicals. The new King Manuel II had a short reign (1908-1910), characterised by coalition governments and great government instability.

D – Republicans at work

The republican takeover of 1910

On the 3rd of October 1910, a republican revolution broke out in Lisbon. After two days of inconclusive fighting, the royal family and that part of the armed forces that remained loyal to the monarchy capitulated and, on the 5th of October 1910, Portugal became a republic.

Political evolution

The republican provisional government enacted some important general reforms (see below) and organised elections for an assembly that prepared a new constitution. The constitution of 1911 established a parliamentary regime. There were a two-chambered Congress (*Congresso*), both chambers being elected by an almost universal (male) suffrage, a President of the Republic (*Presidente da República*) elected by the Congress, and a government chosen by the President, but controlled by the Congress.

As soon as it became a government party, the Republican Party began to splinter. By 1912 it was divided into a huge left wing Democratic Party (*Partido Democrático*) and two small right wing parties, the Unionist Party (*Partido Unionista*) and Evolutionist Party (*Partido Evolucionista*). Between 1911 and 1913, several attempts to form coalition governments among all republican forces led to a period of high political instability. This situation was aggravated by failed attempts by monarchic forces based in Spain to invade the country and to restore the old regime. In 1913, the Democratic Party was able to form a one-party government, to win partial elections, and to become the dominant political force. Thus, the political situation became more stable up until the beginning of the First World War.

General reforms

The most well-known measures of the republican provisional government were in the field of relations between the state and the Catholic Church. The so-called law of separation of State and Church nationalised all Church property. Churches continued as places of worship without compensation, but other buildings belonging to the Church were re-assigned as public-service buildings. At the same time, the government took over several social functions that were still being performed by the Church (such as civil registration), and several legal rules that until then had been much influenced by catholic doctrine were profoundly changed (for instance, divorce rules).

Between 1911 and 1913, two new ministries were formed, showing the concern of the republican governments for the main items of the programme presented before the revolution of 1910: the Ministry of Colonies and the Ministry of Public Instruction. The situation in these fields did not, however, change much in the short period of republican government before the First World War.

As for education, two new universities were created, one in Lisbon, the other in Porto, but they were based on the schools of university level already existing in those two cities. Some additional new schools of university level in technical fields were also created in Lisbon.

In the colonies, a new administration regime, with higher autonomy for local governments was introduced.

Monetary reform

Another important reform of the republican provisional government was the introduction of a new monetary unit. The old Portuguese real was replaced by the Portuguese escudo equal to 1,000 Portuguese réis. The escudo was defined, according to the gold-standard rules, as 1.625 g of gold, but, of course, the immediate return to convertibility was out of the question. Besides the use of a more practical unit (approximately equivalent to the American dollar at the time), the main innovation was the replacement of the subsidiary coins having effigies of the kings with new subsidiary coins bearing republican devices. However, this replacement was not complete by the time the First World War broke out.

Fiscal reform

However, the most important reforms of the republican provisional government were to be found in the fiscal field.

First of all, the formally temporary surtaxes created during the last decades of the monarchy were made formally permanent.

The provisions of the land tax were thoroughly revised, with marked increases in rates, especially for rural property, not affected by the revision of rules of 1899 (see section C, above). Changes in indirect taxation included the repeal of the house rent contribution and a reduction in the rates of consumption taxes. The registration tax was extended to inheritances to desendants and became progressive.

The social intentions of these fiscal measures are easy to grasp. The idea was to tax the affluent classes and the rural part of the country more heavily, as they were assumed to be the supporters of the monarchy, and to stabilise (or even to lighten) the fiscal burden on the urban middle class, which was seen as the principal constituency of the new regime.

Public accounts surpluses

These fiscal reforms paved the way for regular surpluses in public accounts, which began to appear on the eve of the First World War. The Democratic Party, which was in office, and its leader, Afonso Costa, who was Prime Minister and Minister of Finance, were eager to reap the prestige resulting from the attainment of the classical standards of public finance, coming after a long period of heterodox behaviour (which had begun in the 1790s). Returning to convertibility and to international capital markets seemed to be a possibility for the future, but the First World War soon put an end to this optimism.

10.

The epoch of wars and crises, 1914-1947

The impact of the two world wars and the short-term fluctuations of the international economy of the 1920s and 1930s
was, of course, decisive in shaping the evolution of the Portuguese society during these years of wars and crises. It was a
period of social and political unrest and economic difficulties,
even if it is possible to find some long-term improvements.

The short-term perspective must lead the analysis of this
period of the economic history of Portugal. Thus, sections A to
E examine what the First World War, the post-war years, the
mid-1920s, the Great Depression and the Second World War
meant for Portugal. An assessment of the long-term effects of all
these events will be postponed to section F.

A – The First World War

As far as Portugal is concerned, the First World War years
may be divided into two periods: the neutrality period (August
1914-March 1916), and the belligerency period (March 1916-
November 1918).

Portuguese neutrality, 1914-1916

Portugal took no part in the diplomatic process that led to
the beginning of the First World War. Furthermore, as Great

Britain had declared war on Germany on account of a European affair, the 1899 Anglo-Portuguese alliance could not be invoked by Britain to ask for Portuguese intervention in the conflict. Moreover, until February 1916, the British government showed no interest in such an intervention. As a consequence, Portugal remained neutral for a year and a half following the beginning of the hostilities.

This did not prevent Germany from promoting native revolts and border incidents in the south of Angola (from the German colony of the South-West Africa, today Namibia) and in the north of Mozambique (from the German colony of the Tanganyika, to-day part of Tanzania). These problems forced the Portuguese government to send military expeditions to defend the two main Portuguese African colonies, but did not lead Portugal into open belligerency.

Domestic politics during the neutrality period

The Portuguese political situation was not calm during the neutrality period, mainly because of the friction between the supporters of Portuguese intervention in the war and the supporters of Portuguese neutrality. Two governments supported by the Democratic Party led the country between August 1914 and January 1915. They were followed in January 1915 by a right-wing government, which was overthrown in May 1915 in a coup that brought the Democratic Party back to power until March 1916. However, the governments of the Democratic Party, which were supporters of Portuguese intervention in the war, were unable to impose their views upon the British government.

Portuguese belligerency, 1916-1918

In February 1916, the British government asked the Portuguese government to impound the German ships at anchor in Portuguese ports, so that some of them might be lent to Great

Britain to improve the supply efforts, which were threatened by German submarines. As Portugal faced similar problems, in spite of the absence of direct German submarine attacks, the request was promptly complied with. The German government did not contest Portugal's right to this action, but asked the Portuguese government to guarantee that the impounded ships would not be put at the disposal of Germany's enemies. As the Portuguese government refused to give such a guarantee, Germany declared war (March 9, 1916). The impounded ships were divided, as was expected, between the Portuguese and British merchant fleets.

By the time Germany declared war, German South-West Africa had already been occupied by the British dominion of South Africa. Thus, there were no problems along the southern border of Angola. The situation was quite different in Mozambique. British attacks from Kenya and Belgian attacks from the Congo had been unable to subdue the German troops in Tanganyika. Portuguese attacks were added to the efforts of the allies. They met with some success at the beginning and the occupation of southern Tanganyika was achieved in 1916. However, the Portuguese troops were soon repelled, and a German counter-offensive occupied the northern half of Mozambique in 1917. In spite of some Portuguese gains in 1918, German troops left Mozambique only after the general surrender of November 1918.

Meanwhile, a Portuguese expeditionary corps had been sent to Flanders in 1916 to garrison a sector of the western European front. Its fate was to fight the bloody and inconclusive trench war until the spring of 1918, and to be crushed by a German offensive on the 9th of April 1918 (battle of La Lys). Following that defeat, the remaining Portuguese troops in Flanders were attached to the British corps until the end of the war.

Domestic politics during the belligerency period

Meanwhile, the Portuguese political situation had changed a great deal. After the German declaration of war, a coalition government of the Democratic and Evolutionist Parties was formed. It remained in power for thirteen months (March 1916-April 1917). It was then replaced by a government of the Democratic Party, which had to face popular riots in Lisbon, because of food shortages, and was overthrown by a military coup in December 1917. The leader of the coup, Sidónio Pais, a right-wing army officer, tried to organise an authoritarian regime, the New Republic (*República Nova*), which ended, in practice, with his assassination in December 1918. This authoritarian regime was linked to the supporters of neutrality in the war, but was unable to alter the course of Portuguese involvement.

*

During the belligerency period three new ministries were created: the Ministry of Labour and Social Security, the Ministry of Agriculture and the Ministry of Transportation and Supplies. The Ministry of Transportation and Supplies was abolished at the end of the war, but the other two remained in place, due to the increased government intervention in economic affairs after the war: the Ministry of Labour and Social Security existed until 1925, and the Ministry of Agriculture existed until 1940, as will be seen below.

Human losses and demographic evolution

Portuguese casualties in the First World War were around 10,000 men, a small figure that had no significant impact on the demographic evolution of the country. However, the years of 1918 and 1919 were also characterised by a deterioration of the country's health. Typhus and influenza epidemics brought an increase of mortality and the first excess of deaths over births since the mid-19th century.

Financial and economic consequences of the war during the neutrality period

The main problems Portugal had to face during the First World War resided, however, in the economic realm. They may be summed up in two features: shortage and inflation.

On the eve of the war, the Portuguese economy was heavily dependent on foreign supplies for some vital commodities: cereals (mainly wheat) and coal were perhaps the most important items. The war interrupted the supplies of these commodities, either because former suppliers decided to reduce exports, or because transportation facilities were not available. The commodities Portugal needed were also vital for the war effort of the main belligerents, and Portuguese foreign trade was traditionally dependent on British ships, which tended to be allocated to strategically important uses and were falling prey to the German submarine attacks.

The shortage of vital supplies translated into a reduction in the level of economic activity in Portugal. Of course, traditional activities not depending on these foreign supplies, such as agriculture, went on as usual, but the food supply to the cities of Lisbon and Porto, and the fuel and raw materials required for modern industrial activities suffered greatly. The quantitative appraisal of the fall of gross domestic product has been the matter of some debate, and the estimates presented in the statistical appendix may well exaggerate the reduction in the Portuguese standard of living, but the existence of a shortage-driven crisis is undeniable.

Inflation was the result of the combined effects of these shortages and the increase in the money supply. This increase of money supply was the result of the financial problems of the government. The military and economic war effort was very expensive, and it was impossible to increase taxes or to find credit in internal or foreign markets to compensate the entire increase in public expenditure. The solution was to ask for loans from the Bank of Portugal, which implied huge monetary issues. When Germany declared war on Portugal, both the money supply and the consumer price level had increased by one half of the pre-war levels (there was only a rather small increase in the velocity of circulation).

A side effect of inflation was the withdrawal of metallic coins from circulation, as their intrinsic value had become higher than their face value. The role of subsidiary currency came to be filled by a number of (extra-legal) coupons issued by local administrative authorities, in spite of the efforts of the central government to issue new metallic coins of lower intrinsic value.

*

The economic and financial problems brought on by the war led to a sharp rise in state intervention in economic life. This intervention took the form of attempted administrative control of the exchange market and the markets of several key commodities, such as transportation, cereals and fuels, sometimes by means of rationing schemes. On the whole, it may be said that this intervention was quite inefficient and promoted the development of huge black markets.

Financial and economic consequences of the war during the belligerency period

Belligerency did not alter the main aspects of the economic and financial consequences of the war. In a certain sense, it only aggravated them.

After the appropriation of the German ships anchored in Portuguese ports in 1916, the Portuguese merchant fleet was in a position to assume a large share of Portuguese foreign trade, but Portuguese ships thereafter also became targets for German submarine attacks. Food, fuel and raw material shortages only increased.

At the same time, the payment from the British government for the cession of the ex-German ships leased by Portugal and a 22 million pound loan from the Bank of England eased the foreign payments situation of the country and financed the expenditure of the Portuguese troops sent to Flanders. However, the internal financial problems caused by the increasing public deficit worsened and inflation accelerated. Attempts to introduce new war-time surtaxes failed, and though the rates of most taxes were increased, the increase of their revenue was not enough to keep up with the increase in expenditures and prices. By the end of the war, both money supply and the consumer price level had trebled as compared to pre-war levels (the increase in the velocity of circulation was still moderate). Administrative controls of markets continued to flourish as before, as did black markets.

In 1917, the central government gave up its efforts to maintain a proper subsidiary metallic circulation, and decided to replace extra-legal local coupon issues with a legal general coupon issue, to which notes of the Bank of Portugal of very low denominations were added.

*

Military operations in Mozambique struck a severe blow to the economy of the northern half of the colony. The main losers were the private companies that administered most of the territory touched by the war.

The results of the war

As a member of the victorious coalition, Portugal felt entitled to territorial acquisitions and war reparations following the war. However, as the country had made a modest and inefficient contribution to the war effort, these rewards were rather small: the ex-German territory of Quionga was annexed to Mozambique; the German ships impounded in February 1916 became Portuguese property; and Portugal became entitled to 0.75% of the reparations to be paid by the defeated powers (that is to say 49.5 million pounds sterling out of the 6,600 million pounds sterling later fixed by the reparations commission).

In exchange, there was the war debt to Great Britain: 19 million pounds sterling to be paid within two years of the ratification of the peace treaty.

B – The post-war years

Social and political unrest

After the death of Sidónio Pais in December 1918, the authoritarian regime he had attempted to build rapidly disappeared. In January 1919, the supporters of the monarchy tried to seize power, and there followed a civil war during the winter of 1919. In March, the old republican regime had been fully restored.

However, political instability remained the main aspect of Portuguese political and social life until early 1922. There was a reshuffling of the old republican parties: the evolutionists and the unionists merged into the Liberal Party (*Partido Liberal*) later called the Nationalist Party (*Partido Nationalista*), suggesting that a kind of rotating system with the Democratic Party would be possible, but small splinters, such as the Popular Party (*Partido Popular*), the Reconstitution Party (*Partido Reconstituinte*) and the Radical Party (*Partido Radical*), blocked the effort. Several governments of various political persuasions alternated in power, anarchist trade unions tried to organise two general strikes without much success, and in October 1921 a bloody revolution brought the republican radicals to power. The new government was, however, unable to resist the opposition of the traditional parties, and the general elections of January 1922 led to a govern-

Economic and financial problems

In a certain sense, social and political unrest was the inevitable consequence of the economic and financial problems that remained the background of Portuguese life between the end of the war and 1924. Of course, the shortage ended with the repeal of the war restrictions, and production gradually recovered to its pre-war levels. At the same time, administrative controls were gradually dismantled, except in the case of the exchange market, and black markets disappeared as a consequence.

However, inflation went on as it had during the war years, partly as a consequence of the external payments problem and the confidence crisis regarding the value of the Portuguese currency that this problem created. The financing of public accounts deficits by means of loans at the Bank of Portugal and note issues by the bank, a process that went on until 1922, also contributed to inflation. In 1924 the money supply was fifteen times greater than it had been in 1914 and the price level was twenty-four times higher (there was an increase in the velocity of circulation as would be expected in a pre-hyper-inflation context).

*

The cessation of hostilities put an end to the war-time schemes of direct control of commodities markets, but not to the government's attempts to fight inflation. These took the form of interventions in the markets of some basic goods, by means of acquisitions by the state in order to sell the goods at low prices to the consumers, and the practice of artificially fixing low prices in the productive public sector. These attempts were inefficient, because they produced results only in the short run. As a matter of fact, in the long run they contributed to the deficits of public accounts, and acted as an inflationary factor.

Balance of payments and exchange rate

Higher deficits in the balance of payments were perhaps the consequence of capital flights, not compensated by any increase in emigrants' remittances. Official trade deficits increased sharply, but it is likely that these increases were only the consequence of undervaluation of Portuguese exports, or overvaluation of Portuguese imports by import-export firms disguising capital flights abroad. The stagnation of emigrants' remittances was partly the result of the suspension of the emigrants' flow during the war, and partly the consequence of the fact that this flow was unable to recover its growth after the war, due to the closed-door policy of the countries of the New World.

The net financial result of war reparations and war debt was quite favourable to Portugal: it should receive 49.5 million pounds sterling from the defeated powers and pay 19 million pounds sterling to Great Britain. Of course, expectations about the fulfilment of these obligations soon turned sour, and the payments actually received fell far short of the promises: by 1926, Portugal had received only a small share of German commodities as a portion of war reparations and had paid only about 1 million pounds sterling to Great Britain. As a consequence, unpaid interest on the war debt increased its amount by more than 5 million pounds sterling, to a total of around 23.5 million pounds sterling.

However, the main result of this process was not this increase in Portuguese external debt, but the contribution it made to the acceleration of the depreciation of the Portuguese currency, by instigating a confidence crisis resulting from the uncertainty about some decisive variables of the economic situation. During the war the exchange rate had reached the level of 1 British pound = 8 Portuguese escudos (a depreciation which was clearly lower than the price increase); it now entered a period of insanity, ending only in the summer of 1924 at the level of 1 British pound = 157 Portuguese escudos.

During this period, the state tried to maintain schemes of direct control of the exchange market, without success.

Public deficits

Public expenditure decreased with the end of the war, but did not come back to pre-war levels. At the same time, tax increases were unable to keep pace with inflation, because the absence of political stability prevented strong measures in the fiscal area. The only important changes were a few increases in the tax rates and the rule introduced in 1918 that import duties should be paid on a gold basis, that is to say, by an amount of current Portuguese escudos equivalent to the amount of Portuguese réis stipulated in the old 1892 tariff, valued according to the gold definition of the Portuguese escudo enacted in 1911.

The advance of interventionist ideas and practices during the war paved the way for an attempt to increase public revenue by means of the development of the sector of public enterprises. Such an attempt was, however, a failure. As a matter of fact, the most important public enterprises created during the post-war years were a social security institute, the Compulsory Social Insurances and General Social Security Institute (*Instituto de Seguros Sociais Obrigatórios e Previdência Geral*), which, by its own nature, was far from profitable, and a sea transportation company, the State Sea Transportation (*Transportes Marítimos do Estado*), which began its operations with the ex-German ships impounded in 1916 and went bankrupt in 1925. Instead of providing revenue to the Treasury, public enterprises (with the exception of the state savings bank) began to ask for subsidies to cover operating deficits and became a burden to the exchequer.

C – The recovery of the middle and late 1920s

The fiscal reform of 1922

The first step towards the stabilisation of Portuguese economic and financial life was the fiscal reform of 1922.

Concerning the land tax (*contribuição predial*) on rural and urban property and the industrial tax (*contribuição industrial*) on profits, there was an increase in the rates and a change in the rules for calculating the taxable income, so that it might coincide with actual income and not with normal income as before. The interest tax (*contribuição de juros*) and the section of the income tax on bond interests were merged into a capital income tax (*imposto sobre a aplicação de capitais*). The section of the income tax on salaries of civil servants was repealed, and a new personal income tax (*imposto pessoal de rendimento*) on total family income was created.

Changes in indirect taxation were equally important. Almost all consumption taxes including the tax on conspicuous luxury consumption (*contribuição sumptuária*) and several production taxes were repealed and a general transactions tax (*imposto de transacções*) was created. At the same time the rates of the stamp tax (*imposto do selo*) were increased. The same happened with the rates of the registration tax (*contribuição de registo*) on property sales and inheritances.

The tariff reform of 1923

In 1923, the fiscal reform was completed by a tariff reform, which also increased tariff rates (and dropped the rule of payment on a gold basis).

Public accounts and public expenditure

The increase in public revenue resulting from the fiscal reform of 1922 and the tariff reform of 1923 allowed a sharp reduction in the deficit of public accounts. However, balanced accounts were not attained immediately because there was a simultaneous effort to increase some items of public expenditure. Education, the old strategic priority of the republican programme, was certainly the expenditure item that saw the highest relative increase during the mid-1920s. Colonial investment also increased, though less regularly. The economic situation of the colonies, especially Mozambique, certainly improved, but mainly as a consequence of the favourable progress of the international economy.

The end of inflation

The reduction of public deficits combined with the skilful use of short-term monetary policy was able to bring inflation down to zero in 1924. The main aspects of the monetary policy of the years between 1922 and 1924 were the financing of public deficits by means of loans in the market (replacing the loans at the Bank of Portugal, which implied monetary issues), and the intervention in the exchange market as a device to influence the exchange rate (instead of administrative controls). Funds for the intervention in the exchange market were obtained by exporting old Portuguese silver coins, which were being held by the government, and by forcing exporters to sell to the government a significant part of the exchange they obtained by means of an export duty reimbursed against the sale of the exchange. This mechanism of intervention proved effective in obtaining the early result of exchange stabilisation. The confidence that this early result inspired and the optimistic expectations it raised in the market brought true consolidation of the stabilisation.

Meanwhile, events in the international economy were also favourable to the Portuguese recovery. The resumption of the payment of German reparations under the Dawes plan in 1924 and an agreement regarding the payment of war debt to Great Britain (with a sixty-two year delay, that is to say, until 1988), reached in 1926, were especially helpful in overcoming the confidence crisis that had fuelled the inflationary process.

The end of inflation allowed the government to replace coupons with metallic coins as subsidiary currency from 1924 on.

The 1926 revolution and military dictatorship

Financial and economic stabilisation was, however, unable to ensure political stability. The government of the Democratic Party fell in late 1923, and there followed several short-lived governments of various political parties and coalitions. The renewed instability paved the way for a military intervention. On the 28th of May 1926, a military revolution broke out in Braga and was soon supported by another coup in Évora. Negotiations between the government and the army led, two days later, to a compromise that lasted until mid-June. Then, the leader of the Braga coup, General Gomes da Costa, asserted himself as President, only to be pushed out in early July by the leader of the Évora coup, General Óscar Carmona, who managed to retain the presidency until his death in 1951. The military dictatorship had to face several revolts of the supporters of the old democratic republican regime, but was able to overcome all problems and to give birth, in 1933, to the new authoritarian regime, the so-called New State (*Estado Novo*), that would last until 1974.

Public enterprises

According to some views, the attempt of a government of the Democratic Party to create a public enterprise in the tobacco sector, when the period of monopoly of the Tobacco Company of

Portugal ended, was one of the events that triggered the 1926 military revolution. The policy of the military dictatorship was very much against public enterprises. The tobacco sector was restored to free competition (in practice, to a duopoly situation). The state railways were leased to the Portuguese Railway Company, which emerged as the only large railway firm in the country – it later bought all the railways still in the hands of other private firms, and gained control of the whole railway network. This company, in turn, leased the suburban Lisbon-Cascais railway to another firm, the Estoril Society (*Sociedade Estoril*) – Estoril was the main tourism centre near Lisbon – for electrification. There remained in the hands of the government only a savings bank, the posts and telegraphs administration and the social insurances institute.

The consolidation of the financial and economic stabilisation in the late 1920s

The consolidation of financial and economic stabilisation was the main concern of the military dictatorship governments. Formal adoption of the gold-exchange standard according to the rules of the Genoa conference of 1922 and balancing of public finances were perceived as being the main elements of this policy.

Formal adoption of the gold-exchange standard seemed to imply the reinforcement of the gold and exchange reserves of the Bank of Portugal. An attempt was made to raise a foreign loan to provide funds for this reinforcement. Negotiations with London bankers in 1927 were inconclusive, as the would-be creditors asked for a guarantee from the League of Nations. Negotiations with the League of Nations in 1927 and 1928 were disappointing, because the Portuguese government thought it unwise to accept the harsh control conditions demanded. Further negotiations with the London bankers in 1928 proved fruitless. Thus, the Portuguese escudo remained stabilised at a rate of around 1

British pound = 108.25 Portuguese escudos, but no commitment to indirect convertibility was made.

Balancing the public accounts demanded either some reduction in public expenditure, or an increase in public revenues. Efforts at colonial investment were dropped after some hesitation and subsidies to public enterprises were ended, but other expenditure items could bear only marginal reductions. There was no alternative to yet another fiscal reform.

The 1928-1929 fiscal reform

Oliveira Salazar, who was professor of political economy and public finance at the University of Coimbra, and who had been a deputy of the Catholic Party in the early 1920s and Minister of Finance for some days after the military coup in 1926, was called in as technical advisor to the commission that prepared the new fiscal reform (which began to be implemented in 1928 and was completed in 1929).

The 1928 changes consisted mainly of tax rate increases. The only deeper reforms were the repeal of the personal income tax, which was replaced by an addition to all direct taxes, receiving the name of complementary tax (*imposto complementar*), and the reintroduction of a tax on the salaries of civil servants under the name of public salvation tax (*imposto de salvação pública*).

The 1929 changes were more important. With regard to the land tax (*contribuição predial*) on rural and urban property and the industrial tax (*contribuição industrial*) on profits, there was a change in the rules for calculating the taxable income, so that it might reflect normal income and not actual income (thus reversing the goals of the 1922 fiscal reform). A new professional tax (*imposto profissional*) on salaries and wages, which came to include the section of the industrial contribution on the income from free-lance professions, was also created.

Changes in indirect taxation were equally important. The general transactions tax (*imposto de transacções*) was repealed, and new consumption taxes, mainly on sugar and oil derivatives were introduced under the name of national salvation tax (*taxa de salvação nacional*). At the same time, the rates of the stamp tax (*imposto do selo*) were increased, as were the rates of the tax on property sales and inheritances, which was formally divided into two taxes: the excise (*sisa*) on property sales, and the succession and donation tax (*imposto sobre sucessões e doações*) on inheritances and donations.

In 1929, there was also a tariff reform, which increased tariff rates, once again.

Surpluses in public accounts, the political takeover of Oliveira Salazar and the Constitution of 1933

Meanwhile, Oliveira Salazar had become Minister of Finance again in April 1928. In the 1928-1929 fiscal year public accounts showed the first surplus since the pre-First World War years, and translated into a decisive political triumph for the new Minister of Finance. In 1929, he served briefly as Minister of Colonies, and prepared a reform of the constitutional provisions related to the colonies, the so-called Colonial Act (*Acto Colonial*), paving the way to become head of government in July 1932. He then prepared a new constitution and was already the true leader of the new regime when the military dictatorship was replaced by the new constitutional text, enacted after a referendum in 1933.

The Constitution of 1933 introduced a presidential regime. The President of the Republic (*Presidente da República*) was elected by direct vote and then selected the government, which had an extensive legislative power and was not subject to formal parliamentary control. The parliament – National Assembly (*Assembleia Nacional*) – was also elected by direct vote, and saw its legislative functions restrained to constitutional and other fundamental texts and its control powers restricted to recommendations to the government. Male suffrage was restricted to literate adults and to persons paying a certain amount of direct taxes, but women were awarded voting rights for the first time, though with very restricted conditions at first (only women who had university or high-school diplomas or paid rather high taxes).

Political parties were forbidden, which gave the monopoly of legal political activity to the National Union (*União Nacional*) formed to support the authoritarian regime. It included the bulk of the republican and monarchic conservative forces, and managed to establish good relations with the Catholic Church (though the Church claim of the devolution of the property transferred to the state during the early years of the republican regime was, of course, refused, except in the case of church sanctuaries and some unoccupied buildings). The democratic republicans, a small but steadily growing communist party and some fascist and monarchic fringes were the main opposition forces.

Meanwhile the ex-king, Manuel II, died in 1932. As he left no heir, the prospects of a monarchic restoration became almost politically mute.

D – The impact of the Great Depression

Balance of payments and exchange rate

The immediate problems of the Great Depression for the Portuguese economy resided in the area of external payments. Exports decreased, and emigrants' remittances plummeted, not only because Brazil, the main source of Portuguese emigrants' remittances, was severely hurt by the international crisis, but also because the Depression led the New World countries, in general, to tighten the closed-door policy to European emigrants.

Some reduction in Portuguese imports and the return of a good deal of Portuguese capital that had been sent abroad a few years earlier prevented any deep crisis. The exchange rate did not depreciate, which allowed an attempt to be made on the 1st of July 1931 to adopt the gold-exchange-standard rules at the official rate of 1 British pound = 110 Portuguese escudos (amounting to a definition of 1 Portuguese escudo = 66.51 mg of gold).

Eighty-one days later the declaration of inconvertibility of the pound put the Portuguese monetary authorities into a dilemma: to stick to gold or to accept competitive devaluation. The choice of competitive devaluation, so that the competitivity of Portuguese exports might be preserved, was swift and clear: until the beginning of the Second World War the official rate of 1 British pound = 110 Portuguese escudos remained the guideline of the Portuguese exchange policy, except for very short periods of high fluctuations of the British pound.

In the meantime, all payments related to reparations and war debt resulting from the First World War were halted in 1931 as a result of the Hoover moratorium, a situation confirmed in the following year by the Lausanne conference. The final result was rather favourable to Portugal: the Portuguese government managed to receive around 5 million pounds, mainly from Germany, and to pay only around 3 million pounds to Great Britain.

Internal economic activity and the Portuguese response to the Great Depression

The impact of the Great Depression on the Portuguese economy was rather mild, because there was no significant decrease in the gross domestic product, and unemployment was absorbed by rural activities. At the same time, the Portuguese government was able to implement a special and rather successful response to the challenges of the Great Depression.

Promoting economic growth and preserving the balance between supply and demand were the main goals of Portuguese economic policy in the 1930s. To attain these long-term aims, short-term measures were taken to implement some government control of economic activity, to stimulate production and investment and to curb consumption. At the same time, the exchange policy sought to preserve the external competitiveness of the Portuguese economy without triggering internal inflation, as explained above.

Government control of economic activity and the Constitution of 1933

The first measures of government control of economic activity were taken in 1931. These consisted of a scheme of administrative authorisation of large investment projects in some industrial sectors, the so-called industrial conditioning (*condicionamento industrial*). These schemes were justified at the time by the need to avoid the harm that unrestricted competition might bring in the form of closures of productive units and unemployment. They were later extended to almost all non-agricultural sectors and remained in force until the post-Second World War years.

At the same time, a programme to increase the self-sufficiency of the country's cereals consumption, the so-called wheat campaign (*campanha do trigo*), later renamed internal colonisation plan (*plano de colonização interna*) was organised. It produced some short-term results at the cost of serious ecological drawbacks from soil exhaustion. Long-term effects were almost nil.

The Constitution of 1933 included, for the first time in Portuguese constitutional history, important rules about economic life. New public enterprises were forbidden, and the right of the government to control economic activity was clearly stated. At the same time, a so-called corporative organisation based on entrepreneur associations and trade unions was set up as a representative mechanism in the economic field. These organisations remained under tight state control throughout the whole period of the authoritarian regime. Strikes and lock-outs were forbidden by law.

The increase of state control in economic life implied the creation of a new Ministry of Trade and Industry and of a Secretary of State for Corporations. The social insurance institute established after the First World War was replaced by a general social insurance scheme under state control.

Public accounts and the control of aggregate demand

Public finances were the main instrument used in controlling aggregate demand.

Current surpluses were used to curb consumption, directly in the case of public consumption, indirectly in the case of private consumption. The 1928-1929 fiscal reform and the 1929 tariff remained in force throughout the 1930s with only two significant changes. The first was the replacement, in 1933, of the complementary tax by the old personal income tax it had replaced in 1928. However, the name of complementary tax (and a section on business income) remained. The second was the suspension, in 1935, of the public salvation tax on the salaries of civil servants.

At the same time, important public investment programes were organised, mainly in the areas of road and port facilities. In 1936 they were unified in what became the first sketch of an economic plan in the country: the so-called law of economic reconstitution (*lei de reconstituição económica*).

Monetary policy

The monetary policy of the 1930s tried to contribute to the double aim of stimulating investment and avoiding inflation. The interest rate was gradually reduced and the money supply was allowed to expand according to the prevailing balance of payment surpluses and moderate internal credit expansion. These policies met their goals fairly well.

Education

In a certain sense, the economic development policy of the new authoritarian regime after Salazar became Minister of Finance was a return to the old priorities of the liberal blueprint – transportation facilities – and rejected the priorities of the republican blueprint – education and colonies. In any event, the financial effort in education was not reduced (although it did not increase), and the cumulative effects of the whole effort of the 1920s and 1930s began to bear some fruit in the form of a notable reduction of the illiteracy rate and an increase of the average number of school years in the 1940s.

Mention should also be made of the organisation of a Technical University in Lisbon in 1930, joining several technical schools of university level not included in the University of Lisbon in 1911.

The consequences of the Great Depression for the Portuguese colonies

The Great Depression was certainly a severe blow to the prosperity of most of the Portuguese colonies, which saw the international demand and prices of their staple exports fall. As a consequence, traditional self-consumption increased its role in their economic life.

In the case of Mozambique, this brought the private companies that administered most of the north and centre of the colony to a very difficult situation. During the 1930s and 1940s all of them quit their administrative functions, handing back to the Portuguese government the burden of direct administration.

In the case of all other colonies (and also, as far as possible, in the case of Mozambique), the policy of the Portuguese government was to avoid any significant aid to the overseas territories, so that the economic situation of the mother country remained unaffected by colonial economic problems. As it happened, schemes for reinforcement of imperial preferences and for tighter coordination of economic policies were put forward with some success.

E – The Second World War

Portuguese neutrality

The diplomatic situation of Portugal towards the Second World War was very similar to that of the neutrality period during the First World War. Portugal was absent from the diplomatic process that led to the outbreak of the war; as Great Britain had declared war on Germany on account of a European affair, the 1899 alliance, again, could not be invoked by Britain asking for a Portuguese intervention in the conflict, and the British government showed no interest in such an intervention. As a consequence, Portugal remained neutral during the whole war. However, Portuguese neutrality did not prevent an indirect participation in two important military events.

The first of these military events lasted from 1941 to 1945. In December 1941, the Portuguese colony of Timor was occupied by an Australian and Dutch force to prevent its use by the Japanese armed forces as a base against Australia or the Dutch East Indies (today Indonesia). The Portuguese garrison did not resist, but the Portuguese government protested. Negotiations led to an agreement to replace the Australian and Dutch force by a reinforcement of the Portuguese garrison. However, before the arrival of the reinforcement, the Australian and Dutch force was overrun by the Japanese army, and, in spite of new Portuguese protests, Timor remained in Japanese hands from February 1942, to August 1945. It was then restored to Portuguese administration, in spite of some Australian diplomatic efforts to replace Portugal's administration.

The second of these military events began in the autumn of 1943 with the grant of the use of military bases in the Azores to Great Britain (in practice, it was American aircraft that used the bases located on the islands of Terceira and Santa Maria). The German reaction to this hostile Portuguese move did not lead to a declaration of war, because Spain showed no interest in collaborating with Germany in an invasion of Portugal, and the German government preferred to preserve Portugal as a trade partner and a supplier of tungsten (on the question of tungsten exports, see below).

Economic and financial consequences of the war

The main economic consequence of the Second World War was a shortage crisis similar to that which the Portuguese economy had experienced during the First World War. This shortage crisis was due to the same causes and had the same general consequences. The reduction of domestic economic activity was, however, less severe, because of two factors of prosperity that came into play simultaneously. These factors were the exports of tungsten ore and the inflow of capital and remittances.

Tungsten ore exports boomed as a consequence of the demand of the belligerent powers for arms production. Part of the tungsten ore exports were subject to administrative controls, and sold to all belligerents with which Portugal had diplomatic relations (a rule that excluded only the Soviet Union among the main belligerents) according to fixed quotas until 1944. After this date, legal tungsten ore exports were forbidden altogether. However, the bulk of the Portuguese tungsten ore was, in fact, sold in the free marketplace to the highest bidder, which meant that the United States of America and Great Britain obtained almost all of it. Though legally forbidden, these exports continued until the end of the war. The main consequence of the boom of the quantities and prices in the tungsten ore market was a surplus in the

Portuguese trade balance from 1941 to 1943, a unique event in the official records since the first decade of the 19th century.

The capital and remittances inflow was a consequence of the flow of refugees into the country. As a matter of fact, Portugal appeared to many people fleeing from the expanding German (and Italian) power as the easiest passage leading to America, or as a last refuge. Many of these refugees brought liquid assets with them, many others received help from abroad (mainly Jewish refugees supported by the American Jewish community). These inflows pushed the balance of payments to exceptional surpluses throughout the war.

The joint effect of the shortage crisis and the balance of payments surplus was an inflationary process, which more than trebled the money supply and doubled the price level during the war years. It is worth noting that this process was accompanied by neither an external depreciation of the Portuguese currency, nor an increase in the velocity of circulation. As for the exchange rate, the Portuguese escudo appreciated against the British pound to the level of 1 British pound = 100 Portuguese escudos in 1940 and remained stable thereafter. It also remained stable against the American dollar during all the war years at a level of 1 American dollar = 25 Portuguese escudos. The velocity of circulation actually declined, as did the interest rate, due to the abundance of capital.

Attempts to administratively control the markets of several key commodities and black markets accompanied the inflationary process, just as during the First World War. In 1940, the Ministries of Agriculture and of Trade and Industry were merged into a Ministry of Economy in order to improve the coordination of economic policy.

Public accounts

Public accounts showed strong deficits during the war. There were large increases in expenditure, mainly with the armed forces, due to the need to reinforce the garrisons of the Atlantic archipelagoes of the Azores and Cape Verde and the border with Spain to defend against possible German attacks. Moreover, all usual expenditures felt the upward pressure of inflation.

There were some attempts to offset these increases in expenditure with new taxes. The public salvation tax on the salaries of civil servants was re-enacted in 1940 and 1941, but dropped thereafter to avoid an excessive reduction of real salaries because of inflation; a supplementary tax (*imposto suplementar*) on high labour incomes was created in 1940; and a tax on windfall war profits (*imposto sobre lucros excepcionais de guerra*) was created in 1942. Both the supplementary tax and the tax on windfall war profits were dropped after the war. At the same time, a duty on tungsten ore exports provided sizeable revenues, but was not enough to compensate the downturn in import duties resulting from the decrease of imports. These fiscal changes provided some additional revenue, but were unable to keep the public accounts balanced.

However, these deficits had no influence on the inflationary process, because the government was able to cover them with public debt issues in the market, taking advantage of the prevailing low interest rates. Moreover, in 1940, a large part of the remaining foreign public debt was voluntarily converted into internal consolidated debt, profiting from the fears arising from the German occupation of France and the threat of a German invasion of Great Britain.

Anti-inflation policy

Another aim of the issuing of public debt was to fight inflation. By issuing public debt in excess of its immediate financing needs, the state tried to reduce money supply. Thus, it was possible to sterilise part of the balance of payments surpluses.

The immediate post-war years

The immediate post-war years saw a quick reversal of the trends of the war years: the shortage crisis ended; foreign trade and production came back to normal levels; trade deficits and capital outflows restored the deficits of the balance of payments; inflation stopped; and, after some delay, a rough balance of public accounts was also attained.

F – Long-term effects of the epoch of wars and crises

Population

Population growth almost stopped during the First World War, but accelerated thereafter, reaching a yearly accumulated rate above 1%. As a consequence, there were around 7 million people living in Portugal in the early 1930s and 8 million in the mid-1940s. This increase in the rate of population growth was the consequence of lower emigration figures, in turn resulting from the closed-door policy of the New World countries, of clearly declining death rates, and of only slightly declining birth rates.

Regional distribution of population

Trends in the regional distribution of the population were similar to those already identified between 1891 and 1914: a relative increase of the less-populated south of the country and the archipelago of Madeira; a relative decrease of the more-populated north of the country and the archipelago of the Azores.

From a demographic point of view, the higher population growth in the south resulted from the traditional absence of significant emigration and from larger drops in death and birth rates. From an economic point of view, the higher population growth of the south corresponded to a higher economic growth, as well.

Towns

Urban growth was very important during the period under consideration, especially during the 1920s and the 1940s. The population of towns having more than 10,000 inhabitants, which was around 10% of the total population before the First World War, was approaching 20% of the total population following the Second World War. The number of towns having more than 10,000 inhabitants more than doubled. Lisbon and Porto began to expand outside their traditional administrative limits, climbing to more than 800,000 and 300,000 inhabitants, respectively. Braga, Coimbra and Setúbal in the continental part of the country and Funchal in Madeira also became quite important towns, each with more than 30,000 inhabitants.

Macroeconomic aggregates

Real gross domestic product growth clearly exceeded population growth, in spite of the setbacks that resulted from the shortage crises during the world wars. It rose to a yearly accumulated rate of around 2%. This means that per capita real gross domestic product increased during the period under consideration. In the post-Second World War years it was nearly 50% higher than on the eve of the First World War.

*

There is not much to add concerning the evolution of money supply and prices to what has been said with regard to the short-term situations. The only important aspect to stress is that the use of demand deposits as a means of payment began to spread among the population.

Structural changes

As would be expected in a period of growth, structural changes were fairly important in the war periods and the inter-war years.

The distribution of labour force by sectors showed a decrease in agriculture and increase in industry and services. By the mid-20th century, however, around one half of the Portuguese labour force still worked in agriculture; the share for industry slightly exceeded one fourth and the share for services was slightly below that level.

Concerning the distribution of value added by sectors the same pattern prevailed: decrease for agriculture and increases for industry and services. As a matter of fact, the yearly accumulated growth of industrial output was certainly higher than the average (perhaps around 2.5%), while the growth of agricultural output was certainly lower than the average (between 1.0% and 1.5%). No similar estimate is available for the services sector, but it is likely that its growth was similar to that of the industrial sector, as a result of the urban dynamism of the period. By the mid-20th century, the shares of the three sectors in the gross domestic product were roughly similar.

Disaggregation of the output from agriculture shows that cereal output, wine output and fruits, vegetables and animal products output grew at fairly similar rates. Such structural stability was the consequence of the absence of significant changes in the allocation of resources resulting, in turn, from the absence of significant changes in the institutional background (except for the attempt to increase cereal production during the 1930s, already mentioned, which was not successful in the long term).

Disaggregation of the product of industry shows that the most active sectors were the traditional canned fish and cork industries geared towards the export markets, the traditional textile sector geared towards the internal market, and the sector of building inputs, which was favoured by the urban growth and public works programmes. The cement sub-sector was the cradle of one of the most powerful Portuguese economic groups during the inter-war years – a result of the activity of the entrepreneur Henrique Sommer.

No data are available to describe the disaggregation of the services sector. It is possible, however, to suggest that modern sectors, such as transportation, communications, trade, education, health and public administration were more active than traditional personal services.

During the wars and inter-war years, market schemes began to face the growth of planning schemes as an alternative economic system, as has been pointed out above. However, full central planning according to the socialist or communist blueprint was rejected out of hand by all Portuguese governments of the period.

Technological changes

The use of electricity spread during the wars and inter-war years. Higher demand stimulated the development of production methods other than the traditional coal-burning generators. Thus, hydro-electricity gradually assumed a fair share of electricity production in Portugal.

The 1930s saw a spurt in the use of machinery and fertilisers in agriculture, but technological and productivity backwardness persisted in Portuguese agriculture into the immediate post-Second World War years.

Cars and asphalt roads were the main novelty in transportation. Though private cars were rare in Portugal until the Second World War, the use of buses in passenger and commodity transportation was already quite common.

In the communications field, mention must be made of the spread of radio stations during the 1930s.

11.

The second epoch of growth 1947-1974

Between the late 1940s and the early 1970s the Portuguese economy went through a quarter century of uninterrupted growth, which began to close the gap with the most-developed countries, accumulated mainly during the first half of the 19th century and during the stagnation period of the early 20th century.

Section A explains how the Portuguese authoritarian regime was able to survive until 1974. Section B deals with the integration of the Portuguese economy in the new international economic order of the post-Second World War years. Section C turns to the economic policy of the period under consideration. Section D examines the changes associated with the definitive entry of Portugal in the era of modern economic growth.

A – Political evolution

The immediate post-war years

The defeat of the Italian, German and Japanese dictatorships in the Second World War and the absence of Portugal from most of the main international organisations formed immediately after the Second World War generated hopes among the Portuguese political opposition forces that the fall of the Portuguese authoritarian regime would soon follow. The immediate post-war years were politically unstable, with a United Democratic Movement (*MUD – Movimento de Unidade Democrática*) including the democratic republican and communist forces challenging the government.

As the American and British governments decided not to give any great support to the opposition forces, the MUD failed both in its attempts to force the government to organise free elections and in its attempts to prepare a military coup. By the late 1940s, the Portuguese political situation stabilised again. At the same time, Portugal began to take a normal part in international life: it participated in several international economic organisations and in the European economic integration process from the beginning, as explained in section B, below; it was one of the founding members of the North Atlantic Treaty Organization (NATO) in 1949 (it is worth recalling that the American armed forces already had a base in the Azores dating to the Second World War); and it became a member of the United Nations Organization (UNO) in 1955.

Colonial problems and the 1951 constitutional reform

As early as the late 1940s, Portugal began to feel the pressure of the 'winds of change' blowing for decolonisation.

The formal response of the Portuguese government was a constitutional reform in 1951: Angola, Cape Verde, Portuguese Guinea, Portuguese India, Macau, Mozambique, São Tomé e Príncipe and Portuguese Timor ceased to be considered as colonies and became overseas provinces, with special administrative and legal regimes, according to their particular situations.

For a while, these special administrative and legal regimes included the traditional discrimination of non-assimilated indigenous populations. However, ten years later all discrimination rules were abolished, as well. Every Portuguese citizen became formally entitled to the same rights and duties towards the state.

Early colonial losses

Of course, formal responses were unable to stem the tide. During the 1950s, the Portuguese territories in Africa saw the development of independence movements, and the Portuguese territories in India and the Far East were claimed by neighbouring countries (the Indian territories by India, Macau by China, and Timor by Indonesia).

The independent India emerging from the British withdrawal in 1947 was the first to present its claims to put an end to the French and Portuguese presence in some small territories in the Indian Peninsula. An agreement with France was reached and French territories were handed back to India by 1962, but Portugal refused to give up. The Indian reply was with force: in 1954, Dadrá and Nagar Aveli were occupied; and in December 1961, Goa, Damão and Diu also fell to Indian hands.

The story of the Portuguese relations with Dahomey (today Benin) pertaining to the fortress of São João Baptista de Ajudá (formally included in the province of São Tomé e Príncipe, but located on the coast of Dahomey) was very similar. Upon gaining its independence from France in 1961, Dahomey made diplomatic assertions to appropriate São João Baptista de Ajudá from Portugal without success. In August 1961, São João Baptista de Ajudá was occupied by force.

Macau and Timor weathered through these early problems. Both China and Indonesia had more pressing internal problems and foreign conflicts, and did not imitate the Indian conquest of Portuguese India.

Colonial war

Meanwhile, problems were on the rise in other parts of the Portuguese colonial empire. Revolts led by nationalist parties broke out in Angola (February-March 1961), in Portuguese Guinea (1962) and in Mozambique (1964). As a consequence, Portugal became involved in a three-front guerrilla war, in which it received no explicit support, except from South Africa (from the beginning) and from Rhodesia (following the 1965 unilateral declaration of independence). Communist countries and ex-colonies were, of course, clearly anti-Portuguese, and the main Portuguese allies in NATO were, at best, not hostile to the Portuguese position. Moreover, the informal Portuguese support of the Katanga secession from Congo (1961-1964), to the unilateral declaration of independence of Rhodesia (from 1965 on) and to the Biafra secession from Nigeria (1967-1970) did not help to generate a friendly international background.

As the nationalist movements were unable to control the towns or cut the main communication lines, and the Portuguese army was unable to destroy the bases of the nationalist movements in neighbouring countries and in rural areas, the situation became a military stalemate, which dragged on until 1974. The financial cost of the war amounted to around one fifth of all public expenditures. This was enough to jeopardise the traditional balancing of public finances as explained below, but not to put the Portuguese government in excessive difficulties. The human cost of the war was also not unbearable: total casualty figures amounted to around 10,000 men (nearly the same absolute figure as during the First World War, but five times less in relative terms, considering the increased population and the longer duration of the war). Moreover, the maintenance of Portuguese sovereignty had the support of some tribal groups and the population of European origin. It is true that efforts to stimulate emigration from Portugal to the Portuguese overseas territories to strengthen the position of the population of European origin had rather poor results, except in Angola, where the population of European origin was approaching 1 million in the early 1970s. In any event, the population of European origin controlled the economic and social life of Portuguese overseas provinces, and dreams of unilateral independence of the Rhodesian type even developed in Angola and Mozambique. However, the reality of the colonial war and the repression of free political organisation by the government prevented any clear move in that direction.

In 1973, the African Party for the Independence of Guinea and Cape Verde (*PAIGC – Partido Africano para a Independência da Guiné e Cabo Verde*) proclaimed the independence of Portuguese Guinea under the name of Guinea-Bissau. Though a significant part of the territory was already under the control of the PAIGC, the main towns were still under the control of the Portuguese authorities, and the government of the new state had to remain in Conakry in the neighbouring Republic of Guinea.

New internal problems

In the late 1950s and early 1960s there was fresh trouble in the internal political situation, mainly as a consequence of the colonial problems. Though the opposition forces, with the exception of the Communist Party, did not dare to support the independence of the African colonies, or the secession of the Asian colonies, these international problems were a tempting subject for political debate.

Dissidents from the regime joined the opposition in attacking the government. One of them, General Humberto Delgado challenged the government candidate, Admiral Américo Tomás, in the presidential election of 1958 and collected a remarkable 25% of the total vote (he claimed that his defeat was due to electoral fraud; this was true in the sense that free organisation and propaganda of opposition forces was always impossible between 1926 and 1974, but it is doubtful in regard to vote counting).

Others participated in attempts at military coups – the most important was supported, in 1961, by General Craveiro Lopes, former president between 1951 and 1958. However, Oliveira Salazar was able to foil all of these plots and remain in power until 1968.

In 1959, a constitutional reform replaced the direct election of the President by an indirect election by the members of the National Assembly and by representatives of the corporations, municipalities and overseas provinces, making a repetition of the events related to the 1958 presidential election impossible.

In 1966, a new Civil Code replaced the one of 1867. It made no significant changes in the property regime in the country.

Marcelo Caetano

In 1968, Oliveira Salazar became physically incapacitated and had to be replaced by Marcelo Caetano, a professor of the University of Lisbon who had been Minister of Colonies in the 1940s and Minister of Presidency in the 1950s. The new head of government immediately took some measures that seemed to promise a gradual liberalisation of the regime (incidentally, these included, for the first time in Portugal, the same voter eligibility requirements – namely literacy – for men and women). The National Union (*União Nacional*) that had been the political support of Oliveira Salazar was replaced by National Popular Action (*Acção Nacional Popular*) and opposition forces were given broader freedom of action, though not as formal political parties. Marcelo Caetano even tried in the constitutional reform of 1972 to take some steps towards a new approach to the colonial problem, by giving the overseas provinces the status of autonomous regions. However, the seemingly endless course of the colonial wars grew more and more unpopular, and the weight of the conservative forces put an end to all reformist trends. At the same time, most of the communist, socialist and liberal opposition forces formed the Portuguese Democratic Movement (*MDP – Movimento Democrático Português*) trying to profit from the creeping political tension.

The fall of the authoritarian regime

However, it was the use of Portuguese bases by the United States of America to supply Israel during the so-called Yom Kippur War in October 1973 that started the last scene of the last act. As a retaliation, Arab countries organised a boycott against Portugal, which was quite harmful to the oil supply of the country and created a wave of popular discontent paving the way for new attempts of military coups against the regime. The first one, on the 16th of March 1974, failed, but the second, on the 25th of April 1974, put an end to the longest European right-wing authoritarian regime of the 20th century.

Administrative changes

Concerning central administration, the main changes of the period under consideration were the creation of two new ministries, the Ministry of Health and the Ministry of Corporations and Social Security, both linked to the higher intervention of the government in the so-called social field. A new Ministry of Defence was also created to coordinate the activity of the three branches of the armed forces – the air force was separated from the army and the navy in the early 1950s.

In the area of local administration, there were no significant changes between the 1940s and the early 1970s.

B – European and worldwide economic links

The new international economic order of the post-Second World War period

Portugal was absent from the most important conferences that prepared the new international economic order of the post-Second World War period, namely from the 1944 Bretton Woods conference, which organised the new gold-exchange standard international monetary system and created the International Monetary Fund (IMF) and the International Bank for Reconstruction and Development (IBRD), and from the 1947 Geneva negotiations about international trade, which led to the General Agreement on Tariffs and Trade (GATT). Thus, Portugal did not become a member of the IMF, the IBRD, or the GATT during the 1940s.

The Marshall Plan, the OEEC and the EPU

Portugal was one of the European countries that accepted the American aid under the so-called Marshall Plan (Economic Cooperation Administration) in 1947. As a consequence, it became one of the founding members of the Organization for European Economic Cooperation (OEEC) in 1948 and of the clearing scheme of the European Payments Union (EPU) in 1950.

As the Portuguese economy had not suffered from war ravages and did not face serious external payments problems (see below), the amount of Marshall aid to Portugal was small. The country received only five loans from the American government in this context. These loans amounted to some 54 million dollars. Nearly 40 million dollars were invested in Portugal proper, while slightly more than 14 million dollars went toward investments in Mozambique.

Colonial links

The schemes of imperial preference and coordination of economic policies among Portugal and its colonies that already existed during the 1930s and the Second World War were maintained without significant changes until the early 1960s. Neither the GATT rules (which Portugal had not formally accepted), nor the incipient schemes of European integration prevented this situation.

Meanwhile, the international and local economic evolution had restored the economic interest in Portuguese colonies. This led to a return to the policy of public investment in the colonies that had existed until the mid-1920s and also to an increase of private Portuguese and foreign investments.

Balance of payments and exchange rate during the late 1940s and the 1950s

The Portuguese balance of payments deteriorated sharply in the immediate post-war years, but, by the late 1940s, the traditional picture had come back again: imports were clearly higher than exports, but emigrants' remittances and capital movements compensated the trade deficit on the average. Moreover, expenditures from foreign tourists also gradually grew into an important item of the balance of current accounts. As a consequence, Portugal was able to avoid following the depreciation of the British pound in 1949. The Portuguese monetary authorities opted for a smaller depreciation against the dollar, to the exchange rate of 1 American dollar = 28.75 Portuguese escudos.

The rough balance in external payments and the exchange rate stability continued during the 1950s.

European integration and the EFTA

In the late 1950s, the OEEC split into two trade blocs, the European Communities (ECSC – European Coal and Steel Community, Euratom – European Atomic Energy Community and EEC – European Economic Community, created during the 1950s by Belgium, France, the Federal Republic of Germany, Italy, Luxembourg and the Netherlands) and the European Free Trade Association (EFTA, created in 1959 by Austria, Denmark, Great Britain, Norway, Portugal, Sweden and Switzerland, later joined by Finland and Iceland), while Greece, Iceland, Ireland, Spain and Turkey remained outside both areas.

The Portuguese government decided to join the process of European economic integration in order to avoid possible problems with Portuguese exports that might arise from tariff policies of the European trading areas. The decision to join the EFTA bloc instead of the European Communities bloc was taken for three reasons. Firstly, the free trade zone rules of EFTA allowed the maintenance of the scheme of imperial preferences and the possible formation of another separate free trade zone including Portugal and its overseas provinces, while the customs union rules of the European Communities would prevent such situations. Secondly, there were some fears about the economic shock that might result from joining a customs union that included the most-developed European economies. As a matter of fact, even in the EFTA context, a special regime for delaying Portuguese tariff reduction until 1980 was designed, according to annex G of the Stockholm Convention. Thirdly, there were some suspicions about the non-economic, that is to say mainly political, goals of the European Communities, and about the changes they would bring to domestic political life.

The EMA and the OECD

The late 1950s and early 1960s also saw the reshuffling of the European institutions directly linked to the Marshall Plan. In 1958, the EPU gave way to the full convertibility scheme of the European Monetary Agreement (EMA). In 1961, the OEEC was transformed into the Organization for Economic Cooperation and Development (OECD), which now included non-European members, as well – Canada, the United States of America, and later also Japan, Australia and New Zealand. Portugal remained a member of both the EMA and the OECD.

The IMF, the World Bank and the GATT

In the early 1960s, the Portuguese government decided, at last, to link the country to the main world economic organisations. Thus, Portugal became a member of the IMF and the World Bank in 1961 and of the GATT in 1962.

This brought some changes in the monetary, financial and commercial situation of the country. In the monetary field, the exchange rate adopted in 1949 was to remain in force until 1971. In the financial field, the Portuguese government began to call for loans at the World Bank. The first one, in 1963, was loan 362 of IBRD, a 7.5 million dollar loan for a hydroelectric plant on the Douro. In the commercial field, Portugal remained a member of a free trade zone, the EFTA, in Europe and tried to convert the scheme of imperial preferences with its colonies into a Portuguese free trade zone.

The attempt of a Portuguese free trade zone and monetary union

In 1961, legislation to organise a free trade zone and a monetary union between Portugal and its overseas provinces was promulgated. According to this legislation, tariffs and quantitative restrictions to inter-territorial trade would be abolished through the end of 1971, though every territory maintained its own tariffs in trade with other countries. At the same time, a clearing system was set up to ensure a one-to-one parity between the monetary units of all parts of the country. Thus, the Portuguese escudo was the monetary unit in all parts of the Portuguese territory, but there were distinct monetary circulations, the Bank of Portugal (*Banco de Portugal*) being the issuing bank in Portugal, the Bank of Angola (*Banco de Angola*) the issuing bank in Angola and the National Overseas Bank (*Banco Nacional Ultramarino*) the issuing bank in the other overseas provinces. Moreover, current invisible transactions would be liberalised and all barriers to capital movements among the various territories would be abolished.

The whole scheme was a failure. Balance of payments deficits in the main overseas provinces prevented liquidation of inter-territorial payments at sight, and a list of priorities for liquidations was introduced, which, in effect, was nothing more than a multiple exchange rate in disguise. By the late 1960s the amount of delayed payments was becoming unbearable. At the same time, the traditional advantage for Portugal of low price imports of tropical commodities from its colonies was dwindling, because prices tended to fall in world markets, and, for political reasons, the Portuguese government dared not fully reproduce these falls in controlled transactions with overseas provinces. Moreover, Portuguese foreign trade tended to be more and more directed toward the most-developed countries (and to oil producers). As a matter of fact, these trade partners were already the traditional suppliers of the main Portuguese imports and provided more attractive markets for Portuguese exports than did its overseas provinces, because of their purchasing power.

Emigration during the 1960s and early 1970s

During the 1960s, there was a radical change in the traditional patterns of Portuguese emigration. Emigration from the continental part of the country to Brazil, which had recovered to some extent during the 1950s, almost disappeared, and vast numbers of Portuguese emigrants began to cross the Pyrenees, forming sizeable Portuguese communities in some of the most-developed European countries, especially France. In the early 1970s, net emigration peaked at its highest absolute values in the entire history of Portugal. Meanwhile, the traditional flows from Madeira to South America (especially to Venezuela) and from the Azores to the United States of America continued.

Balance of payments and exchange rate during the 1960s and early 1970s

During the 1960s and early 1970s, Portugal had no significant external payment problems. The deficit in the trade balance remained a permanent feature of the Portuguese economy, but this deficit was compensated by several net inflows, some of them quite traditional, others new or at least gaining a new dimension.

Emigrants' remittances remained the most important positive item in the balance of payments, because the increase in emigration figures brought an increase in emigrants' remittances.

Capital inflows also remained an important positive item. Public loans abroad increased: between 1962 and 1968, they amounted to nearly 300 million dollars in American and European markets, used mainly for investment in Portugal; between 1969 and 1974, they exceeded 600 million dollars, more than 500 million dollars being borrowed in European markets and used to finance the building of the Cabora Bassa hydroelectric plant in Mozambique. However, the bulk of capital inflows were private capital movements.

Last but not least, the tourist expenditure in the country also saw a very sharp upturn. It was now that the region of Algarve experienced its first tourist boom, joining Lisbon and Madeira as favoured regions for tourism, and Pope Paul VI also made a pilgrimage in 1967 to the sanctuary of Fátima in Ribatejo, putting it on the map of Catholic pilgrimages of worldwide reputation.

As a consequence of the surpluses in the balance of payments, the gold and exchange reserves of the Bank of Portugal grew in importance when compared to the economic dimension of the country. They climbed to nearly 1,000 metric tonnes of gold in the early 1970s.

Changes in the international background of the Portuguese economy in the early 1970s

The early 1970s saw significant changes in the international background of the Portuguese economy: the breakdown of the Bretton Woods gold-exchange standard international monetary system, the end of the free trade zone with the Portuguese colonies and the free trade agreement with the European Communities.

The breakdown of the Bretton Woods gold-exchange standard international monetary system

The immediate effect of the breakdown of the Bretton Woods gold-exchange standard international monetary system in 1971 was a slight appreciation of the Portuguese monetary unit, because of the balance of payments and gold and exchange reserves of the country, before the adoption of a floating-exchange-rates regime in 1973.

The end of the Portuguese free trade zone and monetary union

Because of the circumstances of the payments of the overseas territories, the 1961 legislation pertaining to the Portuguese free trade zone and monetary union was altered in 1971. Higher protection of the economies of the overseas provinces against Portuguese commodities was introduced in order to ease their balance of payments difficulties. As a consequence, there was a reduction of economic relations between Portugal and its colonies from 1972 on. These measures were formally transient, but the independence of the Portuguese colonies in the mid-1970s would make them definitive.

Free trade agreement with the European Communities

As two EFTA members, Great Britain and Denmark, left the organisation in 1973 to become members of the European Communities, together with Ireland (for a while there was also the expectation that a third EFTA member, Norway, would also leave the organisation and become a member of the European Communities), Portugal had to negotiate a free trade agreement with the European Communities to preserve its commercial links with its ex-EFTA partners. Such a treaty was signed in 1972 and entered into effect in 1973 when the enlargement of the European Communities took place.

C – Economic policy

As soon as the problems resulting from the Second World War ended, the Portuguese government tried to restore the main features of the internal economic policy of the 1930s. However, the changes in the international background and the very success of the process of economic growth brought several new and important factors into play during the 1960s and early 1970s.

Public accounts

During the 1950s current public accounts showed large surpluses, which financed most of the investment programmes to be described below. During the 1960s and early 1970s, in spite of a fiscal reform between 1958 and 1966, public accounts showed large deficits, mainly because of the increased expenditure due to the colonial wars. At the same time, the investment programmes were kept up, and education, health and social security increased their share of public expenditure.

The 1958-1966 fiscal reform

In a certain sense, the fiscal reform gradually enacted between 1958 and 1966 was a second version of the 1922 fiscal reform, which had been abrogated by the 1928-1929 fiscal reform.

Thus, in the realm of direct taxes, the main changes were related to the rules for calculating the taxable income, so that it might reflect current income and not normal income as before. The land tax (*contribuição predial*) on rural and urban property, the industrial tax (*contribuição industrial*) on profits, the capital income tax (*imposto de capitais*) on interests and bond and equity income, the professional tax (*imposto profissional*) on labour income, and the complementary tax (*imposto complementar*) on overall family and firm income remained the main direct taxes. A new tax on agricultural activities (*imposto sobre a indústria agrícola*) on profits of agricultural firms was created, but it was soon suspended, and the taxation of agricultural firms went on as before, mainly related to the land tax.

As for indirect taxes, most consumption taxes and several production taxes were repealed and a general transactions tax (*imposto de transacções*) was created.

There were also minor changes in the stamp tax (*imposto do selo*), in the excise (*sisa*) on property sales and on the inheritance and donation tax (*imposto de sucessões e doações*).

There were significant reductions in tariffs, mainly related to the GATT membership and the free trade zones already mentioned in section B.

Development plans

The investment plan of the law of economic reconstitution (see chapter 10 section D) ended in 1950. It was soon replaced by development plans, which were intended to coordinate the public investment plans and to build up a framework of indicative planning for the whole economy. These were: a First

Development Plan between 1953 and 1958; a Second Development Plan between 1959 and 1964; an Intermediate Development Plan between 1965 and 1967; and a Third Development Plan between 1968 and 1973. A Fourth Development Plan was prepared for the years between 1974 and 1979, but was discarded after the 1974 revolution.

The regional aspects of planning were considered in the Development Plans from their beginnings, but a formal regional division of the country for planning purposes was made for only the Third Development Plan, in the late 1960s. The continental part of the country was divided into four regions: the North (Entre-Douro-e-Minho and Trás-os-Montes) including the administrative districts of Braga, Bragança, Porto, Viana do Castelo and Vila Real; the Centre (Beira Litoral, Beira Alta and Beira Baixa) including the administrative districts of Aveiro, Castelo Branco, Coimbra, Leiria, Guarda and Viseu; Lisbon (Estremadura and Ribatejo) including the administrative districts of Lisbon, Santarém and Setúbal; and the South (Alentejo and Algarve) including the administrative districts of Beja, Évora, Faro and Portalegre. The archipelagoes of Madeira and the Azores, and each of the overseas provinces formed the other planning regions.

Public investment during the period under consideration was partly directed towards traditional public works and partially towards the formation of new enterprises together with private capitals.

In the area of traditional public works, the transportation sector was still the most important, and airports were the chief new developments in this field. In the continental part of the country, three main airports were built: one in Lisbon during the 1940s, another in Porto during the 1950s, and a third in Faro during the 1960s. The main airport of the archipelago of Madeira was built on the island of Porto Santo, because the hilly contours of the main island made a large airport prohibitively expensive. Of course, the existence of only a small airport remained a serious handicap for the main island and a reason for constant complaints.

The main airport of the Azores, which for a while played a very important role in trans-oceanic air transportation, was located on the island of Santa Maria (as a matter of fact, it was the military base built by the American air force during the Second World War, which was converted to civilian use after the war). São Miguel and Terceira, the main islands of the archipelago, also received smaller airports.

The road and railway networks and seaports also received some major improvements. In the road network, the most important additions were several new bridges over the main rivers, especially the bridge over the Tagus in Lisbon. A highway network was also begun during the 1950s, but even by the early 1970s little progress had been made. In the railway network, the most important innovation was the electrification of a second suburban line between Lisbon and Sintra and of the main line between Lisbon and Porto. Regarding seaports, the most important item was the beginning of a new sea port in Sines on the coast of Alentejo, linked with a project of an industrial hub including oil refining and chemical industries.

The other main public works included a few hydroelectric plants, which allowed a decrease in the share of imported fuels used in the power production for the continental part of the country, and several irrigation networks in the region of Alentejo.

The formation of new enterprises, together with private capitals, included a wide range of sectors. The Portuguese Air Transportation (*TAP – Transportes Aéreos Portugueses*), an air transportation company, the National Iron and Steel (*Siderurgia Nacional*), an iron and steel plant, the Lisbon Underground (*Metropolitano de Lisboa*), a company for electric underground urban transportation in Lisbon, and the Portuguese Television (*Radiotelevisão Portuguesa*), which received the monopoly for television broadcasting in the country, were perhaps the most important of these enterprises.

Another very important initiative was the creation of the National Development Bank (*Banco de Fomento Nacional*) with the resources provided by the Marshall loans used in investments in the continental part of the country. This was the origin of the first true investment bank in Portugal.

Industrial conditioning

Industrial conditioning, that is to say, the administrative control of the main investments outside agriculture remained in force. It had been created as a provisional system to face the hardships of the economic situation of the Great Depression, but, once adopted, tended to perpetuate. On one hand, as the established industries produced in an environment lacking competition, there were fewer stimuli to innovation, and the absence of competitivity was given as a justification for maintaining the conditioning. At the same time, political rhetoric justified the conditioning because of its appropriateness to the corporate state and of the need to fight anarchic competition.

An assessment of the role of industrial conditioning cannot be anything but negative. As it prevented the freedom of investment and enterprising capacity in several industrial sectors, the system was responsible for promoting a lack of technological modernisation and for preserving inefficient activities. It did this by disabling the mechanism of natural selection linked to the market context. In practice, it worked as a device to prevent competition in some key sectors of the economy, in which a few large financial and industrial groups began to develop (see below).

Industrial conditioning became expensive and harmful, as well, because of the growing number of applications, the bureaucratic apparatus needed to take decisions and the lack of capacity to police the system. As a matter of fact, the very economic and industrial growth and the process of European integration eroded its significance. In 1966, its scope was drastically reduced,

The Concise Economic History of Portugal: A Comprehensive Guide

and it disappeared in practice in the late 1960s, although it remained, formally, until 1974.

Education

The illiteracy rate continued to decline during the period under consideration. By the early 1970s the proportion of illiterate adult Portuguese was down to less than one fourth of the population. At the same time, compulsory education was increased from three to four years and later to six years, plans to create a secondary school in every municipality were put forward, and the number of state universities doubled: the Universities of Minho (located in Braga and Guimarães), Aveiro, Évora and the New University of Lisbon were added to the Universities of Coimbra, Lisbon, Porto, and Lisbon Tech. Of course, as in earlier periods of deep education reforms, all of these projects were slow in ironing out their problems.

The increased demand for education also led to a flourishing of private primary and secondary schools. In the early 1970s, even a private university, the Portuguese Catholic University (*Universidade Católica Portuguesa*) located in Lisbon and Braga was created.

Colonial economic and education policy

In addition to the imperial preference, the attempt at a free trade zone, the coordination of economic policies and the efforts to stimulate emigration to the Portuguese colonial empire already mentioned in sections A and B, above, mention must also be made of some public works in the colonies.

Main airports were built on the island of Sal in Cape Verde and in the capital cities of the mainland colonies – Bissau, Luanda and Lourenço Marques (today Maputo). Smaller airports were built in São Tomé and in other towns of Angola and

Mozambique – Nova Lisboa (today Huambo) and Beira. Other transportation facilities were also improved, though the colonial wars made internal communications in some zones of the three mainland African colonies rather precarious during the 1960s and early 1970s.

Huge hydroelectric plants were the other main effort of colonial authorities. Cambambe in Angola and Cabora Bassa in Mozambique were the most important of these hydroelectric plants.

The exploitation of the mineral wealth of the colonial empire now added crude oil to the rich resources found in Angola. However, oil exports from Angola were barely beginning when decolonisation came.

*

Investment in education was also important in the colonial empire, though illiteracy rates remained very high (more than 90% of adults were illiterate, except in Cape Verde, where the figure was only around 50%). The plan was to create a primary school in every civil parish and a secondary school in every small province and in every administrative district of the large provinces. Needless to say, the reality was still far off in the early 1970s (of course, the war in Angola, Portuguese Guinea and Mozambique did not help to improve the situation). Two universities were created, one in Angola, located partly in Luanda, partly in Nova Lisboa (today Huambo), partly in Sá da Bandeira (today Lubango), and another in Mozambique, located in Lourenço Marques (today Maputo).

D – The golden era of Portuguese economic growth

Population

Population growth decreased during the late 1940s and 1950s, because of the increase of emigration and the decrease in the birth rate, only slightly compensated by a decrease in the death rate. As a consequence, the number of people living in Portugal reached 9 million in the early 1960s.

During the 1960s and early 1970s the emigration boom even caused a slight population decrease – down to a figure of around 8.5 million in 1973.

Regional distribution of population

Trends of the distribution of the population by region during the period under consideration showed a marked change compared to the preceding periods. The south of Entre-Douro-e-Minho, the north of Beira Litoral and the Estremadura increased their weight in total population. The rest of the country, that is to say, most of the coast and the whole interior of the continental part of the country, and the Atlantic islands saw a decrease in their relative position. During the 1960s and early 1970s, even the absolute population of these regions decreased. This was a consequence of the concentration of the population and of economic activities in the neighbourhood of Lisbon and Porto.

Towns

Urban growth continued its rapid pace during the 1950s, 1960s and early 1970s: the weight of urban population in total population grew from around one fifth to around one fourth and the number of towns having more than 10,000 inhabitants increased by 50%.

The growth of Lisbon and Porto was faster than the growth of total urban population. Both cities swallowed a few more neighbouring zones and increased their population by around 50%, reaching 1.2 million inhabitants in the case of Lisbon and 400,000 in Porto. By the early 1970s, Braga, Coimbra and Setúbal in the continental part of the country and Funchal in Madeira were approaching a population of 50,000, and a few more towns in the continental part of the country (Aveiro, Covilhã, Évora, Faro, Guimarães and Póvoa de Varzim-Vila do Conde) and one in the Azores (Ponta Delgada) had exceeded the 20,000 mark.

Gross domestic product

Real gross domestic product grew at a yearly accumulated rate of 5.4% between 1947 and 1974. Moreover, not a single year in this period showed a negative figure for evolution of real gross domestic product.

The growth of real gross domestic product was clearly higher than the growth of population. This means that per capita gross domestic product also showed strong growth. The average standard of living in Portugal in the early 1970s was four times higher than in the late 1940s.

Thus, it is possible to say that, during the period under consideration, Portugal enjoyed its first epoch of indubitable modern economic growth. As a consequence, the gap towards the main economic powers of Europe and the world closed, though of course, the country lost ground to the new sprinters of growth, such as Japan.

Prices

The price level was rather stable during the late 1940s and 1950s and more than doubled during the 1960s and early 1970s. This stability, followed by an inflationary process, was driven mainly by the balance of payments, as the public deficits during the 1960s and early 1970s were financed by the issuing of public debt in the market and not by credit from the central bank.

At the same time, the use of demand deposits as a means of payment spread to the majority of the population.

Structural changes

Structural changes were, of course, in good evidence during a period of fast growth such as that between the Second World War and the mid-1970s.

In the distribution of labour force by sectors, there was a weighty decrease in the share of agriculture, from nearly one half to around one third, and significant increases in industry and services, from around one fourth to about one third each.

In the distribution of value added by sectors, there was a sharp decrease in the share of agriculture, from around one third to less than one fifth, and significant increases in industry and services, from around one third to more than two fifths each.

To sum up, industrialisation and tertiarisation went hand in hand during this period of modern economic growth in Portugal, while the primary sector experienced a relative decline. Both industry and services posted average yearly rates of growth above 6.0%, while agriculture presented an average yearly rate of growth below 3.5%.

*

Disaggregation of the output from agriculture leads to the conclusion that the output of fruits, vegetables and animal products grew at a rate above the average, that the wine output grew at more or less the same as the average and that the cereal output grew below the average. Such structural changes were the consequence of an allocation of resources resulting mainly from higher exposure of the Portuguese producers of agricultural commodities to the competition and stimuli of external markets.

In the fruits and vegetables sector, the main impetus came from the demand from European markets and from the rise in the standard of living of the Portuguese population. The rise of tomato production in the newly-irrigated areas of Alentejo and Ribatejo, stimulated by the demand from EFTA countries, and the development of a cooperative movement among milk and milk derivatives producers in Estremadura, Alentejo, Beira Litoral and Entre-Douro-e-Minho, to supply the increased demand of the domestic market, are illustrative cases.

In the wine sector, the combined action of the government department for the sector and of the cooperative movement brought some technological progress and quality control. However, the contrast between a small production of high quality to be exported to European and American markets, and a huge production of low quality finding its outlets in the domestic and colonial markets did not disappear.

In the cereal sector, protection from foreign competition decreased but did not disappear. Thus, domestic production with higher costs than imported cereals continued, though losing some relative importance.

*

Disaggregation of the product of industry shows that the chemical and engineering sectors were the most active, while the traditional cork and canned fish sectors stagnated in relative terms, and the textile sector even lost ground in relative terms. Building, public works and energy production also showed some spirit, resulting from urbanisation, public works programmes, an increase in economic activity in general and improvement in the standards of living.

Aircraft and ship repair were the most active sub-sectors in the engineering sector. Portugal was able to profit from its geographic position and from the natural conditions of the region of Lisbon to earn a strong position in these markets.

Oil refining, fertilisers and artificial fibres were the most active sub-sectors in the chemical sub-sector. The region of Lisbon was also the main centre of these industries in the country.

In spite of its relative decline, the textile sector remained the main industrial sector of the country. The main textile industries became concentrated in the region of Porto and were able to profit from the low cost of labour, tariff reductions and technological improvements to increase market quotas in several European countries.

*

Disaggregation of the output of the services sector shows that modern sectors, such as transportation, communications, trade, education, health and public administration were more active than traditional personal services. Tourism was also a very busy sector.

*

During the period under consideration, market schemes continued to face ever more planning schemes as an alternative economic system. Of course, full central planning according to the socialist or communist blueprint was out of the question, but indicative planning progressed in scope and refinement.

Economic groups

Large financial and industrial groups developed in the Portuguese economy during the period under consideration. Two of them had their roots in successful industrial activities of the first half of the 20th century. This was the case of the so-called CUF group (see chapter 9), which originated in the entrepreneurial activities of Alfredo da Silva and his heirs, and of the so-called Champalimaud group (see chapter 10), which emerged from the entrepreneurial activities of Henrique Sommer and António Champalimaud. Others had their roots in commercial banks that began spreading into the entire financial sector and to industrial activities. The most important was perhaps the so-called Espírito Santo group, centred around the bank with the same name.

Technological change and scientific research

Domestic scientific research never played an important role in the technological changes that came to the Portuguese economy. Technological changes during the period under consideration were the result of the spread of innovations occurring abroad, as during the 19th and 20th centuries in general. An interesting indicator of the level of Portuguese scientific research in an international context is the fact that only one Portuguese scientist has ever been awarded a Nobel prize – Egas Moniz, in the field of physiology and medicine, in 1949.

Mechanisation and the use of fertilisers spread through Portuguese agriculture during the period of consideration. Together with the irrigation schemes in some regions of Alentejo and Ribatejo, these improvements allowed some increase in productivity, which, however, remained far below the average European standards.

At the same time, oil and hydroelectric plants became the main power sources. In spite of being a uranium producer, Portugal did not use nuclear technology for economic goals (or for military purposes).

Social movements

In spite of the absence of a free trade union movement and of the weight of agriculture in the economy, the social security schemes were greatly improved and began to cover the majority of the population.

Ecological problems

It is worth noting that urban growth and industrial development brought the first serious pollution problems in the country to the region of Lisbon. Though the windy climate prevented much air pollution, water pollution at the mouth of the Tagus became very serious. As a consequence, beaches ceased to be a main tourist attraction in the region, as they had been before, and tourism in Lisbon had to rely more heavily upon the historical and cultural attractions of the city.

At the same time, the first national park of the country, the National Park of Peneda-Gerês, was created in 1972. It included an area of around 700 square km in the eastern part of Entre-Douro-e-Minho, and in the northwestern part of Trás-os-Montes, near the Spanish border. (Another national park, the National Park of Gorongoza, had also been created in the central part of Mozambique.)

12.

The last quarter of the 20th century and the early 21st century

The beginning of the last quarter of the 20th century saw the end of the uneasy compromise between colonial empire and European integration that had characterised the Portuguese society during the third quarter of the 20th century. Decolonisation and later integration in what is today the European Union were the solutions to the dilemma. At the same time, the authoritarian political regime that supported the compromise was replaced by a typical democratic regime, after a rather unquiet transition period between 1974 and 1976. This transition period will be dealt with in section A of this chapter.

Sections B to D deal with the gradual deepening of Portugal's integration in the European Union. Section B considers the period before membership between 1976 and 1985. Section C describes the transition period until full integration in the economic union in 1993. Section D explains how Portugal came to be a member of the monetary union in 1999. Section E explores the consequences of membership of the economic and monetary union during the early 21st century.

An assessment of the long-term effects of this evolution is presented in section F.

A – The transition period, 1974-1976

Social and political upheavals

After the military revolution of the 25th of April, 1974, the officers that formed the Armed Forces Movement (*MFA – Movimento das Forças Armadas*) replaced the President of the Republic, the government and the parliament by a military National Salvation Committee (*Junta de Salvação Nacional*) headed by General António Spínola, who became the new President of the Republic. The National Popular Action (*Acção Nacional Popular*) that had been the political backbone of Marcelo Caetano (see chapter 11) was outlawed, and the so-called corporative organisations (see chapter 10) that had existed during the authoritarian regime were gradually dismantled or reorganised as elements of the state apparatus.

The new military authorities also lifted all restrictions on trade union and political organisation that had existed for nearly five decades. Social and political forces that had been repressed by the authoritarian regime were soon formed or emerged from underground.

The trade union movement was completely reorganised on a sector basis instead of along professional lines. A trade union confederation, the General Confederation of Portuguese Workers (*CGTP – Confederação Geral dos Trabalhadores Portugueses*) was also created. Claims for higher wages and strikes to support these claims spread all over the country, especially in the industrial zones of Lisbon and Porto. There followed an abrupt rise in nominal wages that jeopardised the financial stability of many firms.

There were, for a while, more than twenty political parties in activity. However, only four of them were to play a decisive role in later events. They were, from left to right: the Portuguese Communist Party (*PCP – Partido Comunista Português*), a thoroughly traditional communist force, well rooted in the rural areas of Alentejo and in the industrial zones of the country; the Socialist Party (*PS – Partido Socialista*), a member of the Socialist International, especially strong in urban areas and among workers of the services sector; the Popular Democratic Party (*PPD – Partido Popular Democrático*), later renamed Social Democratic Party (*PSD – Partido Social-Democrata*), a liberal group, especially strong in the rural areas of the north of the country and in Madeira and the Azores; and the Democratic and Social Centre (*CDS — Centro Democrático e Social*), later renamed Popular Party (*PP – Partido Popular*), a christian democratic group, especially strong in the rural areas of the north of the country.

In May 1974 a provisional government was formed, including representatives of the Communist, Socialist and Popular Democratic Parties, and of the Portuguese Democratic Movement, which had existed during the late years of the authoritarian regime as an alliance of most of the political forces opposed to the authoritarian regime (see chapter 11).

The first provisional government was short lived. In July, a conflict between most of the officers of the Armed Forces Movement and the President led to the formation of a second provisional government, which included a few officers of the armed forces and representatives of the same political forces that had made up the informal coalition of the first provisional government.

This was not to the taste of the President. An attempt to take control of the situation was made in September, and ended with a second triumph of the revolutionary officers. António Spínola was replaced by General Costa Gomes as President, and a third provisional government was formed along the same lines as the second.

The supporters of António Spínola tried to take over by force in March 1975. They were defeated and the political situation fell under the control of the communists and groups of the extreme left, in spite of the fact that the fourth provisional government, formed after the defeat of the coup, still included the usual socialist and popular democratic participation, together with the communists, the members of the Portuguese Democratic Movement and the revolutionary officers. The National Salvation Committee was replaced by a Supreme Revolution Council (*Conselho Superior da Revolução*), which was under the control of the revolutionary officers.

There followed a few radical measures: the banking and insurance sectors and the main industrial, transportation and communication firms were nationalised; the latifundia of Alentejo and Ribatejo were expropriated and collective production units, usually controlled by the Communist Party, were formed in the expropriated lands; the trade union confederation, CGTP, also under communist control, was given a legal monopoly of the workers' representation; and many private firms were subject to state intervention without formal nationalisation.

However, the elections held in April 1975 for a constitutional assembly gave a majority to the socialists and the popular democrats, and these parties claimed an increased role in government decisions. There followed some months of slowly-building tension, with the Armed Forces Movement divided into three groups: the supporters of the extreme left, the supporters of the Communist Party, and the moderates, akin to the Socialist and Popular Democratic Parties. In August the supporters of the Communist Party imposed a fifth provisional government, without formal participation of the political parties. This meant the exclusion of the non-communist groups from power. In September it was the turn of the moderates to impose a sixth provisional government, which was again a communist – socialist – popular democratic coalition with some role for the armed forces officers. In November the extreme left attempted a takeover by force and failed. As the Communist Party chose not to support the coup and to accept the leadership of the moderate group of the Armed Forces Movement, the sixth provisional government was able to go on in office until the new constitutional text was ready.

Decolonisation

Meanwhile, decolonisation had been carried out. After the 1974 revolution, the occupations of the Portuguese Indian territories by India and of São João Baptista de Ajudá by Benin were recognised, and negotiations with the independence movements to grant full independence to the African colonies got under way. In the cases of Portuguese Guinea, Cape Verde, Mozambique and São Tomé e Príncipe the transition was rather easy, because there was only one independence movement and almost no one challenged its transition into the new government. Thus, the independence of Guinea-Bissau was formally recognised in September 1974 under the control of the African Party for the Independence of Guinea and Cape Verde (*PAIGC – Partido Africano para a Independência da Guiné e Cabo Verde*), Cape Verde became independent in July 1975 under the control of the same PAIGC, Mozambique became independent in July 1975 under the control of the Mozambique Liberation Front (*FRELIMO – Frente de Libertação de Moçambique*), and São Tomé e Príncipe became independent in July 1975 under the control of the Liberation Movement of São Tomé e Príncipe (*MLSTP – Movimento de Libertação de São Tomé e Príncipe*). The case of Angola was more complicated, because there were three competing independence movements: the National Front for the Liberation of Angola (*FNLA – Frente Nacional de Libertação de Angola*), the People's Movement for the Liberation of Angola (*MPLA – Movimento Popular de Libertação de Angola*), and the National Union for Total Independence of Angola (*UNITA – União Nacional para a Independência Total de Angola*). In January 1975 an agreement between the Portuguese government and the three independence movements was signed. According to it, general elections would be held during 1975 and Angola would become independent in November 1975. However, a civil war between the MPLA and a FNLA-UNITA alliance broke out before the general elections could be held. Portugal was socially and politically exhausted by the previous colonial war and received almost no help from the international community to cope with the situation. After some unsuccessful attempts to restore peace, the Portuguese authorities abandoned the territory in November as had been earlier agreed. Thus, Angola became independent, but entered a period of protracted civil war.

There remained only the cases of Macau and Portuguese Timor. Macau was recognised as Chinese territory in 1974, though an agreement for implementing a Chinese administration was not reached until 1987. According to this agreement, Portugal remained the administrating power until 1999. Then, Macau became an autonomous region of China, a situation that, according to the 1987 agreement, shall be maintained at least until 2049. In Timor a civil war broke out in 1975 between the supporters of the integration with Indonesia and the supporters of the independence of the territory, and the situation became similar to that in Angola. As the Portuguese authorities lost control of the situation, Indonesia occupied the territory in December 1975. Occupation was followed by annexation, which was not recognised by Portugal or the United Nations, and attempts to crush the independence movement, which were not successful. In 1999, Indonesia had to accept a referendum, which revealed an overwhelming majority in favour of independence, and administration was turned over to the United Nations. East Timor became independent in 2002.

Economic consequences of decolonization

Decolonisation had three main economic consequences for Portugal. Firstly, more than half a million refugees fled from overseas provinces (mainly from Angola) to Portugal, creating very great short-term economic and social hardship. Secondly, trade and other economic relations between Portugal and its former empire plummeted. Thirdly, the Portuguese government remained involved in the property and management of the

Cabora Bassa hydroelectric plant in Mozambique. This was important as a pledge to the foreign debt issued to finance the building of the plant, but proved ruinous. A civil war broke out in Mozambique between the government and the Mozambican National Resistance (*RENAMO* – *Resistência Nacional Moçambicana*), an opposition movement supported by Rhodesia and South Africa, disrupting the functioning of the plant and the distribution of the energy it produced.

Geo-political consequences of decolonization

In a wider perspective, Portuguese decolonisation had some important geo-political consequences. First of all, it was harmful to the apartheid regime of Rhodesia, to the South African occupation of South-West Africa (today Namibia), and to the apartheid regime of South Africa, in spite of a significant emigration of refugees from Angola and Mozambique to South Africa, which reinforced the weight of the white community in this country. Secondly, it put the bulk of the former Portuguese colonial empire under the control of political regimes supported by the Soviet Union, a situation that would last until the late 1980s.

The Constitution of 1976

The Constitutional Assembly was able to bring its task to an end in April 1976. The Constitution of 1976 organised a semi-presidential and semi-parliamentary regime, in which a President of the Republic (*Presidente da República*) and an Assembly of the Republic (*Assembleia da República*) were both elected by direct and universal suffrage, and jointly controlled the government. The military Revolution Council (*Conselho da Revolução*) was retained as something of a constitutional court for a transition period of four years. At the same time, the archipelagoes of Madeira and the Azores became autonomous regions with local parliaments and governments.

The new Constitution included many rules about economic life. Firstly, it proclaimed an ill-defined socialism as the ultimate stage of the Portuguese social evolution. Secondly, it confirmed the agrarian reform (that is to say, land expropriation and the existence of collective production units in Alentejo and Ribatejo) and the nationalisation of large enterprises and of the key sectors of the economy as definitive features of the Portuguese economy. Thirdly, a scheme of short-term yearly plans and medium-term four-year plans was organised. These plans would be imperative for the public sector and indicative for the private sector. Last but not least, an extensive list of economic and social rights, including trade union freedom, protection against unjustified dismissal, and plans for government-provided services, such as education and health, were included as more or less immediate goals of political action.

The new Constitution was voted in by a clear majority of the Constitutional Assembly, which included the communist, socialist and popular democratic parties. However, it soon became a bone of contention, as the Popular Democratic Party changed its position, and became critical of the constitutional text, together with the Democratic and Social Centre, which voted against it in the Constitutional Assembly.

The economic crisis

Besides social and political upheavals, decolonisation and attempts at structural economic reforms, the transition period also witnessed a sharp downturn in the short-term situation of the Portuguese economy. Firstly, the combined effects of the first oil crisis and of the nominal wage rise brought about the first serious recession since the Second World War and an acceleration of inflation. Secondly, the end of the huge emigration movement to European countries and the inflow of refugees from the former Portuguese colonies, together with the economic recession, led to soaring unemployment. Lastly, short-term disturbances in the emigrants' remittances and in the tourist flow, due to the unstable situation of the country, combined to worsen the situation in the balance of payments, already shaken by the impact of the first oil shock on imports and the unfavourable international short-term situation on the exports.

Moreover, it is important to underscore that the presence of around half a million refugees from the African colonies (more than 5% of the population) threatened to escalate into an explosive social situation.

B – Towards the European Communities, 1976-1985

Relations with the European Communities

As privileged relations with the former overseas possessions had been severed by the decolonization process and the upheavals of the transition period had been overcome, soon the Portuguese governments were to sort out a new basis for the relations between Portugal and the European Communities. The free trade treaty of 1972 was upgraded to an association treaty in 1976, and an application for full membership was presented in 1977.

Negotiations for membership dragged on, mostly because the Portuguese case had to be dealt with at the same time as the more difficult (for size reasons) Spanish case. Hopes that full membership could materialise in the early 1980s were disappointed, although a substantial pre-accession aid compensated the country for the delay.

In 1985, however, an agreement was at last hammered out. Transition periods lasting until the early or mid-1990s were agreed upon for the many aspects of the integration of the Portuguese economy into that of the Communities. Thus, Portugal left EFTA and became a member of the European Communities on the 1st of January 1986.

Political evolution

The first parliamentary elections of the new constitutional period were held in April 1976 with results that were quite similar to those of 1975. In June General Ramalho Eanes, leader of the faction that had suppressed the leftist coup of November 1975, was elected President with the support of all main political forces except the communists. In July, the socialist leader Mário Soares was able to form the first constitutional government of the new regime, a socialist government with minority support in parliament.

At the same time, the first regional elections were held in Madeira and the Azores. The Popular Democratic Party won majorities in both regions. Thus, the local popular democratic leaders became the leaders of the regional governments.

The first socialist government fell in December 1977, when it failed a parliamentary vote of confidence, but Mário Soares was able to form a second constitutional government of an informal socialist – christian democrat coalition. This one, too, was short lived, however, and its fall in August 1978 paved the way for a period of governments without formal participation of the political parties, based mainly on presidential support. These governments were no more stable than the socialist ones. The first one, headed by Nobre da Costa, was rejected by the parliament and remained in office for only three months. The second, headed by Mota Pinto, was able to survive only until the summer of 1979. The third, headed by Lourdes Pintasilgo, was a transition government formed only to organise general elections.

For the 1979 general elections, the popular democrats (who had already changed their name to social democrats) and the christian democrats made a formal coalition, the Democratic Alliance (*AD – Aliança Democrática*), which succeeded in winning a parliamentary majority. The social democrat leader, Sá Carneiro, became the new Prime Minister, and there followed a year of bitter conflict between the government and the President, as

Ramalho Eanes refused to remain a passive partner of the new government majority. New parliamentary and presidential elections were held in 1980, and, to the surprise of many, these elections brought no change through ballot: the parliamentary elections were won by the same social democrat – christian democrat coalition, and once again Ramalho Eanes won the presidential seat, in spite of the fact that the parliamentary majority supported another candidate. However, Sá Carneiro died in a plane crash two days before the presidential election (some of his supporters spoke of foul play, and the whole issue has remained cloudy until this day).

The new leader of the Social Democratic Party and of the Democratic Alliance coalition, Pinto Balsemão, was able to avoid further tension between the government and the President, but was less skilful at dealing with internal coalition problems and the economic situation. He had to reshuffle his government as early as 1981 and the alliance was unable to survive a defeat in the municipal elections of 1982. New parliamentary elections were held in early 1983 with results very similar to those of 1975 and 1976.

The socialist leader, Mário Soares, became Prime Minister again, but decided not to form a minority government. Socialists and social democrats (now headed by Mota Pinto) made a coalition government, which was able to carry the negotiations for membership in the European Community all the way through, and to redress the economic situation of the country between 1983 and 1985, though at the cost of growing unpopularity of the coalition leaders. After some internal problems in the Social Democratic Party, its new leader, Cavaco Silva, broke the coalition and forced the President to call for new parliamentary elections.

Administrative reforms

The division of functions and fiscal revenue between the central government and the regional governments of Madeira and the Azores was one of the main concerns of the new authorities. Extensive powers in most fields of government action were given to regional governments. Only foreign relations, defence, general tax collection and economic policy were withheld from the powers of regional governments. The bulk of the fiscal revenue obtained in Madeira and the Azores was left to the regional governments' control.

Plans for new administrative regions in the continental part of the country have been put forward without success. In practice, the planning regions created in the late 1960s gradually became the regional background for economic policy. The map of planning regions underwent some changes during the 1970s and 1980s: the region of the South was divided into two, Alentejo and Algarve; the region of Lisbon became known as Lisbon and Tagus Valley; and several municipalities were transferred from one region to another. Of course, the archipelagoes of Madeira and the Azores remained separate planning regions.

At the same time, municipalities acquired several new functions and also hefty additional revenue: the land tax became revenue of the municipalities, and systematic transfers from central government according to the population, area and degree of development were given to them.

Economic legislation

The first socialist government tried to stabilise the institutional background of Portuguese economic life with a few fundamental laws about the main reforms made during the transition period.

In the agrarian reform, the main goals were to confirm the legal situation of land ownership and to force the collective production units controlled by the Communist Party to acknowledge the public ownership of the land by rent payments. Though a new law of agrarian reform was passed (1977), none of the existing problems were solved, because the former landowners claimed the devolution of their property and the Communist Party did not fully accept the limitations to the action of the collective production units imposed by the law.

Regarding the nationalisation of industrial and services firms, the main goals were to decide which sectors of the economy should be excluded from private initiative and to implement proper management schemes in public firms. A law of delimitation attributing the sectors of banking, insurance, television, radio, air and railway transportation, ports and some industrial branches to public enterprises (except in some cases of foreign or small firms) was passed (1977). Once more, stabilisation did not materialise – this time because private entrepreneurs were not happy being pushed out of so many profitable activities. At the same time, a reorganisation of the public enterprises sector was made in order to improve its efficiency, with mixed results. As a matter of fact, some enterprises (mainly in the industrial sector) were able to achieve good economic results, but others (mainly in the services sector) were used as a device to provide cheap services for political and social purposes and were unable to attain financial stability. Moreover, intervention in firms not formally nationalised was gradually brought to an end.

A decision about payments for land and firm nationalisations was also reached in 1977. The usual complaints about unfair indemnities arose.

As for trade unions, the legal monopoly of the General Confederation of Portuguese Workers ended. After some quarrels between communist, socialist and social democratic trade union leaders, a second trade union confederation, the General Union of Workers (*UGT – União Geral de Trabalhadores*) was created, mainly by trade unions led by socialist and social democrat leaders. The General Confederation of Portuguese Workers became mainly a communist confederation.

At the same time, firm confederations also developed. The Confederation of Portuguese Agriculture (*CAP – Confederação da Agricultura Portuguesa*), the Confederation of Portuguese Industry

(*CIP – Confederação da Indústria Portuguesa*), and the Confederation of Portuguese Commerce (*CCP – Confederação do Comércio Português*) were the most important, although a Portuguese Industrial Association (*AIP – Associação Industrial Portuguesa*) that already existed before 1974, and several other agricultural associations also played some role in economic and social conflicts.

Constitutional reform and institutional changes

The Constitution of 1976 was amended in 1982. Besides the replacement of the military Revolution Council by a normal Constitutional Court (*Tribunal Constitucional*) and some reduction in the control of the President over the government, no major changes occurred. The constitutional economic rules in particular remained unchanged in their main aspects.

However, there followed several important changes in the institutional background of economic life. Earlier rules dividing the public and private sectors were relaxed, and private firms were allowed to compete with public enterprises in most sectors, while a private financial sector began to flourish. The governments of the Democratic Alliance also tried to divide part of the nationalised land in the south of the country into small private holdings without much success. Wider definition of grounds for dismissal and lay-off schemes were established by the socialist – social democratic coalition in an effort to add some flexibility to the rules pertaining to labour. In 1985, house rents in the main towns, which had been frozen since the 1940s seriously impairing the rental housing market, were also allowed to increase according to yearly indexes to be established by the government.

Short-term economic evolution

The short-term evolution of the Portuguese economy during the years between the end of the transition period to a democratic political regime and membership of the European Communities was characterized by sharp fluctuations, resulting from the impact of the oil shocks and of domestic economic policy.

Between mid-1976 and early 1977, economic policy gave priority to social stabilisation, especially to the integration in the Portuguese society of the refugees from the African colonies, mainly by means of the absorption of many in the public administration and public enterprises, of job creation, and of subsidies and other support promoting their own economic activities. This priority implied an expansionist policy, which started growth in internal demand and a recovery of the level of economic activity, but brought higher public deficits, higher public debt, higher inflation, and greater foreign payments problems.

From early 1977 on, priority was given to overcoming the serious foreign payments problems created by the economic crisis of the transition period and by the expansionist policies pursued during the preceding months. A first devaluation of the Portuguese escudo occurred in February 1977 and a few months later Portugal asked, for the first time, for financial and technical assistance from the IMF. This called for implementing the anti-inflationary measures that had become the standard prescription of the IMF. The so-called austerity programme implemented during the second half of 1977 included a reduction of the public deficit and a crawling peg devaluation of the Portuguese escudo. It was rather successful from an economic point of view, and the Portuguese economy was able to overcome its foreign payments problems during the late 1970s. However, the unpopularity of these types of economic measures led to the fall of the first (socialist) constitutional government, and to a period of political instability with four governments between 1977 and 1979, as explained above.

The first Democratic Alliance government tried to take advantage of the economic stabilisation of the late 1970s to come back to an expansionist economic policy in 1980. Public expenditure increased and the Portuguese escudo was revalued in the spring of 1980 to curb inflation, though the crawling peg devaluation went on as usual. This was quite convenient as a lead-in to the parliamentary and presidential elections to be held during the autumn of that year, but was also quite dangerous considering the threats arising from the second oil crisis. The economic results proved disastrous in the medium term. Moreover, 1981 was a year of drought, which brought great harm to agriculture and hydroelectric production. Furthermore, the revaluation of the dollar and the rise of interest rates in international money markets during the early 1980s served to worsen the situation in foreign payments. The economic situation of the country thus deteriorated between 1980 and 1983. These years were characterised by stagnation in the level of economic activity, huge deficits in the balance of payments and higher inflation.

A second wave of financial and technical help from the IMF, and a second austerity programme had to be sought and implemented by the socialist – social democratic coalition between 1983 and 1985. Once again, the stabilisation programme was beneficial from an economic standpoint: the foreign payments problem was brought under control in 1984, economic growth resumed in 1985, and only the persistence of high inflation spoiled the picture. However, austerity was harmful for the popularity of the government, as the results of the 1985 parliamentary election showed.

This period also saw the suspension of investment in the so-called industrial hub of Sines (see chapter 11, above), one of the main projects of the early 1970s, and which takes its place as one of the most unprofitable undertakings of recent decades in Portugal.

C – Towards European economic union, 1985-1992

Relations with the European Community

Soon after the integration of Portugal and Spain, the European Communities agreed upon the so-called Single Act. This treaty merged the three European Communities (ECSC, Euratom and EEC) that had resulted from the formation process in the 1950s into one single European Community, and scheduled the establishment of the economic union among its member states, with free circulation of goods, people and capitals, for 1993.

The late 1980s and early 1990s witnessed the collapse of the communist political regimes and centrally planned economies of Central and Eastern Europe that dated back to the 1940s. This implied a further enlargement of the European Community, which did not consist in the integration of a new member, but in the enlargement of a member state – the absorption of the former German Democratic Republic by the Federal Republic of Germany – and the association of most former communist countries with the European Community with a view to the future integration into the Community itself.

At the same time, negotiations were held which led to the Maastricht Treaty. This treaty created the European Union, by adding two areas of intergovernmental cooperation – external and security policy, and internal affairs and justice – to the European Community. It also included provisions for a monetary union among those member states that could comply with several nominal convergence criteria. These criteria involved low inflation, low interest rates, stable exchange rates and absence of excessive deficits in public accounts or excessive public debt. The monetary union was to be completed in several phases, ending no later than 1999.

Portugal reacted to these transformations of the European Community, which coincided with the transition periods agreed upon for the integration of the Portuguese economy into that of the Community, by trying to keep pace with all developments, and especially to participate in the monetary union from its beginnings. This means that all transition periods were respected (and even sometimes shortened) and that efforts to comply with the nominal convergence criteria were already underway in the early 1990s.

Political evolution

In the 1985 parliamentary elections, the Social Democratic Party came out on top with around 30% of the votes, while the traditional electorate of the Socialist Party split among the socialists, which received only around 20%, and a new Democratic Renovator Party (*PRD – Partido Renovador Democrático*), indirectly headed by Ramalho Eanes, which took more than 15% of the votes. The social democratic leader, Cavaco Silva, was able to form a minority government with the tacit parliamentary support of the Democratic Renovator Party.

However, the social democrats and the democratic renovators were unable to join forces in the 1986 presidential election, allowing victory to go to the socialist leader, Mário Soares. There were fears of renewed tension between the President and the government, but this was not the case. Mário Soares supported the government, and when the democratic renovators joined the socialists to force the government to resign in 1987, he called for new parliamentary elections. These gave the social democrats a parliamentary majority, throwing all the other parties into internal crises until the early 1990s. Thus, Cavaco Silva was able to form a stable government for four years, to support the re-election of Mário Soares as President of the Republic in 1991, and to win a new parliamentary majority in the same year.

Constitutional reform and institutional changes

The Constitution of 1976 was amended again in 1989. This time, political changes were minor, but economic rules underwent profound transformations. Socialism ceased to be proclaimed as the ultimate stage of the Portuguese social evolution, and the agrarian reform and nationalisation of large enterprises and key sectors of the economy ceased to be considered as definitive features of the Portuguese economy.

Even before this constitutional reform, the social democratic government had started the process of privatisation of the expropriated land and public enterprises.

In the case of the expropriated land, privatisation meant giving the land back to its former owners. The resistance of the communist-led collective production units dwindled as the Communist Party itself was weakened by the international evolution of the late 1980s, and the process was complete by the early 1990s.

In the case of public enterprises, privatisation meant equity sales in the market. This was a slow process, because of the need to avoid market saturation, and it was finished only in the early 21st century. There was no systematic policy concerning the problems of nationality or concentration of buyers. Thus, privatisation of public enterprises allowed the penetration of foreign groups into the Portuguese economy, the formation or consolidation of several Portuguese economic groups and some diffusion of stock in the Portuguese middle class.

At the same time, a Social Concert Council (*Conselho de Concertação Social*) was created for regular negotiation of economic and social issues among the government, trade union confederations and firm confederations.

Fiscal reform

The late 1980s witnessed an important fiscal reform that made the Portuguese fiscal system similar to the typical fiscal system of other members of the European Community. In 1986, the transactions tax and several other indirect taxes were replaced by a tax on value added (*IVA – imposto sobre o valor acrescentado*). In 1989, the taxes on different types of income and the complementary tax were replaced by an income tax (*imposto sobre o rendimento*), which included two sections, one on family income (*IRS – imposto sobre o rendimento das pessoas singulares*), the other on collective entity income (*IRC – imposto sobre o rendimento das pessoas colectivas*). Several consumption taxes (the main one on oil derivatives), the stamp tax (*imposto do selo*), the excise (*sisa*) on property sales, and the tax on donations and inheritances (*imposto sobre sucessões e doações*) were retained as the other mainstays of the Portuguese fiscal system. The land tax was replaced as the main fiscal resource of the municipalities by a tax on property value, called local tax (*contribuição autárquica*).

Economic growth during the late 1980s

The success of the stabilisation policies pursued between 1983 and 1985, the short-term effect of the dollar devaluation, the impact of falling interest rates in international money markets and the long-term effect of integration in the European Community combined to produce a marked economic growth, a reduction of inflation, and the end of the problems in foreign payments in Portugal during the late 1980s. Naturally, this situation contributed decisively to securing the political stabilisation that materialised in the social democratic governments of the period.

Many programmes of public investment and job training, profiting from European Community funds, helped to stimulate economic growth. The late 1980s and early 1990s saw the completion of several public works plans such as the basic highways network, designed some two decades before.

At the same time, a programme of financial stabilisation aimed at creating the conditions for the accession of Portugal to the European Monetary System was implemented. Crawling peg devaluation of the Portuguese escudo ceased in the late 1980s and in 1992 the Portuguese currency unit joined the European Monetary System at the central rate of 1 European currency unit = 178.735 Portuguese escudos.

The economic downturn of the early 1990s

The early 1990s were a less happy period for the Portuguese economy. Firstly, because the immediate positive impact of the EU membership ended, and some of its negative social impact became more acute. Secondly, because the downturn of the world (and especially European) economy of the early 1990s clearly affected the Portuguese economy, although, once more, their effects were somewhat delayed by a strong counter-cyclical political intervention in 1991 for electoral purposes. There was a slowdown during 1992, a recession during 1993 and a mild recovery during 1994.

D – Towards European monetary union, 1993-1999

Evolution of the European Union

In 1994, the European Union and the remaining members of EFTA (with the exception of Switzerland, in practice more formal than actual) created the European Economic Area, a cooperation scheme that allowed the negotiation by all members of the main rules to be applied within the common free trade area. In 1995, there was a further enlargement of the European Union, which brought the number of member states to fifteen by the addition of Austria, Finland and Sweden. In 1999, the Maastricht Treaty was replaced as the basic legal framework of the European Union by the Treaty of Amsterdam. However, the efforts to create the conditions to build the European monetary union dominated the life of the European Union throughout the 1990s.

The European monetary union

Between 1992 and 1995, the European monetary system underwent a period of crisis, linked to the difficult short-term economic situation of the early 1990s and the economic and monetary consequences of the German unification, which implied several changes in the parities agreed upon for the different currencies and a general widening of the fluctuation margins. Between 1995 and 1998, all member states did their best to comply with the nominal convergence criteria. When the final decision about participation in the first wave of the monetary union had to be taken, only Greece was clearly unable to be a member of the monetary union. Thus, the European monetary union started in 1999 with eleven members – Austria, Belgium, Finland, France, Germany, Ireland, Italy, Luxembourg, Netherlands, Portugal and Spain. Great Britain, Denmark and Sweden opted to stay out of the monetary union for the time being. An updated version of he European Monetary System was kept as the framework for the relations between the European monetary union and the currencies of the other members of the European Union. A Stability and Growth Pact was adopted as a fiscal behaviour code to ensure that fiscal policy of the member states did not disturb monetary stability of the European monetary union.

Portugal in the European monetary union

Portugal's attitude towards the European monetary union did not differ from that of the other member states. Between 1992 and 1995, there were efforts to prevent the short-term negative evolution of the economy and the impact of eventual speculative attacks against the escudo in exchange markets to jeopardize the achievement of the nominal convergence criteria. Between 1995 and 1998, reducing the public accounts deficit, in order to comply with the upper limit of 3% of gross domestic product (needed for first-wave membership in monetary union), became the main priority of financial and economic policy. In the end, these efforts were successful and Portugal became a member of the European monetary union from 1 January 1999 on. The European currency unit, now called euro, became the new

Portuguese currency unit, with the conversion rate of 1 euro = 200.482 escudos (the 12% depreciation as against the initial central parity in the European monetary system was mainly a consequence of the speculative attacks against the escudo during the 1992-1995 crisis of the European monetary system).

Portuguese economic, political and social evolution

The downturn of the Portuguese economy during the early 1990s had negative political consequences for the social democratic government. Its gradual weakening led to a socialist victory in the 1995 general elections. The socialist leader, António Guterres, organised a new government. The Socialist Party even won the 1996 regional elections in the Azores, although the social democrats retained the control of the regional government of Madeira. Earlier in the same year, the two-term period of Mário Soares as President had come to an end. The new President, Jorge Sampaio, was also a Socialist.

The change of the government impled no significant change in either the main aims or the main instruments of economic policy. Nominal convergence was pursued with equal energy, in order to be able to include Portugal in the group of European countries that would start the European monetary union. Thus, reduction of the deficits of public accounts and the privatisation process continued to shape economic policy. The results were rather good, as the recovery in the world economic situation began to reflect favourably in the Portuguese economy, restarting the process of nominal and real convergence to the European standards.

Social policy, however, showed some innovations. The introduction of a scheme of minimum guaranteed income was perhaps the main novelty. At the same time, the reform of social security, needed because of demographic and financial reasons, became a fundamental issue. Its design and implementation however, proved, quite difficult because of political reasons.

E – Portugal in the economic and monetary union

Evolution of the European Union

In 2001, the Treaty of Amsterdam was replaced by the Treaty of Nice as the basic legal framework of the European Union. In 2004 and 2007, the European Union was further enlarged to include several former communist countries – Bulgaria, Czech Republic, Estonia, Hungary, Latvia, Lithuania, Poland, Romania, Slovakia and Slovenia – and Mediterranean islands – Cyprus and Malta.

Meanwhile, the European monetary union reached its completeness in 2002, when the circulating specie were totally replaced by new specie expressed in euros. The eleven original members were eventually joined by Greece (2001), Slovenia (2007), Cyprus and Malta (2008), and Slovakia (2009).

Also in 2009, the Treaty of Nice was replaced by the Treaty of Lisbon as the basic legal framework of the European Union.

Portuguese economic, political and social evolution

The first decade of the European monetary union was not a bright period in Portugal's economic performance. Economic activity tended to a sluggish growth, caused mainly by foreign payments problems, which led to growing indebtness towards the rest of the world. These problems were the result of traditional trade deficits, coupled with a fall in the traditional emigrants' remmitances and the absence of significant foreign direct investment. The fact that foreign payments problems did not translate into traditional exchange problems, given the framework of the European monetary union, eased the rise of foreign loans, but also prevented the use of traditional exchange solutions. Of course, the sharp downturn of the world economy in 2008 only aggravated the Portuguese economic performance problems even threatning to trigger a sovereign debit problem as we write (2010).

These economic events had a negative impact on political stability. In 2001, the government of the Socialist Party suffered a heavy defeat in local elections and resigned. In 2002, general elections led to a coalition government bewteeen the social democrats and the christian democrats headed by José Manuel Barroso. In 2004, it was the turn of the social democrats – christian democrats government to suffer a stunning defeat at the European elections. As José Manuel Barroso left the Portuguese government to become President of the European Commission, he was replaced briefly by Pedro Santana Lopes at the head of the government. However, a few months later President Jorge Sampaio decided to convene new general elections, which resulted in an absolute majority for the Socialist Party. The socialist leader, José Sócrates formed the new government. The next year, Jorge Sampaio's two-term period as President came to an end. The new President was Aníbal Cavaco Silva, former social democratic leader between the mid-1980s and mid-1990s.

Besides introducing fiscal measures to ensure the end of excessive deficits, José Sócrates' government became involved in several structural reforms in the social field. The reshaping of civil service according to less rigid patterns, the adoption of new social security rules to ensure its financial stability, and the reorganisation of higher education according to the framework of the European Higher Education Area were perhaps the main endeavours. It is fair to say that, at first sight, these reforms produced mixed results.

The most difficult issue Portugal faced during the early years of the monetary union was to abide by the rules of the Stability and Growth Pact. Twice (in 2001 and again in 2005) Portugal broke the rule of excessive deficits. As a consequence, Portugal was subjected to formal pressure to apply fiscal adjustments. Between 2002 and 2004, the demand was for immediate respect of the upper limit of 3% of gross domestic product for the deficit. This led to the use of exceptional revenue as a balancing device, a procedure that left structural problems unresolved and

350 | The Concise Economic History of Portugal: A Comprehensive Guide

led to the 2005 excessive deficit. This time demand was only for a gradual adjustment, which was performed until 2007, allowing for deeper structural adjustments. However, the international economic problems of the late years of the first decade of the 21st century spoiled the situation again as pointed out above.

F – Long-term trends during the last quarter of the 20th century and the early 21st century

Population

The end of large-scale emigration from the continental part of the country to Europe and the inflow of around half a million refugees led to a sizeable population increase in the mid-1970s, which off-set, to some degree, the decrease caused by the emigration of the 1960s and early 1970s. Thus, around 1980, Portugal was approaching the 10 million inhabitants mark.

During the 1980s and early 1990s, the population of Portugal fluctuated below the 10 million level. This was the consequence of a declining birth rate, a stabilisation of the death rate, a decrease of emigration, and an increase of immigration. Birth and death rates reached the 1% level, typical of developed countries with somewhat aged populations. Emigration continued according to the geographic patterns of the third quarter of the 20th century (see chapter 11), but remained clearly below the figures of the 1960s and early 1970s. The immigration inflow came mainly from non-European Portuguese-speaking countries, but also included some ex-emigrants returning from Europe, and reached a yearly average similar to the emigration figure.

The late 1990s and early 21st century witnessed a significant increase of the immigration flow from Eastern Europe (mainly Romania and Ukraine), which ensured a clearly positive net migration figure, and the resumption of a slow but steady population growth, clearly passing the 10 million mark.

Regional distribution of population

Trends in the regional distribution of population from the late 1970s until the early 21st century were similar, in some respects, to those of the third quarter of the 20th century. The south of Entre-Douro-e-Minho, Beira Litoral, Estremadura and the southwest of Ribatejo increased their population. The rest of the country, that is to say, part of the coast and the whole interior of the continental part of the country, and the Atlantic islands saw a decrease in population.

During the 1970s and 1980s, the region of Porto (that is, the south of Entre-Douro-e-Minho and the north of Beira Litoral) showed higher demographic (and economic) energy than the region of Lisbon (that is, Estremadura and the southwest of Ribatejo), something that has not been seen since the mid-19th century. This was the consequence of the higher growth of traditional industrial activities, located mainly in the north, and of the difficulties faced by modern industrial sectors, located mainly in the south (see below). During the 1900s and the early 21st century, the situation became more evened out, as new industrial activities, often driven by foreign direct investment, began to develop also in the region of Lisbon.

Towns

The population of towns having more than 10,000 inhabitants continued to climb in absolute and relative terms during the late 20th and early 21st century. It was approaching half of the total population at the turn of the century.

Lisbon and Porto remained the two principal urban concentrations of the country. They continued growing in area and population, reaching more than 2 million inhabitants (over one fifth of the population of the country) in the case of Lisbon and more than 1 million (over one tenth of the population) in the case of Porto.

Nearly 1 million inhabitants (one tenth of the population) lived in the other towns having more than 10,000 inhabitants in the early 1990s. Braga, Coimbra and Setúbal in the continental part of the country, and Funchal in Madeira remained the main second-rank urban concentrations. These four towns clearly passed the 100,000 mark.

Real growth

In spite of the recessions of the mid-1970s, the early 1980s and the early 1990s, real gross domestic product grew at a yearly accumulated rate above 3.0% between 1974 and the late 1990s. This means that the growth of real gross domestic product was clearly greater than the growth of population and that per capita gross domestic product also increased at a very significant rate. The average standard of living in Portugal in the late 1990s was more than 50% higher than in the mid-1970s. At the same time, the gap toward the main economic powers of Europe and the world continued to narrow, though at a slower pace than during the third quarter of the 20th century.

As pointed out in section E, above, the situation deteriorated during the first decade of the 21st century. The sluggish growth of real gross domestic product meant near stagnation of the standard of living and some lost ground concerning convergence toward the main economic powers of Europe and the world.

Prices

Inflation accelerated during the late 1970s and most of the 1980s, mainly as a consequence of the financing of public deficits by credit from the central bank, calling for fresh monetary issues. Money supply was multiplied by a factor greater than 10 and the consumer price index was multiplied by a factor greater than 15 (thus, there was some increase in the velocity of circulation).

The situation began to change in the late 1980s. The success of the so-called nominal convergence to the European norm meant that by the late 1990s inflation had been reduced to levels that compare to those of the early 1960s. As could be expected, low inflation remained the rule after Portugal joined the European monetary union.

Structural changes

Structural changes were quite rapid during the period under consideration.

In the distribution of labour force by sectors, there was a sharp drop in the share of agriculture, from around one third to less than one tenth, and a slower drop in the share of industry, from around one third to around one fourth, and the share of services was boosted from around one third to around two thirds.

In the distribution of value added by sector, there were decreases in the shares of agriculture, from less than one fifth to less than one twentieth, and of industry, from slightly more than two fifths to less than one third, while the share of services climbed from slightly more than two fifths to around two thirds.

Thus, it may be said that the Portuguese economy entered the epoch in which industrialisation ceased to be a significant trend, and tertiarisation became the main feature of structural change. In fact, while the yearly rate of growth of agricultural output remained below 1.0% and the output of industry presented an average yearly rate of growth of around 2.0%, the output of services posted an average yearly growth rate of around 4.5%.

*

Disaggregation of the agricultural output leads to the conclusion that the output of fruits, vegetables, and animal products grew above the average, and that the wine and cereal outputs grew below the average. Such structural changes were the consequence of an allocation of resources resulting mainly from higher exposure of the Portuguese producers of agricultural commodities to the competition and stimuli of external markets.

In the fruits and vegetables sector and in that of animal products, higher demand came both from European markets and from the rise in the standard of living of the Portuguese population. Mediterranean and tropical fruits production and sheep and swine raising were the fastest growing branches of this sub-sector.

Wine production was restricted because of excess output in the European Union. Plans (and subsidies) for reducing vineyard area and shifting from low-quality mass production to high-quality production were put forward with some success.

Cereal production was restricted for similar reasons and because of the competition coming from less expensive foreign cereals.

In the primary sector, it is also important to stress the increase of forestry output, for both the wood products and the paper pulp industries.

Reference should also be made to the expansion of the dairy sector in the Azores, and to the introduction or expansion of several crops, sometimes as a consequence of the curtailment of forced specialisation with former colonial territories.

Fishing experienced a clear downturn, partly because of the exhaustion of natural resources in the Portuguese exclusive zone (which was significantly enlarged as a consequence of the introduction of the 200 miles rule), and partly because of the closure of traditional fishing zones in the North Atlantic (Canada, Greenland, Iceland) to the fleets of the European Union.

*

Disaggregation of the product of industry shows that both traditional sectors, such as textiles, leather, and wood products, and modern sectors, such as the automotive sector and electronics showed significant dynamism. The traditional sectors benefited from the increase of European demand for Portuguese clothes, shoes and furniture, and from the rising standard of living in the country. The automotive sector and electronics benefited from the introduction of new factories by several multinationals. At the same time, however, some modern sectors, which had expanded during the preceding decades, went through some difficult days. The iron and steel, ship and aircraft repair, and chemical activities were unable to remain competitive in international and even in internal terms.

Construction, public works and energy production also showed significant strength, fuelled by urbanisation, public works programmes, increased economic activity in general, and improvement in the standards of living.

*

Disaggregation of the output of the services sector shows that modern sectors, such as transportation, communications, trade, education, health and public administration fared better than did traditional personal services. Tourism was also a very active sector.

In the media sector, it is important to note that television began to work in Madeira and in the Azores in 1975, and that colour television was introduced in 1979. The late 1980s and early 1990s saw the end of the state monopoly in the sector, first with a wave of pirate radio stations, then with the proper organisation of a private radio sector and a private television sector.

*

During the period under consideration, market schemes were initially and formally threatened by planning schemes in their position as the main economic system, as a consequence of constitutional rules. However, it is important to distinguish between formal planning and state interference by means of nationalisations. The sector of public enterprises was very important in Portugal between the mid-1970s and early 1990s, but the role of formal planning in the coordination of economic life did not increase as a consequence.

Short-term yearly plans were regularly drawn up and passed through parliament, but consisted almost exclusively of broad guidelines for economic policy (often ignored during the year) and lists of public investments. To be precise, they became little more than regular companion documents to the state budget.

Medium-term (four year) plans were prepared for the periods 1977-1980 and 1981-1984, but only the second was formally approved by the parliament. In any event, none of them became a true basis for government action, let alone guidelines for private units' action, because of the need for drastic measures to fight foreign payments problems, as explained above. Medium-term plans were abandoned from 1985 on.

To sum up, market schemes, deeply influenced by economic policy, were the dominant economic system in Portugal throughout the period.

Economic groups

Nationalisations and state interventions dismantled the main private Portuguese economic groups in the mid-1970s. However, the most important of these groups were able to survive on foreign investments made before 1974, and to come back (often to the same firms) when the changes in the delimitation laws and privatisation operations gave ground to their activity. Moreover, some new groups flourished during the period under consideration: the Sonae and Amorim groups, mainly linked to the industrial and commercial sectors, and the Millennium group, mainly linked to the financial sector.

Education

The fall of the illiteracy rate and the rise of the average schooling years continued during the period under consideration, although it is possible to say that the illiteracy rate remained rather high and that the average schooling years were still rather low in the early 21st century for a country with the standard of living already reached in Portugal. In fact, illiterate people still amounted to around one tenth of the adult population, and the rise of compulsory schooling years from six to nine during the 1980s was often not respected, although it is possible to recognise a continuation of the previous positive trends in this domain.

Six new public universities were created during the period under consideration: Trás-os-Montes e Alto Douro (located in Vila Real), Beira Interior (located in Covilhã), Algarve (located in Faro), Azores (located mainly in Ponta Delgada), Madeira (located in Funchal) and an Open University with its headquarters in Lisbon. During the 1980s several private universities were also created in Lisbon, Porto and other communities throughout.

Technological changes

The increase in the use of machinery and fertilisers in agriculture, the increase in the use of modern machinery in industry, and the spread of the use of computers in all sectors were the main technological changes in the period under consideration. This brought strong gains in the productivity levels of the Portuguese economy, together with better organisation and higher quality of human resources.

Ecological problems

The ecological situation of the country certainly worsened during the period under consideration, mainly in the regions of Lisbon and Porto, as a consequence of urban growth. Moreover, the concentration of industrial firms in several zones brought a good deal of local air and river pollution, and oil tankers along the coast also polluted the sea.

However, the situation in Portugal remained fairly good when compared to the average situation in the most-developed countries. Climatic reasons do not favour acid rain, the absence of nuclear power stations means that the only threat of that nature comes from the generators in neighbouring Spain, and several nature reserves were created to preserve exceptional natural resources. Moreover, plans to reduce emissions contributing to the global greenhouse effect were advanced with some success.

Final remarks

History, of course, has no conclusion, but it can certainly help us in our attempts to gaze into the future. Let us now review where we have been and where we are going – this time taking a slightly different perspective. Let us re-examine three of the principal aspects of Portuguese history and culture, which may be crucial to gaining a clearer insight into Portugal's path, both backward and forward in time. The first aspect is that of Portugal's independence, and will be addressed in section A of this conclusion. Section B will look at Portugal's late entry into its phase of modern economic growth. The last aspect is that of the prospects of the Portuguese economy and society in the world that seems to be developing – and will be treated in section C.

A – The problem of Portuguese independence

Pre-medieval roots

It has been suggested that the Portuguese national society finds its roots in human groups established before the 8th century A.D. in the western or northwestern part of the Iberian Peninsula. The Kingdom of the Suevi of the 5th and 6th centuries A.D., the Lusitanian tribes of the 1st millennium B.C. and their resistance to Rome in the 2nd century B.C., and even earlier developments such as the so-called megalithic civilisation of the

3rd millennium B.C. have been put forward by different scholars as candidates for such proto-national influences.

We should be cautious about such hypotheses. As a matter of fact, it is impossible to simultaneously attest the continuity of the ethnic substratum of these societies with the Portuguese society and any individuality compared to neighbouring regions of the Iberian Peninsula.

The origins

The formation of the first County of Portugal, that of the County of Coimbra, and of the second County of Portugal in the Kingdom of Leon between the 8th and the 12th century, and even the independence of the Kingdom of Portugal in the 12th century, may be easily understood in the context of the rather radical feudal structures of the society of Iberian Christendom of that period, as explained in chapter 2. However, similar processes in other regions of the Iberian Peninsula did not lead to stable national societies. Why is it that the Portuguese society was able to survive as a separate national entity?

The answer to such a question should be sought in a comparison between Portugal and societies, such as Aragon, Catalonia and Navarre, which were briefly independent, but later became part of the Spanish national society, in spite of their individuality.

The geographical basis for the existence of Portugal

A first answer to the question of the basis of the political division of the Iberian Peninsula into two states – Spain and Portugal – may come from the geographical characteristics of the Iberian Peninsula.

The analysis of this problem in its geographical aspects may be organised around three factors: easy or difficult internal communications; existence or absence of a capital city capable of polarising political unity and autonomy; and homogeneity or heterogeneity of the territory. In a necessarily brief review of the existing situations, it may be seen that:

a) Concerning the ease or difficulty of internal communications, medieval Iberian kingdoms may be divided into two groups: those that had rather easy internal communications – Aragon, Catalonia, Navarre and Portugal – and those in which internal communications were rather difficult – Castile and Leon.

b) Regarding the existence or absence of a polarising capital city, medieval Iberian kingdoms may again be divided into two groups: those that had an undisputed capital city – Aragon, Catalonia, Navarre and Portugal – and those that did not have an undisputed capital city – Castile and Leon.

c) As for the homogeneity or heterogeneity of the territory, the medieval Iberian kingdoms may once again be divided into two groups: those that presented a clear internal homogeneity – Aragon (a kingdom of almost exclusively semi-continental regions), Catalonia (a kingdom of almost exclusively Mediterranean regions) and Navarre (a kingdom of almost exclusively Atlantic regions) – and those that presented a clear internal heterogeneity – Leon (a kingdom that united Atlantic and semi-continental regions), Castile (a kingdom that united semi-continental and Mediterranean regions, and even Atlantic regions, especially after the absorption of Leon) and Portugal (a kingdom that united Atlantic, semi-continental and Mediterranean regions).

To sum up, it may be suggested that Portugal was, thus, the only peripheral kingdom that gathered all the favourable geographical conditions to preserve its independence: easy internal communications; urban polarisation by its capital city; heterogeneity of the territory. Heterogeneity of the territory thus appears to be the decisive geographical factor affording Portugal a capacity to resist the centralising pressure of Castile, because it is the only one that is lacking in all of the other peripheral kingdoms.

Historical processes

However, it must not be forgotten that, aside from geographical factors, we must consider the historical factors of the independence of Portugal. As we examined above, after the medieval period, during which several independent states existed in the Iberian Peninsula (Aragon, Castile, Catalonia, Leon, Navarre and Portugal were the most important), the modern epoch saw a process of absorption of the other states by Castile, to which only Portugal was able to resist. The question of the historical bases of the political division of the Iberian Peninsula into two states may, thus, be reformulated as follows: which factors, besides the geographical factors already considered above, allowed Portugal to resist the centralising pressure of Castile and were lacking in the other Iberian states that were unable to resist such pressure?

The independence of the various medieval Iberian kingdoms could have simply ended in the late 16th century, had the attempts to build a politically unified Iberian Peninsula been successful. However, these attempts came too late to prevent the development of two destabilising factors: the control of separate colonial empires and the existence of political links with non-Iberian Europe.

The control of separate colonial empires developed during the 15th century and was common to Castile, Portugal and the Aragon-Catalonia union, which had existed since the 12th century. However, there was a very important difference between the colonial empires of Castile and Portugal on one side and the colonial empire of Aragon-Catalonia on the other. While that of Aragon-Catalonia was confined to the Mediterranean, which became a zone in decline during the 17th century, at least in relation to the Euro-Atlantic world-economy, the other two spread to the Atlantic, the cradle of what would become the contemporary world economy. This difference may explain the decisive success of the Portuguese attempt to break the links with the Western Hapsburg Empire in the 17th century and the simultaneous failure of a similar attempt by Catalonia.

The existence of political links with non-Iberian Europe arose with continuity only from the late 15th century on, and only for the union of Castile, Aragon and Catalonia, by then already established. It is doubtful that, except for the links of Aragon and Catalonia with certain Italian regions (namely, Sardinia, Sicily and Naples), which were truly a part of the Aragonese-Catalonian colonial empire, such links were wished and planned for by the Iberian political leaders, as explained in chapter 3. In any event, when the Iberian union was achieved in the late 16th century, it was not purely Iberian (plus colonial empires), but involved political links with other European regions. The fact that not all of the European parties were always peacefully integrated (as was the case of the Low Countries, already in revolt against their common sovereign with the Iberian Peninsula) did not help to consolidate the Iberian union.

Once Portugal had won the so-called Restoration War in the 17th century, there were no more opportunities for an Iberian unification, except for the Spanish dynastic troubles of the late 1860s and early 1870s, an opportunity rejected by Portugal. The idea that Portugal was not a part of a wider Iberian society had become firmly entrenched in the Portuguese psyche, and so it has remained until today.

B – The problem of Portugal's late take-off of modern economic growth

Many generations of Portuguese historians have pointed to themes of decadence following the 16th-century apogee and of retardation when measured against the leading economic powers as key problems haunting Portuguese economic history. However, the take-off of Portuguese modern economic growth, first as something of a false start (between the 1860s and the 1880s), later as a typical modern economic growth process (in the second half of the 20th century), invited a new formulation of the problem as a mere question of late take-off. As a matter of fact, it is pointless to discuss the possibilities of a country of the size of Portugal to maintain the position of hegemony in overseas trade that it held briefly in the 15th and 16th centuries; and it is no longer possible to argue that Portugal is somehow condemned to lag forever behind the leading world powers in the area of economic development.

Traditional explanations for the late take-off of Portuguese modern economic growth have stressed the role of the starting point and international relations as brakes to Portuguese economic growth. Modern explanations tend to shift their attention to the problems of the availability of resources and economic decisions.

The starting point

To stress the weight of the starting point as an explanation for the late take-off of Portugal's modern economic growth is a natural consequence of the concern about Portuguese decadence since the 16th century.

The Portuguese economic situation did not develop well during the 18th century and certainly worsened during the early 19th century, partly as a consequence of external shocks, partly as a consequence of internal problems, as explained in chapters 6 and 7. Thus, it is only fair to accept that the problems faced by the Portuguese economy at the time of the early successful take-offs was detrimental to an immediate imitation of these processes.

The starting point may be a problem in fact, but not one that can explain the main course of the evolution over a long duration. As no shortage of catching up processes illustrate, income gaps are not necessarily self-reproducing; and even Portugal succeeded in starting a process of economic growth in the second half of the 19th century.

The influence of international economic relations

Of course, the influence of international economic relations was decisive in shaping the economic evolution of Portugal during the 19th and 20th centuries, and it is difficult to believe that this influence was always favourable to economic growth. The competition from commodities exported by the leading economic powers of the world was certainly detrimental to the growth of modern sectors; and the same leading powers often pressed for regulations of economic life, especially of foreign trade, that were certainly intended to advance the interests of those that pressed for them.

However, the higher export opportunities and the capital supplies should not be overlooked as stimuli to growth received from the leading world powers. This means that it is also impossible to believe that the influence of international economic relations was always detrimental to economic growth.

It is difficult to ascertain which had a greater impact: the negative or the positive effects. It may be pointed out that the performance of the Portuguese economy seems to have been much better when it was open to freer intercourse with the international economy than when it tried to increase its autarky. This should not be surprising in a small-size economy, which certainly benefited from specialisation (the only way to profit from scale economies and to avoid using resources in inefficient activities).

Natural resources

The appraisal of the influence of the endowment of the Portuguese economy in natural resources in its growth must also lead to a mixed perspective.

As a matter of fact, Portuguese agricultural products were not always good export staples in the world market, and it is quite clear that the innovations that shaped modern economic growth in other countries were often poorly suited to Portuguese economic activities, because of the climate, soil, or other natural factors. At the same time, mineral resources were scarce, and only the tungsten export boom during the Second World War provided any great advantage based on mineral exploitation.

However, Portugal enjoys a natural setting that is not especially hostile to human life, and the use of innovations in contexts different from those for which they were devised is often just a matter of adaptation, something that depends not on natural resources, but on human resources.

Human resources

It is unlikely that any quantitative lack of human resources was ever a barrier to economic growth in Portugal. As a matter of fact, population grew during the 19th and 20th centuries, though usually at a slow pace in a European and world context, and there was a significant emigration flow, suggesting that the level of economic activity was unable to absorb all available workers.

Qualitative lack of human resources is another matter. The survey of the cultural aspects made throughout the book shows that the literacy rate and the average schooling years remained very low until very recently, and that they are still far below the desirable levels in a European and world context in the early 21st century. Thus, the qualitative lack of human resources is perhaps one of the best explanations for the late take-off of Portuguese modern economic growth, and the success of the efforts to overcome this problem during the inter-war years is perhaps one of the best explanations for the success of the Portuguese economic growth seen in the second half of the 20th century.

Produced resources

It is impossible to have a precise idea of the impact of the lack of produced resources in delaying the take-off of the Portuguese economy, because of the absence of statistical data about investment and capital stock. However, data about transportation and communication facilities, building, imports of production goods and capital flows strongly support the thesis that the availability of produced resources played an important role in shaping the evolution of the Portuguese economy. In other words, lack of an adequate capital stock and investment flow was a significant brake upon Portuguese economic growth until the inter-war period, but things tended to change thereafter.

Lack of produced resources may be due to one of three causes: high inter-temporal preferences of economic units, which imply a low level of savings; bad financial institutions, which imply a misuse of the available savings; or lack of entrepreneurial initiative, which also implies a misuse of the available savings.

The problem of the low level of savings is difficult to handle in the case of the Portuguese economy, because of lack of statistical evidence. In any event, even if a significant flow of savings was already available in the period before the First World War, its adequate use was hindered by the lack of good financial institutions. As a matter of fact, the survey of the evolution of financial institutions made in chapters 7 to 12 showed that Portuguese banks came into existence rather late, that they remained confined to short-term activities almost exclusively, and that banking crises contributed to the mistrust of banking services on the part of most of the population. It was only after the 1930s that the situation improved. Thus, it is easy to understand why hoarding was the predominant behaviour until the inter-war period, and why capital imports became vital to stimulate modern economic growth before that epoch. The crucial effect of the financial crisis of the early 1890s, that closed international financial markets to the Portuguese government for several decades, also becomes clear in this context.

The problem of the lack of entrepreneurial initiative must be linked to the problems of the qualitative lack of human resources and of economic decisions. Entrepreneurial initiative is just a special type of human resource, after all, and mistakes of entrepreneurs are just one type of mistake in economic decisions.

Economic decisions

Poor economic decisions of one economic unit may have three different causes: lack of information; error, a case to be related to lack of qualitatively adequate human resources, or to bad luck in uncertain situations; and imposition by other economic units.

It is useful to separate the discussion of the effect of economic decisions in the process of Portuguese economic growth into two parts: one dealing with the problem of private economic decisions; another focusing on the question of economic policy and economic institutions.

Private economic decisions

It is difficult to argue that economic decisions by private units may be a decisive reason for economic stagnation, unless there are private preferences that lead to such a result. As a matter of fact, lack of information and errors in private economic decisions are usually corrected by a process of natural selection, though sometimes only in the long term, and impositions in the context of private economic decisions are usually linked to economic regimes and institutions and must be considered together with economic policies.

Thus, the discussion of the impact of private economic decisions upon economic growth becomes a discussion about whether or not there exists a conflict between the economic goals of private prosperity and economic growth. It is impossible to examine here in detail the Portuguese situation during the 19th and 20th centuries, but it must be stressed that a great number of conflict situations, especially in the sector of agriculture, have been pointed out in literature.

Economic policy and economic institutions

Economic policy and economic institutions are more likely to contribute to economic stagnation than are private economic decisions. As it happens, bad economic policies and economic institutions are only detectable in the long run. Furthermore, impositions in economic policy and economic institutions often come from foreign influences and are harder to counter even when their adverse effects are identified.

The survey of development policies in Portugal during the 19th and 20th centuries, made in chapters 7 to 12, discussed a host of measures intended to promote economic growth that failed (protectionist schemes are perhaps the most important example) and several measures that had desirable effects, but were slow to be implemented and to produce results (building of transportation facilities and the spread of primary and technical education are perhaps the best examples). Once more, it is difficult to present a general picture, although it may be stressed that some poor economic policies and economic institutions (such as industrial conditioning and some degree of agricultural protection) were unable to prevent modern economic growth in the second half of the 20th century.

C – The future of the Portuguese society in a European and world context

Two fundamental problems must be stated at the beginning of this very short excursion into predicting the future: will the

Portuguese society and economy continue as a distinct national society and a distinct national economy? And which European and world context will prevail as the background of any such evolution?

The survival of Portugal as a national society

Two scenarios might endanger the survival of Portugal as a national society: a process of internal disintegration or the possibility of losing its national identity in the process of European integration.

Neither of these seems probable. The claims for regional autonomy, even in the Atlantic archipelagoes, are not likely to lead to true separatist trends. Portugal is a country that is, after all, very homogeneous from a cultural point of view, and unless disrupted by external events (and nothing points to such a thing at this moment) internal continuity is to be expected. Concerning European integration, it may destroy the Portuguese national economy as a distinct economy, and strongly reduce the political autonomy of the country, but certainly not on a scale as to destroy its cultural identity, except perhaps in the very long run.

In any event, the Portuguese society will have to face the problem (as will other European societies) of discovering how to travel two roads at once: participation in the process of European union (indispensable for ensuring the peoples of Europe a proper role in the future of the world), and preservation of its identity (and its cultural links to the peoples outside Europe that share a Portuguese-based culture). As it is a problem that is common to the other European societies, its solution must be found in common with these other European societies within the context of the very process of European union.

The European and world context

Unless profound (and somewhat unlikely) changes occur, the evolution of the Portuguese society and economy in the decades to come will take place in the context of the world society and economy, in general, and of the European Union, in particular.

Such a background will, of course, have positive and negative effects upon the economic development of the country and the well-being of its inhabitants. Judging from previous situations, it is likely that the outcome will be positive. The Portuguese economy has time and again responded with faster growth when it accepted freer intercourse with other economies, as has been pointed out above.

However, any catching up process as against the leading European or world economic powers will still take many decades; and the dangers of the ambiguous position of being one of the less-developed regions inside one of the most-developed economic powers of the world should not be ignored. The Portuguese economy may find it difficult to compete with its most-developed partners in the range of high technology goods, and to compete with thriving outsiders in the range of less-sophisticated goods.

Besides these considerations, we must take into account the role that Portugal, itself and as a part of Europe, may play in the evolution of the world and in the solution of the many problems that mankind faces in our epoch, such as the problem of growth and distribution of the world population, the problem of balanced development of the various regions and peoples, the problem of preserving the world's natural resources, the problem of political stability and world security, or the problem of preserving cultural values in a context of growing intercourse among various cultures.

It is impossible to go into a deep discussion of these questions here, but it is worth noting that the way they will be treated by mankind as a whole will certainly influence the future of Portuguese society and its economy.

Statistical appendix

As explained in the foreword, this statistical appendix is an updated summary of the collection of Portuguese historical statistics released by the Portuguese National Statistics Institute (Instituto Nacional de Estatística) in 2001.

Table 1 – Population

Sources:

– from 1863 to 1889, Maria Eugénia Mata – "As crises financeiras no Portugal contemporâneo" (Clio, 2002);

– from 1890 to 1969, Ana Bela Nunes – "População activa e actividade económica em Portugal dos finais do século XIX à actualidade – uma contribuição para o estudo do crescimento económico português" (Doctoral dissertation presented at the Technical University of Lisbon, 1989);

– from 1970 onwards, computation based on Population Censuses and Demographic Statistics (Estatísticas Demográficas).

Year	Births	Deaths	Immigration – emigration	Population at the end of the year
1863	•	•	•	4 188
1864	147	130	-1	4 204
1865	148	130	0	4 222
1866	149	127	0	4 244
1867	149	127	-2	4 264
1868	150	124	-2	4 288
1869	151	124	-3	4 312
1870	152	122	-4	4 338
1871	153	122	-7	4 362
1872	154	118	-13	4 385
1873	154	118	-9	4 412
1874	155	115	-11	4 441
1875	157	115	-10	4 472
1876	158	113	-6	4 511
1877	159	113	-6	4 551
1878	161	109	-5	4 598
1879	163	110	-8	4 643
1880	164	111	-7	4 689

Year	Births	Deaths	Immigration – emigration	Population at the end of the year
1881	166	112	-9	4 734
1882	167	113	-12	4 776
1883	169	114	-13	4 818
1884	169	115	-11	4 861
1885	170	116	-8	4 907
1886	156	99	-7	4 957
1887	166	109	-10	5 004
1888	164	107	-17	5 044
1889	168	112	-21	5 079
1890	165	127	-12	5 105
1891	162	116	-13	5 138
1892	159	104	-12	5 182
1893	164	110	-17	5 220
1904	177	106	-14	5 670
1905	180	113	-17	5 720
1906	183	125	-19	5 758
1907	176	113	-21	5 800
1908	175	116	-20	5 840
1909	175	112	-19	5 883
1910	187	113	-20	5 937
1911	230	131	-31	6 004
1912	208	120	-85	6 008
1913	194	123	-74	6 004
1914	188	116	-25	6 053
1915	195	123	-18	6 107
1916	193	129	-24	6 147
1917	188	134	-15	6 186
1918	179	249	-11	6 104
1919	166	153	-36	6 082
1920	203	143	-58	6 084
1921	197	126	-6	6 148
1922	204	126	-10	6 216
1923	207	142	-10	6 271

Year	Births	Deaths	Immigration – emigration	Population at the end of the year
1924	207	126	-8	6 344
1925	208	117	-6	6 429
1926	217	128	-11	6 507
1927	203	123	-7	6 580
1928	211	124	-9	6 658
1929	201	119	-11	6 729
1930	203	116	-3	6 812
1931	204	115	+6	6 908
1932	208	119	+6	7 003
1933	204	121	+10	7 096
1934	203	119	+8	7 189
1935	204	123	+10	7 279
1936	206	119	+13	7 379
1937	198	117	+16	7 476
1938	199	115	+15	7 575
1939	199	116	+19	7 677
1940	188	120	+13	7 758
1941	184	135	-7	7 800
1942	188	127	-2	7 859
1943	198	122	-1	7 934
1944	201	119	-3	8 013
1945	209	116	-6	8 101
1946	206	121	-4	8 182
1947	200	110	-14	8 258
1948	221	108	-13	8 358
1949	212	117	-19	8 434
1950	205	103	-25	8 512
1951	208	105	-68	8 547
1952	211	100	-95	8 563
1953	202	97	-80	8 587
1954	198	95	-83	8 607
1955	210	99	-60	8 657

Statistical appendix | 377

Year	Births	Deaths	Immigration – emigration	Population at the end of the year
1956	203	107	-54	8 698
1957	211	102	-71	8 737
1958	212	92	-69	8 789
1959	213	98	-67	8 837
1960	214	95	-65	8 891
1961	218	100	-65	8 944
1962	220	97	-65	9 002
1963	212	98	-76	9 040
1964	217	97	-107	9 053
1965	210	95	-172	8 996
1966	207	100	-232	8 871
1967	202	96	-179	8 798
1968	195	95	-155	8 743
1969	190	101	-135	8 696
1970	173	93	-119	8 657
1971	189	98	-50	8 698
1972	175	90	-54	8 729
1973	172	95	-80	8 726
1974	172	97	+207	9 008
1975	180	98	+351	9 441
1976	187	102	+108	9 634
1977	181	96	-17	9 702
1978	167	96	-19	9 754
1979	160	93	-21	9 800
1980	161	98	-18	9 845
1981	152	96	-17	9 884
1982	151	93	-32	9 910
1983	144	96	-15	9 942
1984	143	97	-15	9 973
1985	130	97	-36	9 970
1986	127	96	-15	9 985
1987	123	95	-27	9 986

378 | The Concise Economic History of Portugal: A Comprehensive Guide

Year	Births	Deaths	Immigration - emigration	Population at the end of the year
1988	122	98	-33	9 977
1989	119	96	-42	9 958
1990	116	103	-53	9 918
1991	116	104	-65	9 865
1992	115	101	+25	9 890
1993	114	106	+32	9 924
1994	109	100	+80	10 030
1995	107	104	+35	10 071
1996	110	107	+16	10 085
1997	113	105	+6	10 094
1998	113	107	+10	10 105
1999	116	108	+41	10 163
2000	120	106	+54	10 243
2001	113	105	+78	10 329
2002	114	106	+70	10 407
2003	113	109	+64	10 475
2004	109	102	+47	10 529
2005	109	107	+39	10 570
2006	105	102	+22	10 599
2007	102	104	+21	10 618
2008	105	104	+8	10 627

Table 2 – Towns

Sources:
1864 to 1991 – Census for the respective year.
2001 – <u>Atlas das Cidades de Portugal</u> (INE, Lisboa, 2002).

Unit – Thousands.

Remarks:
1 – The censuses for the years 1864, 1878, 1890, 1900, 1920 and 1930 do not provide any values for the population of places, but only for the population of parishes. For this reason, the figures relating to the population of cities in the years 1864, 1878, 1890, 1900, 1920 and 1930 are estimates based on the population of totally or partially urban parishes and on the proportion of the urban population in the total population of these parishes in 1911 and 1940, accepting the premise that the proportion of the urban population in the total population of these parishes for the years 1864, 1878, 1890 and 1900 was identical to that of 1911, and for the years 1920 and 1930 was identical to that of 1940. The figures for the population of the cities for the years 1911, 1940, 1950, 1960, 1970, 1981 and 1991 are those shown in the respective censuses.

2 – From 1950 onwards, the boroughs of Lisbon, Almada, Amadora, Barreiro, Cascais, Loures, Moita do Ribatejo, Montijo, Oeiras, Seixal, Sintra and Vila Franca de Xira were grouped together as Greater Lisbon, whilst the boroughs of Porto, Espinho, Gaia, Gondomar, Maia, Matosinhos and Valongo were grouped together as Greater Porto.

1864	
1. Lisbon	190
2. Porto	89
3. Braga	18
4. Funchal	15
5. Ponta Delgada	14
6. Coimbra	12
8 places with more than 10 thousand inhabitants	

1878	
1. Lisbon	241
2. Porto	111
3. Braga	18
4. Funchal	17
5. Ponta Delgada	16
6. Setúbal	13
9 places with more than 10 thousand inhabitants	

1890	
1. Lisbon	301
2. Porto	139
3. Braga	21
4. Funchal	16
5. Coimbra	15
6. Ponta Delgada	15
11 places with more than 10 thousand inhabitants	

1900	
1. Lisbon	356
2. Porto	168
3. Braga	22
4. Setúbal	19
5. Funchal	17
6. Coimbra	16
12 places with more than 10 thousand inhabitants	

1911	
1. Lisbon	435
2. Porto	194
3. Setúbal	26
4. Braga	22
5. Funchal	20
6. Coimbra	18
11 places with more than 10 thousand inhabitants	

1920	
1. Lisbon	486
2. Porto	203
3. Setúbal	31
4. Funchal	20
5. Braga	20
6. Coimbra	19
13 places with more than 10 thousand inhabitants	

1930	
1. Lisbon	594
2. Porto	232
3. Setúbal	38
4. Funchal	31
5. Coimbra	26
6. Braga	25
17 places with more than 10 thousand inhabitants	

1940	
1. Lisbon	709
2. Porto	262
3. Funchal	40
4. Setúbal	37
5. Braga	29
6. Coimbra	27
23 places with more than 10 thousand inhabitants	

1950	
1. Greater Lisbon	1 157
2. Greater Porto	652
3. Setúbal	44
4. Coimbra	42
5. Funchal	37
6. Braga	32
27 places with more than 10 thousand inhabitants	

1960	
1. Greater Lisbon	1 365
2. Greater Porto	746
3. Coimbra	46
4. Setúbal	44
5. Funchal	43
6. Braga	41
31 places with more than 10 thousand inhabitants	

1970	
1. Greater Lisbon	1 649
2. Greater Porto	832
3. Coimbra	57
4. Setúbal	51
5. Braga	50
6. Funchal	40
34 places with more than 10 thousand inhabitants	

1981	
1. Greater Lisbon	2 269
2. Greater Porto	1 001
3. Setúbal	77
4. Coimbra	42
5. Braga	63
6. Funchal	44
39 places with more than 10 thousand inhabitants	

1991	
1. Greater Lisbon	2 315
2. Greater Porto	1 035
3. Funchal	99
4. Coimbra	90
5. Braga	86
6. Setúbal	83
43 places with more than 10 thousand inhabitants	

2001	
1. Greater Lisbon	2 390
2. Greater Porto	1 123
3. Braga	109
4. Coimbra	101
5. Funchal	101
6. Setúbal	89
66 places with more than 10 thousand inhabitants	

Table 3 – Active population by sectors of activity

Source – Population Censuses.

Unit – Thousands.

Year	1890	1900	1911	1930	1940
Total active population	2 530	2 457	2 545	2 517	2 775
Agriculture	1 536	1 508	1 442	1 237	1 424
Fishing	27	21	19	39	37
Mining and quarrying	4	4	9	11	19
Manufacturing industry	448	455	548	337	433
Building and public works	(a)	(a)	(a)	125	127
Electricity, gas, water and sewage	(a)	(a)	(a)	6	6
Transport	52	66	77	72	84
Trade	103	142	154	145	190
Administration and defence	58	52	54	88	101
Services	302	208	241	456	354

(a) Added to manufacturing industry.

Year	1950	1960	1970	1981	1991	2001
Total active population	3 196	3 316	3 061	3 848	4 128	4 680
Agriculture	1 523	1 398	966	705	419	216
Fishing	46	47	37	33	27	16
Mining and quarrying	25	26	12	18	16	18
Manufacturing industry	593	691	737	1 009	1 078	1 039
Building and public works	155	227	256	442	442	570
Electricity, gas, water and sewage	10	14	16	29	27	34
Transport	107	122	147	192	190	209
Trade	255	309	377	582	801	1 025
Administration and defence	115	119	156	253	329	369
Services	367	362	357	586	799	1 184

Disaggregation of manufacturing industry:

Year	1930	1940	1950	1960	1970	1981	1991	2001
Food, drinks and tobacco	37	66	77	73	61	106	99	96
Textiles, clothing and footwear	163	199	240	254	264	312	439	337
Wood, cork and furniture	40	59	92	101	108	117	69	63
Paper, printing and publishing	9	13	18	27	31	50	55	54
Non-metallic minerals	8	16	26	39	48	65	70	70
Chemicals	3	9	10	31	40	75	64	54
Metals, machinery, electrical and transport equipment	53	57	84	144	159	246	219	293
Sundry manufacturing industries	24	15	44	21	26	37	63	72

Table 4 – Gross domestic product

Source – Nuno Valério – "Avaliação do produto interno bruto de Portugal. I – Aproximação macroeconómica" (Working Paper no. 32 of the Gabinete de História Económica e Social, Instituto Superior de Economia e Gestão, 2008).

year	gross domestic product current prices 10^6 escudos	price index 1914 basis	gross domestic product 1914 prices 10^6 escudos	population thousands	per capita gross domestic product 1914 prices escudos
1776	140	0.44	318	2 869	111
...					
1800	312	1.03	303	3 165	96
1801	295	0.97	304	3 186	95
1802	273	0.93	294	3 189	92
...					
1812	205	1.34	153	3 229	47
...					
1817	260	1.02	255	3 249	78
...					
1821	188	0.55	342	3 282	104
...					
1827	176	0.59	298	3 412	88
...					
1842	159	0.54	294	3 756	78
1843	168	0.50	336	3 776	89
...					
1855	210	0.74	284	4 018	71
1856	232	0.93	249	4 039	62
...					
1861	266	0.80	332	4 144	80
...					
1865	287	0.77	373	4 222	88
1866	292	0.80	365	4 244	86
1867	309	0.86	359	4 264	84
1868	299	0.80	374	4 288	87
1869	302	0.79	382	4 312	89
1870	324	0.74	438	4 338	101
1871	320	0.72	444	4 362	102

384 | The Concise Economic History of Portugal: A Comprehensive Guide

year	gross domestic product current prices 10^6 escudos	price index 1914 basis	gross domestic product 1914 prices 10^6 escudos	population thousands	per capita gross domestic product 1914 prices escudos
1872	341	0.72	474	4 385	108
1873	364	0.95	383	4 412	87
1874	370	0.78	474	4 441	107
1875	398	0.79	504	4 472	113
1876	391	0.80	489	4 511	108
1877	408	0.91	448	4 551	99
1878	383	0.90	426	4 598	93
1879	385	0.86	448	4 643	96
1880	406	0.80	508	4 698	108
1881	411	0.82	501	4 734	106
1882	421	0.83	507	4 776	106
1883	413	0.79	523	4 818	109
1884	431	0.73	590	4 861	121
1885	441	0.70	630	4 907	128
1886	472	0.72	656	4 957	132
1887	462	0.70	660	5 004	132
1888	490	0.70	700	5 044	139
1889	510	0.76	671	5 079	132
1890	510	0.86	593	5 105	116
1891	497	0.83	599	5 138	117
1892	493	0.85	580	5 182	112
1893	503	0.87	578	5 220	111
1894	502	0.89	564	5 251	107
1895	538	0.84	640	5 275	121
1896	551	0.85	648	5 297	122
1897	557	0.92	605	5 331	114
1898	597	0.96	622	5 365	116
1899	602	0.94	640	5 407	118
1900	639	0.91	702	5 450	129
1901	616	0.90	684	5 497	125

Statistical appendix | 385

year	gross domestic product current prices 10⁶ escudos	price index 1914 basis	gross domestic product 1914 prices 10⁶ escudos	population thousands	per capita gross domestic product 1914 prices escudos
1902	613	0.87	705	5 552	127
1903	643	0.90	714	5 613	127
1904	658	0.96	685	5 670	121
1905	649	0.95	683	5 720	119
1906	659	0.95	694	5 758	120
1907	675	0.95	711	5 800	123
1908	694	0.96	723	5 840	124
1909	702	0.97	724	5 883	123
1910	732	0.93	787	5 937	133
1911	714	0.99	721	6 004	120
1912	756	0.98	771	6 008	128
1913	786	1.01	779	6 004	130
1914	711	1.00	711	6 053	117
1915	840	1.12	750	6 107	123
1916	1 141	1.37	833	6 147	135
1917	1 211	1.62	748	6 186	121
1918	1 600	2.93	546	6 104	89
1919	2 122	3.35	633	6 082	104
1920	3 881	5.80	669	6 084	110
1921	4 829	9.09	531	6 148	86
1922	8 048	10.99	732	6 216	118
1923	12 903	17.26	748	6 271	119
1924	16 958	23.99	707	6 344	111
1925	17 084	23.06	741	6 429	115
1926	17 139	22.08	776	6 507	119
1927	18 262	23.71	770	6 580	117
1928	20 690	22.69	912	6 658	137
1929	21 667	23.61	918	6 729	136
1930	20 818	22.43	928	6 812	136
1931	18 528	19.90	931	6 908	135

386 | The Concise Economic History of Portugal: A Comprehensive Guide

year	gross domestic product current prices 10^6 escudos	price index 1914 basis	gross domestic product 1914 prices 10^6 escudos	population thousands	per capita gross domestic product 1914 prices escudos
1932	18 354	19.49	942	7 003	134
1933	19 536	19.48	1 003	7 096	141
1934	20 361	19.68	1 035	7 189	144
1935	21 153	19.72	1 073	7 279	147
1936	21 134	20.22	1 045	7 379	142
1937	22 935	21.02	1 091	7 476	146
1938	23 329	20.37	1 145	7 575	151
1939	23 481	19.18	1 224	7 677	159
1940	24 503	20.09	1 220	7 758	157
1941	28 903	22.58	1 280	7 800	164
1942	34 134	27.58	1 238	7 859	157
1943	36 082	31.18	1 157	7 934	146
1944	35 216	32.08	1 098	8 013	137
1945	36 223	34.97	1 036	8 101	128
1946	42 079	39.80	1 057	8 182	129
1947	46 583	41.03	1 135	8 258	137
1948	47 406	38.31	1 237	8 358	148
1949	48 462	39.20	1 236	8 434	147
1950	50 682	38.19	1 327	8 512	156
1951	57 297	38.72	1 480	8 547	173
1952	58 751	38.78	1 515	8 563	177
1953	58 993	39.13	1 508	8 587	176
1954	62 564	39.44	1 586	8 607	184
1955	65 447	40.03	1 635	8 657	189
1956	69 943	41.28	1 694	8 698	195
1957	74 250	41.91	1 772	8 737	203
1958	79 191	42.14	1 879	8 789	214
1959	84 042	43.00	1 954	8 837	221
1960	88 994	43.47	2 047	8 991	228
1961	92 648	43.67	2 122	8 944	237

Statistical appendix | 387

year	gross domestic product current prices 10^6 escudos	price index 1914 basis	gross domestic product 1914 prices 10^6 escudos	population thousands	per capita gross domestic product 1914 prices escudos
1962	103 987	44.37	2 344	9 002	260
1963	107 438	44.12	2 435	9 040	269
1964	116 626	45.16	2 583	9 053	285
1965	135 681	48.01	2 826	8 996	314
1966	144 812	49.03	2 954	8 871	333
1967	162 217	52.75	3 075	8 798	350
1968	175 432	54.27	3 233	8 743	370
1969	188 229	56.86	3 310	8 696	381
1970	212 358	59.12	3 592	8 648	415
1971	245 768	61.94	3 968	8 642	459
1972	289 955	66.21	4 379	8 622	508
1973	342 817	74.58	4 597	8 545	538
1974	405 744	85.77	4 731	8 891	532
1975	469 776	104.67	4 488	9 457	475
1976	561 947	122.40	4 591	9 685	474
1977	722 257	148.38	4 868	9 737	500
1978	893 364	172.88	5 168	9 772	529
1979	1 135 905	205.24	5 535	9 800	565
1980	1 476 316	254.62	5 798	9 828	590
1981	1 773 726	299.38	5 925	9 884	599
1982	2 144 820	354.36	6 053	9 939	609
1983	2 740 339	448.39	6 112	9 970	613
1984	3 365 099	556.43	6 048	10 008	604
1985	4 131 014	672.06	6 147	10 014	614
1986	5 048 501	794.93	6 351	10 007	635
1987	5 948 432	870.21	6 836	9 981	685
1988	7 100 357	986.08	7 201	9 955	723
1989	8 388 429	1 092.35	7 679	9 920	774
1990	10 072 063	1 216.04	8 283	9 873	839
1991	11 549 381	1 348.93	8 562	9 865	868

year	gross domestic product current prices 10^6 escudos	price index 1914 basis	gross domestic product 1914 prices 10^6 escudos	population thousands	per capita gross domestic product 1914 prices escudos
1992	12 984 390	1 470.51	8 830	9 896	892
1993	13 579 306	1 548.53	8 769	9 935	883
1994	14 722 964	1 654.30	8 900	9 988	891
1995	16 165 000	1 747.70	9 249	10 026	923
1996	17 246 000	1 800.10	9 581	10 056	953
1997	18 603 000	1 868.30	9 957	10 092	987
1998	20 192 000	1 939.95	10 409	10 128	1 028
1999	22 539 000	1 999.39	11 273	10 178	1 108
2000	24 454 000	2 060.55	11 868	10 243	1 159
2001	25 862 000	2 135.68	12 109	10 329	1 172
2002	27 087 000	2 219.57	12 204	10 407	1 173
2003	27 505 000	2 280.77	12 060	10 475	1 151
2004	28 606 000	2 318.82	12 336	10 529	1 172
2005	29 825 000	2 377.56	12 544	10 570	1 187
2006	31 089 000	2 444.92	12 716	10 599	1 200
2007	32 610 000	2 517.40	12 954	10 618	1 200
2008	33 287 000	2 570.54	12 949	10 627	1 219

Figures for recent years (million euros)

year	gross domestic product current prices	gross domestic product prices of previous year
1999	112 695	109 324
2000	122 270	118 660
2001	129 308	124 735
2002	135 434	130 290
2003	137 523	133 831
2004	143 029	140 682
2005	149 123	145 439
2006	155 446	151 163
2007	163 051	158 357
2008	166 433	162 992

Statistical appendix | 389

Table 5 – Money supply

Sources:
– from 1834 to 1853, M0 according to Rita Sousa – "Money supply in Portugal 1834-1891" (Estudos de Economia, volume XII, no. 1, 1991);
– from 1854 to 1890, M0 according to the same source; other items computed using data from Jaime Reis – A evolução da oferta monetária portuguesa: 1854-1912 (Banco de Portugal, Lisboa, 1990);
– from 1891 to 1912, Jaime Reis – A evolução da oferta monetária portuguesa: 1854-1912 (Banco de Portugal, Lisboa, 1990) excluding gold coins;
– from 1913 to 1946, computed using data from Nuno Valério – A moeda em Portugal, 1913-1947 (Sá da Costa, Lisboa, 1984);
– from 1947 to 1993, Maximiano Pinheiro et al. – Séries longas para a economia portuguesa (Banco de Portugal, Lisboa, 1997);
– from 1994 onwards, Estatísticas Monetárias e Financeiras.

Unit – Million escudos.

Remark – Statistics relating to the banking system are incomplete until 1946. Coverage is particularly poor between 1893 and 1912: during this period there are data relating only to joint-stock banks.

Year	M0	M1	M2	Liquidity	Monetary base
1834	36	?	?	?	?
1835	36	?	?	?	?
1836	36	?	?	?	?
1837	36	?	?	?	?
1838	36	?	?	?	?
1839	37	?	?	?	?
1840	37	?	?	?	?
1841	38	?	?	?	?
1842	38	?	?	?	?
1843	39	?	?	?	?
1844	39	?	?	?	?
1845	40	?	?	?	?

Year	M0	M1	M2	Liquidity	Monetary base
1846	37	?	?	?	?
1847	36	?	?	?	?
1848	36	?	?	?	?
1849	35	?	?	?	?
1850	35	?	?	?	?
1851	37	?	?	?	?
1852	40	?	?	?	?
1853	41	?	?	?	?
1854	37	38	38	38	47
1855	39	41	41	41	47
1856	41	43	43	43	48
1857	43	45	45	45	48
1858	44	47	47	47	47
1859	44	47	47	47	50
1860	49	52	52	52	51
1861	51	54	54	54	53
1862	55	59	59	59	59
1863	57	61	61	61	61
1864	55	60	60	60	61
1865	53	59	59	59	58
1866	53	58	58	58	58
1867	52	58	58	58	57
1868	51	56	56	56	57
1869	51	57	57	57	58
1870	53	60	60	60	58
1871	56	65	65	65	63
1872	58	69	69	69	64
1873	60	75	75	75	69
1874	61	78	78	78	70
1875	63	87	87	87	74
1876	63	78	78	78	76
1877	66	80	80	80	74

Statistical appendix | 391

Year	M0	M1	M2	Liquidity	Monetary base
1878	70	84	84	84	78
1879	69	83	83	83	78
1880	72	86	86	86	81
1881	75	92	92	92	85
1882	75	91	91	91	85
1883	80	96	96	96	89
1884	83	101	101	101	92
1885	87	105	105	105	96
1886	92	116	116	116	107
1887	99	127	127	127	114
1888	106	140	140	140	120
1889	114	151	151	151	130
1890	121	152	152	152	134
1891	50	71	71	71	58
1892	68	86	86	86	75
1893	69	81	81	81	73
1894	71	84	84	84	72
1895	74	88	88	88	73
1896	75	91	91	91	76
1897	82	95	95	98	83
1898	89	105	105	117	89
1899	90	108	108	121	90
1900	90	108	108	123	90
1901	92	112	112	129	90
1902	93	113	113	132	93
1903	94	113	113	133	93
1904	93	113	113	135	91
1905	91	113	113	129	90
1906	95	115	115	144	91
1907	98	116	116	144	94
1908	98	119	119	147	94
1909	95	113	113	144	92

Year	M0	M1	M2	Liquidity	Monetary base
1910	105	126	126	155	92
1911	109	131	131	159	95
1912	109	134	134	165	94
1913	106	146	160	192	114
1914	117	165	179	209	125
1915	135	183	199	234	142
1916	161	213	231	263	169
1917	198	261	285	344	219
1918	262	348	386	463	294
1919	284	570	660	759	319
1920	547	820	951	1033	584
1921	655	1056	1286	1487	721
1922	965	1521	1866	2127	1035
1923	1298	1963	2354	2660	1365
1924	1599	2420	2822	3092	1691
1925	1709	2500	2921	3487	1814
1926	1761	2583	3116	4158	1900
1927	1780	2711	3360	4463	1910
1928	1870	2974	3715	4929	1983
1929	1898	3335	4340	5493	2060
1930	1857	3674	4600	5479	2003
1931	1875	3846	4723	5538	2154
1932	1885	4252	5221	5911	2429
1933	1925	4417	5408	5632	2458
1934	2069	5121	6150	6155	2827
1935	2090	5526	6549	6550	2872
1936	2188	5777	6757	6757	3113
1937	2192	5839	6920	6920	3250
1938	2212	6081	7150	7150	3283
1939	2468	6447	7607	7607	3339
1940	2815	7617	8726	8726	4133
1941	4244	10985	12109	12109	7345

Year	M0	M1	M2	Liquidity	Monetary base
1942	5267	16192	17497	17497	11805
1943	6656	19425	20770	20770	14541
1944	7230	23265	24444	24444	16943
1945	7734	26314	27380	27380	18859
1946	8253	28307	29347	29347	19214
1947	8371	21646	24654	24654	15391
1948	8323	21194	24029	24029	13265
1949	8104	20049	22954	22954	11949
1950	8096	20988	24029	24029	12692
1951	8849	23474	26775	26775	15058
1952	8994	23879	27278	27278	15699
1953	9236	25290	29183	29183	17229
1954	9747	27615	31767	31767	18429
1955	10274	28716	33558	33558	18897
1956	10677	30546	35820	35820	19924
1957	11267	32958	38787	38787	20212
1958	11842	35113	41764	41764	21028
1959	12507	37135	44628	44628	21843
1960	13151	38877	47378	47378	22252
1961	15246	39212	48418	48418	22655
1962	16119	42710	54480	54480	23957
1963	17505	48746	61888	61888	25487
1964	17994	55837	72287	72287	28366
1965	22126	60311	79681	79681	30817
1966	23577	69202	90649	90650	32229
1967	24363	76924	104643	104644	35182
1968	25402	83589	121076	121077	38855
1969	26772	91349	139887	139957	41238
1970	29848	96464	163017	163152	45685
1971	32061	106663	195601	196060	52173
1972	36269	120532	239568	239988	62239
1973	38418	164696	308520	309174	70201

Year	M0	M1	M2	Liquidity	Monetary base
1974	69881	181062	350495	351544	94353
1975	109994	221363	390217	391522	130190
1976	109107	245666	459163	466614	141394
1977	113208	274123	534817	573076	149421
1978	121280	312374	645888	731508	174402
1979	142119	396557	851779	1001555	228200
1980	165162	481426	1093506	1347044	274964
1981	188372	524514	1356367	1733009	376369
1982	219457	610479	1683896	2195451	486244
1983	240051	666197	1969213	2645821	552713
1984	267349	772320	2458328	3379336	577540
1985	318982	980559	3056227	4310376	609329
1986	399256	1334154	3656960	5274648	686246
1987	457686	1611614	4280151	6110495	875485
1988	509544	1951198	5059103	7132188	990262
1989	577349	2242559	5717246	7999273	1893017
1990	623876	2352222	6229915	8885620	2052595
1991	683079	2704682	7801571	10644870	2514967
1992	708190	3163733	9106545	12356165	2781634
1993	752931	3392599	9758933	13498835	3031088
1994	795800	3641400	10654400	11743800	3558200
1995	841000	3972200	11522000	12848500	3692100
1996	867200	4302200	12468200	13721400	3317000
1997	776100	4901900	13289200	14673300	3015900
1998	923600	5757400	14401300	15713500	3029600

Table 6 – Bank of Portugal discount rates

Source – <u>Banco de Portugal, Relatório do Conselho de Administração</u>, various years

Unit – Percentage.

Date	Discount rate	Date	Discount rate	Date	Discount rate
1891-01-13	6	1943-04-08	3	1985-11-26	19
1896 (a)	5.5	1943-08-16	2.5	1986-04-09	17.5
1908-01-09	6	1944-01-12	2	1986-06-28	16
1913-06-23	5.5	1965-09-01	2.5	1987-01-06	15.5
1920-07-03	6	1969-01-06	2.75	1987-03-20	15
1920-07-15	6.5	1970-04-25	3.5	1987-10-15	14.5
1920-09-03	7	1971-02-05	3.75	1988-02-05	14
1923-05-01	8	1972-12-18	4	1988-09-15	13.5
1923-09-12	9	1973-12-21	5	1989-03-18	14.5
1926-07-27	8	1974-07-10	6.5	1993-05-20	13.5
1930-06-02	7.5	1974-12-21	7.5	1994-01-20	12
1931-08-10	7	1975-12-19	6.5	1994-09-30	10.5
1932-04-04	6.5	1977-02-28	8	1996-02-01	8.75
1933-03-13	6	1977-08-26	13	1996-04-23	8.25
1933-12-11	5.5	1981-07-16	18	1996-12-12	7
1934-12-13	5	1982-04-20	19	1997-05-06	6
1936-05-11	4.5	1983-03-23	23	1998-02-25	5
1937-08-11	4	1985-01-11	25	1998-11-06	4.25
1941-03-31	3.5	1985-08-03	23	1998-12-19	3.25

(a) The date of alteration is not shown in the Report of the Bank of Portugal.

Table 7 – Prices

Sources:
Legal price of gold – calculated on the basis of Valério, 1991.
Market price of gold – Banco de Portugal, Relatório do Conselho de Administração, various years.
Legal price of silver – calculated on the basis of Valério, 1991.
Price index – Valério, 1997, extended with the consumer price index of the National Statistical Institute.
Legal factor of correction – From 1369 to 1473, Godinho, 1981-1983. From 1900 onwards, Government Regulations.

Note concerning the legal factor of correction – From 1369 to 1473, base 1369 = 1. From 1900 onwards, base 1914 = 100. The two sections of the series are not linked together.

Year	Legal price of gold (escudos/kg)	Market price of gold (escudos/kg)	Legal price of silver (escudos/kg)	Price index (base 1914 = 100)	Legal factor of correction (see note)
1253	0.011	?	0.001	?	-
...					
1329	0.011	?	0.001	?	-
1330	0.019	?	0.002	?	-
...					
1359	0.019	?	0.002	?	-
1360	0.026	?	0.003	?	-
...					
1366	0.026	?	0.003	?	-
1367	0.026	?	0.004	?	-
1368	0.026	?	0.004	?	-
1369	0.053	?	0.026	?	1
1370	0.053	?	0.031	?	1
1371	0.038	?	0.022	?	1
1372	0.038	?	0.004	?	1

Year	Legal price of gold (escudos/kg)	Market price of gold (escudos/kg)	Legal price of silver (escudos/kg)	Price index (base 1914 = 100)	Legal factor of correction (see note)
...					
1382	0.038	?	0.004	?	1
1383	?	?	0.006	?	1
1384	?	?	0.006	?	1
1385	?	?	0.013	?	1
1386	?	?	0.013	?	1
1387	?	?	0.022	?	1
1388	?	?	0.022	?	1
1389	?	?	0.045	?	5
1390	?	?	0.067	?	5
1391	?	?	0.275	?	5
...					
1397	?	?	0.275	?	5
1398	?	?	0.157	?	5
1399	?	?	0.157	?	15
1400	?	?	0.157	?	15
1401	?	?	0.314	?	15
...					
1403	?	?	0.314	?	15
1404	?	?	0.468	?	15
...					
1407	?	?	0.468	?	15
1408	?	?	0.314	?	15
1409	?	?	0.314	?	50
...					
1414	?	?	0.314	?	50
1415	?	?	1.242	?	50
1416	4.082	?	1.242	?	50
1417	?	?	1.242	?	250
...					
1421	?	?	1.242	?	250

Year	Legal price of gold (escudos/kg)	Market price of gold (escudos/kg)	Legal price of silver (escudos/kg)	Price index (base 1914 = 100)	Legal factor of correction (see note)
1422	?	?	1.242	?	500
...					
1429	?	?	1.242	?	500
1430	?	?	3.765	?	500
...					
1432	?	?	3.765	?	500
1433	40.816	?	3.765	?	500
1434	40.816	?	3.765	?	500
1435	34.864	?	3.803	?	500
1436	34.864	?	3.803	?	700
...					
1440	34.864	?	3.803	?	700
1441	40.675	?	4.564	?	700
...					
1450	40.675	?	4.564	?	700
1451	53.749	?	6.466	?	700
...					
1456	53.749	?	6.466	?	700
1457	63.416	?	6.466	?	700
...					
1459	63.416	?	6.466	?	700
1460	71.870	?	6.466	?	700
...					
1471	71.870	?	6.466	?	700
1472	91.316	?	9.052	?	700
1473	91.316	?	9.052	?	980
...					
1488	91.316	?	9.052	?	-
1489	107.101	?	10.840	?	-
...					
1498	107.101	?	10.840	?	-

Statistical appendix | 399

Year	Legal price of gold (escudos/kg)	Market price of gold (escudos/kg)	Legal price of silver (escudos/kg)	Price index (base 1914 = 100)	Legal factor of correction (see note)
1499	107.101	?	10.982	?	-
...					
1503	107.101	?	10.982	?	-
1504	109.914	?	10.982	?	-
...					
1516	109.914	?	10.982	?	-
1517	112.740	?	11.410	?	-
...					
1519	112.740	?	11.410	?	-
1520	112.740	?	11.410	6	-
1521	112.740	?	11.410	6	-
...					
1523	112.740	?	11.410	?	-
1524	112.740	?	11.410	8	-
1525	112.740	?	11.410	3	-
...					
1527	112.740	?	11.410	?	-
1528	112.740	?	11.410	6	-
1529	112.740	?	11.410	8	-
1530	112.740	?	11.410	?	-
1531	112.740	?	11.410	9	-
...					
1533	112.740	?	11.410	?	-
1534	112.740	?	11.410	6	-
...					
1536	112.740	?	11.410	?	-
1537	119.574	?	11.410	?	-
1538	121.966	?	11.410	?	-
1539	121.966	?	11.885	?	-
1540	121.966	?	11.885	9	-
...					

400 | The Concise Economic History of Portugal: A Comprehensive Guide

Year	Legal price of gold (escudos/kg)	Market price of gold (escudos/kg)	Legal price of silver (escudos/kg)	Price index (base 1914 = 100)	Legal factor of correction (see note)
1542	121.966	?	11.885	?	-
1543	121.966	?	11.885	10	-
...					
1548	121.966	?	11.885	?	-
1549	121.966	?	11.885	9	-
1550	121.966	?	11.885	?	-
1551	121.966	?	11.885	12	-
1552	121.966	?	11.885	?	-
1553	121.966	?	11.885	8	-
1554	121.966	?	11.885	?	-
1555	141.824	?	12.361	?	-
1556	141.824	?	12.361	14	-
1557	141.824	?	12.361	?	-
1558	141.824	?	11.410	?	-
1559	141.824	?	11.410	?	-
1560	141.824	?	11.695	8	-
1561	141.824	?	11.695	14	-
...					
1563	141.824	?	11.695	?	-
1564	141.824	?	11.695	12	-
1565	141.824	?	11.695	11	-
1566	141.824	?	11.695	15	-
1567	141.824	?	11.695	14	-
1568	141.824	?	11.695	11	-
1569	141.824	?	11.695	11	-
1570	141.824	?	11.695	14	-
1571	141.824	?	11.695	14	-
1572	141.824	?	11.695	13	-
1573	141.824	?	12.599	13	-
...					
1576	141.824	?	12.599	?	-

Statistical appendix | 401

Year	Legal price of gold (escudos/kg)	Market price of gold (escudos/kg)	Legal price of silver (escudos/kg)	Price index (base 1914 = 100)	Legal factor of correction (see note)
1577	141.824	?	12.599	16	-
1578	141.824	?	12.599	20	-
1579	141.824	?	12.599	20	-
1580	141.824	?	12.599	13	-
1581	141.824	?	12.599	?	-
1582	141.824	?	12.741	20	-
1583	141.824	?	12.741	23	-
1584	141.824	?	12.741	20	-
1585	141.824	?	12.741	17	-
1586	141.824	?	12.741	17	-
1587	141.824	?	12.741	22	-
1588	141.824	?	13.312	26	-
1589	141.824	?	13.312	25	-
1590	141.824	?	13.312	?	-
1591	141.824	?	13.312	22	-
1592	141.824	?	13.312	22	-
1593	141.824	?	13.312	23	-
1594	141.824	?	13.312	19	-
1595	141.824	?	13.312	27	-
1596	141.824	?	13.312	28	-
1597	141.824	?	13.312	29	-
1598	141.824	?	13.312	32	-
1599	141.824	?	13.312	29	-
1600	141.824	?	13.312	27	-
1601	141.824	?	13.312	?	-
1602	141.824	?	13.312	24	-
1603	141.824	?	13.312	?	-
1604	141.824	?	13.312	35	-
1605	141.824	?	13.312	?	-
1606	141.824	?	13.312	34	-
1607	141.824	?	13.312	30	-

Year	Legal price of gold (escudos/kg)	Market price of gold (escudos/kg)	Legal price of silver (escudos/kg)	Price index (base 1914 = 100)	Legal factor of correction (see note)
1608	141.824	?	13.312	31	-
...					
1611	141.824	?	13.312	?	-
1612	141.824	?	13.312	23	-
1613	141.824	?	13.312	25	-
1614	141.824	?	13.312	22	-
1615	141.824	?	13.312	22	-
1616	141.824	?	13.312	23	-
1617	141.824	?	13.312	28	-
1618	141.824	?	13.312	33	-
1619	141.824	?	13.312	25	-
1620	141.824	?	13.312	26	-
1621	141.824	?	13.312	27	-
1622	141.824	?	13.312	?	-
1623	141.824	?	13.312	18	-
1624	141.824	?	13.312	17	-
1625	141.824	?	13.312	21	-
1626	141.824	?	13.312	32	-
1627	141.824	?	13.312	28	-
...					
1629	141.824	?	13.312	?	-
1630	141.824	?	13.312	34	-
1631	141.824	?	13.312	39	-
1632	141.824	?	13.312	36	-
1633	141.824	?	13.312	22	-
1634	141.824	?	13.312	26	-
1635	141.824	?	13.312	39	-
1636	141.824	?	13.312	43	-
1637	141.824	?	13.312	41	-
1638	141.824	?	13.312	27	-
1639	141.824	?	13.312	20	-

Statistical appendix | 403

Year	Legal price of gold (escudos/kg)	Market price of gold (escudos/kg)	Legal price of silver (escudos/kg)	Price index (base 1914 = 100)	Legal factor of correction (see note)
1640	141.824	?	13.312	?	-
1641	141.824	?	16.164	19	-
1642	267.451	?	16.237	23	-
1643	267.451	?	19.016	30	-
1644	267.451	?	19.016	?	-
1645	267.451	?	19.016	26	-
1646	312.012	?	19.016	27	-
1647	312.012	?	19.016	25	-
...					
1650	312.012	?	19.016	?	-
1651	312.012	?	19.016	45	-
1652	312.012	?	19.016	33	-
1653	312.012	?	19.016	36	-
1654	312.012	?	19.016	26	-
1655	312.012	?	19.016	26	-
1656	312.012	?	19.016	?	-
1657	312.012	?	19.016	24	-
1658	312.012	?	19.016	36	-
1659	312.012	?	19.016	38	-
1660	312.012	?	19.016	32	-
1661	312.012	?	19.016	?	-
1662	356.506	?	19.016	31	-
1663	356.506	?	23.771	49	-
1664	356.506	?	23.771	40	-
1665	356.506	?	23.771	?	-
1666	356.506	?	23.771	33	-
1667	356.506	?	23.771	?	-
1668	392.157	?	23.771	19	-
1669	392.157	?	23.771	19	-
...					
1671	392.157	?	23.771	?	-

404 | The Concise Economic History of Portugal: A Comprehensive Guide

Year	Legal price of gold (escudos/kg)	Market price of gold (escudos/kg)	Legal price of silver (escudos/kg)	Price index (base 1914 = 100)	Legal factor of correction (see note)
1672	392.157	?	23.771	18	-
1673	392.157	?	23.771	22	-
1674	392.157	?	23.771	24	-
1675	392.157	?	23.771	22	-
1676	392.157	?	25.197	21	-
1677	405.680	?	25.197	24	-
1678	405.680	?	25.197	28	-
1679	405.680	?	25.197	22	-
1680	405.680	?	25.197	31	-
1681	405.680	?	25.197	27	-
1682	405.680	?	25.197	24	-
1683	405.680	?	25.197	26	-
1684	405.680	?	25.197	28	-
1685	405.680	?	25.197	32	-
1686	405.680	?	25.197	22	-
1687	405.680	?	25.197	18	-
1688	486.855	?	31.496	19	-
1689	486.855	?	31.496	20	-
1690	486.855	?	31.496	25	-
1691	486.855	?	31.496	27	-
1692	486.855	?	31.496	29	-
1693	486.855	?	31.496	29	-
1694	486.855	?	31.496	39	-
1695	486.855	?	31.496	38	-
1696	486.855	?	31.496	34	-
1697	486.855	?	31.496	33	-
1698	486.855	?	31.496	43	-
1699	486.855	?	31.496	45	-
1700	486.855	?	31.496	37	-
1701	486.855	?	31.496	31	-
1702	486.855	?	31.496	40	-

Statistical appendix | 405

Year	Legal price of gold (escudos/kg)	Market price of gold (escudos/kg)	Legal price of silver (escudos/kg)	Price index (base 1914 = 100)	Legal factor of correction (see note)
1703	486.855	?	31.496	57	-
1704	486.855	?	31.496	50	-
1705	486.855	?	31.496	34	-
1706	486.855	?	31.496	32	-
1707	486.855	?	31.496	38	-
1708	486.855	?	31.496	38	-
1709	486.855	?	31.496	56	-
1710	486.855	?	31.496	65	-
1711	486.855	?	31.496	69	-
1712	486.855	?	31.496	74	-
1713	486.855	?	31.496	47	-
1714	486.855	?	31.496	49	-
1715	486.855	?	31.496	43	-
1716	486.855	?	31.496	39	-
1717	486.855	?	31.496	30	-
1718	486.855	?	31.496	24	-
1719	486.855	?	31.496	30	-
1720	486.855	?	31.496	37	-
1721	486.855	?	31.496	38	-
1722	486.855	?	31.496	35	-
1723	486.855	?	31.496	30	-
1724	486.855	?	31.496	33	-
1725	486.855	?	31.496	35	-
1726	486.855	?	31.496	38	-
1727	486.855	?	31.496	32	-
1728	486.855	?	31.496	34	-
1729	486.855	?	31.496	32	-
1730	486.855	?	31.496	36	-
1731	486.855	?	31.496	35	-
1732	486.855	?	31.496	39	-
1733	486.855	?	31.496	39	-

Year	Legal price of gold (escudos/kg)	Market price of gold (escudos/kg)	Legal price of silver (escudos/kg)	Price index (base 1914 = 100)	Legal factor of correction (see note)
1734	486.855	?	33.279	41	-
1735	486.855	?	33.279	41	-
1736	486.855	?	33.279	43	-
1737	486.855	?	33.279	70	-
1738	486.855	?	33.279	53	-
1739	486.855	?	33.279	35	-
1740	486.855	?	33.279	43	-
1741	486.855	?	33.279	44	-
1742	486.855	?	33.279	37	-
1743	486.855	?	33.279	41	-
1744	486.855	?	33.279	45	-
1745	486.855	?	33.279	41	-
1746	486.855	?	33.279	42	-
1747	486.855	?	35.656	43	-
1748	486.855	?	35.656	39	-
1749	486.855	?	35.656	39	-
1750	486.855	?	35.656	44	-
1751	486.855	?	35.656	44	-
1752	486.855	?	35.656	43	-
1753	486.855	?	35.656	45	-
1754	486.855	?	35.656	42	-
1755	486.855	?	35.656	44	-
1756	486.855	?	35.656	40	-
1757	486.855	?	35.656	44	-
1758	486.855	?	35.656	46	-
1759	486.855	?	35.656	42	-
1760	486.855	?	35.656	40	-
1761	486.855	?	35.656	41	-
1762	486.855	?	35.656	43	-
1763	486.855	?	35.656	43	-
1764	486.855	?	35.656	49	-

Statistical appendix | 407

Year	Legal price of gold (escudos/kg)	Market price of gold (escudos/kg)	Legal price of silver (escudos/kg)	Price index (base 1914 = 100)	Legal factor of correction (see note)
1765	486.855	?	35.656	45	-
1766	486.855	?	35.656	41	-
1767	486.855	?	35.656	41	-
1768	486.855	?	35.656	45	-
1769	486.855	?	35.656	49	-
1770	486.855	?	35.656	43	-
1771	486.855	?	35.656	41	-
1772	486.855	?	35.656	43	-
1773	486.855	?	35.656	41	-
1774	486.855	?	35.656	45	-
1775	486.855	?	35.656	45	-
1776	486.855	?	35.656	44	-
1777	486.855	?	35.656	47	-
1778	486.855	?	35.656	49	-
1779	486.855	?	35.656	46	-
1780	486.855	?	35.656	53	-
1781	486.855	?	35.656	49	-
1782	486.855	?	35.656	47	-
1783	486.855	?	35.656	52	-
1784	486.855	?	35.656	54	-
1785	486.855	?	35.656	50	-
1786	486.855	?	35.656	53	-
1787	486.855	?	35.656	52	-
1788	486.855	?	35.656	51	-
1789	486.855	?	35.656	61	-
1790	486.855	?	35.656	66	-
1791	486.855	?	35.656	60	-
1792	486.855	?	35.656	60	-
1793	486.855	?	35.656	67	-
1794	486.855	?	35.656	63	-
1795	486.855	?	35.656	62	-

408 | The Concise Economic History of Portugal: A Comprehensive Guide

Year	Legal price of gold (escudos/kg)	Market price of gold (escudos/kg)	Legal price of silver (escudos/kg)	Price index (base 1914 = 100)	Legal factor of correction (see note)
1796	486.855	?	35.656	64	-
1797	486.855	?	35.656	69	-
1798	486.855	?	35.656	80	-
1799	486.855	?	35.656	79	-
1800	486.855	?	35.656	103	-
1801	486.855	?	35.656	97	-
1802	486.855	?	35.656	93	-
1803	486.855	?	35.656	101	-
1804	486.855	?	35.656	115	-
1805	486.855	?	35.656	98	-
1806	486.855	?	35.656	92	-
1807	486.855	?	35.656	91	-
1808	486.855	?	35.656	98	-
1809	486.855	?	35.656	101	-
1810	486.855	?	35.656	130	-
1811	486.855	?	35.656	156	-
1812	486.855	?	35.656	134	-
1813	486.855	?	35.656	112	-
1814	486.855	?	35.656	96	-
1815	486.855	?	35.656	96	-
1816	486.855	?	35.656	91	-
1817	486.855	?	35.656	102	-
1818	486.855	?	35.656	85	-
1819	486.855	?	35.656	65	-
1820	486.855	?	35.656	52	-
1821	486.855	?	35.656	55	-
1822	570.451	?	35.656	64	-
1823	570.451	?	35.656	68	-
1824	570.451	?	35.656	70	-
1825	570.451	?	35.656	63	-
1826	570.451	?	35.656	63	-

Statistical appendix | 409

Year	Legal price of gold (escudos/kg)	Market price of gold (escudos/kg)	Legal price of silver (escudos/kg)	Price index (base 1914 = 100)	Legal factor of correction (see note)
1827	570.451	?	35.656	59	-
1828	570.451	?	35.656	54	-
1829	570.451	?	35.656	58	-
1830	570.451	?	35.656	52	-
1831	570.451	?	35.656	58	-
1832	570.451	?	35.656	53	-
1833	570.451	?	35.656	46	-
1834	570.451	?	35.656	56	-
1835	570.451	?	36.845	70	-
1836	570.451	?	36.845	63	-
1837	570.451	?	36.845	49	-
1838	570.451	?	36.845	49	-
1839	570.451	?	36.845	51	-
1840	570.451	?	36.845	58	-
1841	570.451	?	36.845	61	-
1842	570.451	?	36.845	54	-
1843	570.451	?	36.845	50	-
1844	570.451	?	36.845	42	-
1845	570.451	?	36.845	42	-
1846	570.451	?	36.845	54	-
1847	608.643	?	36.845	51	-
1848	608.643	?	36.845	45	-
1849	608.643	?	36.845	48	-
1850	608.643	?	36.845	55	-
1851	608.643	?	36.845	50	-
1852	608.643	?	36.845	49	-
1853	608.643	?	36.845	62	-
1854	615.063	?	-	76	-
1855	615.063	?	-	74	-
1856	615.063	?	-	93	-
1857	615.063	?	-	77	-

410 | The Concise Economic History of Portugal: A Comprehensive Guide

Year	Legal price of gold (escudos/kg)	Market price of gold (escudos/kg)	Legal price of silver (escudos/kg)	Price index (base 1914 = 100)	Legal factor of correction (see note)
1858	615.063	?	-	70	-
1859	615.063	?	-	78	-
1860	615.063	?	-	75	-
1861	615.063	?	-	80	-
1862	615.063	?	-	81	-
1863	615.063	?	-	77	-
1864	615.063	?	-	80	-
1865	615.063	?	-	77	-
1866	615.063	?	-	80	-
1867	615.063	?	-	86	-
1868	615.063	?	-	80	-
1869	615.063	?	-	79	-
1870	615.063	?	-	74	-
1871	615.063	?	-	72	-
1872	615.063	?	-	72	-
1873	615.063	?	-	95	-
1874	615.063	?	-	78	-
1875	615.063	?	-	79	-
1876	615.063	?	-	80	-
1877	615.063	?	-	91	-
1878	615.063	?	-	90	-
1879	615.063	?	-	86	-
1880	615.063	?	-	80	-
1881	615.063	?	-	82	-
1882	615.063	?	-	83	-
1883	615.063	?	-	79	-
1884	615.063	?	-	73	-
1885	615.063	?	-	70	-
1886	615.063	?	-	72	-
1887	615.063	?	-	70	-
1888	615.063	?	-	70	-

Statistical appendix | 411

Year	Legal price of gold (escudos/kg)	Market price of gold (escudos/kg)	Legal price of silver (escudos/kg)	Price index (base 1914 = 100)	Legal factor of correction (see note)
1889	615.063	?	-	76	-
1890	615.063	?	-	86	-
1891	615.063	693	-	83	-
1892	615.063	784	-	85	-
1893	615.063	766	-	87	-
1894	615.063	792	-	89	-
1895	615.063	779	-	84	-
1896	615.063	801	-	85	-
1897	615.063	899	-	92	-
1898	615.063	980	-	96	-
1899	615.063	878	-	94	-
1900	615.063	864	-	91	89
1901	615.063	873	-	90	89
1902	615.063	782	-	87	89
1903	615.063	763	-	90	89
1904	615.063	740	-	96	96
1905	615.063	656	-	95	96
1906	615.063	626	-	95	96
1907	615.063	635	-	95	96
1908	615.063	712	-	96	96
1909	615.063	710	-	97	96
1910	615.063	669	-	93	96
1911	615.063	668	-	99	100
1912	615.063	680	-	98	100
1913	615.063	718	-	101	100
1914	615.063	768	-	100	100
1915	615.063	924	-	112	112
1916	615.063	963	-	137	137
1917	615.063	1 056	-	162	172
1918	615.063	1 119	-	293	241
1919	615.063	1 287	-	335	315

412 | The Concise Economic History of Portugal: A Comprehensive Guide

Year	Legal price of gold (escudos/kg)	Market price of gold (escudos/kg)	Legal price of silver (escudos/kg)	Price index (base 1914 = 100)	Legal factor of correction (see note)
1920	615.063	3 819	-	580	476
1921	615.063	7 128	-	909	730
1922	615.063	10 559	-	1 099	985
1923	615.063	15 926	-	1 726	1 610
1924	615.063	20 336	-	2 399	1 913
1925	615.063	13 448	-	2 306	2 219
1926	615.063	12 896	-	2 208	2 219
1927	615.063	12 558	-	2 371	2 219
1928	615.063	14 807	-	2 269	2 219
1929	615.063	14 844	-	2 361	2 219
1930	615.063	14 813	-	2 243	2 219
1931	15 035.333	16 318	-	1 990	2 219
1932	15 035.333	20 466	-	1 949	2 219
1933	15 035.333	21 683	-	1 948	2 219
1934	15 035.333	24 223	-	1 968	2 219
1935	15 035.333	25 022	-	1 972	2 219
1936	15 035.333	24 698	-	2 022	2 219
1937	15 035.333	24 408	-	2 102	2 286
1938	15 035.333	25 175	-	2 037	2 286
1939	15 035.333	27 419	-	1 918	2 286
1940	15 035.333	28 402	-	2 009	2 716
1941	15 035.333	27 701	-	2 258	3 058
1942	15 035.333	27 948	-	2 758	3 541
1943	15 035.333	28 024	-	3 118	4 159
1944	15 035.333	28 024	-	3 208	4 898
1945	15 035.333	28 024	-	3 497	4 898
1946	15 035.333	28 024	-	3 980	4 898
1947	15 035.333	28 024	-	4 103	4 898
1948	15 035.333	28 024	-	3 381	4 898
1949	15 035.333	29 239	-	3 920	4 898
1950	15 035.333	32 378	-	3 819	4 898

Statistical appendix | 413

Year	Legal price of gold (escudos/kg)	Market price of gold (escudos/kg)	Legal price of silver (escudos/kg)	Price index (base 1914 = 100)	Legal factor of correction (see note)
1951	15 035.333	32 378	-	3 872	5 341
1952	15 035.333	32 378	-	3 878	5 341
1953	15 035.333	32 378	-	3 913	5 341
1954	15 035.333	32 378	-	3 944	5 341
1955	15 035.333	33 865	-	4 077	5 341
1956	15 035.333	33 626	-	4 256	5 341
1957	15 035.333	33 395	-	4 257	5 341
1958	15 035.333	33 472	-	4 318	5 680
1959	15 035.333	33 278	-	4 375	5 680
1960	15 035.333	33 449	-	4 472	5 680
1961	32 351.990	34 749	-	4 461	5 680
1962	32 351.990	33 453	-	4 459	5 680
1963	32 351.990	33 127	-	4 575	5 680
1964	32 351.990	33 204	-	4 799	5 943
1965	32 351.990	33 572	-	4 955	6 168
1966	32 351.990	33 605	-	5 081	6 458
1967	32 351.990	33 978	-	5 293	6 904
1968	32 351.990	37 656	-	5 398	6 904
1969	32 351.990	39 390	-	5 543	6 904
1970	32 351.990	37 691	-	5 822	7 455
1971	33 292.273	39 691	-	6 253	7 833
1972	33 292.273	53 553	-	6 778	8 380
1973	34 614.053	82 850	-	7 299	9 216
1974	-	151 394	-	10 064	12 019
1975	-	181 385	-	11 929	14 066
1976	-	146 660	-	14 391	16 801
1977	-	189 920	-	19 136	21 889
1978	-	287 250	-	24 257	27 984
1979	-	505 710	-	30 103	35 456
1980	-	968 750	-	35 641	39 354
1981	-	925 290	-	41 372	48 122

414 | The Concise Economic History of Portugal: A Comprehensive Guide

Year	Legal price of gold (escudos/kg)	Market price of gold (escudos/kg)	Legal price of silver (escudos/kg)	Price index (base 1914 = 100)	Legal factor of correction (see note)
1982	-	1 038 600	-	50 639	57 909
1983	-	1 594 710	-	63 552	72 554
1984	-	1 856 200	-	81 855	93 490
1985	-	1 810 650	-	97 899	111 854
1986	-	1 836 360	-	109 451	123 629
1987	-	2 108 700	-	119 470	134 706
1988	-	2 172 050	-	131 354	149 139
1989	-	2 070 210	-	147 905	166 297
1990	-	1 878 180	-	167 724	186 055
1991	-	?	-	186 845	209 961
1992	-	?	-	203 474	227 776
1993	-	?	-	216 700	245 641
1994	-	?	-	227 968	259 194
1995	-	?	-	237 315	268 451
1996	-	?	-	244 672	276 346
1997	-	?	-	250 055	280 471
1998	-	?	-	256 056	289 101
1999	-	?	-	261 690	293 618
2000	-	?	-	269 017	300 665
2001	-	?	-	280 854	321 223
2002	-	?	-	290 965	332 594
2003	-	?	-	300 567	341 665
2004	-	?	-	307 780	347 992
2005	-	?	-	314 859	357 934
2006	-	?	-	324 620	368 462
2007	-	?	-	332 735	375 831
2008	-	?	-	341 017	387 106

Statistical appendix | 415

Table 8 – Public accounts and public debt

Sources:

a) Effective expenditure, tax revenue, other effective revenue, and balance of public accounts – From 1833-1834 to 1882-1883, Conta da Receita e Despesa do Tesouro Público; from 1883-1884 to 1919-1920, Conta Geral da Administração Financeira do Estado; from 1920-1921 onwards, Conta Geral do Estado. As from 1964, the values are as presented by the source itself. For the years until 1963, the values are constructed from the source using the same criteria.

b) Effective public debt – Mata, 1993 and Valério, 1994, extended using the same criteria, based on the Conta Geral do Estado as from 1948.

Remarks:

Fiscal years from 1833-1834 to 1933-1934 began on 1 July of each civil year and ended on 30 June of the following civil year; the fiscal year 1934-1935 began on 1 July 1934 and ended on 31 December 1935; fiscal years from 1936 onwards coincided with civil years.

The account for 1833-1834 refers only to the flows relating to the constitutional government of Lisbon, and therefore excludes the flows relating to the absolutist government of Santarém.

Unit – Million escudos.

Year	Effective expenditure	Tax revenue	Other effective income	Balance of public accounts	Effective public debt
1833-1834	10	3	3	- 4	?
1834-1835	14	6	2	- 6	?
1835-1836	12	7	1	- 5	?
1836-1837	10	6	3	- 1	?
1837-1838	8	6	1	- 1	?
1838-1839	7	7	+ 0	+ 0	?
1839-1840	8	7	+ 0	- 1	?
1840-1841	8	6	1	- 2	?
1841-1842	14	7	2	- 5	?
1842-1843	14	7	1	- 6	?
1843-1844	12	8	2	- 2	?
1844-1845	11	8	1	- 2	?
...					
1851-1852	10	9	1	+ 0	91

Year	Effective expenditure	Tax revenue	Other effective income	Balance of public accounts	Effective public debt
1852-1853	13	10	1	- 2	76
1853-1854	11	9	1	- 0	92
1854-1855	13	10	1	- 3	92
1855-1856	13	10	1	- 2	93
1856-1857	14	10	1	- 3	107
1857-1858	17	10	3	- 5	106
1858-1859	17	11	2	- 5	112
1859-1860	15	10	1	- 3	124
1860-1861	15	11	1	- 3	136
1861-1862	20	12	1	- 7	141
1862-1863	21	13	1	- 7	148
1863-1864	20	13	2	- 5	170
1864-1865	20	15	2	- 3	183
1865-1866	20	13	2	- 5	184
1866-1867	22	13	2	- 7	193
1867-1868	29	14	2	- 13	226
1868-1869	20	14	2	- 5	246
1869-1870	31	15	2	- 15	261
1870-1871	21	15	2	- 4	308
1871-1872	24	16	2	- 6	307
1872-1873	23	17	3	- 3	308
1873-1874	27	19	4	- 4	343
1874-1875	29	20	3	- 5	351
1875-1876	31	21	4	- 6	363
1876-1877	36	21	5	- 10	380
1877-1878	34	22	4	- 8	404
1878-1879	34	24	3	- 7	406
1879-1880	31	20	3	- 8	421
1880-1881	33	22	3	- 8	417
1881-1882	36	25	4	- 7	433
1882-1883	33	23	4	- 6	444
1883-1884	34	25	4	- 5	441

Statistical appendix | 417

Year	Effective expenditure	Tax revenue	Other effective income	Balance of public accounts	Effective public debt
1884-1885	39	26	4	- 8	489
1885-1886	40	27	4	- 9	494
1886-1887	40	29	5	- 7	502
1887-1888	43	32	5	- 7	513
1888-1889	49	32	6	- 12	526
1889-1890	52	32	6	- 14	539
1890-1891	49	33	6	- 11	583
1891-1892	53	32	5	- 15	587
1892-1893	46	35	5	- 5	625
1893-1894	44	39	5	+ 0	600
1894-1895	45	38	5	- 1	599
1895-1896	48	43	7	+ 2	610
1896-1897	54	40	7	- 7	671
1897-1898	54	40	7	- 7	665
1898-1899	52	41	7	- 4	615
1899-1900	57	44	5	- 7	665
1900-1901	51	45	7	+ 1	695
1901-1902	52	43	6	- 3	683
1902-1903	54	45	6	- 3	594
1903-1904	55	47	6	- 2	610
1904-1905	55	48	8	+ 0	646
1905-1906	57	48	8	- 0	649
1906-1907	57	47	8	- 1	628
1907-1908	70	50	17	- 4	627
1908-1909	68	50	15	- 2	628
1909-1910	69	51	18	- 1	670
1910-1911	63	50	15	+ 2	656
1911-1912	64	51	10	- 3	661
1912-1913	76	56	23	+ 4	657
1913-1914	62	53	16	+ 7	648
1914-1915	95	46	22	- 27	744
1915-1916	134	47	39	- 48	806

418 | The Concise Economic History of Portugal: A Comprehensive Guide

Year	Effective expenditure	Tax revenue	Other effective income	Balance of public accounts	Effective public debt
1916-1917	144	50	39	- 56	883
1917-1918	179	49	43	- 87	994
1918-1919	271	64	37	- 170	1 164
1919-1920	347	88	71	- 188	1 553
1920-1921	418	131	88	- 199	2 860
1921-1922	550	173	147	- 230	4 002
1922-1923	1 187	321	216	- 649	6 963
1923-1924	1 171	555	215	- 401	8 048
1924-1925	1 428	734	428	- 266	8 401
1925-1926	1 508	815	284	- 409	8 900
1926-1927	1 821	907	280	- 634	9 365
1927-1928	1 667	1 069	442	- 155	9 573
1928-1929	1 757	1 444	604	+ 291	9 547
1929-1930	1 862	1 549	396	+ 83	9 432
1930-1931	1 730	1 439	481	+ 190	9 583
1931-1932	1 845	1 482	412	+ 49	9 867
1932-1933	1 931	1 497	423	- 11	7 394
1933-1934	1 973	1 548	435	+ 10	7 270
1934-1935	2 879	2 426	610	+ 157	7 208
1936	1 984	1 612	401	+ 29	7 186
1937	2 035	1 663	475	+ 104	7 238
1938	2 257	1 752	498	- 7	7 200
1939	2 357	1 684	485	- 188	7 154
1940	2 382	1 727	491	- 164	6 391
1941	2 786	1 911	532	- 343	6 615
1942	2 928	2 364	603	+ 39	8 243
1943	3 619	2 453	806	- 359	8 760
1944	3 456	2 526	847	- 83	9 410
1945	3 835	2 570	763	- 502	9 884
1946	4 394	2 968	932	- 494	10 437
1947	5 621	3 386	918	- 1 317	10 297
1948	5 631	3 494	939	- 1 198	10 230

Statistical appendix | 419

Year	Effective expenditure	Tax revenue	Other effective income	Balance of public accounts	Effective public debt
1949	5 581	3 687	1 003	- 891	10 258
1950	5 024	3 842	983	- 198	10 504
1951	5 493	4 280	1 280	+ 67	11 018
1952	5 701	4 548	1 332	+ 179	11 133
1953	6 238	4 539	1 722	+ 23	11 120
1954	6 520	4 777	1 594	- 149	11 652
1955	7 156	5 134	1 716	- 306	11 686
1956	7 389	5 465	1 897	- 27	11 717
1957	8 009	5 790	2 238	+ 19	11 734
1958	8 453	6 256	2 221	+ 24	14 790
1959	9 494	6 637	2 264	- 593	15 330
1960	11 057	7 269	2 426	- 1 362	16 174
1961	13 158	8 247	2 694	- 2 217	17 552
1962	14 542	8 680	3 406	- 2 456	21 524
1963	15 355	9 428	3 124	- 2 803	24 731
1964	16 789	9 750	3 922	- 3 117	28 276
1965	17 241	11 527	4 469	- 1 245	30 570
1966	18 647	12 631	5 109	- 907	32 413
1967	21 982	14 928	5 848	- 1 206	33 152
1968	24 051	16 409	6 259	- 1 383	33 304
1969	26 842	18 873	6 897	- 1 072	34 981
1970	30 811	23 011	8 097	+ 297	38 658
1971	35 651	24 798	9 033	- 1 820	42 723
1972	39 756	29 658	8 689	- 1 409	46 499
1973	47 609	35 498	9 684	- 2 427	53 626
1974	61 865	42 878	9 295	- 9 692	62 809
1975	84 850	48 235	10 161	- 26 454	100 340
1976	122 387	65 884	11 800	- 44 703	151 397
1977	155 582	91 297	18 607	- 45 678	210 549
1978	210 548	110 655	23 055	- 76 838	292 530
1979	273 312	139 896	30 624	- 102 792	253 773
1980	364 740	192 868	46 195	- 125 677	466 918

Year	Effective expenditure	Tax revenue	Other effective income	Balance of public accounts	Effective public debt
1981	481 708	257 171	73 287	- 151 250	709 702
1982	582 141	323 628	78 986	- 179 527	938 834
1983	737 019	434 492	120 050	- 182 477	1 302 540
1984	913 647	511 125	144 980	- 257 542	1 773 625
1985	1 202 886	629 366	149 748	- 423 772	2 343 372
1986	1 456 744	760 617	241 775	- 454 352	2 858 292
1987	1 637 359	1 008 140	204 061	- 425 158	3 768 076
1988	1 911 442	1 313 692	176 013	- 421 737	4 511 583
1989	2 296 570	1 621 140	321 367	- 354 063	5 180 194
1990	2 836 654	1 891 002	443 524	- 502 128	5 671 315
1991	3 356 655	2 295 918	479 643	- 581 094	6 584 002
1992	4 124 947	2 845 346	750 794	- 528 807	7 048 897
1993	4 218 861	2 786 209	507 033	- 925 619	8 225 777
1994	4 465 535	3 160 372	496 339	- 808 824	9 328 602
1995	4 865 022	3 396 930	719 547	- 748 545	10 509 910
1996	5 247 879	3 651 423	890 293	- 706 163	11 161 220
1997	5 933 355	3 992 462	1 461 024	- 489 869	11 365 911
1998	5 918 724	4 397 031	1 133 610	- 388 083	11 677 376
1999	6 137 003	4 790 746	933 832	- 412 425	12 621 556
2000	6 813 372	5 150 290	1 160 352	- 502 730	13 266 943
2001	6 862 753	5 248 715	717 917	- 896 121	14 525 163

Unit – Million euros.

Year	Effective expenditure	Tax revenue	Other effective income	Balance of public accounts	Effective public debt
2002	39 123	28 509	4 740	- 5 873	79 319
2003	36 630	28 593	3 088	- 4 949	83 276
2004	42 463	28 382	4 302	- 9 779	90 560
2005	43 156	30 436	2 926	- 9 794	101 575
2006	43 065	32 627	3 298	- 7 140	108 367
2007	44 454	35 628	3 780	- 5 036	112 804
2008	46 571	35 595	5 261	- 5 715	118 463

Table 9 – Foreign economic relations

Source:
– exports, imports, import duties until 1920 and monetary operations until 1930, <u>Estatísticas do Comércio Externo</u>, published under different titles;
– import duties from 1921 onwards, <u>Conta Geral do Estado</u>;
– monetary operations from 1931 onwards, <u>Relatório do Conselho de Administração do Banco de Portugal</u>;
– invisible flows, computed as imports - exports - monetary operations.

Unit – million escudos.

Remark – Data for the period 1891-1930 are of lower quality.

Year	Exports	Imports	Import duties	Invisible flows	Monetary operations
1776	9	10	?	?	?
1777	8	9	?	?	?
...					
1796	21	24	?	?	?
1797	11	19	?	?	?
...					
1799	32	33	?	?	?
1800	31	33	?	?	?
1801	35	34	?	?	?
1802	32	29	?	?	?
1803	30	28	?	?	?
1804	30	30	?	?	?
1805	30	35	?	?	?
1806	31	31	?	?	?
1807	27	29	?	?	?
1808	7	3	?	?	?
1809	12	14	?	?	?

Year	Exports	Imports	Import duties	Invisible flows	Monetary operations
1810	13	21	?	?	?
1811	8	43	?	?	?
1812	9	39	?	?	?
1813	10	38	?	?	?
1814	20	32	?	?	?
1815	23	37	?	?	?
1816	21	30	?	?	?
1817	21	27	?	?	?
1818	23	31	?	?	?
1819	16	24	?	?	?
1820	16	21	?	?	?
1821	14	22	?	?	?
1822	14	19	?	?	?
1823	10	17	?	?	?
1824	10	17	?	?	?
1825	13	16	?	?	?
1826	9	15	?	?	?
1827	11	16	?	?	?
1828	10	12	?	?	?
1829	9	12	?	?	?
1830	9	13	?	?	?
1831	7	10	?	?	?
...					
1842	7	10	2	- 3	0
1843	7	12	3	- 5	0
...					
1848	8	11	3	+ 2	0
...					
1851	8	12	4	+ 6	- 2
...					
1854	?	?	?	?	- 3
1855	12	16	4	+ 7	- 3

Year	Exports	Imports	Import duties	Invisible flows	Monetary operations
1856	15	19	4	+ 5	- 1
...					
1861	14	25	5	+ 13	- 2
1862	?	?	?	?	- 4
1863	?	?	?	?	- 2
1864	?	?	?	?	0
1865	16	24	8	+ 5	+ 3
1866	17	25	7	+ 8	0
1867	16	26	7	+ 9	+ 1
1868	16	24	7	+ 7	+ 1
1869	17	22	6	+ 5	0
1870	20	24	7	+ 5	- 1
1871	21	24	6	+ 6	- 4
1872	23	27	8	+ 6	- 2
1873	24	30	8	+ 11	- 4
1874	23	27	8	+ 5	- 1
1875	24	34	10	+ 11	- 2
1876	21	30	9	+ 12	- 3
1877	23	31	10	+ 7	+ 1
1878	18	29	10	+ 12	- 2
1879	18	33	12	+ 14	+ 1
1880	25	32	9	+ 11	- 3
1881	21	33	10	+ 16	- 3
1882	23	34	11	+ 12	- 1
1883	23	31	12	+ 11	- 3
1884	23	33	13	+ 13	- 3
1885	23	33	14	+ 13	- 3
1886	26	37	15	+ 20	- 9
1887	21	37	16	+ 20	- 4
1888	23	38	14	+ 21	- 6
1889	23	42	14	+ 26	- 8
1890	22	44	15	+ 27	- 4

Year	Exports	Imports	Import duties	Invisible flows	Monetary operations
1891	21	40	13	- 8	+ 26
1892	25	31	10	+ 2	+ 4
1893	23	38	14	+ 9	+ 6
1894	24	36	14	+ 9	+ 3
1895	27	40	16	+ 13	0
1896	26	40	15	+ 9	+ 4
1897	27	40	13	+ 11	+ 2
1898	31	49	12	+ 19	- 1
1899	29	51	15	+ 20	+ 2
1900	31	60	16	+ 27	+ 2
1901	28	58	15	+ 28	+ 1
1902	28	56	14	+ 27	0
1903	31	59	16	+ 28	0
1904	31	62	17	+ 29	+ 2
1905	29	61	17	+ 34	- 2
1906	31	60	17	+ 28	+ 2
1907	30	62	16	+ 31	0
1908	28	67	17	+ 38	+ 1
1909	31	65	16	+ 38	- 4
1910	36	70	16	+ 30	+ 4
1911	34	68	16	+ 38	- 4
1912	34	75	17	+ 42	- 2
1913	35	89	20	+ 51	+ 3
1914	27	69	17	+ 43	- 1
1915	34	76	12	+ 44	- 2
1916	56	129	12	+ 73	0
1917	55	137	11	+ 83	- 1
1918	83	178	10	+ 97	- 2
1919	107	229	14	+ 121	+ 1
1920	222	691	26	+ 470	- 1
1921	225	933	40	+ 709	- 1
1922	444	1 252	69	+ 809	0

Statistical appendix | 425

Year	Exports	Imports	Import duties	Invisible flows	Monetary operations
1923	684	2 229	147	+ 1 545	0
1924	949	2 958	198	+ 2 037	- 28
1925	862	2 484	213	+ 1 630	- 8
1926	736	2 342	271	+ 1 608	- 2
1927	723	2 663	342	+ 1 933	+ 7
1928	1 029	2 679	455	+ 1 645	+ 5
1929	1 073	2 529	554	+ 1 455	+ 1
1930	945	2 406	565	+ 1 462	- 1
1931	812	1 674	552	+ 1 850	- 988
1932	791	1 707	539	+ 1 181	- 265
1933	802	1 905	555	+ 1 209	- 106
1934	909	1 965	595	+ 1 041	+ 15
1935	923	2 294	612	+ 1 302	+ 69
1936	1 026	1 994	599	+ 1 178	+ 210
1937	1 202	2 353	578	+ 1 382	- 231
1938	1 139	2 300	619	+ 996	+ 165
1939	1 336	2 077	543	+ 1 132	- 391
1940	1 619	2 441	483	+ 1 481	- 659
1941	2 972	2 468	528	+ 3 214	- 3 718
1942	3 939	2 477	421	+ 3 066	- 4 528
1943	4 035	3 323	437	+ 993	- 1 705
1944	3 166	3 920	479	+ 3 429	- 2 675
1945	3 237	4 050	510	+ 2 669	- 1 856
1946	4 587	6 857	867	+ 2 772	- 502
1947	4 307	9 445	1 131	+ 2 339	+ 2 799
1948	4 295	10 351	1 073	+ 2 794	+ 3 262
1949	4 089	9 043	1 225	+ 4 869	+ 85
1950	5 334	7 879	1 071	+ 3 731	- 1 186
1951	7 559	9 472	1 348	+ 4 256	- 2 343
1952	6 811	9 988	1 488	+ 3 672	- 495
1953	6 283	9 513	1 357	+ 5 205	- 1 975
1954	7 297	10 085	1 484	+ 4 213	- 1 425

Year	Exports	Imports	Import duties	Invisible flows	Monetary operations
1955	8 165	11 453	1 641	+ 3 722	- 434
1956	8 621	12 725	1 738	+ 5 112	- 1 008
1957	8 289	14 422	1 845	+ 6 225	- 92
1958	8 299	13 809	1 874	+ 5 705	- 195
1959	8 351	13 681	1 990	+ 5 705	- 375
1960	9 408	15 695	2 273	+ 6 165	+ 122
1961	9 373	18 863	2 548	+ 7 113	+ 2 377
1962	10 632	16 830	2 299	+ 11 239	- 5 041
1963	12 024	18 866	2 390	+ 8 709	- 1 867
1964	14 831	22 377	2 341	+ 10 684	- 3 138
1965	16 573	26 553	3 029	+ 12 206	- 2 226
1966	17 812	29 406	2 992	+ 15 622	- 4 028
1967	20 166	30 453	3 112	+ 14 876	- 4 589
1968	21 917	33 858	3 112	+ 16 357	- 4 416
1969	24 526	37 262	3 533	+ 15 226	- 2 490
1970	27 299	45 495	4 896	+ 20 421	- 2 225
1971	30 248	52 416	4 786	+ 31 412	- 9 244
1972	35 255	60 684	4 890	+ 33 094	- 7 665
1973	45 410	74 776	4 725	+ 39 200	- 9 834
1974	58 014	118 095	5 128	+ 46 866	+ 13 215
1975	49 328	99 474	5 581	+ 25 194	+ 24 952
1976	55 089	130 859	8 916	+ 42 487	+ 33 283
1977	77 685	190 684	12 797	+ 53 524	+ 59 475
1978	106 451	230 128	11 650	+ 133 033	- 9 356
1979	176 051	331 927	10 551	+ 194 233	- 38 357
1980	231 623	475 486	12 107	+ 278 863	- 35 000
1981	256 913	609 014	15 600	+ 340 881	+ 11 220
1982	331 743	756 981	19 087	+ 432 460	- 7 222
1983	508 568	899 340	23 006	+ 303 456	+ 87 316
1984	760 580	1 160 633	19 721	+ 459 374	- 59 321
1985	971 747	1 326 529	22 041	+ 522 634	- 167 852
1986	1 082 261	1 444 026	16 236	+ 328 704	+ 33 061

Year	Exports	Imports	Import duties	Invisible flows	Monetary operations
1987	1 311 003	1 965 315	18 449	+ 920 896	- 266 584
1988	1 581 957	2 570 265	18 899	+ 1 180 683	- 192 275
1989	2 015 711	3 003 196	18 956	+ 1 536 600	- 549 115
1990	2 335 798	3 589 570	21 703	+ 1 746 832	- 493 060
1991	2 354 083	3 811 076	19 697	+ 2 042 256	- 585 263
1992	2 475 202	4 087 577	12 365	+ 1 857 584	- 245 209
1993	2 474 401	3 882 777	1 725	+ 1 863 473	- 455 097
1994	2 975 639	4 514 296	132	+ 1 006 762	+ 531 900
1995	3 501 819	5 028 697	175	+ 788 978	+ 737 900
1996	3 795 868	5 427 132	89	+ 461 964	+ 1 169 300
1997	4 195 050	6 139 709	242	+ 2 164 759	- 220 100
1998	4 461 034	6 914 779	394	+ 2 549 645	- 95 900
1999	4 616 280	7 519 209	32	+ 2 961 309	- 58 380
2000	5 288 467	8 672 286	53	+ 3 464 839	- 81 020

Unit – million euros.

Year	Exports	Imports	Import duties	Invisible flows	Monetary operations
2001	26 918 320	44 093 881	9 337	+ 5 667 149	+ 11 508 412
2002	27 398 284	42 466 265	120	+ 6 129 337	+ 8 938 644
2003	28 092 290	41 753 699	—	+ 7 885 443	+ 5 775 966
2004	29 576 450	45 861 484	—	+ 7 560 265	+ 8 724 769
2005	30 664 698	49 179 110	—	+ 6 137 203	+ 12 377 209
2006	34 511 054	53 100 312	—	+ 4 132 780	+ 14 456 478
2007	37 588 758	57 055 625	—	+ 4 489 136	+ 14 977 631
2008	37 949 405	61 174 478	—	+ 4 175 237	+ 19 049 836

428 | The Concise Economic History of Portugal: A Comprehensive Guide

Table 10 – Exchange rates

Sources:
– from 1891 to 1946, Banco de Portugal, Relatório do Conselho de Administração, various years;
– from 1947 onwards, Estatísticas Financeiras and Estatísticas Monetárias e Financeiras.

Unit – Escudos.

Year	Pound sterling	American dollar	French franc	European Currency Unit
1891	4.832	?	?	—
1892	5.735	?	?	—
1893	5.600	?	?	—
1894	5.790	?	?	—
1895	5.698	?	?	—
1896	5.853	?	?	—
1897	6.575	?	?	—
1898	7.108	?	?	—
1899	6.416	?	?	—
1900	6.320	?	?	—
1901	6.382	?	?	—
1902	5.722	?	?	—
1903	5.581	?	?	—
1904	5.413	?	?	—
1905	4.793	?	?	—
1906	4.582	?	?	—
1907	4.642	?	?	—
1908	5.199	?	?	—
1909	5.185	?	?	—
1910	4.895	?	?	—
1911	4.889	?	?	—
1912	4.974	?	?	—
1913	5.235	?	?	—

Statistical appendix | 429

Year	Pound sterling	American dollar	French franc	European Currency Unit
1914	5.663	?	?	—
1915	6.746	?	?	—
1916	7.032	?	?	—
1917	7.726	?	?	—
1918	7.901	?	?	—
1919	8.196	?	?	—
1920	18.329	?	?	—
1921	39.384	?	?	—
1922	65.084	?	?	—
1923	109.714	?	?	—
1924	133.950	?	?	—
1925	99.210	?	?	—
1926	94.770	?	?	—
1927	108.360	?	?	—
1928	108.250	?	?	—
1929	108.250	?	?	—
1930	108.250	?	?	—
1931	109.369	23.861	0.936	—
1932	110.061	31.601	1.240	—
1933	109.103	26.603	1.292	—
1934	110.453	21.867	1.436	—
1935	110.363	22.396	1.484	—
1936	110.377	22.172	1.355	—
1937	110.375	22.291	0.903	—
1938	110.385	22.553	0.649	—
1939	110.270	24.944	0.624	—
1940	102.726	27.564	0.597	—
1941	100.200	25.198	0.578	—
1942	100.200	25.054	0.580	—
1943	100.200	25.050	0.580	—
1944	100.200	24.977	0.580	—
1945	100.200	24.920	0.565	—

Year	Pound sterling	American dollar	French franc	European Currency Unit
1946	100.200	24.940	0.208	—
1947	100.200	25.014	0.212	—
1948	100.200	25.065	0.097	—
1949	94.791	26.150	0.079	—
1950	80.650	28.900	0.084	—
1951	80.659	28.900	0.083	—
1952	81.100	28.900	0.083	—
1953	81.100	28.900	0.083	—
1954	81.100	28.900	0.083	—
1955	81.100	28.900	0.083	—
1956	81.100	28.900	0.083	—
1957	81.100	28.900	0.078	—
1958	81.100	28.900	0.069	—
1959	82.000	28.780	0.060	—
1960	80.310	28.790	5.870	—
1961	80.270	28.860	5.880	—
1962	80.260	28.800	5.880	—
1963	80.280	28.870	5.890	—
1964	80.260	28.940	5.910	—
1965	80.240	28.900	5.900	—
1966	80.240	28.940	5.890	—
1967	78.980	28.960	5.880	—
1968	68.660	28.850	5.820	—
1969	68.190	28.680	5.520	—
1970	68.510	28.740	5.190	—
1971	68.710	28.310	5.140	—
1972	67.570	27.170	5.385	—
1973	59.780	24.650	5.541	—
1974	59.310	25.520	5.305	—
1975	56.470	25.670	5.980	—
1976	54.530	30.340	6.347	—
1977	66.920	38.410	7.824	—

Statistical appendix | 431

Year	Pound sterling	American dollar	French franc	European Currency Unit
1978	84.710	44.090	9.808	—
1979	103.970	49.080	11.541	?
1980	116.540	50.220	11.880	?
1981	124.180	61.710	11.360	?
1982	139.170	79.300	12.020	?
1983	167.730	110.950	14.500	?
1984	196.330	146.560	16.770	?
1985	222.700	170.580	19.090	?
1986	219.880	149.800	21.640	147.220
1987	231.050	141.090	23.480	162.730
1988	256.500	144.240	24.579	170.360
1989	258.130	157.770	25.095	173.670
1990	254.020	142.555	26.286	181.429
1991	255.260	144.482	25.621	178.833
1992	234.660	134.998	25.504	174.438
1993	241.382	160.780	28.358	187.804
1994	253.914	166.076	29.908	180.128
1995	236.667	149.984	30.063	193.898
1996	240.897	154.244	30.153	193.170
1997	287.033	175.313	30.028	197.958
1998	298.480	180.216	30.553	202.064

Cartographic appendix

Map 1 – Orography and hydrography of Continental Portugal

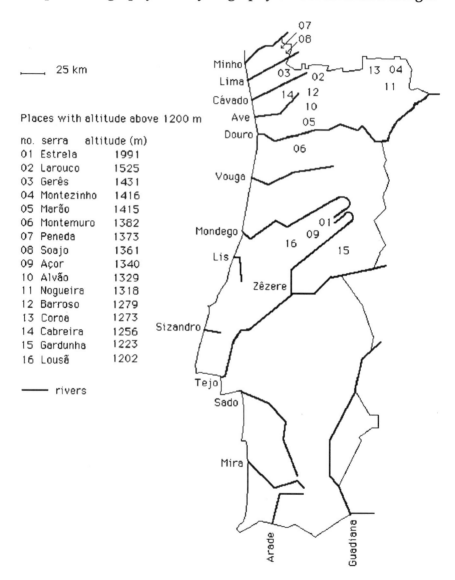

Map 2 – Geology of Continental Portugal

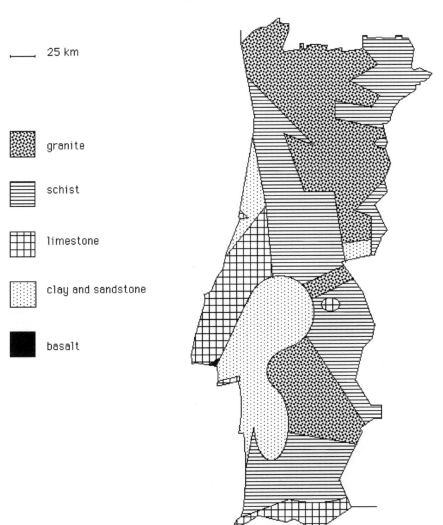

Map 3 – Regions and main towns of Continental Portugal

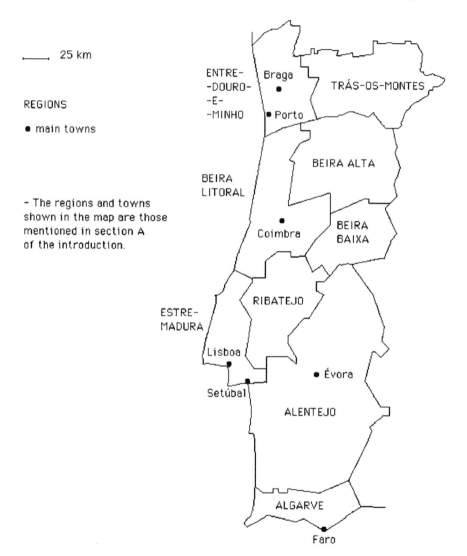

Cartographic appendix | 437

Map 4 – Regions and main towns of Madeira

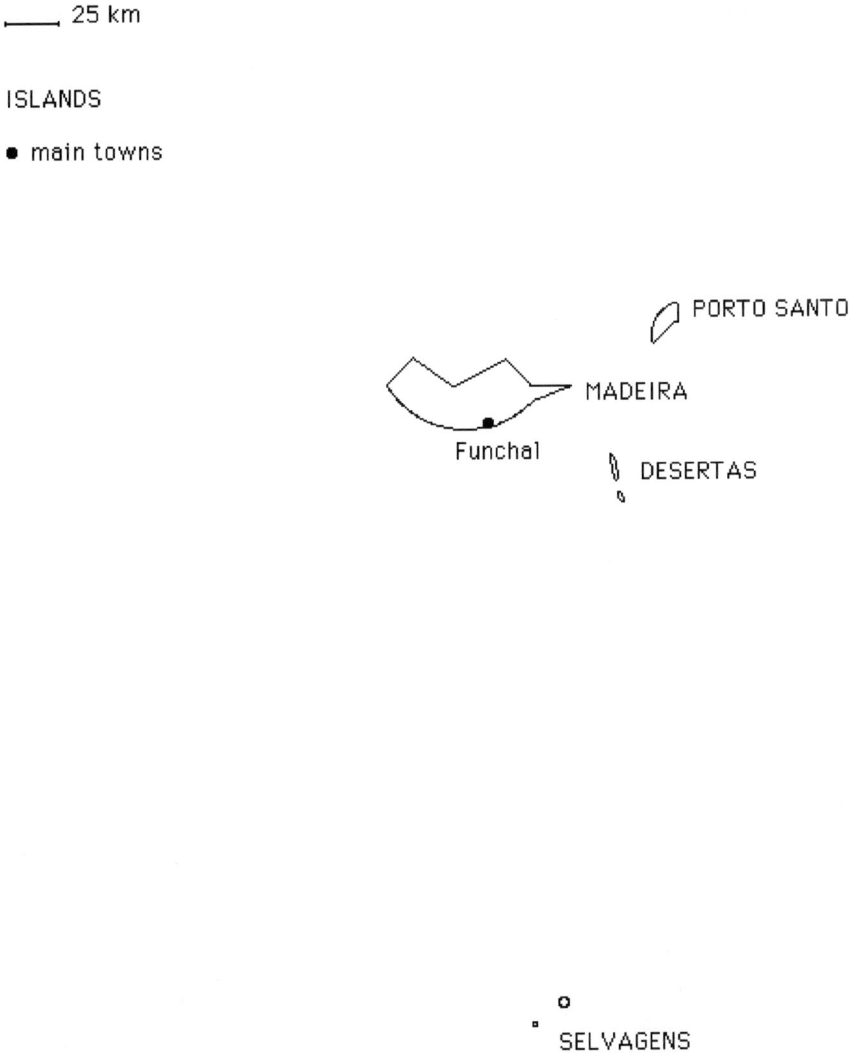

⌐——⌐ 25 km

ISLANDS

● main towns

PORTO SANTO

MADEIRA

Funchal

DESERTAS

SELVAGENS

438 | The Concise Economic History of Portugal: A Comprehensive Guide

Map 5 – Regions and main towns of the Azores

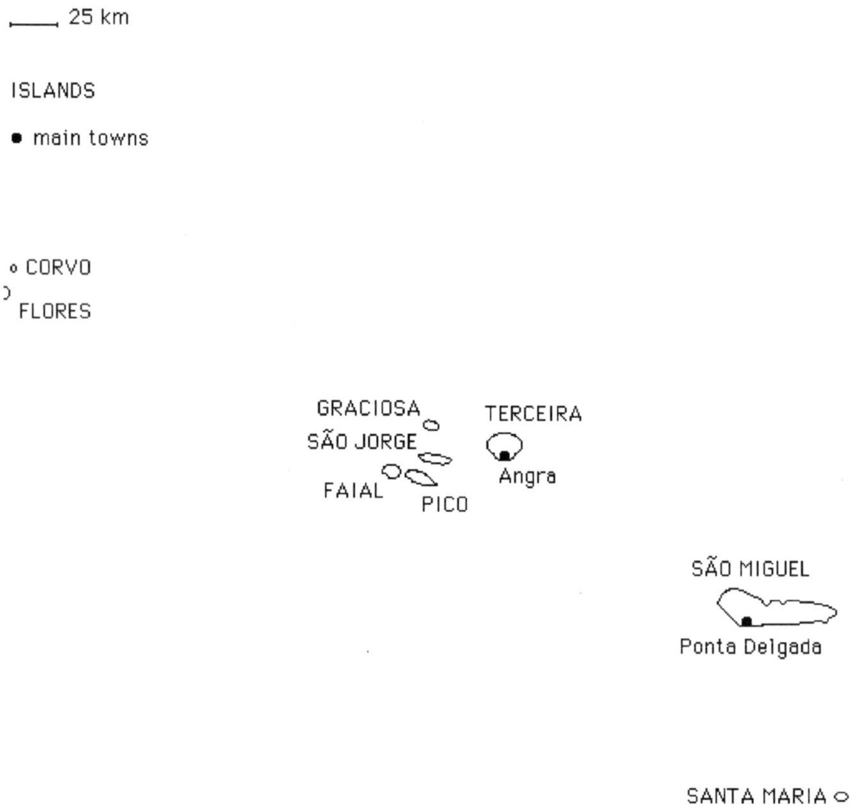

⊢—⊣ 25 km

ISLANDS

● main towns

○ CORVO

) FLORES

GRACIOSA
SÃO JORGE
FAIAL
PICO

TERCEIRA
Angra

SÃO MIGUEL
Ponta Delgada

SANTA MARIA ○

Map 6 – Provinces and main towns of the future Portuguese continental territory during the Roman and Visigothic rules

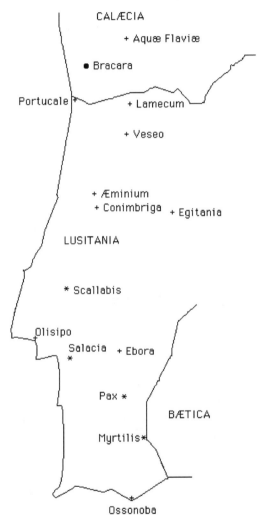

440 | The Concise Economic History of Portugal: A Comprehensive Guide

Map 7 – Formation of Portugal

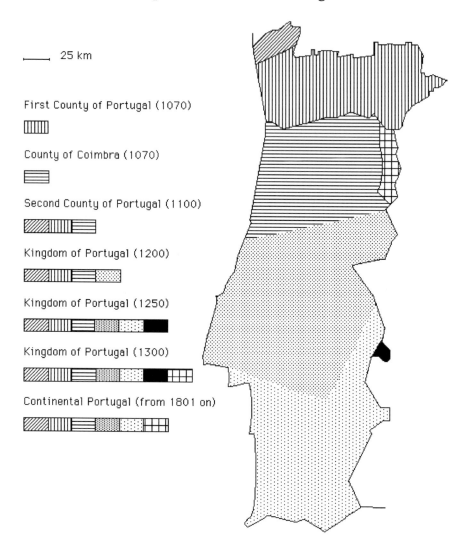

Cartographic appendix | 441

Map 8 – Provinces of Continental Portugal (14th-19th centuries)

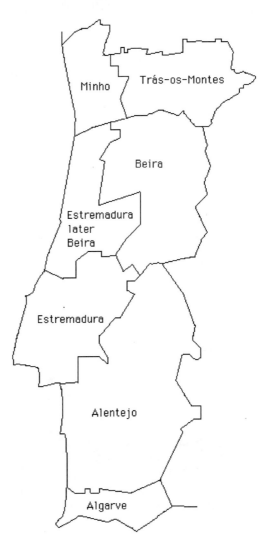

Map 9 – Administrative districts of Continental Portugal (19th-21st centuries)

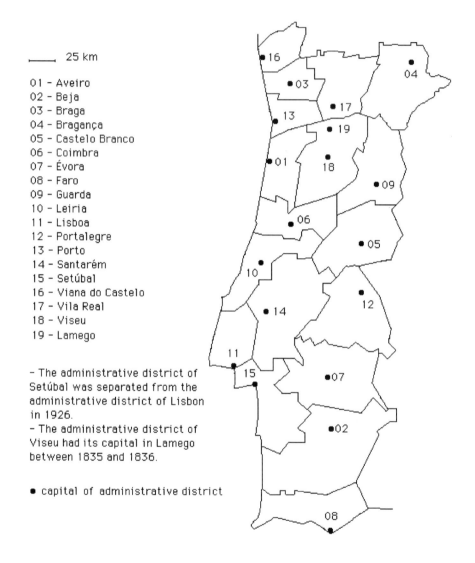

25 km

01 - Aveiro
02 - Beja
03 - Braga
04 - Bragança
05 - Castelo Branco
06 - Coimbra
07 - Évora
08 - Faro
09 - Guarda
10 - Leiria
11 - Lisboa
12 - Portalegre
13 - Porto
14 - Santarém
15 - Setúbal
16 - Viana do Castelo
17 - Vila Real
18 - Viseu
19 - Lamego

- The administrative district of Setúbal was separated from the administrative district of Lisbon in 1926.
- The administrative district of Viseu had its capital in Lamego between 1835 and 1836.

• capital of administrative district

Map 10 – Railroads built in Portugal

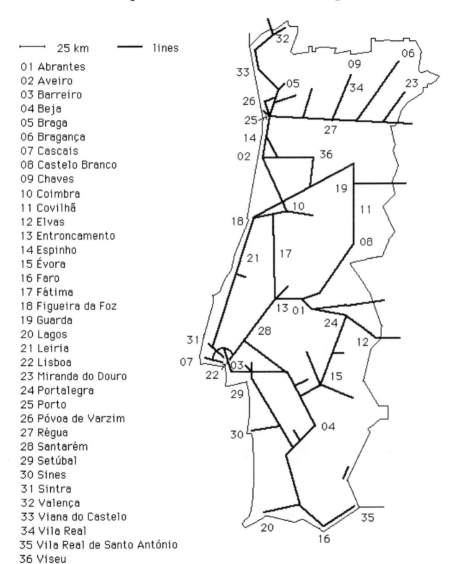

⊢—— 25 km   —— lines

01 Abrantes
02 Aveiro
03 Barreiro
04 Beja
05 Braga
06 Bragança
07 Cascais
08 Castelo Branco
09 Chaves
10 Coimbra
11 Covilhã
12 Elvas
13 Entroncamento
14 Espinho
15 Évora
16 Faro
17 Fátima
18 Figueira da Foz
19 Guarda
20 Lagos
21 Leiria
22 Lisboa
23 Miranda do Douro
24 Portalegre
25 Porto
26 Póvoa de Varzim
27 Régua
28 Santarém
29 Setúbal
30 Sines
31 Sintra
32 Valença
33 Viana do Castelo
34 Vila Real
35 Vila Real de Santo António
36 Viseu

Map 11 – Portuguese colonial empire (15th century)

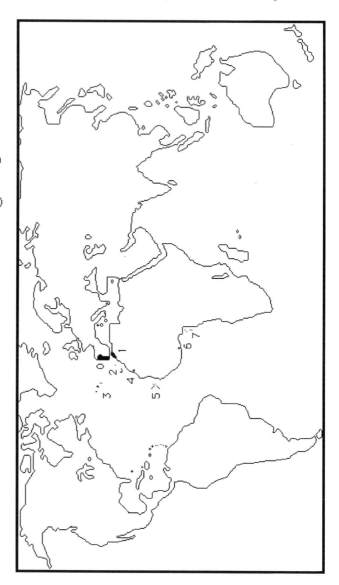

— 1 000 km

0 – Continent

1 – Possessions in Morocco (Ceuta, Alcacer Ceguer, Arzila and Tânger)

2 – Madeira

3 – Açores

4 – Arguim

5 – Cabo Verde

6 – São Jorge Mina

7 – Islands of the Gulf of Guinea

Map 12 – Portuguese colonial empire (16th century)

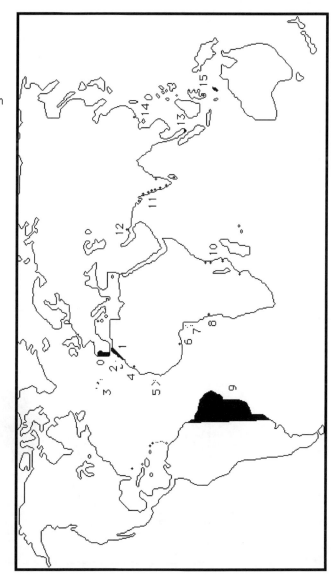

← 1 000 km

0 – Continent

1 – Possessions in Morocco (Ceuta, Alcácer Ceguer, Arzila, Tânger, Azamor, Mazagão, Safim and Gué)

2 – Madeira

3 – Açores

4 – Arguim

5 – Cabo Verde

6 – São Jorge da Mina

7 – Islands of the Gulf of Guinea

8 – São Paulo de Luanda

9 – Brasil (legal boundaries)

10 – East Africa possessions

11 – Indian possessions

12 – Ormuz

13 – Malaca

14 – Macau

15 – Molucas + + Solor + Timor

Map 13 – Portuguese colonial empire (17th-18th centuries)

├── 1 000 km

0 – Portugal
(Continent +
+ Madeira +
+ Açores)

1 – Mazagão

2 – Cabo Verde

3 – Cacheu + Bissau

4 – São João
Baptista de Ajudá

5 – Islands of the
Gulf of Guinea

6 – Angola

7 – Brasil
(legal boundaries)

8 – Moçambique

9 – Indian
possessions

10 – Macau

11 – Solor + Timor

Cartographic appendix | 447

Map 14 – Portuguese colonial empire (19th-20th centuries)

⊢——⊣ 1 000 km

0 – Portugal
(Continent +
+ Madeira +
+ Açores)

1 – Cabo Verde

2 – Guiné

3 – São Tomé e
Príncipe (including
São João Baptista
de Ajudá)

4 – Angola
(including Cabinda)

5 – Moçambique

6 – Índia (Goa +
+ Damão + Diu +
+ Dadrá + Nagar-
-Aveli)

7 – Macau

8 – Timor

Bibliography

The list that follows includes the books and articles used directly in preparing the text. They are classified by subject in order to allow an easier choice of material for those who wish to go further in the study of the economic history of Portugal.

General studies about the history of Portugal

Godinho, Vitorino Magalhães – *Ensaios 2 – sobre história de Portugal* – Sá da Costa, Lisboa, 1978 (2nd edition).

Godinho, Vitorino Magalhães – "L'émigration portugaise (XVe – XXe siècles)" – *Revista de História Económica e Social*, no. 1, 1978.

Godinho, Vitorino Magalhães – "Reflexão sobre Portugal e os portugueses na sua história" – *Revista de História Económica e Social*, no. 10, 1982.

Lains, Pedro; Silva, Álvaro Ferreira da (editors) – *História Económica de Portugal 1700-2000* – Imprensa de Ciências Sociais, Lisboa, 2005 (3 volumes).

Marques, A. H. de Oliveira – *History of Portugal* – Columbia University Press, New York and London, 1972 (2 volumes). Translation in Portuguese – *História de Portugal* – Palas, Lisboa, 1977 (2 volumes, 6th edition).

Martinez, Pedro Soares – *História diplomática de Portugal* – Verbo, Lisboa, 1986.

Martins, Oliveira – *História da civilização Ibérica* – Guimarães & Cª, Lisboa, 1954 (posthumous edition).

Martins, Oliveira – *História de Portugal* – Guimarães & Cª, Lisboa, 1977 (posthumous edition).

Mattoso, José (editor) – *História de Portugal* – Círculo de Leitores, Lisboa, 1992-1994 (7 volumes).

450 | The Concise Economic History of Portugal: A Comprehensive Guide

Peres, Damião (editor) – *História de Portugal* – Portucalense, Barcelos, 1938-1940 (8 volumes).

Ramos, Rui; Bernardo Vasconcelos e; Monteiro, Nuno – *História de Portugal* – Esfera dos Livros, Lisboa, 2009.

Rodrigues, Manuel Ferreira; Mendes, José Maria Amado – *História da indústria portuguesa da Idade Média aos nossos dias* – Associação Industrial Portuense – Publicações Europa-América, Mem Martins, 1999.

Sérgio, António – *Breve interpretação da história de Portugal* – Sá da Costa, Lisboa, 1972 (posthumous edition).

Serrão, Joel – *Cronologia geral da história de Portugal* – Iniciativas Editoriais, Lisboa, 1977 (3rd edition).

Serrão, Joel (editor) – *Dicionário de História de Portugal* – Iniciativas Editoriais, Lisboa, 1981 (6 volumes, 2nd edition).

Telo, António – "Treze teses sobre a disfunção nacional" – *Análise Social*, nº 142, 1997.

Valério, Nuno – "Sobre a divisão da história de Portugal em períodos" – *Estudos e ensaios – em homenagem a Vitorino Magalhães Godinho* – Sá da Costa, Lisboa, 1988.

Valério, Nuno – "A guerra na história de Portugal: uma avaliação quantitativa" – *Política Internacional*, nº 21, 2000.

Valério, Nuno – "La division politique de la Péninsule Ibérique et les particularités de l'Espagne et du Portugal: un essai d'éxplication" – *Revista de História Económica e Social*, 2nd series, no. 2, 2001.

Valério, Nuno (editor) – *Portuguese historical statistics* – Instituto Nacional de Estatística, Lisboa, 2001 (2 volumes). Translation in Portuguese: *Estatísticas históricas portuguesas* – Instituto Nacional de Estatística, Lisboa, 2001 (2 volumes).

The geographical background of the history of Portugal

Lema, Paula; Rebelo, Fernando – *Geografia de Portugal* – Universidade Aberta, Lisboa, 1997.

Mattoso, José; Daveau, Suzanne; Belo, Duarte – *Portugal. O sabor da Terra. Um retrato histórico e geográfico por regiões* – Círculo de Leitores, Lisboa, 2010 (2nd edition).

Medeiros, Carlos Alberto – *Geografia de Portugal* – Estampa, Lisboa, 1996.

Bibliography | 451

Ribeiro, Orlando – *Portugal, o Mediterrâneo e o Atlântico* – Sá da Costa, Lisboa, 1986 (3rd edition).

Ribeiro, Orlando – *Introduções geográficas à história de Portugal* – Imprensa Nacional-Casa da Moeda, Lisboa, 1977.

Sérgio, António – *Introdução geográfico-sociológica à história de Portugal* – Sá da Costa, Lisboa, 1973 (posthumous edition).

Monetary, banking, and financial history

Bastien, Carlos – "Para a história da Casa da Moeda de Lisboa – aspectos técnicos e organizativos da produção da moeda metálica" – *Estudos de Economia*, volume XII, no. 1, 1991.

Valério, Nuno – "Periodização da história monetária de Portugal" – *Estudos de Economia*, volume XII, no. 1, 1991.

Valério, Nuno – "Os preços em Portugal (séculos 13 a 20)" – Reis, Jaime; Dias, Fátima Sequeira; Fonseca, Helder (editors) – *História do crescimento económico em Portugal* – Associação Portuguesa de História Económica e Social, Ponta Delgada, 1997.

Valério, Nuno – *O escudo – a unidade monetária portuguesa 1911-2001 / The escudo – the Portuguese currency unit 1911-2001* – Banco de Portugal, Lisboa, 2001.

Valério, Nuno (editor) – *As finanças públicas no parlamento português* – Assembleia da República – Afrontamento, Lisboa – Porto, 2001.

Valério, Nuno; Nunes, Ana Bela; Bastien, Carlos; Mata, Maria Eugénia; Costa, Sandra Domingos – *Os orçamentos do Estado português – propostas governamentais, orçamentos aprovados e rectificados e contas de exercício* – Instituto Nacional de Estatística, Lisboa, 2006.

Valério, Nuno; Nunes, Ana Bela; Bastien, Carlos; Sousa, Rita Martins de; Costa, Sandra Domingos – *History of the Portuguese banking system (volume I)* – Banco de Portugal, Lisboa, 2006. Translation in Portuguese: *História do sistema bancário português (volume I)* – Banco de Portugal, Lisboa, 2006.

Valério, Nuno (editor) – *Os impostos no parlamento português – sistemas fiscais e reformas fiscais durante os séculos 19 e 20* – Assembleia da República – Dom Quixote, Lisboa, 2006.

Valério, Nuno (editor) – *Os orçamentos no parlamento português* – Assembleia da República – Dom Quixote, Lisboa, 2006.

Non-economic aspects

Caetano, Marcelo – *História do direito português* – Verbo, Lisboa, 1981.

Carvalho, Rómulo de – *História do ensino em Portugal* – Fundação Calouste Gulbenkian, Lisboa, 1986.

Oliveira, César; Monteiro, Nuno – *História dos municípios e do poder local em Portugal (dos finais da Idade Média à União Europeia)* – Círculo de Leitores, Lisboa, 1996.

Oliveira, Miguel de – *História eclesiástica de Portugal* – Europa-América, Mem Martins, 1994.

Pereira, Luísa; Ribeiro, Filipe M. – *O património genético português – A história humana preservada nos genes* – Gradiva, Lisboa, 2010 (4th edition).

Saraiva, António José – *Para a história da cultura em Portugal* – Europa-América, Lisboa, 1967-1969 (2 volumes).

Saraiva, António José; Lopes, Óscar – *História da literatura portuguesa* – Porto Editora, Porto, 1992 (16th edition).

Teyssier, Paul – *Histoire de la langue portugaise* – Presses Universitaires de France, Paris, 1980. Translation in Portuguese: *História da língua portuguesa* – Sá da Costa, Lisboa, 1982.

Portuguese expansion

Bethencourt, Francisco; Chaudhuri, Kirti – *História da expansão portuguesa* – Círculo de Leitores, Lisboa, 1998-1999 (5 volumes).

The period before the existence of Portugal

Alarcão, Jorge (editor) – *Portugal das origens à romanização* – Presença, Lisboa, 1990.

Amaral, João Ferreira do; Amaral, Augusto Ferreira do – *Povos antigos em Portugal* – Quetzal, Lisboa, 1997.

Arnaud, José Morais – "Le néolithique ancien et les processus de néolithisation au Portugal" – *Le néolithique ancien méditerranéen* – Fédération Archéologique de l'Hérault, Montpellier, 1981.

Ciffyn, André – *Le Bronze final atlantique dans la Péninsule Ibérique* – Boccard, Paris, 1985.

Bibliography | 453

Daveau, Suzanne – "Espaço e tempo. Evolução do ambiente geográfico de Portugal ao longo dos tempos pré-históricos" – *Clio*, volume 2, Lisboa, 1980.

Díaz-Andreu, Margarita; Keay, Simon – *The archaeology of Iberia – the dynamics of change* – Routledge, London – New York, 1997.

Gamito, Teresa – *Social complexity in southwest Iberia* – Doctoral dissertation presented at the University of Cambridge, 1988 (mimeographed).

Harrison, R. J. – *The bell beaker cultures of Spain and Portugal* – Harvard University Press, Cambridge (Massachussets), 1977.

Silva, Armando Coelho Ferreira da – *A cultura castreja no Noroeste de Portugal* – Câmara Municipal de Paços de Ferreira / Museu Arqueológico de Sanfins, Paços de Ferreira, 1986.

Zbyzewski, Georges – "L'âge de la pierre taillée au Portugal" – *Les dossiers de l'archéologie*, no. 4, 1974.

The formation of the Portuguese society and medieval Portugal

Azevedo, J. Lúcio de – *Elementos para a história económica de Portugal – séculos XII a XVII* – Inapa, Lisboa, 1990 (posthumous edition).

Barros, Henrique de Gama – *História da administração pública em Portugal nos séculos XII a XIV* – Sá da Costa, Lisboa, 1945-1954 (4 volumes).

Castro, Armando – *A evolução económica de Portugal (séculos XII-XV)* – Portugália, Lisboa, 1964-1966 (5 volumes).

Castro, Armando – *Portugal na Europa do seu tempo. História sócio-económica medieval comparada* – Seara Nova, Lisboa, 1977.

Coelho, António Borges – *Portugal na Espanha Árabe* – Seara Nova, Lisboa, 1970-1974 (4 volumes).

Coelho, Maria Helena da Cruz; Homem, Armando Luís de Carvalho (editors) – *Portugal em definição de fronteiras – do Condado Portucalense à crise do século XV* – Presença, Lisboa, 1996.

Cortesão, Jaime – *Os factores democráticos na formação de Portugal* – Portugália, Lisboa, 1966 (posthumous edition).

Hespanha, António – *A história das instituições: épocas medievais e moderna* – Almedina, Coimbra, 1982.

Marques, A. H. de Oliveira – *Introdução à história da agricultura em Portugal: a questão cerealífera* – Cosmos, Lisboa, 1978 (3rd edition).

454 | The Concise Economic History of Portugal: A Comprehensive Guide

Marques, A. H. de Oliveira – *Portugal na crise dos séculos XIV e XV* – Presença, Lisboa, 1987.

Marques, A. H. de Oliveira (editora) – *Portugal das invasões germânicas à "reconquista"* – Presença, Lisboa, 1993.

Mattoso, José – *Identificação de um país: ensaio sobre as origens de Portugal 1096-1325* – Estampa, Lisboa, 1988 (2 volumes).

Serrão, Joel – *O carácter social da revolução de 1383* – Horizonte, Lisboa, 1976.

Tavares, Maria José Pimenta Ferro – "Judeus e Mouros no Portugal dos séculos XIV e XV" – *Revista de História Económica e Social*, no. 9, 1982.

Portugal in the Euro-Atlantic world-economy

Araújo, A.; Cardoso, J. L.; Monteiro, Nuno; Rossa, W.; Serrão, J. (editors) – *O terramoto de 1755; impactos históricos* – Horizonte, Lisboa, 2007.

Braudel, Fernand – *La Méditerranée et le monde méditerranéen à l'époque de Philippe II* – Armand Colin, Paris, 1979 (3 volumes). Translation in Portuguese: *O Mediterrâneo e o mundo mediterrânico* – Dom Quixote, Lisboa, 1983-1984 (2 volumes).

Cardoso, José Luís, Cluny, Isabel; Costa, Fernando Dores; Costa, Leonor; Andrade Martins, Conceição; Monteiro, Nuno; Pedreira, Jorge (editors) – *O Tratado de Methuen (1703): diplomacia, guerra, política e economia* – Horizonte, Lisboa, 2003.

Carreira, António – *As companhias pombalinas* – Presença, Lisboa, 1983.

Costa, F. Marques; Domingues, F. Contente; Monteiro, N. Gonçalo (editors) – *Do antigo regime ao liberalismo: 1750-1850* – Vega, Lisboa, 1990.

Dias, João José Alves (editor) – *Portugal do Renascimento à crise dinástica* – Presença, Lisboa, 1989.

Fisher, H. E. S. – *The Portugal trade – a study of Anglo-Portuguese commerce 1700-1770* – Methuen, London, 1971. Translation in Portuguese: *De Methuen a Pombal – o comércio anglo-português de 1700 a 1770* – Gradiva, Lisboa, 1984.

Godinho, Vitorino Magalhães – *Prix et monnaies au Portugal 1750-1850* – Armand Colin, Paris, 1955.

Godinho, Vitorino Magalhães – *Estrutura da antiga sociedade portuguesa* – Arcádia, Lisboa, 1980 (4th edition).

Bibliography | 455

Hanson, Carl – *Economy and society in barroque Portugal 1668-1703* – MacMillan, London, 1981. Translation in Portuguese: *Economia e sociedade no Portugal barroco 1688-1703* – Dom Quixote, Lisboa, 1986.

Hespanha, António – *L'espace politique dans l'ancien regime* – Gráfica Coimbra, Coimbra, 1983.

Macedo, Jorge Borges – *Problemas da história da indústria portuguesa no século XVIII* – Querco, Lisboa, 1982 (2nd edition).

Macedo, Jorge Borges – *A situação económica no tempo de Pombal – Alguns aspectos* – Morais, Lisboa, 1982.

Macedo, Jorge Braga de; Silva, Álvaro Ferreira da; Sousa, Rita Martins de – "War, taxes and gold: the inheritance of the real" – Bordo, Michael; Cortés-Conde, Roberto (editors) – *Transferring wealth and power from the Old to the New World* – Cambridge University Press, Cambridge, 2001.

Madureira, Nuno – *Mercado e privilégios: a indústria portuguesa entre 1750 e 1834* – Estampa, Lisboa, 1997.

Magalhães, Joaquim Romero – *Para o estudo do Algarve económico no século XVI* – Cosmos, Lisboa, 1973.

Magalhães, Joaquim Romero – *O Algarve económico 1600-1773* – Estampa, Lisboa, 1988.

Martins, Maria da Conceição – *Memória do vinho do Porto* – Instituto de Ciências Sociais, Lisboa, 1990.

Meneses, Avelino de Freitas (editor) – *Portugal da Paz da Restauração ao ouro do Brasil* – Presença, Lisboa, 2001.

Oliveira, João Nunes – *A Beira Alta de 1700 a 1840 – gentes e subsistências* – Palimage, Viseu, 2002.

Rau, Virgínia – *Estudos sobre a história económica e social de antigo regime* – Presença, Lisboa, 1984 (posthumous edition).

Schneider, Susan – *O marquês de Pombal e o vinho do Porto. Dependência e subdesenvolvimento em Portugal no séc. XVIII* – A Regra do Jogo, Lisboa, 1980.

Sideri, Sandro – *Trade and power* – Rotterdam University Press, Rotterdam, 1970. Translation in Portuguese: *Comércio e poder* – Cosmos, Lisboa, 1978.

Sousa, Rita Martins de – *Moeda e metais preciosos no Portugal setecentista (1688-1797)* – Doctoral dissertation presented at the Instituto Superior de Economia e Gestão da Universidade Técnica de Lisboa, 1999 (mimeographed).

Tomaz, Fernando – "As finanças do Estado Pombalino" – *Estudos e ensaios – em homenagem a Vitorino Magalhães Godinho* – Sá da Costa, Lisboa, 1988.

Valério, Nuno – "Local economies and the world-economy – nineteenth-century Trás-os-Montes" – *Review*, volume XVI, nº 1, 1993.

Portuguese expansion until the 19th century

Albuquerque, Luís – *Os descobrimentos portugueses* – Alfa, Lisboa, 1983.

Albuquerque, Luís – *A cartografia portuguesa dos séculos XV e XVI* – Academia das Ciências, Lisboa, 1986.

Albuquerque, Luís – *Astronomical navigation* – Comissão Nacional para as Comemorações dos Descobrimentos Portugueses, Lisboa, 1988.

Albuquerque, Luís (editor) – *Dicionário de história dos descobrimentos portugueses* – Círculo de Leitores, Lisboa, 1994 (2 volumes).

Albuquerque, Luís; Vieira, Alberto – *The archipelago of Madeira in the XVth century* – Secretaria Regional do Turismo e Cultura, Funchal, 1988.

Almeida, Pedro Ramos – *História do colonialismo português em África. Cronologia – séculos XV-XVIII* – Estampa, Lisboa, 1978.

Barreto, Luís – *Descobrimentos e Renascimento – Formas de ser e de pensar nos séculos XV e XVI* – Imprensa Nacional-Casa da Moeda, Lisboa, 1983.

Boxer, Charles – The *Portuguese seaborne empire* – Hutchinson, London, 1969. Translation in Portuguese: *O império colonial português (1415--1825)* – Edições 70, Lisboa, 1981.

Cortesão, Jaime – *A expansão dos portugueses no período henriquino* – Portugália, Lisboa, 1966 (posthumous edition).

Cortesão, Jaime – *Os descobrimentos portugueses* – Portugália, Lisboa, 1966 (posthumous edition).

Cortesão, Jaime – *A expansão dos portugueses na história da civilização* – Horizonte, Lisboa, 1983 (posthumous edition).

Costa, Fontoura da – *A ciência náutica dos portugueses na época dos descobrimentos* – Comissão Executiva das Comemorações do Quinto Centenário da Morte do Infante D. Henrique, Lisboa, 1958 (posthumous edition).

Costa, Maria Leonor Freire – "Naus e galeões na Ribeira de Lisboa" – M. A. thesis presented at the Universidade Técnica de Lisboa, 1993 (mimeographed).

Costa, Maria Leonor Freire – "O transporte no Atlântico: as frotas do açúcar e a Companhia Geral do Comércio do Brasil (1580-1633)" – Doctoral dissertation presented at the Instituto Superior de Economia e Gestão da Universidade Técnica de Lisboa, 2000 (mimeographed).

Diffie, Bailey – *Prelude to empire* – University of Nebraska Press, Lincoln, 1960.

Diffie, Bailey; Winius, George – *Foundations of the Portuguese empire 1415-1580* – University of Minnesota Press, Minneapolis, 1977.

Godinho, Vitorino Magalhães – *A economia dos descobrimentos henriquinos* – Sá da Costa, Lisboa, 1962.

Godinho, Vitorino Magalhães – "Os descobrimentos: inovação e mudança nos séculos XV e XVI" – *Revista de História Económica e Social*, no. 2, 1978.

Godinho, Vitorino Magalhães – *Os descobrimentos e a economia mundial* – Presença, Lisboa, 1981-1983 (4 volumes – 2nd edition).

Godinho, Vitorino Magalhães – *Les finances de l'Etat portugais des Indes Orientales (1517-1635) – Matériaux pour une étude structurale et conjoncturelle* – Fundação Calouste Gulbenkian, Paris, 1982.

Godinho, Vitorino Magalhães – "La Méditerranée dans l'horizon des Européens de l'Atlantique" – *Revista de História Económica e Social*, no. 17, 1986.

Godinho, Vitorino Magalhães – *Mito e mercadoria, utopia e prática de navegar* – Difel, Lisboa, 1990.

Heintze, Beatrix – "The Angolan vassal tributes of the 17th century" – *Revista de História Económica e Social*, no. 6, 1980.

Johnson, Harold; Silva, Maria Beatriz Nizza da (editors) – *O império luso-brasileiro 1500-1620* – Estampa, Lisboa, 1992.

Lopes, David – *A expansão em Marrocos* – Teorema, Lisboa, 1989 (posthumous edition).

Matos, Artur Teodoro de (editor) – *A colonização atlântica* – Estampa, Lisboa, 2005 (e volumes).

Marques, A. H. de Oliveira (editor) – *A expansão quatrocentista* – Estampa, Lisboa, 1998.

Marques, Alfredo Pinheiro – *Guia de história dos descobrimentos e expansão portuguesa* – Biblioteca Nacional, Lisboa, 1988.

Mauro, Frédéric – *Le Portugal et l'Atlantique au XVIIe siècle 1570-1670* – SEVPEN, Paris, 1960.

458 | The Concise Economic History of Portugal: A Comprehensive Guide

Mauro, Frédéric – *Études économiques sur l'éxpansion portugaise (1500--1800)* – Fundação Calouste Gulbenkian, Paris, 1970.

Mauro, Frédéric – *Le Brésil: du 15e à la fin du 18e siècle* – Société d'Edition de l'Enseignement Superieur, Paris, 1977.

Mauro, Frédéric – *Portugal, o Brasil e o Atlântico* – Estampa, Lisboa, 1988 (2 volumes).

Mauro, Frédéric (editor) – *O império luso-brasileiro 1620-1750* – Estampa, Lisboa, 1991.

Morison, S. E. – *Portuguese voyages to America in the fifteenth century* – Harvard University Press, Cambridge, 1940. Translation in Portuguese: *As viagens portuguesas à América* – Teorema, Lisboa, 1990.

Pearson, M. N. – *The Portuguese in India* – Cambridge University Press, Cambridge, 1988. Translation in Portuguese: *Os portugueses na Índia 1505-1961* – Teorema, Lisboa, 1990.

Pedreira, Jorge – "'To have and to have not'. The economic consequences of empire: Portugal (1415-1822)" – O'Brien, Patrick; Prados, Leandro (editors) – *The costs and benefits of European imperialism from the conquest of Ceuta, 1415, to the Treaty of Lusaka, 1974* – Marcial Pons, Madrid, 1998.

Santos, João Marinho dos – *Os Açores nos séculos XV e XVI* – Secretaria Regional da Educação e Cultura, Ponta Delgada, 1989 (2 volumes).

Silva, Maria Beatriz Nizza da (editor) – *O império luso-brasileiro: 1750-1822* – Estampa, Lisboa, 1986.

Portugal in the 19th and 20th centuries

Eichengreen, Barry; Reis, Jaime; Macedo, Jorge Braga de (editors) – *Historical perspective on the gold standard. Portugal and the world* – Banco de Portugal, Estudos Gerais da Arrábida, Fundação Luso-Americana para o Desenvolvimento, Lisboa, 1994.

Fontoura, Paula; Valério, Nuno – "Foreign economic relations and economic growth in Portugal, 1840s-1990s: a long term view" – *Economies et Sociétés*, 3/2000.

Franco, A. Sousa – "Ensaio sobre as transformações estruturais das finanças públicas portuguesas, 1900-1980" – *Análise Social*, no. 72--73-74, 1982.

Lains, Pedro; Reis, Jaime – "Portuguese economic growth 1833-1985: some doubts" – *The Journal of European Economic History*, volume 20, no. 2, 1991.

Mata, Maria Eugénia – "Actividade revolucionária no Portugal contemporâneo – uma perspectiva de longa duração" – *Análise Social*, no. 112-113, 1991.

Mata, Maria Eugénia; Valério, Nuno – "Normas de direito financeiro nas constituições portuguesas" – *Revista de História económica e social*, no. 3, 1979.

Mata, Maria Eugénia; Valério, Nuno – "Foreign public debt and economic growth in Portugal 1830-1985" – *Estudos de Economia*, volume XI, no. 4, 1991.

Mata, Maria Eugénia; Valério, Nuno – "Monetary stability, fiscal discipline and economic performance – the experience of Portugal since 1854" – Macedo, Jorge Braga de; Eichengreen, Barry; Reis, Jaime (editors) – *Currency convertibility* – Routledge, London, 1996.

Neves, João César das – *The Portuguese economy. A picture in figures. XIX and XX centuries* – Universidade Católica Editora, Lisboa, 1994.

Nunes, Ana Bela – "População activa e actividade económica em Portugal dos finais do século XIX à actualidade – uma contribuição para o estudo do crescimento económico português" – Doctoral dissertation presented at the Universidade Técnica de Lisboa, 1989 (mimeographed).

Nunes, Ana Bela – "A rede urbana portuguesa e o moderno crescimento económico" – study presented at the Universidade Técnica de Lisboa for Doctoral examination, 1989 (mimeographed).

Nunes, Ana Bela; Mata, Maria Eugénia; Valério, Nuno – "Portuguese economic growth 1833-1985" – *The Journal of European Economic History*, volume 18, no. 2, 1989.

Nunes, Ana Bela; Mata, Maria Eugénia; Valério, Nuno – "Portuguese economic growth 1833-1985: some comments on Pedro Lains' and Jaime Reis' doubts" – *The Journal of European Economic History*, volume 20, no. 2, 1991.

Nunes, Ana Bela; Bastien, Carlos; Valério, Nuno – "Nationalisations et privatisations au Portugal" – *Entreprises et Histoire*, nº 37, 2004.

Pereira, Pedro Telhado; Mata, Maria Eugénia (editors) – *Urban dominance and labour market differentiation of a European capital city, Lisbon 1890-1990* – Kluwer, Boston – London – Dordrecht, 1996.

460 | The Concise Economic History of Portugal: A Comprehensive Guide

Telo, António; Torre, Hipolito de la Torre – *Portugal e Espanha nos sistemas internacionais contemporâneos* – Cosmos, Lisboa, 2000.

Valério, Nuno – "Monetary evolution, public finance and balance of payments: Portugal 1891-1990" – Bovykine, Valery; Broder, Albert; Maranhão, Roberto (editors) – *Public debt, public finance, money and balance of payments in debtor countries, 1890-1932/1933* – Fondación Fomento de la Historia Económica, Madrid, 1998.

Portuguese colonies in the 19th and 20th centuries

Clarence-Smith, Gervase – *The third Portuguese empire 1825-1975. A Study in Economic Imperialism* – Manchester University Press, Manchester, 1985.

Lains, Pedro – "An account of the Portuguese African empire, 1885-1975" – O'Brien, Patrick; Prados, Leandro (editors) – *The costs and benefits of European imperialism from the conquest of Ceuta, 1415, to the Treaty of Lusaka, 1974* – Marcial Pons, Madrid, 1998.

Lains, Pedro – "Causas do colonialismo português em África 1822-1975" – *Análise Social*, no. 146-147, 1998.

Lima, Mesquitela – "L'anthropologie africaniste et la traite négrière" – *Revista de História Económica e Social*, no. 3, 1979.

Telo, António – *Economia e império no Portugal contemporâneo* – Cosmos, Lisboa, 1994.

Valério, Nuno – "O significado económico do Império Colonial para um pequeno poder – o caso de Portugal (de finais do século XIX ao terceiro quartel do século XX)" – Telo, António; Torre, Hipolito de la (editors) – *I Encuentro Peninsular de Historia de las Relaciones Internacionales* – Fundación Rei Afonso Henriques, Zamora, 1998.

Portugal in the 19th century (also until the First World War or the inter-war years)

Alegria, Maria Fernanda – "A organização dos transportes em Portugal (1850-1910). As vias e o tráfego" – Doctoral dissertation presented at the Universidade de Lisboa, 1989 (mimeographed).

Baganha, Maria Joannis Benis – "International labor movements: Portuguese emigration to the United States 1820-1930" – Doctoral dissertation presented at the University of Pennsylvania, 1988 (mimeographed).

Bibliography | 461

Baganha, Maria Joannis Benis – "Social marginalization, government policies and emmigrants' remittances. Portugal 1870-1930" – *Estudos e ensaios – em homenagem a Vitorino Magalhães Godinho* – Sá da Costa, Lisboa, 1988.

Brandão, Maria de Fátima Silva – "Land, inheritance and family in Northwestern Portugal: the case of Mosteiro in the nineteenth century" – Doctoral dissertation presented at the University of East Anglia, 1988 (mimeographed).

Cabral, Manuel Villaverde (editor) – *Materiais para a história da questão agrária em Portugal, séculos XIX e XX* – Inova, Porto, 1974.

Cabral, Manuel Villaverde – *O desenvolvimento do capitalismo em Portugal no século XIX* – Regra do Jogo, Lisboa, 1976.

Cabral, Manuel Villaverde – *Portugal na alvorada do século XX. Forças sociais, poder político e crescimento económico de 1890 a 1914* – Regra do Jogo, Lisboa, 1979.

Castro, Armando – *Introdução ao estudo da economia portuguesa (fins do século XVIII a princípios do século XX* – Cosmos, Lisboa, 1947.

Castro, Armando – *A economia portuguesa do século XX (1900-1925)* – Edições 70, Lisboa, 1973.

Castro, Armando – *A revolução industrial em Portugal no século XIX* – Limiar, Porto, 1978 (2nd edition).

Dias, Fátima Sequeira – *Uma estratégia de sucesso numa economia periférica. A Casa Bensaúde e os Açores* – Jornal de Cultura, Ponta Delgada, 1996.

Ferreira, Jaime – "Questões de abastecimento de cereais e farinhas na abertura da contemporaneidade portuguesa" – Doctoral dissertation presented at the Universidade de Coimbra, 1989 (3 volumes, mimeographed).

Ferreira, Jaime – *Farinhas, moinhos e moagens* – Âncora, Lisboa, 1999.

Fonseca, Helder – "Economia e práticas económicas no Alentejo oitocentista" – Doctoral dissertation presented at the Universidade de Évora, 1993 (mimeographed).

Justino, David – *A formação do espaço económico nacional* – Vega, Lisboa, 1988 (2 volumes).

Justino, David – *Preços e salários em Portugal (1850-1912)* – Banco de Portugal, Lisboa, 1989.

Lains, Pedro – *Evolução da agricultura e da indústria em Portugal (1850-1913): uma interpretação quantitativa* – Banco de Portugal, Lisboa, 1990.

462 | The Concise Economic History of Portugal: A Comprehensive Guide

Lains, Pedro – "Foreign trade and economic growth in the European periphery: Portugal, 1851-1913" – Doctoral dissertation presented at the European University Institute, 1992 (mimeographed).

Macedo, Jorge Borges – *O bloqueio continental* – Gradiva, Lisboa, 1990.

Marques, A. H. de Oliveira (editor) – *Portugal e a instauração do liberalismo* – Presença, Lisboa, 2002.

Marques, A. H. de Oliveira (editor) – *Portugal da Monarquia para a República* – Presença, Lisboa, 1991.

Martins, Oliveira – *Economia e finanças* – Guimarães & Cª, Lisboa, 1956 (posthumous edition).

Martins, Oliveira – *Portugal contemporâneo* – Guimarães & Cª, Lisboa, 1976-1979 (2 volumes, posthumous edition).

Mata, Maria Eugénia – *As finanças públicas portuguesas da Regeneração à primeira guerra mundial* – Banco de Portugal, Lisboa, 1993.

Mata, Maria Eugénia – *Câmbios e política cambial na economia portuguesa 1891-1931* – Sá da Costa, Lisboa, 1987.

Mata, Maria Eugénia – "As três fases do fontismo: projectos e realizações" – *Estudos e ensaios – em homenagem a Vitorino Magalhães Godinho* – Sá da Costa, Lisboa, 1988.

Mata, Maria Eugénia – "Conjuntura económica e conjuntura política em Portugal (1851-1910)" – *Economia*, volume XIV, no. 1, 1990.

Mata, Maria Eugénia – "Exchange rate and exchange policy in Portugal 1891-1931 revisited" – *Estudos de Economia*, volume XII, no. 1, 1991.

Mata, Maria Eugénia – "A Companhia das Obras Públicas de Portugal" – *Estudos de Economia*, vol. XIX, no. 1, 1999.

Mata, Maria Eugénia – "Economic Ideas and Policies in Nineteenth-Century Portugal" – *The Luso-Brazilian Review*, XXXVIII, II, 2001.

Mata, Maria Eugénia; Valério, Nuno – "O Banco de Portugal, único banco emissor (1891-1931)" – *Revista de História Económica e Social*, no. 10, 1982.

Mata, Maria Eugénia; Valério, Nuno – "As finanças constitucionais portuguesas entre duas guerras civis (1833-1845)" – *Revista de História Económica e Social*, 2nd series, no. 1, 2001.

Mata, Maria Eugénia; Valério, Nuno – "Dívida pública externa e crescimento económico em Portugal 1830-1914" – *Notas Económicas*, no. 11, 1998.

Mateus, Margarida; Mateus, Abel – "Technological change, trade regimes and the response of agriculture in Portugal during the 19th century" – Working Papers, no. 52 – Faculdade de Economia, Universidade Nova de Lisboa, Lisboa, 1984.

Pedreira, Jorge – "Social structure and the persistence of rural domestic industry in XIXth century Portugal" – *The Journal of European Economic History* volume 19, no. 3, 1990.

Pedreira. Jorge – *Estrutura industrial e mercado colonial: Portugal e Brasil (1780-1830)* – Difel, Lisboa, 1994.

Pereira, Miriam Halpern – *Assimetrias de crescimento e dependência externa* – Seara Nova, Lisboa, 1974.

Pereira, Miriam Halpern – *Revolução, finanças e dependência externa (de 1820 à convenção de Gramido)* – Sá da Costa, Lisboa, 1979.

Pereira, Miriam Halpern – *Política e economia. Portugal nos séculos XIX e XX* – Horizonte, Lisboa, 1979.

Pereira, Miriam Halpern – *Livre-câmbio e desenvolvimento económico* – Sá da Costa, Lisboa, 1983 (2nd edition).

Pereira, Miriam Halpern; Ferreira, Maria de Fátima; Serrão, João (editors) – *O liberalismo na Península Ibérica na primeira metade do século XIX* – Sá da Costa, Lisboa, 1982.

Reis, Jaime – "O atraso económico português em perspectiva histórica (1860-1913)" – *Análise Social*, no. 80, 1984.

Reis, Jaime – *A evolução da oferta monetária portuguesa: 1854-1912* – Banco de Portugal, Lisboa, 1990.

Reis, Jaime; Mónica, Maria Filomena; Santos, Maria Lurdes Lima (editors) – "O século XIX em Portugal" – *Análise Social*, no. 61-62, 1980.

Reis, Jaime – *O Banco de Portugal – das origens a 1914* – Banco de Portugal, Lisboa, 1996.

Serrão, Joel – *Demografia portuguesa* – Horizonte, Lisboa, 1973.

Serrão, Joel – *A emigração portuguesa* – Horizonte, Lisboa, 1974 (2nd edition).

Serrão, Joel – *Temas oitocentistas* – Horizonte, Lisboa, 1980 (2nd edition).

Serrão, Joel – *Da "Regeneração" à república* – Horizonte, Lisboa, 1990.

Serrão, Joel; Martins, Gabriela (editors) – *Da indústria portuguesa: do antigo regime ao capitalismo* – Horizonte, Lisboa, 1978.

Silbert, Albert – *Do Portugal de antigo regime ao Portugal oitocentista* – Horizonte, Lisboa, 1973.

Silbert, Albert – *Le Portugal méditerranéen à la fin de l'Ancien Regime* – INIC, Lisboa, 1978 (2nd edition).

464 | The Concise Economic History of Portugal: A Comprehensive Guide

Silva, António Martins da – "Desamortização e venda dos bens nacionais em Portugal na primeira metade do século XIX" – Doctoral dissertation presented at the Universidade de Coimbra, 1989 (mimeographed).

Sousa, Fernando – *A demografia portuguesa em finais do Antigo Regime* – Sá da Costa, Lisboa, 1983.

Sousa, Fernando; Marques, A. H. de Oliveira (editors) – *Portugal e a Regeneração* – Presença, Lisboa, 2004.

Sousa, Rita – "Money supply in Portugal 1834-1891" – *Estudos de Economia*, volume XII, no. 1, 1991.

Valério, Nuno – "A Companhia Confiança Nacional (1844-1846)" – *Revista de História Económica e Social*, no. 13, 1984.

Vieira, António Lopes – "Investimentos britânicos nos transportes urbanos e suburbanos em Portugal na segunda metade do século XIX – fracasso e sucesso. A Lisbon Steam Tramways Company e a Lisbon Electric Tramways Company" – *Revista de História Económica e Social*, no. 7, 1981.

Vieira, António Lopes – "The role of Britain and France in the finance of the Portuguese railways, 1850-1890. A comparative study in speculation, corruption and inefficiency" – Doctoral dissertation presented at the University of Leicester, 1983 (mimeographed).

Vieira, António Lopes – "Speculation on the growth of the Portuguese domestic market in the 19th century: government policy, dependence and availability of resources. An agenda for research" – *Estudos de Economia*, volume VI, no. 2, 1986.

Portuguese colonies in the 19th century (also until the First World War or the inter-war years)

Almeida, Pedro Ramos – *História do colonialismo português em África. Cronologia – século XIX* – Estampa, Lisboa, 1979.

Alexandre, Valentim – *Origens do colonialismo português moderno (1822-1891)* – Sá da Costa, Lisboa, 1979.

Alexandre, Valentim; Dias, Jill (editors) – *O império africano 1825-1890* – Estampa, Lisboa, 2001.

Hammond, Richard – *Portugal and Africa, 1815-1910: a study in uneconomic imperialism* – Stanford University Press, Stanford, 1966.

Marques, A. H. de Oliveira (editor) – *O império africano 1890-1930* – Estampa, Lisboa, 2001.

Martins, Oliveira – *O Brasil e as colónias portuguesas* – Guimarães e Cª, Lisboa, 1978 (posthumous edition).

Pélissier, René – *História da Guiné – portugueses e africanos na Senegâmbia 1841-1936* – Estampa, Lisboa, 1989 (2 volumes).

Portugal in the 20th century

Almeida, Carlos; Barreto, António – *Capitalismo e emigração em Portugal* – Prelo, Lisboa, 1970.

Barreto, António (editor) – *A situação social em Portugal* – Instituto de Ciências Sociais, Lisboa, 1996.

Brito, José Maria Brandão de – *A industrialização portuguesa no pós-guerra (1948-1965) – o condicionamento industrial* – Dom Quixote, Lisboa, 1989.

Brito, José Maria Brandão de – "The Portuguese response to the Marshall Plan" – *Estudos de Economia*, volume X, no. 4, 1990.

Carneiro, Roberto – *Educação e emprego em Portugal – uma leitura de modernização* – Fundação Calouste Gulbenkian, Lisboa, 1988.

Castro, Armando – *Desenvolvimento económico ou estagnação* – Dom Quixote, Lisboa, 1970.

Castro, Armando Antunes; Torres, Adelino; Silveira, Joel; Lima, Aida Valadas – "La campagne du blé et le protectionisme céréalier au Portugal: 1929-1960" – *Estudos de Economia*, volume III, no. 4, 1981.

Confraria, João – *Condicionamento industrial: uma análise económica* – Direcção-Geral da Indústria, Lisboa, 1992.

Constâncio, Maria José – "Evolução da política económica desde 1974" – *Evolução recente e perspectivas de transformação da economia portuguesa (volume I)* – CISEP, Lisboa, 1984.

Costa, A. Bruto da; Silva, Manuela; Pereirinha, J.; Matos, Madalena – *A pobreza em Portugal* – Caritas, Lisboa, 1985.

Courlet, Claude; Silva, Mário Rui – "Transitions industrielles en Espagne et au Portugal" – *O comportamento dos agentes económicos e a reorientação da política económica (volume I)* – CISEP, Lisboa, 1986.

Cutileiro, José – *A Portuguese rural society* – Clarendon Press, Oxford, 1971.

Cravinho, João – "Sources of output growth in the Portuguese economy (1959-1974)" – *Estudos de Economia*, volume VIII, no. 1, 1987.

Dauderstädt, Michael – "The EC's pre-accession aid to Portugal. A first appraisal" – *Estudos de Economia*, volume VII, no. 4, 1987.

Dias, J. N. Ferreira – *Linha de rumo – notas de economia portuguesa* – Livraria Clássica Editora, Lisboa, 1945.

Ferreira, Eduardo de Sousa; Opello, Walter (editors) – *Conflict and change in Portugal 1974-1984* – Teorema, Lisboa, 1985.

Ferreira, José Medeiros – *Posição de Portugal no mundo* – Fundação Calouste Gulbenkian, Lisboa, 1988.

Garrido, Álvaro (editor) – *A pesca do bacalhau – história e memória* – Editorial Notícias, Lisboa, 2001.

Garrido, Álvaro – *O Estado Novo e a campanha do bacalhau* – Círculo de Leitores, Lisboa, 2010.

Gaspar, Jorge – *Ocupação e organização do espaço. Retrospectiva e tendências* – Fundação Calouste Gulbenkian, Lisboa, 1987.

Godinho, Vitorino Magalhães – *O socialismo e o futuro da Península* – Horizonte, Lisboa, 1968.

Gomes, Miguel Costa; Tavares, José – "Democracy and business cycles: evidence from the Portuguese economic history" – *European Review of Economic History*, vol. 3, part 3, 1999.

Labisa, António – *Política cambial portuguesa em tempo de dificuldades: 1918-26* – Banco de Portugal, Lisboa, 2001.

Leite, João Pinto Costa – *Economia de guerra* – Livraria Tavares Martins, Porto, 1943.

Lopes, Ernâni; Grilo, Marçal; Nazareth, José Manuel; Aguiar, Joaquim; Gomes, Amaral; Amaral, J. Pena do – *Portugal: o desafio dos anos 90* – Presença, Lisboa, 1989.

Lucena, Manuel – *Salazarismo* – Perpectivas e Realidades, Lisboa, 1976.

Lucena, Manuel – *Marcelismo* – Perpectivas e Realidades, Lisboa, 1976.

Marques, Alfredo – *Política económica e desenvolvimento em Portugal (1926-1959)* – Livros Horizonte, Lisboa, 1988.

Marques, Alfredo; Romão, António – "Croissance et crise de l'économie portugaise (1960-1982)" – *Estudos de Economia*, volume IV, no. 1, 1983.

Marques, A. H. Oliveira – "The Portuguese 1920's: a general survey" – *Revista de História Económica e Social*, no. 1, 1978.

Marques, A. H. Oliveira – *A Primeira República Portuguesa – alguns aspectos estruturais* – Horizonte, Lisboa, 1975 (2nd edition).

Marques, A. H. Oliveira (editor) – *História da 1ª República Portuguesa. As estruturas de base* – Iniciativas Editoriais, Lisboa, 1973.

Marques, A. H. Oliveira – *Guia de história da Primeira República portuguesa* – Estampa, Lisboa, 1981.

Marques, A. H. Oliveira – *Ensaios de história da Primeira República portuguesa* – Horizonte, Lisboa, 1988.

Martins, António Viana – *Da I República ao Estado Novo* – Iniciativas Editoriais, Lisboa, 1976.

Martins, Rogério – *Caminho de país novo* – Gris, Lisboa, 1970.

Mata, Maria Eugénia; Valério, Nuno – "As finanças das regiões autónomas 1977-2000" – *Revista de História Económica e Social*, 2ª série, nº 5, 2003.

Mateus, Abel – *Economia portuguesa: crescimento no contexto internacional (1910-1998)* – Verbo, Lisboa, 1998.

Matos, Luís Salgado – *Os investimentos estrangeiros em Portugal* – Seara Nova, Lisboa, 1973.

Medeiros, Fernando – *A sociedade e a economia portuguesas nas origens do salazarismo* – A Regra do Jogo, Lisboa, 1978.

Medina, João (editor) – *História contemporânea de Portugal* – Amigos do Livro Editores, Lisboa, 1985 (5 volumes).

Morais João; Violante, Luis – *Contribuição para uma cronologia dos factos económicos e sociais. Portugal,1926-1985* – Livros Horizonte, Lisboa, 1986.

Moura, Francisco Pereira de; Pinto, Luís Manuel Teixeira; Nunes, Jacinto – "Estrutura da economia portuguesa" – *Revista do Centro de Estudos Económicos*, no. 14, 1954.

Moura, Francisco Pereira de – *Por onde vai a economia portuguesa?* – Seara Nova, Lisboa, 1973 (4th edition).

Murteira, Mário – *Desenvolvimento, subdesenvolvimento e o modelo português* – Presença, Lisboa, 1979.

Nazareth, José Manuel – *Unidade e diversidade da demografia portuguesa no final do século XX* – Fundação Calouste Gulbenkian, Lisboa, 1988.

Nunes, Ana Bela; Valério, Nuno – "A Lei de Reconstituição Económica e a sua execução – um exemplo dos projectos e realizações da política económica do Estado Novo" – *Estudos de Economia*, volume III, no. 3, 1983.

Nunes, Ana Bela; Bastien, Carlos; Valério, Nuno – "Privatization and transnationalization of network services in Portugal" – Judith

468 | The Concise Economic History of Portugal: A Comprehensive Guide

Clifton, Francisco Comín e Daniel Diaz-Fuentes (editors) – *Transforming public enterprise in Europe and North America – Networks, Integration and Transnationalization* – Palgrave, Houndmills, 2007.

Pinheiro, Maximiano; et allii – *Séries longas para a economia portuguesa* – Banco de Portugal, Lisboa, 1997.

Pintado, V. Xavier – *Structure and growth of the Portuguese economy* – EFTA, Geneva, 1964.

Pinto, A. Sevinate (editor) – *A agricultura portuguesa no período 1950- -1980: de suporte do crescimento industrial a travão ao desenvolvimento económico* – Imprensa Nacional-Casa da Moeda, Lisboa, 1984.

Pinto, António Costa; Moreira, António; Costa, Fernando Marques da; Rosas, Fernando; Serra, João; Brito, José Maria Brandão de; Teixeira, Nuno Severiano (editors) – *O Estado Novo – das origens ao fim da autarcia 1926-1959 (volume I)* – Fragmentos, Lisboa, 1987.

Rafael, Francisco (editor) – *Portugal, capitalismo e o Estado Novo – algumas contribuições para o seu estudo* – Afrontamento, Porto, 1976.

Rollo, Fernanda – "Portugal e o Plano Marshall: história de uma adesão a contra-gosto (1947-1952)" – *Análise Social*, no. 128, 1994.

Rolo, José Manuel – *Capitalismo, tecnologia e dependência em Portugal* – Presença, Lisboa, 1977.

Rosas, Fernando – *O Estado Novo nos anos trinta, 1928-1938* – Estampa, Lisboa, 1986.

Rosas, Fernando – *Portugal entre a paz e a guerra: estudo do impacto da II guerra mundial na economia e na sociedade portuguesa 1939-1945* – Estampa, Lisboa, 1990.

Rosas, Fernando (editor) – *Portugal e o Estado Novo* – Presença, Lisboa, 1992.

Rosas, Fernando; Brito, J. M. Brandão de (editors) – *Dicionário de história do Estado Novo* – Círculo Leitores, Lisboa, 1996-1997 (2 volumes).

Rosas, Fernando; Rollo, Maria Fernanda (editors) – *História da Primeira República Portuguesa* – Tinta da China, Lisboa, 2010 (2nd edition).

Santos, Boaventura Sousa – *O Estado e a sociedade em Portugal (1974-1988)* – Afrontamento, Porto, 1990.

Sarmento, Judite – "A política económica em Portugal no pós 25 de Abril de 1974" – *O comportamento dos agentes económicos e a reorientação da política económica (volume II)* – CISEP, Lisboa, 1986.

Silva, Maria Manuela (editor) – *Portugal contemporâneo. Problemas e perspectivas* – Instituto Nacional de Administração, Oeiras, 1986 (2 volumes).

Telo, António – *Decadência e queda da I República Portuguesa* – Vega, Lisboa, 1980-1984 (2 volumes).

Telo, António – *Portugal na segunda guerra 1939-1941* – Vega, Lisboa, 1988.

Telo, António – *Portugal na segunda guerra 1941-1945* – Vega, Lisboa, 1991.

Telo, António – *Portugal e a NATO – o reencontro da tradição atlântica* – Cosmos, Lisboa, 1996.

Valério, Nuno – *A moeda em Portugal, 1913-1947* – Sá da Costa, Lisboa, 1984.

Valério, Nuno – "The Portuguese Economy in the inter-war period" – *Estudos de Economia*, volume V, no. 2, 1985.

Valério, Nuno – *As finanças públicas portuguesas entre as duas guerras mundiais* – Cosmos, Lisboa, 1994.

Valério, Nuno – "Oliveira Salazar (1889-1970) et le régime autoritaire portugais (1926-1974)" – *Estudos de Economia*, vol. XIII, no. 2, 1993.

Valério, Nuno – "O Banco de Portugal, banco central privado 1931-1974" – *Ensaios de homenagem a Manuel Jacinto Nunes* – Instituto Superior de Economia e Gestão, Lisboa, 1996.

Valério, Nuno – "Portugal e a integração européia" – *Revista ANPEC*, no. 3, 1998.

Valério, Nuno – "The Portuguese national question in the twentieth century: from Spanish threat to European bliss" – Teichova, Alice; Matis, Herbert; Pátek, Jaroslav (editors) – *Economic change and the national question in twentieth-century Europe* – Cambridge University Press, Cambridge (UK), 2000.

Valério, Nuno – "The role of the Bank of Portugal as a central bank (1931-1999)" – *The Journal of European Economic History*, special issue, 2001.

Valério, Nuno – "Nationalizations and privatizations in Portugal during the last quarter of the 20th century: were they profitable to the State?" – *Revista de História Económica e Social*, 2ª série, nº 7, 2004.

Portuguese colonies in the 20th century

Almeida, Pedro Ramos – *História do colonialismo português em África. Cronologia – século XX* – Estampa, Lisboa, 1979.

Ferreira, Manuel Ennes – *Angola – Portugal – do espaço económico português às relações pós-coloniais* – Escher, Lisboa, 1990.

Leite, Joana Pereira – "La reproduction du réseau impérial portugais: quelques précisions sur la formation du circuit d'or Mozambique/ Portugal 1959-1973" – *Estudos de Economia*, volume X, no. 3, 1990.

Torres, Adelino – "Le processus d'urbanisation d'Angola dans la période coloniale (années 1940-1970)" – *Estudos de Economia*, volume VII, nº 1, 1986.

Valério, Nuno – "The escudo zone – a failed attempt at a colonial monetary union (1962-1971)" – Lars Jonung and Jürgen Nautz (editors) – *Conflict potentials in monetary unions* – Franz Steiner Verlag, Stuttgard, 2007.

Valério, Nuno; Tjipilica, Palmira – "Economic activity in the Portuguese Colonial Empire: a factor analysis approach" – *Économies et Sociétés*, Série Histoire économique quantitative, AF, nº 39, 9/2008.